Hamilton County, Ohio Burial Records

Volume 5

Crosby and Whitewater Township Cemeteries

Hamilton County Chapter of the Ohio Genealogical Society
P. O. Box 15865
Cincinnati, Ohio 45215-0865

HERITAGE BOOKS
2010

HERITAGE BOOKS
AN IMPRINT OF HERITAGE BOOKS, INC.

Books, CDs, and more—Worldwide

For our listing of thousands of titles see our website
at
www.HeritageBooks.com

Published 2010 by
HERITAGE BOOKS, INC.
Publishing Division
100 Railroad Ave. #104
Westminster, Maryland 21157

International Standard Book Numbers
Paperbound: 978-1-55613-917-8
Clothbound: 978-0-7884-8317-2

INTRODUCTION

Whitewater township was named in 1803 as a territorial division of Hamilton county, Ohio, to include all that part of the county west of the Great Miami river. In 1804 this area was subdivided again to form Crosby township. Today Whitewater township is bounded on the west by Dearborn county, Indiana, on the north by Harrison and Crosby townships and on the east and south by the Great Miami river. Crosby township is bounded on the south by the Great Miami river and Whitewater township, on the west by Harrison township, on the north by Butler county, and on the east by the Great Miami river, separating it from Colerain township.

A brief history and present status report for the cemeteries in the above named townships is given in an introduction together with the existing records. A list of standard abbreviations and their meaning, as used to record information about burials, can be found on page five. The names for each burial in a cemetery are listed by row or section and lot, as found, to keep the family units of information together. Names listed in the Veterans Grave Registration File at the Hamilton county, Ohio, courthouse as of 1940 were cross referenced and notations made for military service. Gravestones for the following Revolutionary soldiers were not found in either township: Ephraim Buell, died 1820, Moses (Medagh) Maddock, date unknown, John Cavender, died 1837, Francis Kelsimere, died 1826, Thomas Lacy, died 1835, Asa Harvey, died 1826. Othniel Looker, aged 83 years, was residing in Crosby township for the 1840 census of military pensioners. Also, a gravestone was not found for Charles Cone, a veteran of the War of 1812, who died 26 April 1853.

The Maple Grove cemetery is located in Whitewater township and is owned by Miami township. Their records were published in volume four. The Miami cemetery records listed some names as reinterrments and those named as removals from Old Ground at Miamitown may have been from the first Public cemetery. The Old Ground may have been located on the east side of Hamilton-Cleves road and north of Harrison road. Other reinterrments were made from Foster (from Colerain township), Shear (from Green township). and William M. Orr (township not listed) family farm burying ground. Information given in the early records of Miami cemetery, such as place of birth, place of death, occupation, cause of death and kindred information were added to the gravestone inscription. Gravestone inscriptions are the only records for Miami cemetery from December 1881 thru July 1904 and from January 1906 thru January 1976 as records are missing for these periods of time.

We are particularly appreciative of all the time and effort spent by Mrs. Hazel L. Berry in abstracting and coordinating these cemetery records of Crosby and Whitewater townships. This is the first time for the majority of these records to be published.

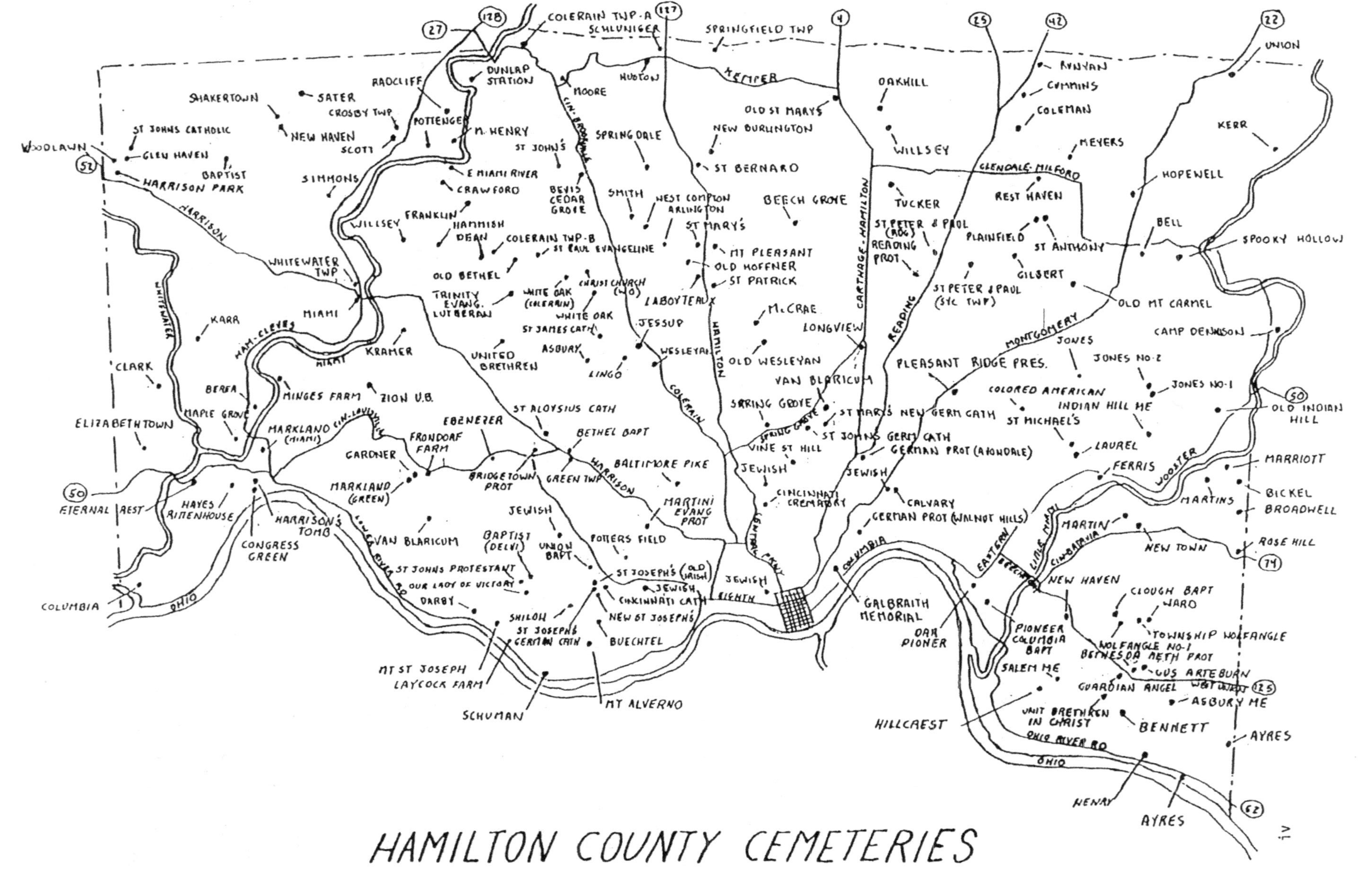

HAMILTON COUNTY CEMETERIES

TABLE of CONTENTS

ABBREVIATIONS

AE	age
b.	born
BD	birth date
b/o	brother of
Bur.	buried
Co.	County or company in military
d	days
d.	died
DD	death date
DI	date interred
d/o or dau	daughter of
E	east
emb.	emblem
F. & A.M.emb.	Member of Masons
f/o	father of
geb.	geboren/born
gest.	gestórben/died
Gr.	grave
grd.	grand
h/o	husband of
Jr.	Junior
LO	Lot owner
m or mos.	month (s)
mkr.	marker
m/o	mother of
N	north
O.E.S.	Order of Eastern Star
pos.	possibly
Res.	resided/residence
S	south
Sec.	Section
s/o	son of or sister of
Sp.	spelling uncertain
Sr.	Senior
ssa	same stone as name above
tochter	daughter
Twp.	township
Vet.	veteran
von	of
W	west
w'd	widowed spouse
wk	week (s)
w/o	wife of
WW I	World War I
WW II	World War II
y or yrs.	year (s)
&	and
?	not known or uncertain
----	missing data
pos	possible

AL	Alabama
AK	Alaska
AZ	Arizona
AR	Arkansas
CA	California
CO	Colorado
CT	Connecticut
DE	Delaware
DC	District of Columbia
FL	Florida
GA	Georgia
HI	Hawaii
ID	Idaho
IL	Illinois
IN	Indiana
IA	Iowa
KS	Kansas
KY	Kentucky
LA	Louisana
ME	Maine
MD	Maryland
MA	Massachusetts
MI	Michigan
MN	Minnesota
MS	Mississippi
MO	Missouri
MT	Montana
NE	Nebraska
NV	Nevada
NH	New Hampshire
NJ	New Jersey
NM	New Mexico
NC	North Carolina
ND	North Dakota
NY	New York
OH	Ohio
OK	Oklahoma
OR	Oregon
PA	Pennsylvania
PR	Puerto Rico
RI	Rhode Island
SC	South Carolina
SD	South Dakota
TN	Tennessee
TX	Texas
UT	Utah
VT	Vermont
VA	Virginia
WA	Washington
WV	West Virginia
WI	Wisconsin
WY	Wyoming

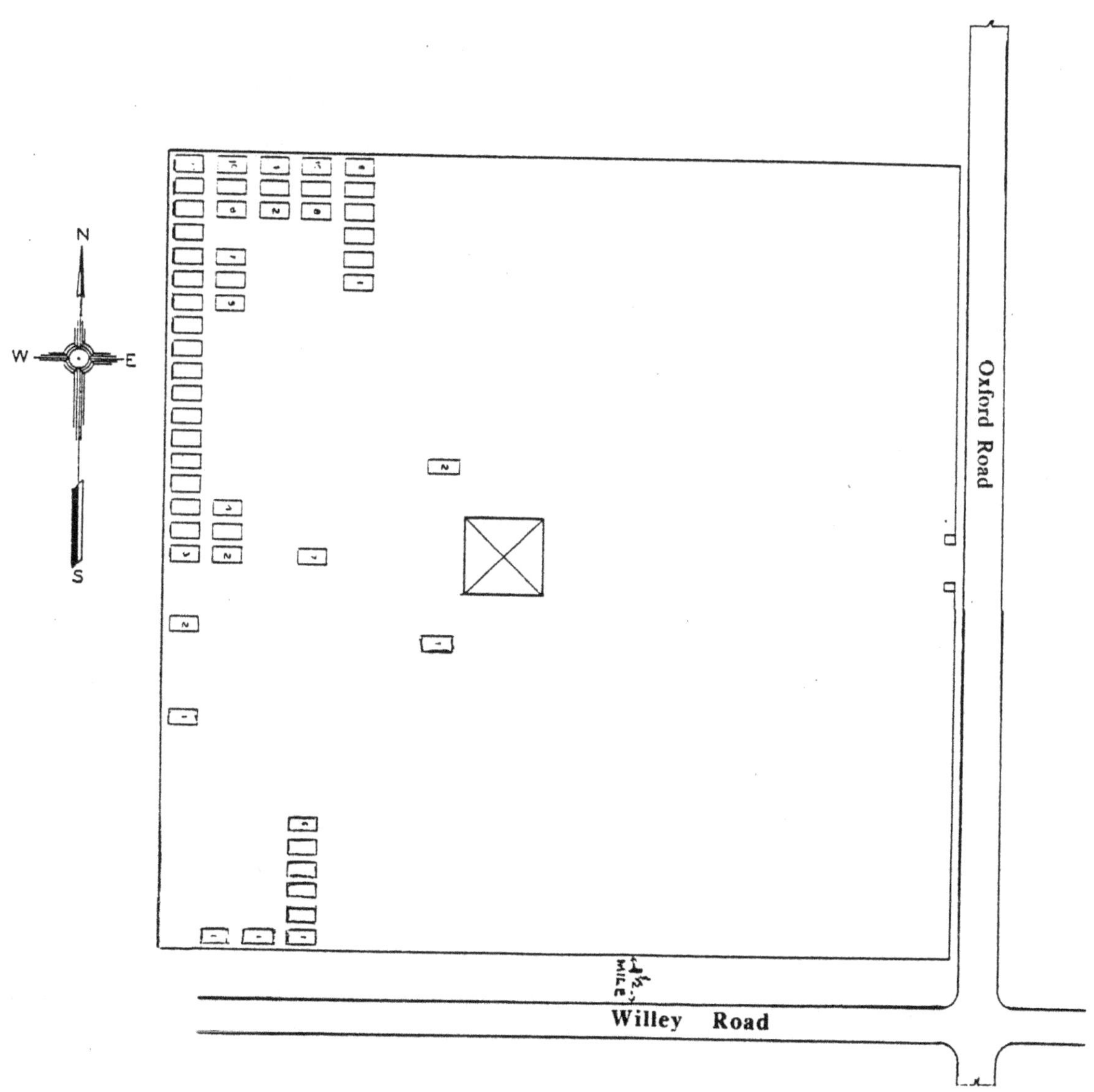

SHAKERTOWN CEMETERY

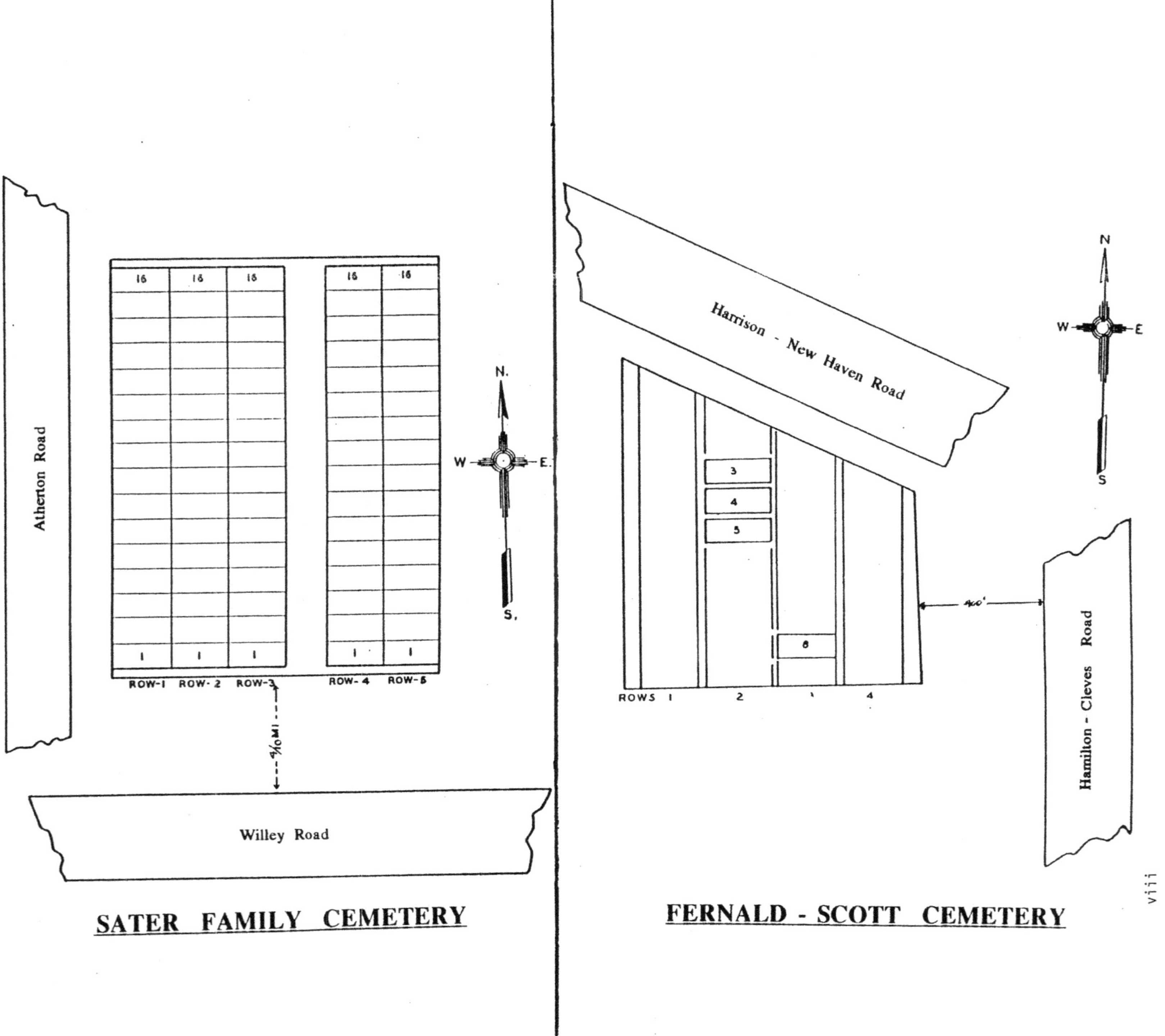

Atherton Road
ROW-1
ROW-2
ROW-3
ROW-4
ROW-5
N.
W
E.
S.
Willey Road
SATER FAMILY CEMETERY
Harrison - New Haven Road
N
W
E
S
3
4
5
8
ROWS 1
2
4
Hamilton - Cleves Road
FERNALD - SCOTT CEMETERY

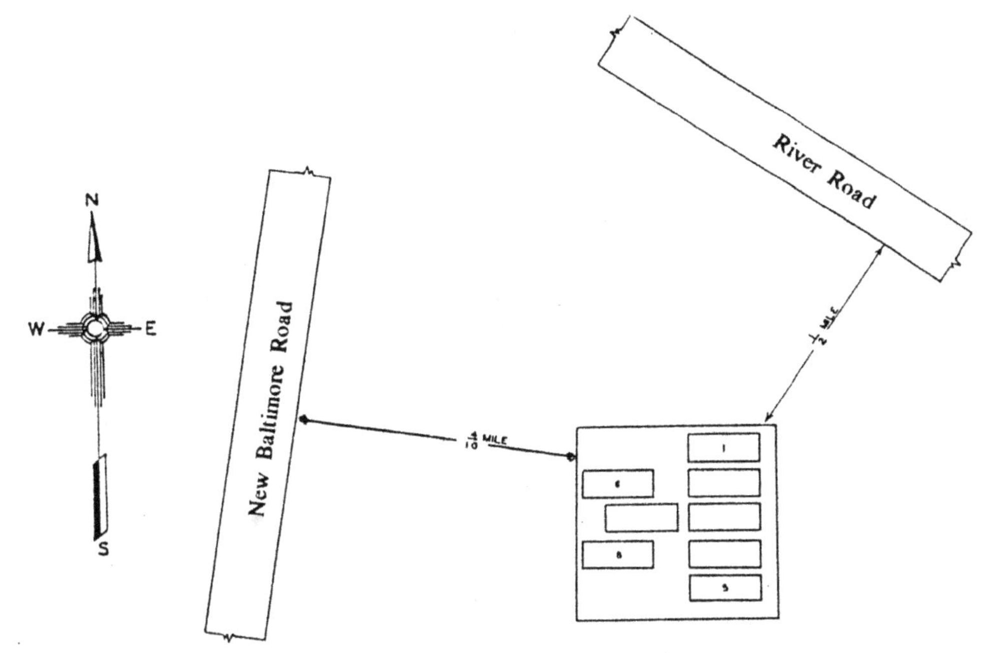

McHENRY FAMILY CEMETERY

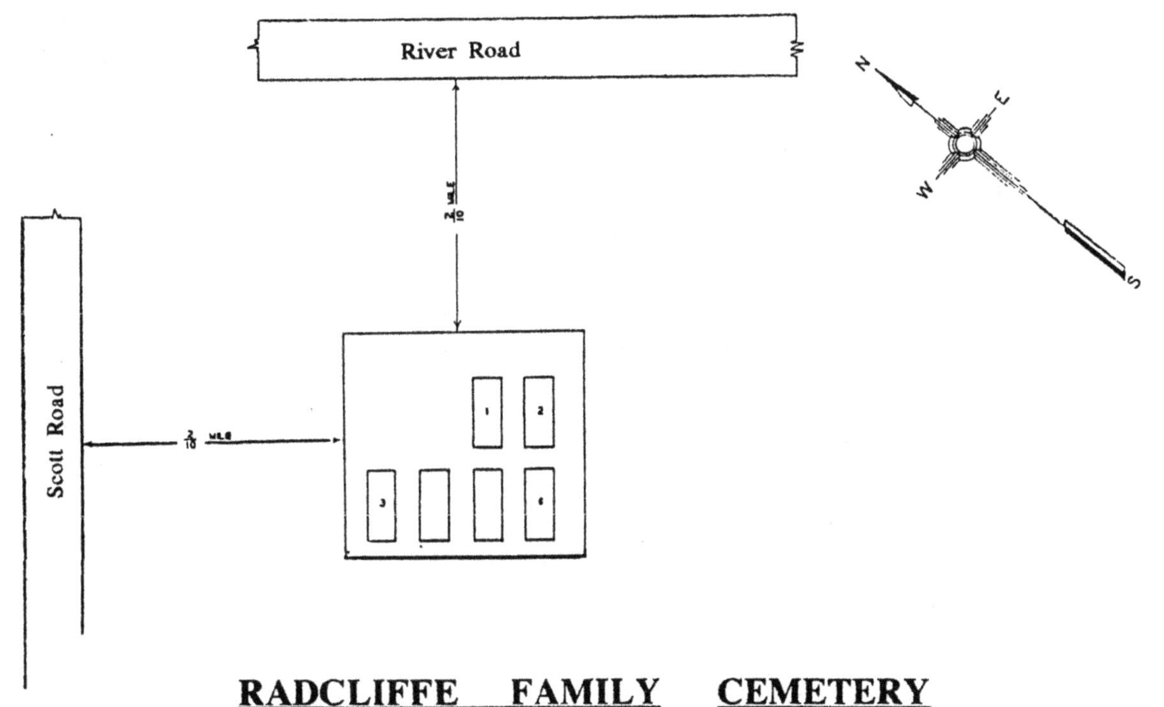

RADCLIFFE FAMILY CEMETERY

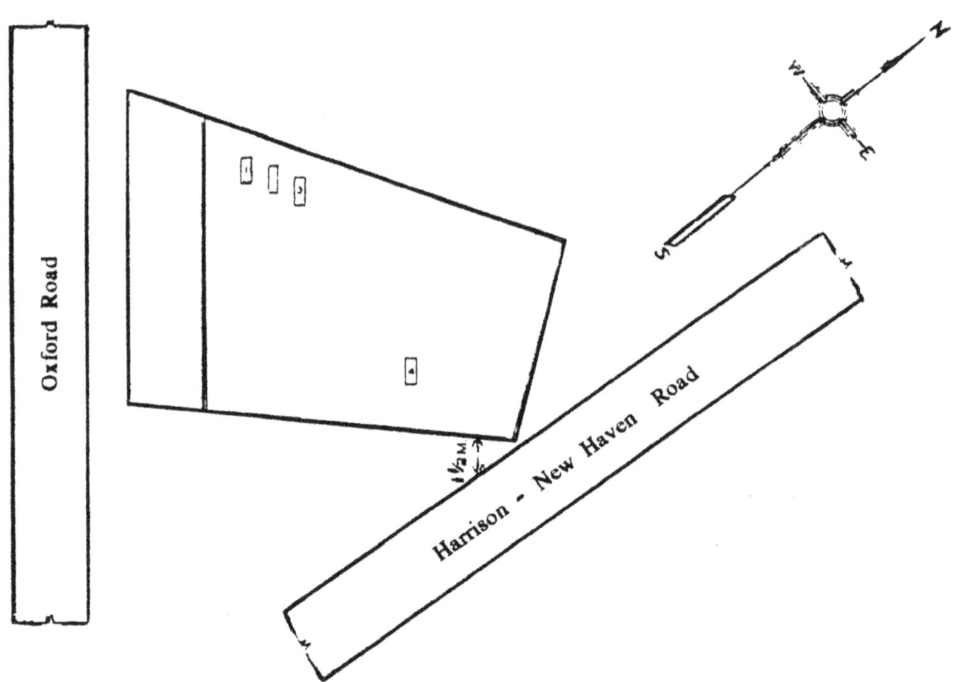

POTTENGER FAMILY CEMETERY

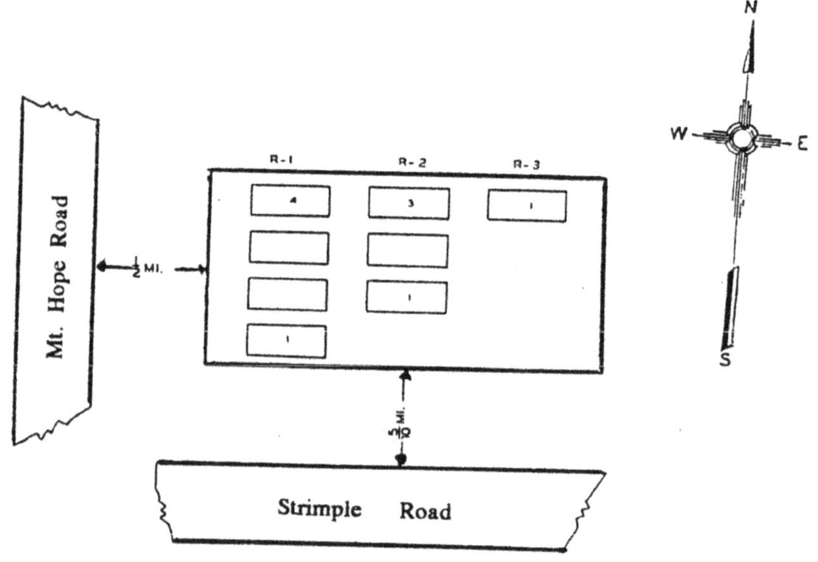

SIMONS-SIMMONDS FAMILY CEMETERY

x

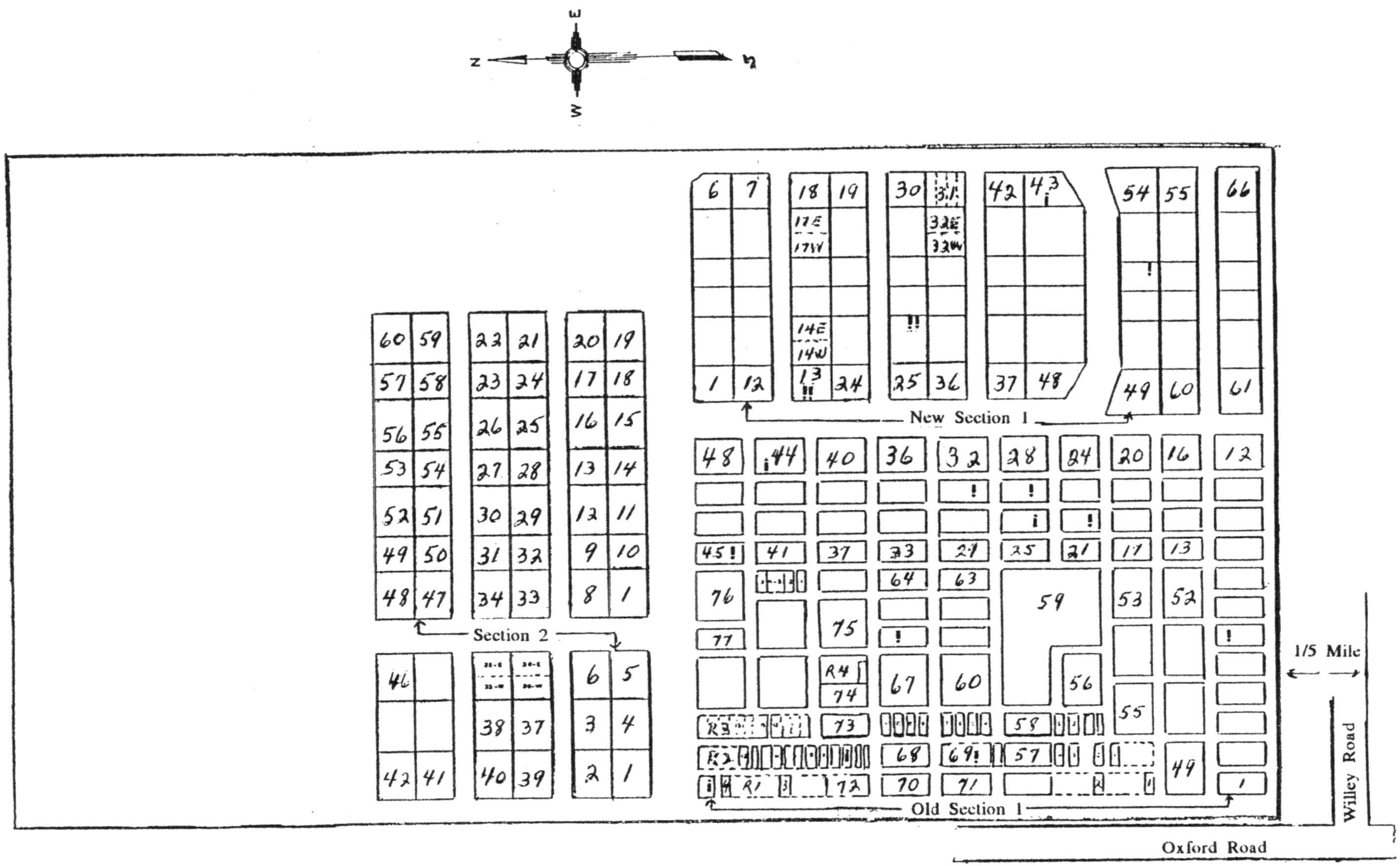

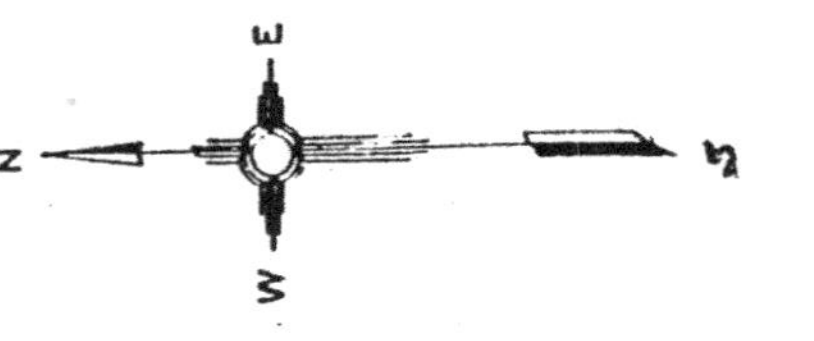

N
E
W
New Section 1
Section 2
Old Section 1
1/5 Mile
Willey Road
Oxford Road

NEW HAVEN CEMETERY

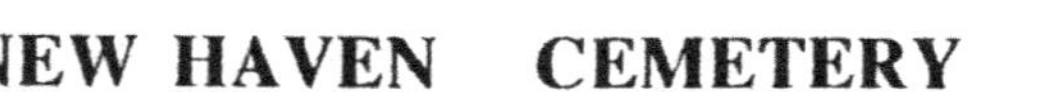

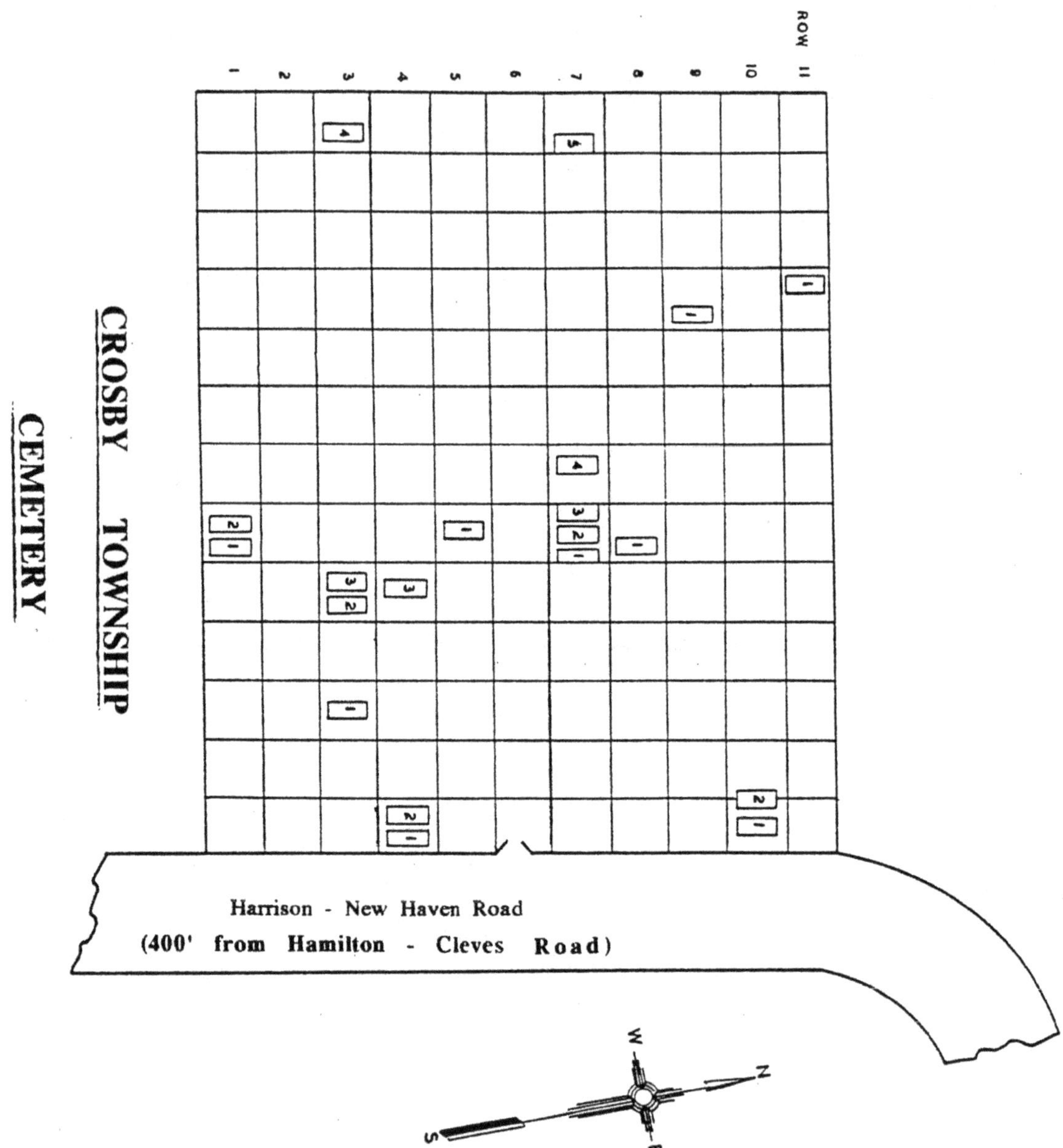

CROSBY TOWNSHIP
CEMETERY
ROW
1
2
3
4
5
6
7
8
9
10
11
Harrison - New Haven Road
(400' from Hamilton - Cleves Road)
W
N
E
S

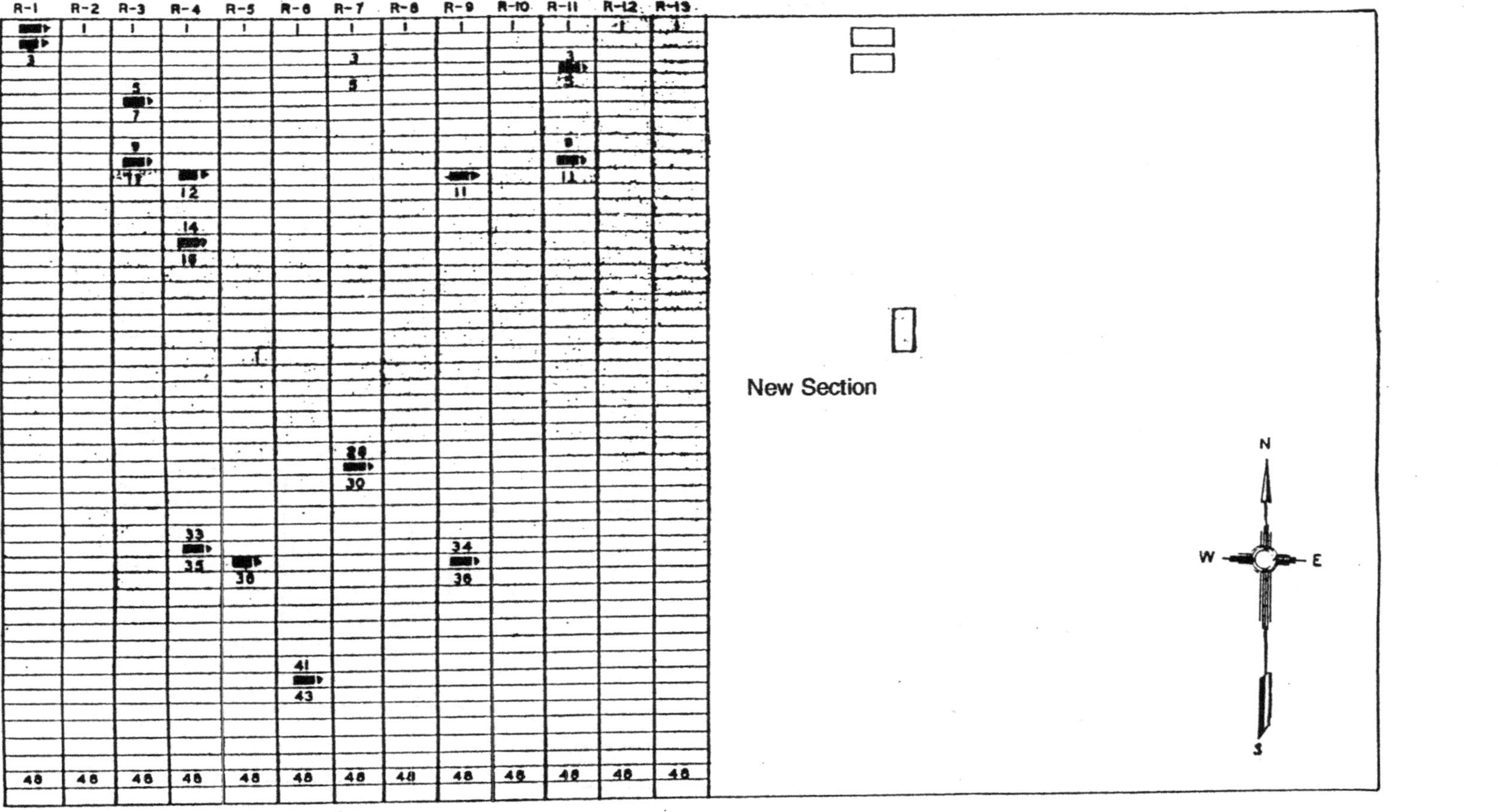

Stephens Road

ELIZABETHTOWN CEMETERY

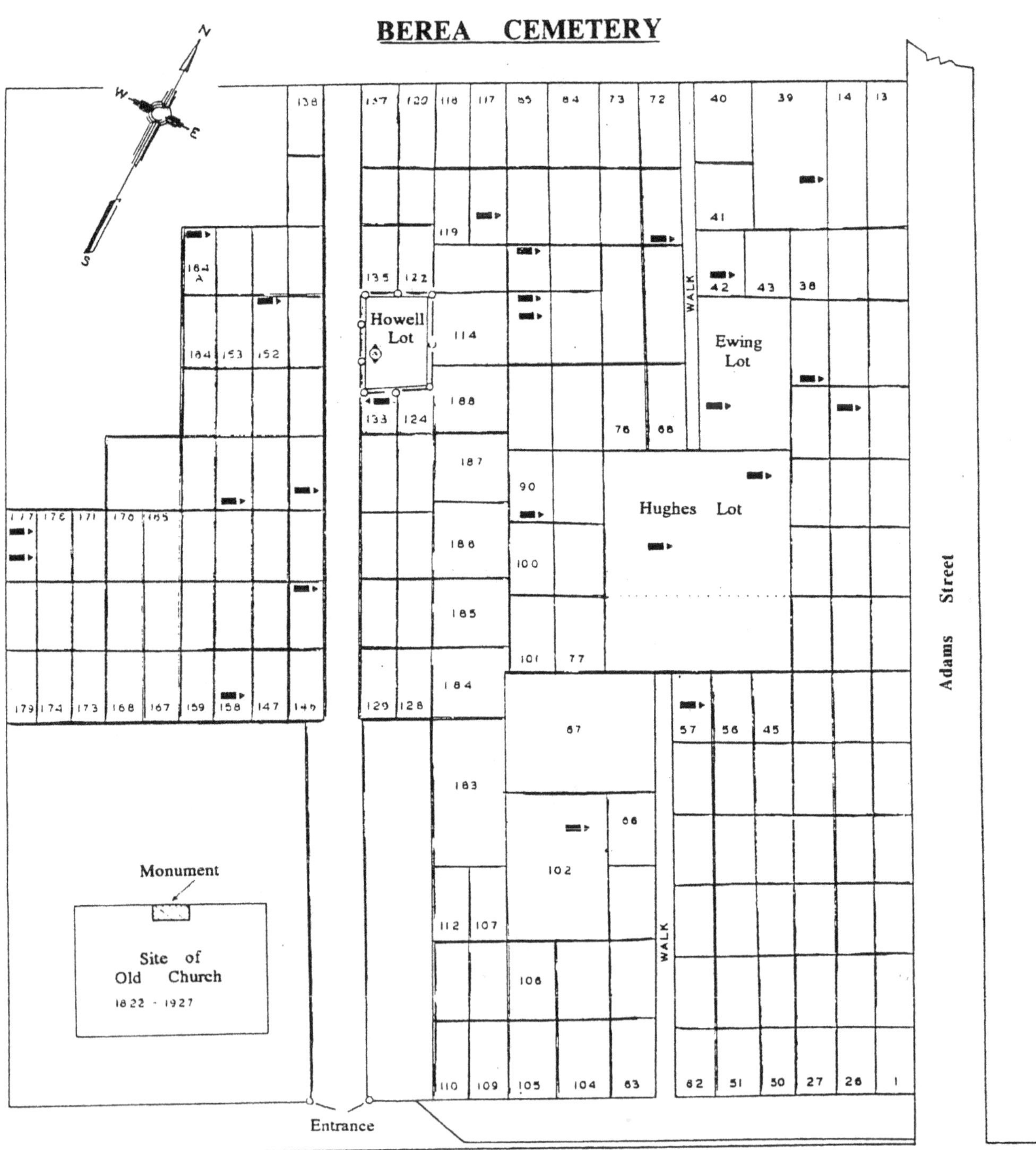
BEREA CEMETERY
N
W
E
S
Howell Lot
Ewing Lot
Hughes Lot
WALK
WALK
Monument
Site of Old Church
1822 - 1927
Entrance
Adams Street
Brotherhood Road
To U.S. Bypass 50

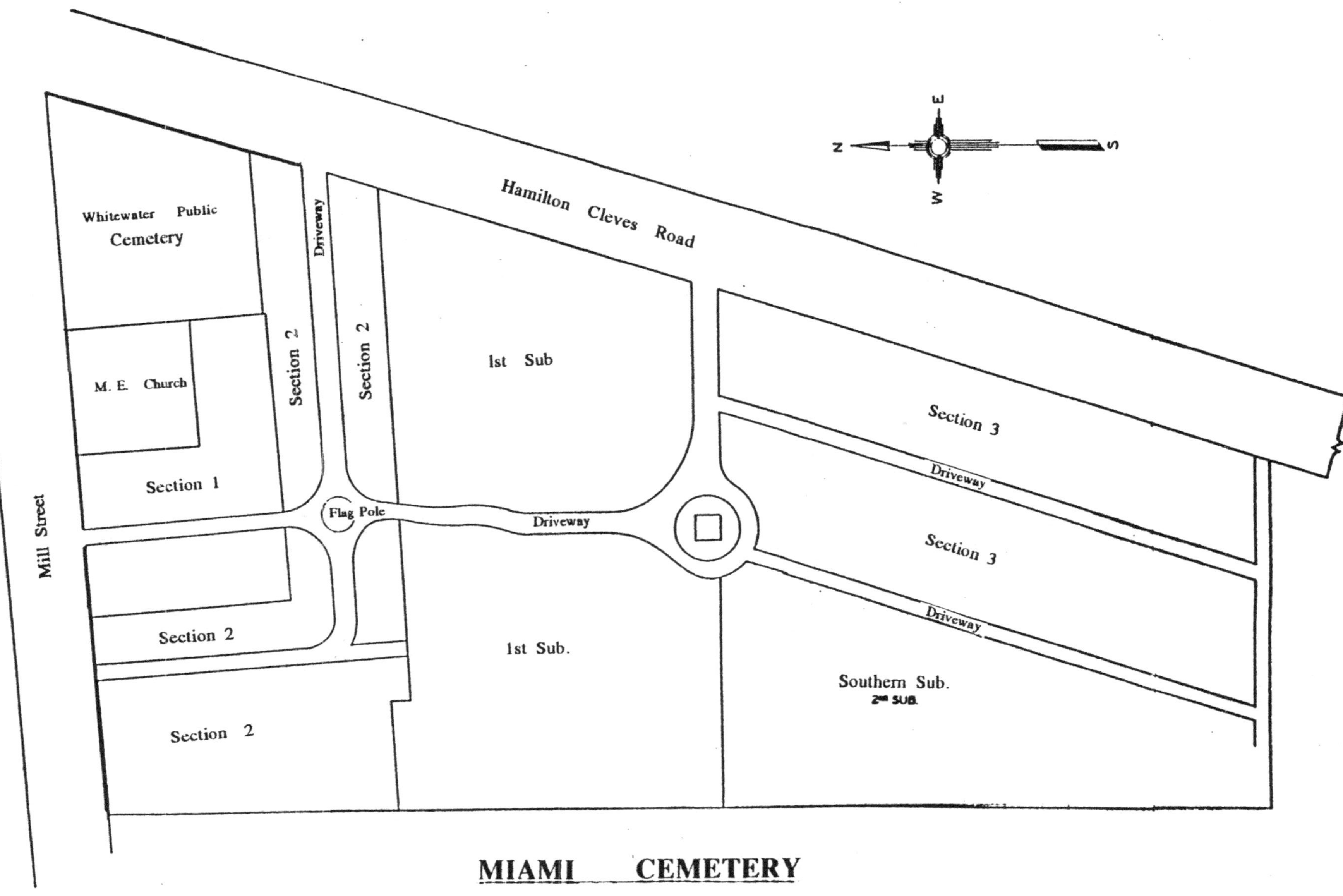

MIAMI CEMETERY

Hamilton Cleves Road

S
E
W
N

Exit

Driveway

Flag Area Vets.

Section 2

Whitewater Township
Cemetery No. 2

M. E. CHURCH

Driveway

Section 1

Driveway

Mill Street

Exit

Exit

MIAMI CEMETERY

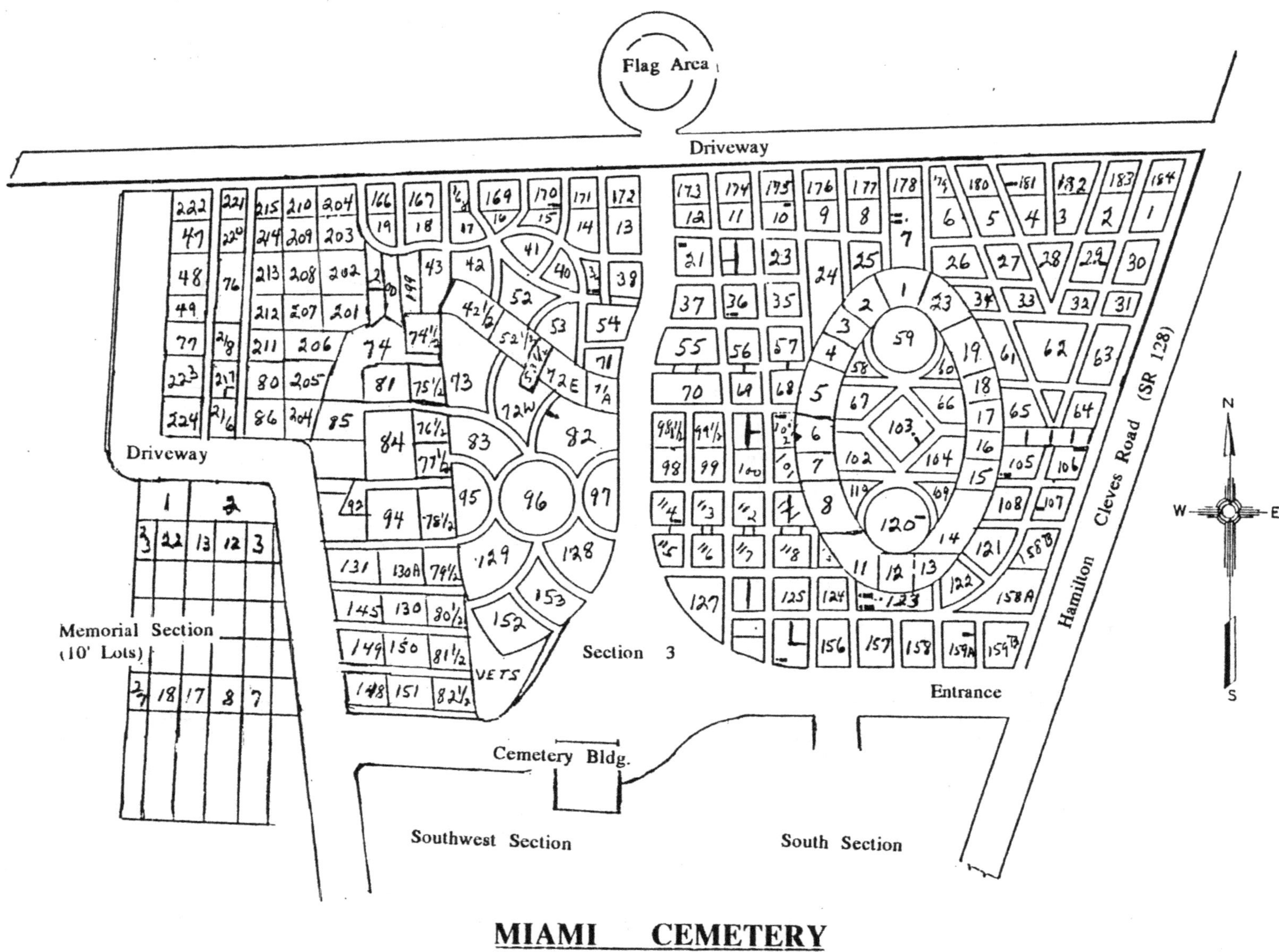
Flag Area
Driveway
Driveway
Hamilton Cleves Road (SR 128)
N
W
E
S
Memorial Section
(10' Lots)
VETS
Section 3
Entrance
Cemetery Bldg.
Southwest Section
South Section
MIAMI CEMETERY

MIAMI CEMETERY
Mausoleum
Memorial Section
Driveway
Southwest Section
South Section
Driveway
South Section
Hamilton - Cleves Road (U.S. 128)
Driveway
Section 3
Entrance
N
S
E
W

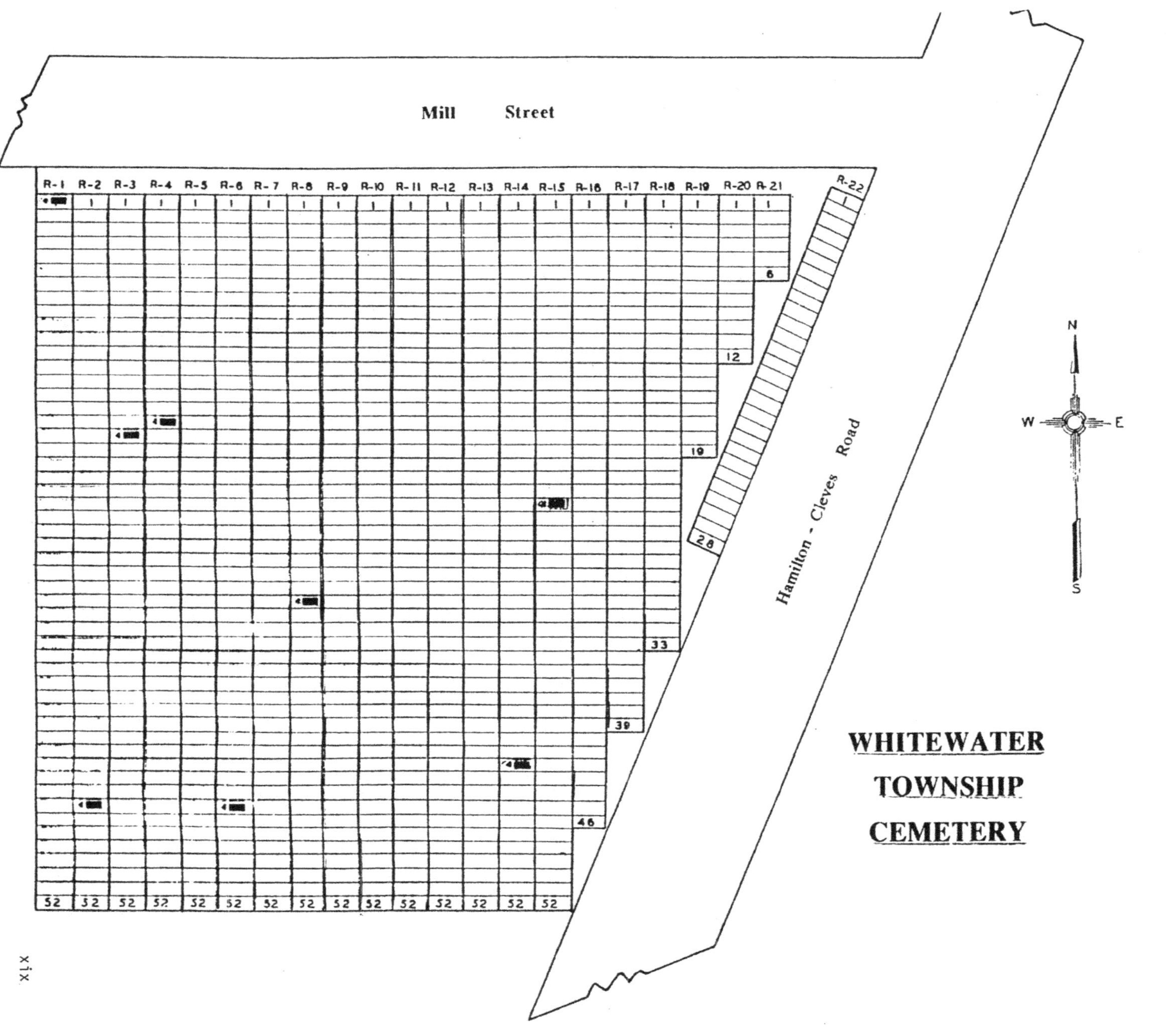

WHITEWATER TOWNSHIP CEMETERY

The Shakertown Cemetery is located in Section 3 of Crosby Township in Hamilton County, Ohio on west side of Oxford Road and about one mile north of intersection with Willey Road in New Haven, Ohio. The wrought iron fencing around the site is deteriorating and gravestones are in need of repair. The township trustees are responsible for maintaince. There are some loose fieldstones piled around trees and on tree stumps that may or may not be head-stones. The courthouse record indicates that this cemetery was established November 11, 1852 for one acre of land. These inscriptions were copied by H. L. Berry in October 1982. Rows were copied from west to east and each row was copied from north to south.

On a stone monument as you enter the cemetery: "Erected by Society of Shakers Whitewater Village, an order of celebate Christian communists to honor the memory of the members whose mortal remains are interred in this lot, 1827-1916. They have done good unto the resurrection of life whose abiding place is immortality."

Adam POE, a contemporary of Daniel Boone, reportedly killed Big Foot in the nearby Whitewater Forest. Big Foot was a Shawnee Indian chief and it is uncertain if he or A. Poe are buried in this cemetery.

Name	Born	Died	Row
BALL, Elaner - b. England (70y & 14d)	7- 8-1786	7-22-1856	Row 1
STROUD, Reese - b. Bucks Co. PA (77y 1m21d)	12-10-1781	1-31-1859	Row 1
MORRISON, Jane - b.Scotland (28y 1m 1d)	2-13-1831	3-14-1859	Row 1
EASTABROOKS, John - b.Providence, RI	78y 4m 5d	10-18-1865	Row 1
BANISTER, Phebe - broken stone	66y 7m21d	11-21-1863	Row 1
BURNHAM, Josiah - b.Marion Co. OH (42y-16d)	1-27-1822	2-13-1864	Row 1
HOBART, John - b. Worcester Co. Mass.	8-18-1792	10-11-1866	Row 1
______, foundation for stone only	----	----	Row 1
BALL, Wm. b. England (84y4m16d)	6- 4-1784	10-20-1868	Row 1
AGNEW, Joseph B. b. Bergen Co. NJ	12-21-1787	7-11-1870	Row 1
E. D. - (initials only) with star emblem:	----	----	Row 1
FARADAY, Mary A. - Our Mother b.Bristol Co. PA	9-27-1806	8- 6-1868	Row 1
RUBUSH, George - Our Father b. Franklin Co. PA - 77y 4m 15d	2-22-1799	7- 7-1876	Row 1
McMAKIN, Albert - 4y 4m25d	6-21-1874	10-16-1878	Row 1
______, Fieldstone without inscription	----	----	Row 2
______, Fieldstone without inscription.	----	----	Row 2
H.M. (Very worn)	----	----	Row 2
McGUIRE, Minerva G. (83y ?m ?d) Erected by her devoted son, J.G. McGUIRE; Stone is broken into 3 pieces.)	9-24-1791	1- 4-1875	Row 2
CARTER, Eliza - b. Boston, Mass.	12?-10?-17(9?)6	illegible	Row 2
RUBUSH, Susan - Our Mother b. in Rockingham Co. VA (74y10m21d)	1-12-1804	12- 3-1878	Row 2
GASS, Elizabeth - Mother - b. Colchester Essex, England (74y 1m10d)	11-20-1814	12-30-1888	Row 2
FARADAY, Mary	5- 6-1841	6-21-1892	Row 2
C. P.	----	----	Row 3
M. C.	----	----	Row 3
A. H.	----	----	Row 4
______, Fieldstone without inscription	----	----	Row 4
BRYANT, E.	----	----	Row 4
E. S.	----	----	Row 4
______, 3 loose fieldstones without inscriptions	----	----	Row 4
______, Fieldstone without inscription	----	----	Row 4
SHERMAN, Ezra (age 74y 4m) Broken stone	9-22-1805	1-22-1882	Row 4
______, Fieldstone without inscription	----	----	Row 4
______, 4 Fieldstones without inscriptions by tree	----	----	Row 4
______, Fieldstone without inscription	----	----	Row 5
A. W.	----	----	Row 5
Z. B.	----	----	Row 5
DURBIN, H.	----	----	Row 5
PARKER, Lucinda - Mother - Erected by her son, nephew, and grandchildren	9- 4-1833	10-27-1911	Row 5
______, Foundation without a stone (possibly S.R.'s)		----	Row 5
J.L.G. (Possibly J.L.C.)	----	----	Row 5
W. W.	----	----	Row 5
S. R. (Broken off & leaning against J.B.'s)	----	----	Row 5
J. B.	----	----	Row 5
W. H.	----	----	Row 5
E. S.	----	----	Row 5
H. D.(?) - very worn stone. Stone monument erected to the Society...quote in above paragraph.	----	----	Row 5
E. R. B. - 3 initials as they appear on worn stone. 7(8?)y		8-2?-1852/9	Row 6

WILLEY FAMILY CEMETERY

This family farm of one hundred and thirty five acres was located in Section 8, Crosby Township of Hamilton County, Ohio on west side of Hamilton-Cleves Road (SR 128) on the south side of intersection with Willey Road. Area is now a cultivated field. Reinterrments were made May 12, 1904 to Venice Cemetery at Venice, (now called Ross), Ohio of the following names as listed. This information was provided by Mrs. Elmer (Ruth) Early.

Name	Age	Died
WILLEY, Elvira	11	7- 4-1837
WILLEY, Amanda	25y & 11d	3-24-1847
WILLEY, Judah, Jr.	58y 4m 1d	8- 5-1852
WILLEY, William	32y	2-28-1858
WILLEY, Caroline	41y11m16d	2-11-1842
WILLEY, Judah, Sr.	85y	1848
WILLEY, Anna B.	21y 5m12d	3-11-1853

Reinterrment of the following was made to Miamitown Cemetery circa 1920.

Name	Born	Died
WILLEY, Samuel s/o Judah WILLEY, Jr. & Caroline (BUELL) WILLEY	1828	1858
WILLEY, Patience E. WALKER w/o Samuel WILLEY & d/o Edward B. & Ann (?) WALKER	1831	ca 1861

PADDY'S RUN CEMETERY

The burial site is supposedly located at the mouth of Paddy's Run and Big Miami River. (Supposedly west of Paddy's Run (the road or the creek ??) and north of SR 128.) The following was taken from the "Scott Family History" by Cora SCOTT:

Andrew Scott born September 23, 1741 in Roxburyshire, Scotland. Emigrated to United States in 1787, landing in Philadelphia in May, 1787 and moved to Redstone, PA where his wife died. He moved on to North Bend, Ohio and then to the mouth of Paddy's Run where he died January 31, 1831, aged 89 years, 4 months and 8 days. Children: Isabella, born in Kelso, Roxburyshire, Scotland. Unmarried, died December (9?), 1838 in her 66th year.

Ann, born in Kelso, November 8, 1779, married a Mr. REED, died June 25, 1849 and buried with her father, Andrew Scott, and sister, Isabella Scott, in Paddy's Run Cemetery.

Daughter, Elizabeth, married William MILLER. She died on April 10, 1835, following birth of an infant which died May 27, 1835. Elizabeth was 29 years, 3 months and 2 days old when she died and both she and the infant are buried in the cemetery at the mouth of Paddy's Run.

Name	Born / Age	Died
SCOTT, Andrew - b. Roxburyshire, Scotland 89y 4m 8d	9-23-1741	1-31-1831
SCOTT, Isabella - b. Kelso, Roxburyshire, Scotland	In 66th yr.	12- 9-1838
REED, Ann nee SCOTT - b. Kelso, Scotland	11- 8-1779	6-25-1849
MILLER, Elizabeth nee REED, w/o Wm. MILLER	29y 3m 2d	4-10-1835
MILLER, Infant of Elizabeth & Wm.	----	5-27-1835

SATER FAMILY CEMETERY

The Sater Cemetery is located in Section 11 of Crosby Township, Hamilton County, Ohio on the east side of Atherton Road and one fourth mile north of intersection with Willey Road. Courthouse record states that it was established March 1, 1854 for (.05) five hundredths of an acre of land. The area is enclosed with a fence and maintained by the township. The rows were copied from west to east and each row from north to south in October 1982 by Mrs. Hazel L. Berry. There is one fieldstone without inscription and only a couple of sunken areas without markers that may indicate there were other burials.

Name	Age	Date	Row
SATER, Anson s/o John J. & Nancy S. SATER	3m 4d	8- 5-1863	Row 1
(Loose stone leaning against N. fence.)			
SATER, Infant d/o Hannah E. Sater	29d	7-30-1862	Row 1
SATER, Infant s/o John & Nancy S. Sater	4m28d	5-24-1862	Row 1
SATER, Ira Merrill s/o John J. & Nancy	4y 1m 5d	9-29-1860	Row 1
SATER, Amos	21y 2m13d	1- 5-1856	Row 1
SATER, Jonathan L.	21y 4m14d	5-14-1862	Row 1
SATER, Nancy S. w/o John J. SATER	44y 7m 5d	5- 2-1863	Row 1
SATER, John J.	49y 9m24d	4- 3-1864	Row 1
MORGANS, Infant s/o E. J. & M. MORGANS	7-27-1862	7-27-1862	Row 2
(Loose stone leaning against N. fence.)			
SATER, Hannah w/o Joseph SATER	90y 2m23d	4- 9-1854	Row 2
SATER, Joseph	79y10m 2d	10-27-1833	Row 2
KILBORN, Dorcas w/o Henry KILBORN & d/o Joseph & Hannah SATER	10-31-1796	7-18-1839	Row 2
______, ---- fieldstone without inscription	----	----	Row 2
KILBOURN, Henry	In 51st yr.	11-11-1845	Row 2
SATER, Willard F. s/o Wm. V. & E. SATER	1y 18d	12-15-1862	Row 3
"ssa , Infant s/o Wm. V. & E. SATER	----	8-28-1865	Row 3
SATER, Evaline w/o Wm. V. SATER	24y 5m 7d	8-29-1865	Row 3
SATER, Hannah d/o Wm. & Nancy SATER	19 or 13d	7-29-1816	Row 3
SATER, Infant s/o Wm. & Nancy SATER	6- 1-1821	6- 1-1821	Row 3
SATER, William - Our Father	55y 4m13d	1-30-1849	Row 3
" ssa, Nancy - Our Mother - w/o Wm. SATER	81y & 1m	9- 3-1871	Row 3
SATER, Wm. Thomas s/o Oliver & Marie SATER	24y 4m13d	8-15-1878	Row 3
SATER, Oliver	31y 4m19d	11- 9-1860	Row 3
SATER. Oliver F. s/o Oliver & Maria	1m31d	9-18-1859	Row 3
SATER, Infant s/o Oliver & Maria SATER	3- 1-1858	3- 1-1858	Row 3
SATER, Infant s/o Oliver & Maria SATER	----	12- 7-1860	Row 3
L. S. (Initials on footstone)			Row 3
GWALTNEY, Mary E. d/o James & Sarah	27d	11-10-1848	Row 4
GWALTNEY, Infant s/o James & Sarah	9- 7-1849	9- 7-1849	Row 4
GWALTNEY, Anis E. d/o James & Sarah	2y 8m15d	3-18-1856	Row 4
SATER, Hannah Jane d/o Joseph & Eliza Ann	3m28d	7-28-1850	Row 5
(Stone is leaning against east fence but matches foundation in this row.)			
SATER, George L. s/o Joseph & Eliza A.	4m 2d	12-22-1853	Row 5
SATER, William s/o Joseph & Eliza Ann	4y 2m27d	4- 1-1856	Row 5

McHENRY CEMETERY

Record at the Hamilton County Courthouse states that this burial site was first established October 9, 1807 for (.01) one hundredth of an acre of land. It is a small area in a large area known as Fort Scott which is owned by the Archdiocese of the Catholic Church for a summer campground. The exact location is in Section 16, Crosby Township, on the south side of River Road, four tenths of a mile east of intersection of River Road, New Baltimore Road and Blue Rock Road in New Baltimore, Ohio.

McHENRY, VanBuren	8-20-1844	11-30-1862
McHENRY, Celia (75y 4m12d)	11-19-1812	3-31-1888
McHENRY, William s/o Celia & Armis	1m	3- 5-1852
McLLAND, Rebecca w/o James E. McLAND & d/o A. & C. McHENRY	18y 1m25d	8-27-1865
McH, B. (Initials on a footstone)	----	----

POTTENGER CEMETERY

This family cemetery is located in Section 17, Crosby Township, Hamilton County, Ohio, north of New Haven Road, one half mile east of intersection with Hamilton-Cleves Road (SR 128). The cemetery is located in a woods on a hill behind the brick residence of a tenant on the farm owned by Loren Hann. The tombstones have all been broken off...courthouse record indicates that it was first established June 17,1820 for (.15) fifteen hundredths of an acre. H. L. Berry was able to find these inscriptions in 1982.

CROWELL, Nelson	16y 6m19d	3-31-1851
POTTENGER, Royal s/o J.W. & Mary	11-23-1848	2-13-1849
POTTENGER, James W. s/o J.W. & Mary	4m 8d	11-25-1842
POTTENGER, Susannah w/o Samuel POTTENGER	In 56th Yr.	10-20-1829
POTTENGER, Samuel	In 60th Yr.	10-.1-1827

RADCLIFFE CEMETERY

This small burial site is located in Section 16, Crosby Township, Hamilton County, Ohio on the west side of River Road, seven tenths of a mile NE of intersection of River Road, New Haven Road and Blue Rock Road in New Baltimore, Ohio. The cemetery is just outside the south side of a chain link fence enclosing Ft. Scott Summer Camp. The cemetery is surrounded by rusty woven wire fence, with a gate on the south side. It is quite brushy and covered with vines, but someone has taken some care of the cemetery in the past. One older type tombstone, 2 or 3 inches thick, two feet by four feet tall, has fallen over and broken into three pieces. They were placed within a metal frame on the ground but are not cemented together. The other tombstones appear to be of a later type (replacements?). Courthouse record indicates that this burial site was establised November 3, 1821 for two hundredths of an acre. The following inscriptions were copied in November 1982 by H. L. Berry.

RADCLIFFE, ----- s/o J.M. & M.A.	----	1851
RADCLIFFE, Eliza J. CORNICK	1815	1848
RADCLEFF, Margaret w/o James RADCLEFF* Native of Yorkshire, England (*This is the spelling used on the old tombstone that's broken.)	60y 7m28d	11-15-1838
RADCLIFFE, ----- s/o J. & E. RADCLIFFE	----	1844
RADCLIFFE, ----- d/o G.W. & E.S.	----	1882
RADCLIFFE, James - Native of Yorkshire, Eng.	1786	1864
________, ----- Fieldstone, possibly a footstone for James.		

SIMMONS (SIMMONDS)CEMETERY

Hamilton County courthouse record indicates that on October 25, 1880 a burial site for two hundredths of an acre was recorded in this name. In Section 24 of Crosby Township about one tenth mile north of Mt. Hope Road on SR 128, and west side of road along the line fence was found, two gravestone bases, one headstone in two pieces and one footstone. One hundred feet north of the first site, same side of SR 128 and two hundred feet back a lane on the left side was found -(2nd site) the following as reported by Harvey Crihfield.

CORNICK, Eliza Ann d/o John & Susan	ca 3y	8- 1-1837
CORNICK, John	35y & 11d	2-28-1840
CORNICK, David	67y	12-15-1834
J. C. footstone		

The New Haven Cemetery is located in Section 11 of Crosby Township, Hamilton County, Ohio on the east side of Oxford Road and two tenths of a mile north of intersection with New Haven Road in New Haven, Ohio. In 1818 this cemetery was conveyed by Charles Cone and James Comstock to the Baptist and Congregation Churches as part of the original town site for approximately three acres. At present the cemetery is maintained by a Board of Directors who are decendants of the deceased buried in this cemetery or own burial lots.

Cemetery records date from 1895 to the present and they were copied in 1987 by Gene Woefel. The gravestone inscriptions were copied in 1988 by H. L. and L. A. Berry. The old part of the cemetery was copied by rows from west to east and from south to north. Stones with the same surname will be grouped together in the lists even though they may be buried in different rows. Cemetery records refer to this Section as the "Old Yard", Section A, or sometimes as Section 3. At one time Preston was the name designated by the post office for New Haven. This is the first time for these records to be published.

The following symbols were used as a key in typing these records:
* = no gravestone on lot. The name and dates were obtained from cemetery records.
' = gravestone on lot. It was illegible and/or missing date(s) were obtained from cemetery records.
( ) = data copied from cemetery records or additional information not on stones or in the records.
+ = data copied from gravestones in 1959 by Stanley W. McClure; no gravestone on the lot as of 1988.

OLD YARD or "A" SECTION

NAME BD or AE DD Row - No.
_____, _____ (stone cross, no inscription) 1 1
BRANDENBURG, Elizabeth 10-20-1840 12-31-1866 1 2
+BRANDENBURG, Joab (?) 37y 5-31-1831 1+ 3 [Jacob,War of 1812] [Stone set in concrete-no dates]
HALL, Jonathan 2-18-1818 7-11-1889 1 4
HALL, Catherine BRANDENBURG 11-10-1823 1901' 1 5 w/o Jonathan;Mother
CHRISMAN, Elias 73y10m25d 9- 2-1858 1 6
CHRISMAN, Susannah 12-27-1791 9-22-1875 1 7
HAMIL(TON?), David -footstone type headstone 1 8
with hand carve letters & no dates.
TEMPLE, Charlotte d/o 1y 1m 5d 10- 1-1851 1 9 S.C. & Nancy TULL
TULL, Euphama w/o Richard 56y 2m 11d 10- 6-1851 1 10 TULL; d/o S.C. &
L. TULL
TULL, William A. b.MD 7- 9-1828 1-20-1913 1 11(Res. Barthol Co.)
THOMAS, Robert L. 1903 1921 1 12 s/o James & Zelma
SMITH THOMAS; Res. Johnson's Fork, IN
LENHOFF, Peter 69y' 1908' 1 13 Civil War Vet.
Co. E. 2nd KY Inf.
OTTO, Hazel M.(d/o J. & L.) 1897 1899 2 1 (Res. Preston, OH)
STONE, Eugene Donald 10- 8-1930 5-16-1960 2 2 (s/o Eugene & Edith
OTTO STONE; Ohio Pfc Artillery, WW II Vet.; Res. Bradenton, FL)
OTTO, Lida Ellen (NOES) 1869 1931 2 3 (w/o John) Mother
" ssa, John - Father 1865 1943 2+ (Res.Harrison,OH)
CONOVER, M. (Footstone type headstone) ---- 2 4
DILL, Elias Ferree 19y 7m 6d 6-10-1862 2 5 s/o John & Ann
Co. G 5th Ohio Cav. Civil War Vet.
BAUGHMAN, Samuel A.-s/o 1y 7m29d 4-24-1834 2 6 John & Lucinda S.
MILHOLLAND, Infant 4m27d 2- 3-1863 3 1 s/o C. & M.L.
SHUCK, Elizabeth 74y 4-30-1850 3 2
SHUCK, George 13y 7m 5d 7- 7-1831 3 3
HAYDEN(?), Gilbert s/o 17y10m13d 7- 5-1859 3 4 Enoch & Elizabeth
DUBOIS, Clark S. 7-16-1858 4- 2-1873 3 5
" ssa , Alvah I. 7- 2-1851 3-18-1873
" ssa , John W(arren) 10-22-1819 12-28-1902 (Res.Preston,OH)
" ssa , Nancy WARD 6-22-1821 2-15-1873 w/o John W.
WARD, Harriet L. 24y 5m12d 10-24-1842 3 6 w/o R. WARD & d/o
James & Darcus BANISTER
PATTERSON, Jehu 22y 5m 1d 9-11-1865 3 7 s/o Jehu &
Elizabeth; Co. K 4th Ohio Cav.-Civil War Vet.
PATTERSON, Jehu 83y 12- 8-1867 3 8
+CLEMENS(?), Mary C. & 28y -m26d+ 12-1?-1872+ 3+ 9 d/o J. & E.
PATTERSON; w/o C.
+CLEMENS(?), Elizabeth ---- ---- d/o Mary C.
CLENDENING, Evert 6-18-1806 8-31-1878 3 10
CLENDENING, Maggie A.M. 24y 4m16d 7-10-1871 3 11 d/o E. & A.
CLENDENING, Thomas W. 21y 2m 5d 11-20-1848 3 12 s/o E. & M.
BUTTS, Alice E. 19y10m22d 3-26-1873 4 1 w/o William H.
BUTTS, Henry 60y 8m 8d 10- 1-1872 4 2
" ssa, Charlotte 70y.& 18d 4-14-1887 w/o Henry
" ssa, Thomas 20y 9m11d 1- 2-1865 s/o H. & C.
THOMAS, Wm.- MD 54y 3-17-1853 4 3
CORYELL, John 50y ?m15d 5- 7-1843 4 4 of Lycoming Co.PA
F & AM member & OES star emblem
RITTENHOUSE, John L. 76y ?m15d 6- 2-1839 4 5
RITTENHOUSE, Maria 73y 7m 9d 4- 5-1836 4 6
LEMON, William In 74th yr. 3- 6-1851 5 1
LEMON, Margaret 56y 11-14-1835 5 2 w/o William
WRIGHT, Lavina HUDSON 74y 12-30-1882 5 3 w/o J. WRIGHT
SEFTON, Elizabeth 1- 1-1777 12-21-1841 5 4 b. in Ireland
SEFTON, Henry, Sr. 66y 8m17d 7-27-1834 5 4
FRENCH, Mrs. Charlotte 25y 1m 6-12-1834 5 6 d/o Henry &
Elizabeth SEFTON
LONG, Hester ATHERTON 38y 6m26d 11- 2-1834 5 7 w/o Daniel
leaving 8 daughters & 2 sons
MORRISON, Rebecca 24y 3m18d 6-12-1866 5 8 d/o Wm. & Rebecca
MORRISON, Amos W. 4m20d 8- 1-1862 5 9 s/o Jas.A. & Susana

BD or AE DD Row - No.
KREWSON, Amy 72y 3m12d 12- 8-1854 5 10 w/o John J.
KREWSON, Alexander Infant ---- 5 11 s/o Amos D. & Mary
KREWSON, John H.-Infant 3m28d 1-11-1848 5 12 s/o Amos D. & Mary
KREWSON, William M.-Infant 27d 9-19-1846 5 13 s/o Amos D. & Mary
LURTON, Franklin Joshua 1m24d 7-24-1852 5 14 Adopted s/o B.F. &
Mary STEEL
KELCH, J. J.(Jackson Jefferson)1828 1900 5 15 Res. Preston, OH
" ssa, Mary 11- 2-1833 11-20-1890 w/o J. J.
" ssa, Mary E. 11- 6-1856 8-24-1871
" ssa, Thomas J. 7- 5-1860 12-11-1882
HALL, Sarah Ann 1855 1928 5 16(w/o J.J. KELCH &
Henry HALL; Res. New Haven, OH)
WAKEFIELD, Mollie DeARMOND 1856 1924 6 1 (w/o Elijah)Lot 4A
WAKEFIELD, Elijah 1854 1926 6 2 (h/o Mollie; Res.
Butler Co. OH, Lot 4A)
WAKEFIELD, Emma 7-25-1861 9- 7-1892 6 3 nee AGNEW; Mother
WICKARD, Ella-Mother 1855 1896 6 4 (Ellen Jane, 1st
w/o Joseph WICKARD)
WICKARD, Jos.-Father 1855 1924 6 5 (Sr., h/o Mattie,
Res. New Baltimore, OH)
WICKARD, Martha-Mother;Lot28 1860 1943 6 6 (w/o Joseph, Sr.)
WICKARD, Lowry 1y 1896* Old Yard*
LITTLE, Philena (Set in Concrete-no dates) 6 7 w/o Dr. George
LITTLE, Dr. George 70y 6m24d 9-13-1852 6 8 F & AM Emblem
LITTLE, Jane H. 18y 2m23d 9- 3-1833 6 9 d/o Dr. G. & P.
LITTLE, Hester Ann 5m17d 8-21-1820 6 10 d/o Dr. G. & P.
COMSTOCK, Joab 57y 1m10d 5-14-1825 6 11
BARTLIT, Eunice B. 20y & 30d 8- 7-1831 6 12 Consort of David
BARTLETT (two different spellings on the stone)
BARTLETT, Phebe D. 5- ?-1818 4-17-1855 6 13 w/o D. BARTLETT
BARTLETT, David 62y 6m18d 9-27-1870 6 14
RADCLIFFE, John W. 1846 1912 7 1 Lot 5A
RADCLIFFE, Eliza Ann 1843 1929 7 2 (w/o John-Lot 5A)
RADCLIFFE, Eliza Jane 10- 6-1866 6- 2-1894 7 3 d/o J.W. & E. A.
MYERS, James W.-Brother 11-11-1852 8- 9-1935+ 7 4 (s/o Daniel & Anna
Res. Springfield, OH)
MYERS, Daniel-Father 6-11-1826 4- 4-1887 7 5
MYERS, Ann E(liza)Mother 11-16-1830 7-20-1907 7 6 (w/o Daniel)
CONE, James S. 21y 4m 2d 9-10-1827 7 7 s/o Charles & Jane
WHIPPLE, Joab 46y 3m15d 7- 4-1859 7 8
" ssa , Jane J(OHNSON) 98y 6m19d 6- 7-1916 LUTES his wife.
(w/o Joab-Res. Crosby Township)
" ssa , Charlie 5m 6d 2- 9-1857 s/o J. & J.J.
" ssa , Mary A(lbina) 20y 2m 3d 2-23-1860 7 9 d/o Joab & Jane J.
" ssa , David J. 16y10m14d 11-10-1870 7 10 s/o Joab & Jane J.
COMSTOCK, Amy Eloisa 8m 9d 3-13-1827 7 11
BREVOORT, Emma F. 2y 6m 5-16-1843 7 12
COMSTOCK, Chloe 43y 5m 7d 8-17-1834 7 13
PIERCE, Edith 12-19-1851 2- 2-1853 7 14
MILHOLLAND, John C. 7m 5-25-1864 7 15 s/o G.W. & R.
" ssa , Rebecca 49y 2m 8d 9-19-1878 w/o Geo. W.
HYATT, Margaret 23y 6m 5d 4-24-1865 7 16 d/o John & Martha
SMITH, Sally 3-12-1796 1- 6-1851 7 17 54y 9m25d
PULSE, Peter, Sr. 68y 6m27d 1-26-1844 7 18
PULSE, Sarah 74y 8m 1d 4- 3-1872 7 19 w/o Peter
PROVINCE, Neal 1870 1955 8 1 (h/o Ida-Res. Green
Township-Lot 6 Sec.A)
PROVINCE, Ida DEAN 1871 1965 8 2 (w/o Neal-Lot 6 & 7
Sec. A-Res. Cincinnati, OH)
PROVINCE, Joseph L. 12- 4-1892 11-18-1967 8 3 (s/o Neal & Ida)
Ohio 1st Sgt. Co. L 330 Infantry WW I Vet.-Res. Cincinnati, OH
BLACKBURN, R. H. 75y & 13d 3-25-1888 8 4
" ssa , Catherine (C.)83y 5m15d 11-19-1898 w/o R.H.(Res.
Preston, OH)

NAME BD or AE DD Row-No.
BUTTS, Lillian 4y11m 2d 10- 9-1887 8 5 d/o G.E. & M.L.
MARSH, Sarah Annett 26y 7m 7d 2- 8-1856 8 6 w/o Moses
WEBER, Louis 7- 4-1831 1- 7-1906 9 1 Civil War Vet.
Co. H 183 Ohio Inf. & Co. H 185 O.V.I. (Lot 6 & 7 Sec.A)
" ssa, Elizabeth 10-20-1836 1-17-1892 w/o Louis
TURK, Frank J. 10-15-1859 11-22-1884 9 2 (F-L-T in overlapping ovals as an emblem)
VANSICKLE, Eliza 7-26-1851 1-16-1893 9 3
VANSICKLE, Baxter 74y 3-12-1872 9 4
VANCLEVE, John, Sr. 68y11m22d 9- 6-1850 9 5
VANCLEVE, Jane CLARK 75y 6m18d 4-28-1866 9 6 w/o John
VANSICKLE, Rachel 10- 7-1821 1- 9-1850 9 7 w/o Baxter & d/o John & Jane VANCLEVE - aged 28y 3m 3d
BARTLETT, Euphemia ---- ---- 9 8 d/o Wm. H. & Eliza
" ssa , Horatio ---- ---- s/o Wm. H. & Eliza
BARTLIT, Anna In 56th year 8- 5-1832 9 9
BARTLETT, Josiah 12- 2-1767 11- 1-1856 9 10
BARTLETT, Nancy COMSTOCK 43y 1m 2d 4-17-1840 9 11 Mother; w/o Latham S.
BARTLETT, Latham S. 63y 7m27d 6-13-1862 9 12
BARTLETT, Harriet 2m 3d 5- 9-1836 9 13 d/o L.S. & Nancy
BARTLETT, Josiah 3y10m24d 11- 3-1827 9 14 s/o L.S. & Nancy
HARDY, Hannah 18m16d 12-23-1843 9 15
WILLIAMSON, Elias C. 7-23-1814 1-12-1855 9 16
" ssa , Barbara SMITH 3-27-1820 4-21-1841 w/o Elias C.
" ssa , Josiah T. 4-14-1841 8- 4-1841 s/o E.C. & B.S.
WILLIAMSON, Rebecca B. 23y10m24d 4-21-1842 9 17 SHANNON w/o Wm. K.
COULTHARD, Geo. 26y 9m27d 10- 5-1865 9 18 Civil War Vet. in U.S. Navy
KENDALL, Lizzie-b.England 6-20-1842 1- 6-1863 9 19 d/o Joseph & Ann
JEANES, Ellen Anna 21y 6m 3d 1-11-1873 9 20 w/o John Thomas JEANES
COWGUILL, Madison 41y 7m 3- 4-1859 9 21 Husband
COWGUILL, Henry G. 6y 9m20d 5-16-1855 9 22 s/o M. & E.
COWGUILL, Thomas M. 7-22-1850 2-11-1878 9 23 s/o Madison & Eliza J.
COWGUILL, Washington 7-28-1817 9-14-1855 9 24 (38y 1m16d)
THOMPSON, Lydia In 45th year 9-13-1849 9 25 Consort of Josiah
COWGUILL, Elizabeth In 65th year 8-14-1845 9 26 Consort of John
PASSMORE, George W. 1859 5-28-1938' 10 1 (h/o Emma; Lot 6 & 7 Sec. A - Res. New Haven, OH)
" ssa , Emma (WEBER) 61y' 12- 5-1930 (w/o George)
MORTEN, Carrie E. 67y' 8-31-1917 10 2 (Caroline WEBER)
BARTLETT, Wm. H.-MD 1-27-1806 8-13-1884 10 3
" ssa , Matilda S. 9-27-1827 12-25-1896 w/o Wm. H. (Res. Preston, OH)
THOMPSON, Elijah F. 1y 1m13d 12-13-1832 10 4 s/o E.W. & C.A.
_____, ____Illegible 10y11m14d ?-10-1835?10 5
THOMPSON, Clinton W. 2y11m 5d 1-26-1832?10 6 s/o E.W. & C.A.
NUTT, Adam 11-16-1752 9-27-1833 10 7 (80y10m11d)
NUTT, Nancy 12-15-1757 3-13-1835 10 8 w/o Adam; DAR Marker
SAVIN, Mary 58y 7m 9- 7-1835 10 9 w/o Peter Robert
ESTABROOKS, Manda Jane In 30th year 3-21-1866 11 1 w/o William
CAVENDER, A. P. 54y 2m28d 12-16-1842 11 2
M.A.C. (footstone only) ---- ---- 11 3
------, July -illegible ---- 7-18-1828 11 4
A.H.C. ---- 7-21-1832 11 5
A. C. ---- 7-23-1832 11 6
CAVENDER, S. ---- 8- 8-1832 11 7
L. C. ---- 8-30-1832 11 8
A. C. ---- ---- 11 9
------, ------ Illegible ---- ---- 11 10
BROWN, Mary In 19th year 10- ?-1835 11 11 Consort of Robert D.
SHROYER, George 1852 1852 11 12
" ssa , John,Sr. 1798 1864 11 13 Father
" ssa , Delila RUTHERFORD 1804 1835 11 14 w/o John, Sr.
" ssa , Infant One date 1837 11 15
" ssa , Catherine (d/o John) 1845 1916 11 16 (Res.Butler Co.OH)
" ssa , Delila 1840 1919 11 17 (s/o Thomas SHROYER & Res. Butler Co. OH)
" ssa , Margaret NELSON 1810 1891 11 18 w/o John,Sr.-Mother
" ssa , John, Jr. 1843 1868 11 19
SCOTT, Mary Elizabeth 8m 6d 8-20-1859 11 20 d/o Wm. Henry & Elizabeth Ann
SCOTT, Infant One date 5- 6-1853 11 21 d/o Wm. Henry & Elizabeth Ann
SCOTT, William Olin 11m 9d 8-10-1856 11 22 s/o Wm. Henry & Elizabeth Ann
HOPPING, Forest M(cKinley) 1900 1978 12 1 (w/o Ella-Res. Lawrenceburg, Dearborn Co. IN-Lot 13A)
" ssa , Ella 1902 ----
PERLEE, John 2- 4-1824 3- 4-1897 12 2 (Res. Harrison, OH)
" ssa , Sara A. BARTLETT 6-30-1830 10-14-1918 w/o John (Lot 17A Sec.3
BARTLETT, Lewis L. 27y 7m25d 9- 6-1873 12 3
" ssa , Herbert L. 8m21d 1-19-1873 s/o Lewis L. & Emma

COULTHARD, Sarah 1-11-1811 8-11-1880 12 4 w/o John; b. in Yorkshire, England
ssa THOMAS, Mary (COULTHARD) 1841 1927 w/o Joseph
" ssa , John 5-11-1810 8- 4-1878 b. in Yorkshire, England
" ssa , Sarah 12-23-1852 6- 6-1873 d/o John & Sarah
PASSMORE, Stephen-Father 1830 1911 12 5 (h/o Rachel; Res. New Haven, OH - Lot 33A Sec.3)
" ssa , Rachel 1823 1904 w/o Stephen; Mother
PASSMORE, Infant ---- 1896* __ __ s/o Amos;Lot33A Sec.3
DUVALL, J. L.(James) ---- 1900' 12 6 Co. B. 181 Ohio Inf. Civil War Vet. (Lot 45A Sec. 3)
DUVALL, Marietta 1848 1897 12 7 (Lot 45A Sec. 3)
CORSON, Syl'r (Sylvester) 1851 1914 13 1 (Res. Millcreek Township; Lot 18 Sec. ?)
" ssa , Alice (L.CREIGHTON) 1854 1910
CREIGHTON, Lorenia (GOSHORN)3-31-1827 8-12-1874 13 2 w/o Wm., Sr.
CREIGHTON, Jacob G. 1-30-1844 12-11-1915 13 3 Corp'l 2 Ohio L.A. Civil War Vet. (Member of Freemonts Body Guards)
" ssa , Harriot L. 6-19-1845 9-28-1888 13 4 DUBOIS; Mother; w/o J. B.
" ssa , Nellie M. 1- 7-1872 3-14-1873 13 5
" ssa , Minnie M. 6- 1-1870 3-12-1873 13 6
COULTHARD, Catherine OPPERMAN 6-24-1850 8-2-1882 13 7 b. France; Sister
ssa OPPERMAN, Charles J. 8-15-1842 8-20-1874 Co. B 167 Ohio Inf. Civil War Vet.; born in France.
OPPERMAN, John B. 3- 9-1812 10-26-1873 13 8
" ssa , Rosina 11-15-1815 1-30-1870 w/o John B.
McBAYLES, Robert 81y 1911* -- - (Res. Cambridge City, IN; Run over by a train; Lot 30 Sec.?)
McBAYLES, Mary C. 1831 1903 13 9 w/o R.(Res.Dublin,IN)
McBAYLES, William A. 7y10m28d 3-22-1868 13 10 s/o R.Mc & M. C.
STARLIN, Eliza 8-19-1842 2- 8-1873+ 13 11 w/o S.
STARLIN, Samuel K. 2-10-1838 8-26-1883 13 12
STARLIN, Daniel 12- 2-1841 3-13-1919 13 13 (h/o Elizabeth)
" ssa , Eliza J. 9-24-1843 9-16-1872 RADCLIFFE;w/o Daniel
STARLIN, William 9-11-1812 5-25-1896 13 14 (h/o Anna; Res. Preston, OH; Lot 38 Sec. 3)
" ssa , Anna SMITH 11-17-1809 4-20-1883
STARLIN, Elizabeth 1836 1927 13 15 (Lot 38A Sec. ?)
SPOHR, John Henry 1851 1939 13 16 (h/o Inez; Lot46A)
" ssa, Inez CARTER 1850 1917
SPOHR, Blanche Baby ---- ---- 13 17
SPOHR, Retha or Letha 58y 1958* -- - w/o Forrest (Res. Morgan Township, Butler Co. OH; Lot 46A)
SPOHR, Forrest ---- ----* -- - h/o Retha or Letha
CAMPBELL, William H(enry) 1866 1942 14 1 (Lot 11 Sec. ?)
" ssa , Lulu M(ay) (BUELL) 1866 1945 (w/o Wm. H.)
ANDREWS, James T.(Lot 19A) 1851 1905 14 2 (Res. Seven Mile,OH)
" ssa , Elizabeth A. 1854 1918 (w/o James;Lot 6)
CASE, **Geo.** 1831 1879 14 **3**
CASE, Sarah 1846 1878 14 4
CASE, Etta 1869 1874 14 5
CADY, Robert J. 9m13d 7-19-1872 14 6 s/o D. & A.
DAWSON, Henry-Civil War Vet. ---- ---- 14 7 Co. A 76 Ohio Inf.
CARTER, John C. 7-29-1837 3-10-1871 14 8
" ssa , James Harvey 12-26-1834 7- 1-1910 Co. F 93 Ohio Inf. Civil War Vet. (Res. in Iowa; Lot 31 Sec. A
" ssa , Blanche M. 11-30-1855 ---- (Buried in Iowa)
" ssa , Robert B. 11-15-1894 1-11-1898 s/o J.H. & B.M. (Res. Vincennes, IN; Lot 31 Sec. A)
" ssa , John 2-16-1800 10- 1-1876
" ssa , Nancy 12-10-1809 6- 4-1894
HARPER, John 1822 1904 14 9 (Lot35A-Res.New Haven)
" ssa , Mary (TIMMONS) 1830 1904 w/o John (Bur. in Gr.of John)
SCHEERING, Charles 1840 1875 14 10
SCHEERING, Wilhelmina 1841 1914 (Res.Butler Co.OH;Lot39)
PASSMORE, Charles A. 1893 1956 15 1
PASSMORE, A(lfred) T. 1859 1928 15 2 Metal marker "**Mt.** Healthy Council #244" Jr. Order UAM (f/o C.A. PASSMORE, Res.Mt. Healthy,OH Lot 12 Sec. 1)
PASSMORE, Charles Alfred 9y 1928* -- -(s/o C.A.,Sr.-Lot12A)
PASSMORE, Norman 1y 1923 -- - (s/o Chas.-Lot 12A)
*DINN, Crystal Mae 1y 1901 (grd d/o A.T. PASSMORE)
RITTENHOUSE, Wright 3?- ?-1851 ---- 15 3 s/o George & Eliza [bottom of stone is broken off]
RITTENHOUSE, Frank E.(Lot16) 37y 1905* -- - (Res.Cincinnati, OH)
RITTENHOUSE, G. William " 44y 1906* -- - (Res.Cincinnati,OH)
RITTENHOUSE, Eliza " 75y 1906* -- - (Res.Cincinnati,OH)
RITTENHOUSE, Mary S. " ---- 1940* -- - (Res.Cincinnati,OH
MONTGOMERY, _______ Our Baby ---- 15 4
MONTGOMERY, L. ---- ---- 15 5
MONTGOMERY, Andrew 6m24d 2-20-1873 15 6 s/o Hugh & Phoebe
MONTGOMERY, **George W.[dates set in concrete]** 15 7 s/o Hugh & Phoebe

OLD YARD or "A" SECTION - Continued

NAME BD or AE DD Row No.

MONTGOMERY, James H. 1-29-1854 4-10-1889 15 8 [Married Hattie E. SEFTON, 28 Feb. 1878]
PASSMORE, Elias (Lot 36) 1825 1904 15 9 (h/o Ann; Res. Preston, OH)
PASSMORE, Ann GOSHORN DENNING 1821 1911 15 10 (w/o Elias)
BERNARD, Margaret DENNING SPRINGER-1841 1890 15 11
DENNING, Arthur I. 1852 1890 15 12
SMITH, John V.(VanTREESE) 1845 1915 15 13 Civil War Vet. Res. Harrison, OH

SECTION I

Lot -Sec.

McCLURE, Barney S(IMONSON) 1866 1945 1 1 (h/o Grace) (Res. New Haven, OH)
McCLURE, Grace H(OUSTON) 1873 1938 Mother(w/o Barney)
McCLURE, William W.-Father 1830 1918 2 1 (h/o Martha A.)
" ssa , Martha A.(SIMONSON) 1832 1915 Mother (w/o Wm.)
" ssa , William 1871 1871 s/o W.W. & M.A.
" ssa , Martha A. 1877 1878 d/o W.W. & M.A.
CREIGHTON, Wm. W. 1868 1907 3 1 (h/o Ada CHRISTY)
F-L-T- in 3 ovals on metal marker emblem.
CREIGHTON, Addella (w/o Wm. W.) 1877 1911 (Res. Crosby Twp.)
" ssa , Alvah 1901 1912 (s/o Wm. & Addie)
CREIGHTON, Ezra S. (s/o Jacob) 1880 1949 (Res.College Corner,OH)
CREIGHTON, Lillian H. KING 1889 1975 4 1 (w/o Charles B.)
CREIGHTON, Charles B. 1884 1845 (h/o Lillian)
CREIGHTON, Carrie E(dith) 1866 1941 (d/o Jacob;Res.Harrison,OH)
CREIGHTON, George 1882 1938 (s/o Jacob,Res.Hamilton,OH)
KELHOFFER, Maebell E(thel) 1912 1918 5 1 (d/o Martin)
KELHOFFER, Elizabeth L(ulu) 1884 1925 (w/o Martin)
KELHOFFER, Martin(Res.Hamilton,OH)1879 1957 (h/o Lulu)
KELHOFFER, Albert 1876 1933 s/o Frank, Sr.
KELHOFFER, Frank A. (Sr.)Father 1847 1926 (h/o Barbara,Res.Hamilton,OH KUTCHENRIDER, Res. New Haven, Crosby Twp.)
" ssa , Barbara DIEFENBACHER 1852 1918 w/o Frank A.,Sr.
" ssa , Amelia 1895 1913 d/o Frank & Barbara
KELHOFFER, Henrietta-Mother 1885 1913 (w/o Alex,Res.Butler Co.OH
6 1 No burials
MOORE, Creighton C.(Res.Hamilton,OH)1897 1960 7 1 (s/o Wm. & Lucy)
MOORE, Nannie-wife(Res.Hamilton,OH) 1897 1933 (w/o Creighton)
MOORE, William S.-Father- " 1874 1947 (h/o Lucy)
MOORE, Lucy W.-Mother- " 1877 1974' (Lucy Nellie CREIGHTON) (w/o William MOORE)
MOORE, Helen E.-(Res.Hamilton,OH)1903 1919 (d/o Lucy & Wm.)
SCHWING, Emma 1876 1959 8 1 (d/o Jacob)
SCHWING, Jacob-(Res.New Haven,OH)1853 1928 (h/o Sarah)
" ssa Sarah (Res.Hamilton,OH) 1853 1919 (w/o Jacob)
SCHWING, William (Res.Harrison Twp.)1879 1959 9 1 (h/o Mabel)
SCHWING, Mabelle (UNDERWOOD) 1882 1967 (Res.Harrison,OH)
SCHWING, Theadore (Wm.) Infant 1922 (s/o Wm. & Mary)
SCHWING, Julia (Gertrude) 1915 1916 (d/o Wm.-Crsoby Twp.)
SCHWING, Charles (Homer) 1908 1925 (s/o Wm. & May)
HATHAWAY, Henry (E.)(h/o Adelia) 1859 1924 10 1 Knights of Pythias member. (Res. Cincinnati, OH)
HATHAWAY, Adelia (M.) nee CAMPBELL-1862 1908 (w/o H.E., Res.New Haven)
CALEY, C.W. (Dr.)(Res.New Haven) 1856 1915 11 1 (h/o Mary)
CALEY, Mary M. (McCLURE-w/o Dr.C.W.)1868 1946 (Res.Miami, FL)
CALEY, Lois (d/o Dr.C.W.) 1891 1962 (Res.Miami, FL)
DRAKE, Mary CALEY-(Res.Preston,OH) 1827 1902 12 1 (m/o Wilbur)
DRAKE, Wilber-Father-F & AM emblem 1857 1929 (h/o Ella-Res.Indianapolis,IN)
DRAKE, Ella (AGNEW) Mother 1867 1954 (w/o Wilbur ")
WALKER, John-(Res. Crosby Twp.) 78y* 1911*13 1 Co. F 93 Ohio Inf. Civil War Vet.
WALKER, Owen , Corp'l ---- ---- Co. F 93 Ohio Inf. Civil War Vet.
WALKER, Abbie ---- ----
WALKER, Jane BROOKS 90y 1902*13* 1 (Res. Sater, OH)
WALKER, John C.-(Res.New Baltimore,OH)66y 1939*13* 1
WALKER, George A. " " 1852 1924 14 1 (b/o Abagail)
WALKER, Mary J. (Res.Crosby Twp.) 1856 1917 (w/o George)
WALKER, Abagail-Res.New Baltimore,OH)74y 1924*14 1 (s/o George)
WELLING, George J.(Sr.) 1890 1934 14* 1 (h/o Mabel)
WELLING, Mabel WALKER 76y 1965* (w/o George)
ADAMS, Clyde W(illiam) 1899 1968 (Res. Livonia, MI)
ADAMS, Earl 10- 8-1891 8-28-1912
WERT, Harry (Res.Harrison,OH)1-25-1887 7-13-1948 15 1 Pfc 322 Field Arty 83 Div WW I Vet.
WERT, Dorothea ---- 1931*15* 1 d/o Lena OWENS WERT
OWENS, J(oseph) M. 1862 1923
OWENS, Ida May (Res.New Haven) 1868 1906 (w/o Jos.)
OWENS, Willis C(lark)(Res.Harrison Twp)1895 1910 (s/o Mark OWENS)
PERKINS, Ida May d/o Lena ---- 1925*15* 1 OWENS PERKINS
BURNETT, Alfred-(Res.Shandon,OH) 1871 1939 16 1
BURNETT, Mary HALL 1851 1910 (Res.NewHaven,OH)
BURNETT, David Richard 1844 1916 (Res.Harrison,OH)

Lot-Sec.

MYERS, Joseph Daniel 4- 3-1907 4-15-1957 17 1 Ohio TSgt 1560 Service Unit, WW II (h/o Anna Flora)
MYERS, William R. 1860 1926 (h/o Edith,Res. Shandon,OH)
MYERS, Edith M(ae McHENRY) 1864 1929 (w/o Wm., Res.Shandon, OH)
ADAMS, Fannie M. 1891 1988 18 1
"ssa , Claude L. 1885 1960 (h/o Fannie,Res.Harrison,OH)
ADAMS, Norma R(uth) 1921 1926 (d/o Claude & Fannie)
HOPPING, Robert 1866 1930
HOPPING, Mary A.(BIBEE) 1871 1941 (Res.Harrison, OH)
KELHOFFER, Frank, Jr.-husband 1869 1946 19 1 (h/o Martha-New Haven)
KELHOFFER, Martha - Wife 1867 1929 (w/o Frank,Jr.-Harrison,OH)
MEARS, Flodie L.(s/o Charles) 1887 1956 20 1 (Res.Washington, DC)
MEARS, Charles (h/o Lillian) 1900 1978 (Res. Harrison, OH)
" ssa, Lillian A. (AMISS) 1906 ----
CLEAVER, Henry 1866 1950 21 1 (Res.Pendleton, IN)
" ssa , Alice BRISBIN 1852 1926
" ssa , Ida (Ida Mae BRISBIN) 1882 1911 (w/o Henry,Res.Crosby Twp.)
CLEAVER, Edward Ellswroth 1y 1905*22* - s/o Ed & Justin
CLEAVER, Mary Eloise 1y 1910*22* d/o Ed & Justin
CLEAVER, Nancy 72y 1912*22* (Res.Harrison Twp.)
MILLER, Lawrence-Father 1838 1918 23 1
" ssa , Louisa LANDWERTH-Wife 1853 1913 w/o Lawrence
KUTCHENRIDER, Mary MILLER 45y* 1916*23* 1 (1st w/o George
POTTENGER, David Francis 1861 1941 24 1 (s/o David,Res. College Corner, OH)
" ssa , Carrie Bell WEST 1865 1910 Wife (w/o Frank,Res. Ross,OH)
POTTENGER, Harry Ross (Res.Preston,OH)2m6d 12-1-1901 s/o Frank & Carrie
POTTENGER, Earl F(rancis) 21y' 1912' (s/o Frank & Carrie,Ross,OH)
BECKER, George W.(Res.Butler Co.OH)1848 1913 25 1
" ssa , Gertrude WALKER 1857 ---- w/o George
" ssa , Willie-(Res.Preston,OH)1896 1900 (s/o George)
NOES, Clifford, Sr.(Res.Cincinnti,OH)1884-1961 26 1 (h/o Martha)
"ssa, Martha G. HAMMITT 1886 1976 (w/o Clifford)
NOES, Clark Allen 1907 1908 s/o James & Myrtle
FLOWERS, Carrie B(elle) 1873 1904 w/o R.C.FLOWERS (d/o Ben & Lavina NOES, Res. Ross, Butler Co. OH)
NOES, Leonard B.(Jack) 50y' 3-18-1937 Ohio Pvt 324 HV Fld Arty 83 Div WW I Vet. (s/o Lavina & Benj.)
NOES, Benjamin J. 1841 1908 Co. F 93 Ohio Inf. Civil War Vet. (h/o Lavina, Res.Mt. Hope, Crosby Twp.)
"ssa, Lavina PROVINCE-Wife 1846 1937 (Res. New Haven, OH
BRISBIN, Robert H. ("Pink") 1846 1927 27 1 (Res. Crosby Twp.)
BRISBIN, Walter 61y 1939*27* 1 (Res. Crosby Twp.)
BRISBIN, Leroy(Res.Preston,OH) 1y 1903*27* 1 s/o W. & A.
BRISBIN, Infant 0y 1906*27* 1 (Res. Butler Co.OH)
BRISBIN, Adaline(Res.ButlerCo.OH 30y 1910*27* 1 (w/o Walter,Sr.)
BRISBIN, Margaret(Res.Butler Co.OH) 1y 1910*27* 1
WICKARD, Susan McHENRY 11-15-1825 3-4-1910 28 1 (Res.Centerville,IN)
JONES, Kate W.(Katherine WICKARD)1875 1939 (w/o James, Res.Richmond,IN)
JONES, James 73y 1932*28* 1 (h/o Kate,Res. Okeana, Butler Co. OH)
NUGENT, Phoebe (Julia) 1863 1932 29 1 (s/o Inez GWALTNEY) Res. Harrison, OH
GWALTNEY, Charles E. 1901 1936 32 Degree Mason Emblem (s/o Joseph, Res. Cincinnati, OH)
GWALTNEY, Infant of Charles 0y 1919*29* 1
GWALTNEY, Arthur V(ernon) 1882 1952 (s/o Josiah, Res. New Haven,OH)
GWALTNEY, Clifford E. 1884 1963 Thirty-Second Degree Mason Emblem (Res. New Haven, OH)
GWALTNEY, Inez A. (NUGENT)10-16-1875 10-16-1952 (w/o Joseph,Res.Crosby Twp.)
GWALTNEY, Joseph A(aron) 1-14-1880 5-20-1958 (h/o Inez,Res.New Haven, OH)
GWALTNEY, Catherine-Mother 1843 1921 (w/o Josiah,Res.Butler Co.OH)
GWALTNEY, Gertrude G. 1878 1923 (d/o Josiah & Catherine)
GIFFORD, William H. 1890 1946 30 1 (b/o John,Res. Mercer Co. OH)
GIFFORD, John Henry 1892 1963 (h/o Mary,Res.Circleville,OH)
" ssa , Mary (OTTO) 1895 ----
GIFFORD, Herbert 1895 1969 (b/o John,Res.Circleville,OH)
GIFFORD, Ernest R. 1941 1941
GIFFORD, Violet-Infant d/o 0y' 12- 6-1925 John & Mary GIFFORD
RUGG, Chaffin Walter 78y 1914*31* 1 (Res. Butler Co.OH)
RUGG, Mary (Res.Harrison,OH) 52y 1924*31* 1 (w/o H.H. RUGG
RUGG, Abigail CHISMAN 92y 1935*31* 1 (Res.Indianapolis,IN)
HAUK, Benjamin (Res.Harrison,OH)1851 1922 32 1 (h/o Ellen)

NAME BD or AE DD Lot Sec.

HAUK, Ellen M. (MONTGOMERY) 1850 1929' (w/o Benjamin)
MONTGOMERY, Thomas 64y 1921*-- - (h/o Kate)
MONTGOMERY, Catherine ADAMS 73y 1936*32* 1 (w/o Thomas)
(Res. Harrison, OH)
MONTGOMERY, Harry (Res.Crosby Twp)--- 1918*32* 1 (s/o Thos. & Cath.)
MONTGOMERY, Sadie (Sarah E.) 53y' 1912'33 1 (Res. Crosby Twp.)
" ssa , Aaron 66y' 1916'(s/o Hugh,Res.Crosby Twp)
" ssa , William 70y' 1935' (Res. Lima,OH)
" ssa , Nannie(Mamie Sadie?) 53y' 1922'(Res. Harrison, OH)
KINNETT, Nannie A.(MONTGOMERY) 1892 1974 (d/o Thomas &
Kate MONTGOMERY, Res. Lawrenceburg, Dearborn Co. IN)
SCHARDINE, Val(entine h/o Lena) 1852 1930 34 1 (Res.New Haven,OH)
" ssa , Lena (Magdelina BARNHART)1858 1944 (w/o Valentine)
" ssa , Fay (Louise,Res.Preston,OH)1893 1902 (d/o V. & L.)
McHENRY, Joseph 1834 1903 35 1 (Res. Preston,OH)
" ssa , Rachel A.(ATHERTON) 1838 1911 w/o Joseph
McHENRY, John Lowry, MD 1868 1933 (ftr? Lee,Res.Cincinnati)
CRAIG, Laura A(nne) 10-22-1864 7- 3-1897 36 1 w/o Wm. A.
(d/o A. & M. SEALS, Res. Preston, OH
"ssa , Wm. A(aron) , 1-30-1859 5-16-1938 (Res.New Baltimore, OH)
CRAIG, Olive Beatrice 1y 1904*36* 1 (grd d/o Wm. CRAIG)
(Res. Shandon, OH)
GRIMM, Mary A. CRAIG 21y 1907*36* 1 (Res.Hamilton, OH)
CLEAVER, James H(arvey) 9-27-1863 7-20-1895 37 1 (Res. Preston, OH)
CLEAVER, Florence (Catherine)1-21-1863 9-20-1943 (w/o James, Res.
Okeana, OH)
WAKEFIELD, Ferree C.(s/o Elijah) 1876 1943 38 1 (Res. Dayton, OH)
WAKEFIELD, J.L.(John Lowry) 5-20-1852 12- 9-1917 (h/o Mary E.,Res.
Crosby Twp.)
" ssa , Mary E. SATER 12-30-1856 4-29-1929 w/o J. L. (Res.
Harrison, OH
" ssa , Joseph McCOY 4-19-1880 11-16-1895 s/o J.L. & M.E.
(Res. Preston, OH)
WAKEFIELD, Charlotte A. 1907 1910 (d/o Mack WAKEFIELD)
(Res. New Haven, OH)
MYERS, J. Edgar (Jesse Edgar)1- 8-1871 2- 5-1907 39 1 (h/o Fanny)Mother
(Res. Harrison, OH)
MYERS, Fanny (Frances)GWALTNEY 1868 1961 (w/o Ed., Res.
Cincinnati, OH)
MYERS, Klayton M(illard) 4-28-1898 11- 8-1900 s/o J.E. & F.
(Res. Crosby Twp.)
GWALTNEY, Charles W., (Sr.) 1860 1925 40 1 FCB 653 Knights of
Pythias (h/o Sarah, Res. Harrison Twp.;records give yr of death as 1924)
GWALTNEY, Infant (s/o C.W.,Res.Preston,OH) 1901
GWALTNEY, Sarah E. ROUDEBUSH 1861 1947 w/o Charles W.
(Res. Harrison, OH)
SATER, Thomas E.-Father 1831 1909 41 1 (h/o Mary, Res.
Crosby Twp.)
SATER, Olive M.(Res.Cincinnati) 1861 1946 (d/o Thomas)
SATER, Mary G.(GWALTNEY) Mother 1828 1912 (w/o Thomas E.)
AMISS, John L. 1846 1933 42 1 (h/o Elizabeth)
" ssa, Elizabeth (M. JONES) 1860 1952 (w/o J.L. AMISS)
(Res. Harrison, OH
AMISS, Charles T(homas) 1890 1904 (s/o John &
Elizabeth, Res. Preston, OH)
JONES, Elizabeth (Res.New Haven,OH)1823 1906(m/o Mrs. John AMISS)
COULTHARD, John - Civil War Vet. 1843 1932 43 1 Co. D 123 Ind.Vol.
Inf. (h/o Sarah Jane, Res. Harrison, OH)
" ssa , Sarah Jane DENNING 1847 1935 w/o John
COULTHARD, George H. 1866 1943 (s/o John & Sarah)
CAMPBELL, Clinton C. (Res.Crosby Twp.)1874 1955 (h/o Alice)
CAMPBELL, Sarah Alice COULTHARD 1874 1962 (w/o Clinton)
COULTHARD, Charles R(aymond) 1872 1961 44 1 (h/o Clara, Res.
Fairborn, OH)
" ssa , Clara B. (CONE) 1877 1958 (w/o Charles)
GRASSANE, Gertrude S. PHILLIPS 8-12-1892 7- 3-1947 Mass Nurse ANC WW I
RUSH, Charles A. - WW II Vet. 1911 1969 (h/o Eleanor, Res.
Washington, DC
" ssa, Eleanor C. 1908 ----
SCHEERING, John - Father 11-29-1820 4- 5-1904 45 1 (h/o Catherine,
Res. Preston, OH
" ssa , Catherine WEICK 9-24-1831 12-17-1901 w/o John;Mother
WALTHERS, Katherine(SCHEERING)8-10-1870 2- 3-1900 (w/o F. WALTHERS,
Res. Shandon, OH)
SCHEERING, John (Res.New Haven,OH) 1855 1935 (s/o John, Sr.)
SCHEERING, Jacob (Res.NewHaven,OH) 1864 1942 (s/o John)
SCHEERING, Amelia (" " ") 1875 1946 (d/o John)
SCHEERING, George (" " ") 1864 1950 (h/o Julia)
SCHEERING, Julia (MOLTER) 1873 1966 (w/o George, d.
Warren Co. OH at Otterbein Home)
SCHEERING, J. Martin 8-18-1818 1-31-1900 46 1 (Res.Preston, OH)
SCHEERING, Caroline KAPPEL 11-27-1833 4-22-1911 w/o J. Martin
TAYLOR, Emma S.(Res.Hamilton,OH) 1873 1957(d/o J. Martin SCHEERING)

NAME BD or AE DD Lot Sec.

MOLTER, Louise May 1879 1910 46 1 (w/o Chas. R. MOLTER
Res. Hamilton, OH)
SCHEERING, Charles M(artin) 1875 1934 (s/o Martin)
SCHEERING, Katherine 1871 1939 (d/o J. Martin, Res.
Hamilton, OH)
SCHEERING, David (s/o Martin)1861 1939 (Res. Hamilton, OH)
SATER, Joseph 11-20-1824 2- 9-1915 47 1 (h/o Eliza, Res.
Crosby Twp., New Haven, OH)
"ssa , Eliza A(nne) 1-11-1826 5-19-1904 w/o Joseph
"ssa , Hannah J. 3-30-1850 7-28-1850 d/o Joseph & Eliza
"ssa , William 1- 5-1852 4- 1-1856 s/o Joseph & Eliza
"ssa , George L. 8-20-1853 12-22-1853 s/o Joseph & Eliza
WAKEFIELD, Walter S(ater) Sr. 4-22-1897 10-28-1956 (h/o Florence)
(Res. Crosby Twp.)
WAKEFIELD, Florence JOHNSON 10-31-1905 3-19-1980 (w/o Walter, Res. at
Morrow, OH, DAR Marker)
McCLURE, Russell 4-16-1911 2-23-1982 48 1 (s/o James & Almina,
Res. Harrison, OH)
McCLURE, James R.-Father 1873 1951 (h/o Almina, Res.
Crosby Twp.)
McCLURE, Almina E.(WAKEFIELD)1874 1948 (w/o James)
McCLURE, Stanley W. 7-10-1905 ----
HAWK, (Stanley) Howard 1901 1961 49 1 (s/o J.C. & Elizabeth)
Res. Crosby Twp.
HAWK, Joseph C.(Res.Crosby Twp.)1866 1932 h/o Elizabeth
" ssa, Elizabeth S.(McCLURE) 1864 1939 (w/o Joseph C.)
CAMPBELL, Olive (H.) 1865 1947 50 1 (d/o Alexander,
Res. New Haven, OH)
CAMPBELL, Alex.(Alexander) 1844 1936 (h/o Sophia, Res.
New Haven, OH)
CAMPBELL, Sophia OYLER 1843 1907 w/o Alexander
HUFFMAN, Geo. D(avid) 1852 1895 51 1 (Res.Harrison, OH)
HUFFMAN, Eliza (CREIGHTON) 1854 1943 (Res.Harrison, OH)
HUFFMAN, Minnie 1877 1960*51* 1 (d/o George & Lida,
Res. Harrison, OH)
SCOTT, Isaac (Res.Green Twp.)1842 1912 52 1 Co. D 5th Ohio Vol.
Cav., Civil War Vet.
SCOTT, Lydia M(argaret) 1842 1895 (w/o Isaac, Res.
Preston, OH)
SCOTT, Leonard L. 1867 1913
WHITE, Robert - Father 1849 1929 53 1 F & AM Emblem on
stone.(h/o Elizabeth)(Res. New Haven, OH)
WHITE, Elizabeth STEPHENSON 1850 1929 Mother; w/o Robert
SCHWING, Albert 1882 1957 54 1 (h/o Jessie)
" ssa , Jessie M.(WOOD) 1881 1940 (w/o Albert, Res.
New Haven, OH)
" ssa , Albert Jacob, Jr. 1906 1908 (s/o Albert & Jessie)
CORSON, Amanda 7-26-1828 7-26-1909 (m/o Sarah SCHWING)
(Res. Colerain Twp.)
SCOTT, Andrew Jay-Father 1853 1929 55 1 (Res.New Haven, OH)
" ssa, Sarah Jane-Mother 1855 1908 (w/o A.J.)
" ssa, Lillian M(ary) 1882 1955 (d/o A.J.)
OYLER, Clara L(ena) 1874 1964 56 1 (w/o David P., Res.
Hamilton, OH Butler Co.)
OYLER, David P. 1871 1951
OYLER, Edith M. CONE 1870 1907 (w/o David,New Haven)
JEFFERIES, John C.(Res.Hamilton,OH)1869 1941 57 1 (h/o Cora M.)
JEFFERIES, Mary E. 1904 1924 (d/o J.C.)
JEFFERIES, Cora M. 1875 1927 (w/o J.C.)
JEFFERIES, Emma Louella 1870 1897 (w/o J.C.,Res.Okeana)
WILLIAMSON, Mary F(rances) 1861 1899 58 1 (Res. Preston, OH)
WILLIAMSON, Katie Marie 1898 1898 (d/o J. & M.)
PENNELL, Dessolyn (WILLIAMSON)1887 1938 (Res.Middletown, OH)
KNOSE, F. A.(Frank A.) 4-11-1847 12-14-1911 59 1 (Res. Crosby Twp.)
KNOSE, Edward (Res.Crosby Twp.)35y 1909*59* 1 (h/o Lulu DEAN KNOSE)
TEETERS, George E. 1909 1930 60 1 (s/o Philip & Tena,
Res. Harrison, OH)
TEETERS, Philip B. 1881 1964 60 1 Married 22 Feb. 1903
to Tena, Res. Crosby Twp.)
TEETERS, Tena (Christina L.KRAUS)1880 1973 (w/o Philip)
TEETERS, Lois Leda 1y* 1908* 9? - (d/o Philip & Tena)

Lots 61-64, Section 1 have no burials indicated.

BREHM, Paul 1915 ---- 65 1
" ssa, Gertrude I. 1918 ----
CLEAVER, George 1864 1936 66 1 (h/o Nellie, New Haven)
" ssa , Nellie (BRISBIN) 1884 1956 (w/o George, Res.
Harrison, OH)
BAYLES, William A. 7y 10m 28d 22 Mar.1868 s/o R.M. & M.C. BAYLES
BAYLES, Mary C. 1831 1903 w/o R.M. BAYLES

NAME	BD or AE	DD	Lot	Sec.	
FRYER, Carl L(eslie)	1930	1984	1	2	(h/o Elsie)
(Res. Harrison, OH					
THOMPSON, Christena - Mother	1848	1916	2	2	Erected by her son
Lambert (Res. Crosby Twp.)					
GLADY, Herbert(Res.Mt.Hope)	1874	1942	2	2	
RUSSELL, Helen BREHM (Res.Okeana)	1908	1937	3	2	(d/o Charles BREHM)
RUSSELL, Robert Lee	1932	1933			(s/o Rufus & Helen)
BREHM, Charles H.(Res.St.Charles)	1883	1965			(h/o Charlotte)
BREHM, CHarlotte	1884	1929			(w/o Charles)
PROVINCE, Joe N. (Joseph)	1-26-1871	2-13-1956	4	2	(h/o Laura, Res.
New Haven, OH)					
PROVINCE, Laura (WEBER)	58y'	1-24-1931			(w/o Joseph)
DEAN, Clinton A. (Res.Mt.Hope)	1879	1960			(h/o Clara)
DEAN, Clara E. (PROVINCE)	1885	1953			(w/o Clinton)
KRAUS, Blanche A.	1889	1985	5	2	(aunt of Hilda
("Patsy"), Res. New Haven, OH)					
KRAUS, George (Res.New Haven,OH)	1857	1926			(h/o Mary)
KRAUS, Mary (EPP)	1857	1933			(w/o George)
KRAUS, Lura C.(Res.New Haven,OH)	1886	1973			(m/o Hilda LACEY)
KRAUS, Arlo Frederick	7- 4-1893	5-16-1955			Ohio 2nd Lt.V.C.Res.
WW I Vet. (D.V.S.) (h/o Florence, Res. Ross, OH)					
KRAUS, Florence Ida	4-19-1890	6- 3-1981			(w/o Arlo F.)
LACEY, Frank F.(Res.New Haven,OH)	1907	1964			F & AM Emblem
(h/o Hilda W.)					
" ssa, Hilda	1907	----			OES Emblem
GIMPEL, Ruth Esther - Daughter	1912	1926	6	2	(d/o Chas. & Louise)
(Res New Haven, OH)					
GIMPEL, Charles - Father	1862	1956			(h/o Louise, Res.
Dayton, OH)					
GIMPEL, Louise C(atherine BREHM)	1872	1940			(w/o Charles,
Res. New Haven, OH); mother					
GIMPEL, Edith A.-Daughter	1897	1984			(s/o Blanche
McCLAIN, Res. Cincinnati, OH)					
FUCHS, (Jacob*) Father	1864	1948	7	2	(Res. Crosby Twp.)
FUCHS, (Anna Margaret*)Mother	1869	1913			(w/o Jacob,Sr.)
FUCHS, Hilda (Res.Cincinnati,OH)	1898	1963			FATAL emblem(OES?)
(d/o Jacob, Sr.)					
FUCHS, Jacob C., Jr.(h/o Mary)	1889	1983			F & AM emblem
(Res. Harrison, OH)					
" ssa, Mary E(lizabeth ARN---)	1888	19--			OES emblem
" ssa, Helen M.	1923	1928			(d/o Jacob & Mary)
*FUGHS, Evelyn (Res.Crosby Twp)	0y*	1917*7*		2	(twin d/o Wm. &
Bertha					
*FUCHS, Eleanor (twin d/o Wm. &	0y*	1917*7*		2	Bertha)
FAGALY, Edward F. (Res.New Haven)	1874	1917	8	2	(h/o Salina)
" ssa , Salina E. NOES (KLENK)	1881	1976			(w/o Mike KLENK
& Edw. FAGALY, Res. Okeana, OH)					
KLENK, Michael (Res.Butler Co.OH)	1873	1955			(h/o Lina)
SPANTON, Thomas M. (h/o Fannie)	1861	1938	9	2	(Res.Washington,DC)
SPANTON, Fannie N.(NUGENT)	1866	1924			(w/o Thomas, Res.
Colerain Twp.)					
WAKEFIELD, Amos (Res.New Haven)	1849	1919	10	2	(h/o Sarah)
WAKEFIELD, Sarah (SCOTT)	1849	1932			(w/o Amos)
WAKEFIELD, Alma (Res.New Haven)	1874	1930			(d/o Amos & Sarah)
WAKEFIELD, Willard " "	1875	1935			(s/o Amos)
WAKEFIELD, Leroy (s/o Amos & Sarah)	1873	1939			(Res.Cincinnati,OH)
FLIEHMAN, Harry Milton (h/o Ida)	1890	1924	11	2	Knights of Pythias
(Res. Harrison, OH)					
FLIEHMAN, (Ida) Frances CRAWFORD	1893	1984			(m/o Dorothea &
Vera, Res. Harrison, OH)					
LEHMAN, Frederick J.	12- 6-1920	----			Korean War Vet.
" ssa , Vera F.	4-18-1921	----			
FLIEHMAN, Minnie Mae	1885	1970			(d/o Henry & Julia,
Res. Crosby Twp.)					
FLIEHMAN, Henry M.-Father	1856	1936			(h/o Julia)
FLIEHMAN, Julia C. SCHLEMMER	1857	1945			(w/o Henry, Res.
New Haven, OH)					
FLIEHMAN, Ethel S. (Res. Lebanon,OH	1898	1980			(d/o Henry & Julia)
BAUER, (Charles) Lummie	1894	1960	12	2	(s/o Chas. & Mattie)
BAUER, Charles	1859	1927			(h/o Mattie)
BAUER, Mattie (Martha)	1865	1938			(w/o Charles)
BAUER, Phene (Josephine)	1873	1933			(1st w/o Jesse,
Res. Harrison, OH)					
BAUER, Jesse Leroy (Res.Crosby Twp.)	1887	1967			(h/o Ethel)
BAUER, Ethel CONGLETON	1895	1984			(w/o Jesse, d. West--)
BADER, Joseph E. (Res.Shandon,OH)	1889	1981	13	2	(h/o Dona)
BADER, Dona L. OYLER (Res.Crosby Twp.)	1892	-1947			(w/o Joseph)
BADER, Hazel M(arie)	1923	1925			(d/o Jos. & Dona)
KNOSE, Bernard Lee (Res.New Haven)	1915	1922	14	2	(s/o W.J. & Elva)
KNOSE, Walter J(ames)	1872	1959			(h/o Elva)
KNOSE, Orie J.	1923	----			
KNOSE, Charles W.	1908	1929			(s/o W.J. & Elva)
KNOSE, Elva V. HAEHURST	1886	1966			(w/o Walter J.)

NAME	BD or AE	DD	Lot	Sec.	
HENRY, Kathryn L. (SIEFTON)	1917	1954	15	2	(d/o Harvey & Hazel
SIEFTON, Res. Cincinnati, OH)					
TAYLOR, Hazel A. (w/o Walter)	1900	1981			(Res. Miamitown, OH)
" ssa , Walter	1892	1955			(h/o Hazel)
WEBER, George J. (h/o Anna)	1871	1947			(Res. Cincinnati, OH)
" ssa, Anna (CONWAY)	1871	1931			(w/o George)
WEBER, Mattie J. (MACK?)	1895	1950			(2nd w/o George)
*MACK, Charles H.	65y*	1950*15*		2	(b/o Mattie WEBER)
(Res. Cincinnati, OH)					
*MACK, Roseann AMANNS	65y*	1957*15*		2	(w/o Charles, Res.
Amelia, OH)					
*CONWAY, William	----*	1922*15*		-	
RADCLIFFE, James B.,Jr.	1868	1930	16	2	Order UAM emblem
(h/o Minnie, Res. Harrison, OH)					
RADCLIFFE, Winifred (WABNITZ)	1880	1962			(w/o James, Sr., Res.
Cincinnati, OH)					
RADCLIFFE, Lillian B.	1912	1983			(sister-in-law of
Marg, Res. Cincinnati, OH)					
RADCLIFFE, James K. (Res.Harrison,OH)	1907	-1968			(h/o Margaret)
RADCLIFFE, Margaret (TEETERS)	1915	----			
NOES, Minnie (FEIGHT) Mother	1888	1926	17	2	(w/o John, Res. Crosby
Twp.)					
NOES, Joseph Roy (Res.New Haven)	1890	1970			(h/o Helen)
NOES, (Deborah) Helen SMITH	1906	1977			(2nd w/o Joseph)
NOES, Baby	----	1944			
WRIGHT, Eric	4-29-1964	4-30-1964			
" ssa , Dennis	4-29-1964	4-30-1964			
HACKER, Ivan	2-13-1914	1-19-1981	18	2	(h/o Carrie, Res. Eliza-
bethtown, OH)					
" ssa , Carrie E. HARPER	10-27-1905	2- 3-1982			(w/o Ivan, Res. Lawrence-
burg, IN)					
REINER, Mildred Marie	3- 4-1924	3- 5-1924			(d/o Clarence, Res.
Harrison Twp.)					
DONAWERTH, Albert L.	8- 7-1896	10- 9-1968	19	2	Ohio Pvt 2 Recruit SQ
Air SVC WW I Vet.; 32 Degree Mason; (h/o Florence,Res.Harrison, OH)					
" ssa , Florence R. FAGALY	1892	1984			(w/o Albert L.)
DONAWERTH, Richard (Charles)	3-21-1946	3-23-1946			(s/o Charles & Hazel)
DAVIES, Ethel D.(DONAWERTH)	1922	1975			(w/o Hugh,Res.Harrison,OH)
SIEFFERMAN, William H.-Father	1878	1955	20	2	F & AM emblem (h/o Anna,
Res. Cincinnati, OH)					
" ssa , Anna C.(COULTHARD)	1879	1951			Mother O.E.S. emblem
(w/o William, Res. Cincinnati, OH)					
PICKETT, John K. (h/o Alice)	1902	1982			F & AM emblem
" ssa , Alice S.(SIEFFERMAN)	1914	----			O.E.S. emblem (Res.
Cincinnati, OH)					
JACOBS, John G.	1882	1969	21	2	(h/o Daisy, Res.New Haven)
" ssa , Daisy E.	1884	1970			(w/o John) " "
JACOBS, Norbert E. (h/o Rose)	1909	1970			(Res. New Haven, OH)
" ssa , Rose J. (GRUBBS)	1911	----			
FITZPATRICK, Garrett B.	9-11-1940	11- 9-1979	22	2	III U.S. Navy(h/o Linda,
Res. Oxford, OH)					
FITZPATRICK, Linda Lee (CLARK)	12-2-1940	11-9-1979			Mother (w/o Garrett)
BURRILL, Irma C.	1927	1987	23?	2	
MYERS, Mildred J.	1906	----	24	2	
" ssa, Leroy W. (h/o Mildred)	1903	1971			(Res. New Haven, OH)
NUGENT, William S(teel)	1870	1955	25	2	(h/o Pearl, Res.Mt.Hope)
NUGENT, Pearl E. (BRISBIN)	1875	1966			(w/o Wm., Res.Spring-
field, M---)					
FRYMAN, Rev. Charles E.	1888	1961			(h/o Lona, Res.Crosby TWP)
FRYMAN, Lona (GOOD)	1888	1968			(w/o Rev. Charles, Res.
Harrison, OH)					
FRYMAN, Forest("Frosty")	9-23-1915	6-10-1984			(h/o Esther KNOSE FRYMAN
Res. Harrison, OH)					
LANE, Leon	1916	----	26	2	F & AM emblem
"ssa, Hilda (LACEY)(w/o Leon)	1923	1985			O.E.S. emblem (Res. White-
water Twp.)					
LACEY, Grace (TAYLOR)	1890	1962			(w/o Allen,Res.Crosby Twp)
"ssa , Allan (Res.Harrison,OH)	1896	1976			(h/o Grace)
NUGENT, Francis S.	1-19-1904	10-29-1966	27	2	(h/o Marie HOWARD NUGENT,
Res. Colerain Twp.)					
NUGENT, Charlotte E.(GIERINGER)	4-16-1902	7-14-1985			(w/o Lee,Res. Butler
Co. OH)					
NUGENT, William Lee	3-17-1898	3- 6-1987			(h/o Charlotte)
HATHAWAY, Rollin B.(h/o Blanche)	1884	1932	28	2	F & AM emblem
"ssa , Blanche E.(WAKEFIELD)	1886	1959			O.E.S. emblem(w/o Rollin,
Res. Saylor Park, OH)					
CONGLETON, Dorothy M.(BAUER)	1915	----	29	2	
" ssa , Roy E. (h/o Dorothy)	1909	1972			(Res. Crosby Twp.)
DEAN, Virginia	7-14-1914	3-23-1973			(w/o Kenneth, Res. Mt.
Hope, Crosby Twp.)					
DEAN, Kenneth	11- 7-1902	5-11-1982			(h/o Virginia)
ESTES, Herbert A.(h/o Verdie)	1909	1973			(Res. New Haven, OH)
" ssa, Verdie	1910	----			

NAME BD or AE DD Lot Sec.

KOLB, Edward A. 1883 1961 30 2 (h/o Margaret, Res. Harrison, OH)
KOLB, Margaret (CRAWFORD) 1886 1949 (w/o Edw. A., Res. Crosby Twp.)
FLIEHMAN, Royal R. 1895 1939 31 2 (s/o Julia & Henry, Res. Cincinnati, OH)
FLIEHMAN, Catherine (Ann)(FUCHS)1896 1980 (m/o Eugene, Res. Cincinnati, OH)
CAMPBELL, Mary A(nn) GWALTNEY 1868 1931 32 2 w/o S.E. (1st w/o S.E., Res. Hamilton Co. OH)
CAMPBELL, Sylvester E. 1874 1964 (h/o Sadie & Mary; Res. Logsdon Rest)
CAMPBELL, Sadie E. (SCOTT) 1887 1958 (w/o S.E., Res. Crosby Twp.)
GWALTNEY, Sarah Elizabeth 1859 1945 33 2 (Aunt of Dr. O.J. SMITH, Res. New Haven, OH)
GWALTNEY, Matilda A.(AGNEW) 1854 1938 (Tillie, w/o James B., Res. Harrison, OH)
" ssa , James B. 1857 1934 (h/o Matilda)
ENGLISH, Albert L.(h/o Ella) 1866 1946 (Res. New Haven)
" ssa , Ella Mae (McHENRY) 1864 1933 (w/o A. L.)
DICKERSON, Ruth ENGLISH (KYLE)1899 1977 (s/o Walter ENGLISH, Res. FL)
COLEGATE, Frank D. 1916 ----
" ssa , Daisy J. 1920 ----
SCHAICH, Herbert 1894 1981 34 2 (h/o ?Helen SCHOENLING SCHAICH, Res. Harrison, OH)
SCHAICH, Daisy (Lavina NOES) 1894 1943 (w/o Herbert)
LAWYER, Thomas I.(h/o Alma) 1899 1953 35 2 WW I Vet. (Res. Crosby Twp.)
" ssa , Alma S.(SCHLEMMER) 1899 1978 (Marie)(w/o Thomas)
LAWYER, William E.(s/o Thos.) 1926 1937 (Res. New Haven, OH)
LAWYER, Floyd P(hilip) 1936 1955 (s/o Thos. & Alma)
GAISER, Henrietta C.(BADER) 1897 ----
" ssa , Walter E. 1899 1988 (h/o Henrietta, Res. Harrison, OH)
BADER, Lester W. 1902 1983 (b/o Etta GAISER & Irene ----, Res. Harrison, OH)
BADER, Sophia M. 1896 19--
" ssa, Carl R(aymond) 1899 1935 (h/o Sophia,Res. Shandon, OH)
SCHLEMMER, Edward N. 1869 1934 36 2 (h/o Sophia, Res. Harrison, OH)
" ssa , Sophia K.(KLENK) 1871 1944 (w/o Edward)
BADER, John H(enry) 1871 1962 (h/o Cora, Res.Crosby)
"ssa , Cora E(llen COX) 1874 1948 (w/o John)
BADER, Clarence A.(s/o John) 1905 1934 (Res. Harrison, OH)
DOWNARD, Jimmy Dale 1935 1941 37 2 (s/o Clifford, Res. New Haven, OH)
DOWNARD, Carla Lou Ann 1y' 1968 (d/o Denver & Ruth, Res. Cincinnati, OH)
DOWNARD, Clifford A. 10-27-1905 11-14-1979 Married 27 Apr. 1925
" ssa , Louise F. (LYTLE)2-19-1906 ---- w/o Clifford A., Res. Harrison, OH)
PURDY, Lewis 1-11-1875 11- 1-1938 (Res. Hamilton, OH
PURDAY, Emma (Arnetta) 4-24-1880 9-20-1955 (w/o L.H.)
PARKER, Bernard W. 1916 1981 U.S. Coast Guard, WW II Vet. (h/o Marie DOWNARD PARKER, Res. Harrison, OH)
DOWNARD,Rebecca Lynn 4- 1-1960 12-20-1984 38 2 (d/o Clifford & Barbara, Res. Trenton, OH)
KNOSE, David P(aul) 1920 1965 38E 2 (h/o Mary, Res. New Haven, Crosby Twp.)
" ssa, Mary E.(DOWNARD) 1926 ----
BIBEE, Arthur Wm. 1907 1984 38W 2 ((h/o Dorothy, Res. Harrison, OH)
" ssa, Dorothy F. (HAWK) 1913 ----
BELL, Harvey T. 1909 ----
"ssa, Grace M(arie HAWK) 1911 1964 (w/o Harvey, Res. Collinsville)
WALTZ, John E. (h/o Gracie) 1889 1945 39 2 (Res. Peru, IN)
WALTZ, Grace M.(ADAMS) 1889 1966 (w/o John E.)
STORMES, Jacob (h/o Susie) 1864 1948 (Res. New Haven,OH)
STORMES, Susie (NOES) 1876 Aged 79 yrs. (w/o Jacob, Res. Otterbein Home, Warren Co. OH)
WRIGHT, W. O. (Wilbert Oscar) 1873 1947 (h/o Pearl, Res. New Haven, OH)
WRIGHT, Pearl V(iola SLEET) 1872 1966 (w/o W.O.)
DREW, Charles (h/o Wilmouth) 1879 1947 (Res. Addyston, OH)
"ssa, Wilmouth OWENS 1886 1967 (w/o Charles, Res. Berea, KY)
SIMONSON, George W. (h/o Nellie)1867 1948 40E 2 (Res. Hamilton, OH)
" ssa , Nellie G. BUELL 1868 1949 (w/o George)
SCHRIER, Louis C(hristopher) 1869 1948 (Res. Cheviot, OH)

SCHRIER, Amanda L. 1882 1963 40E 2 (Res. Harrison, OH was on the same stone as Louis C. SCHRIER
MOORE, Laura B.-Mother 12-11-1895 ---- 40W 2
MOORE, Herbert 1925 1946 Cox U.S.N. WW II (brother-in-law of Clare----, Res. Harrison, OH)
MOORE, Neal 5-23-1888 11- 2-1966 (Res. Harrison, OH)
MORGAN, Andrew H. 1882 1968 41 2 (h/o Helen, Res. Harrison, OH)
" ssa , Helen M. (HAMMITT) 1915 1983 (w/o Andrew)
HAWK, Leslie E(arl) (h/o Amelia)1886 1950 (Res. New Haven, OH)
" ssa, Amelia (ARNOLD) 1891 1977 (Res. New Haven, OH)
LARUE, William F(rancis) 1889 1976 (h/o Loraine HEIS LARUE, Res. Harrison, OH)
" ssa, Carrie M. (w/o William) 1888 1951 (Res. Crosby Twp.)
SNYDER, Doris M.-Mother 1897 1978 (w/o Walter, Res. Harrison, OH)
" ssa , Walter F.-Father 1894 1951 (Res. Colerain Twp.)
LANE, Infant 0y 1960* (d/o Allen & Jane BIBEE LANE
POWELL, Wm. Alfred (h/o Flora) 1866 1953 42 2 (Res. Cincinnati, OH
" ssa , Flora (w/o Alfred) 1870 1944 (Res. Cheviot, OH)
FIELDS, Matt (h/o Elizabeth) 1879 1957 (Res.Mt. Hope,Crosby Twp)
" ssa , Elizabeth (h/o Matt) 1883 1961 (Res. Hamilton, OH)
CORSON, Earl (h/o Grace) 1906 1968 (Res. Harrison, OH)
" ssa , Grace (ROESSLER) 1904 ----
CORSON, Clarence (h/o May) 1884 1956 (Res. New Haven, OH)
CORSON, May (Elizabeth) 1886 1962 (w/o Clarence, Res. New Baltimore, OH)
WEBSTER, Dorothy Edna 1911 ---- 42? 2
LUSTER, Earl (h/o Amanda) 1887 1967 43 2 (Res. Indiana)
LUSTER, Amanda (w/o Earl) 1894 1969 (Res. Harrison, OH)
MITCHELL, Earl Joseph 8-24-1892 1-16-1966 43SE 2 (Barney) Ohio Pvt 35 Co. 158 Depot Brigade WW I Vet. (Res. New Haven, Crosby Twp.)
MITCHELL, Blanche (WRIGHT)7-18-1899 8- 7-1973 (w/o Earl)
STROTHMAN, Hazel (SNYDER) 1914 1956 44 2 (d/o Charles, Res. Phoenix, AZ)
SNYDER, Pansy E. (w/o Charles) 1894 1961 (Res.Morgan Twp. Butler Co. OH)
" ssa , Charles H. (h/o Pansy) 1887 1968 (Res. Butler Co.OH)
KUTCHENRIDER, Lena M. (WEBER) 1885 1967 (w/o George, Res. New Haven, OH)
" ssa , George (h/o Lena)1874 1962 (Res. New Haven, OH)
BRISBIN, Earl W. 1900 1960 (Res. Ross, OH)
" ssa , Bessie M. (w/o Earl) 1900 1979 (Res. Ross, OH)
HAWK, Charles B.(h/o Thelma L.)1906 1961 45 2 (Res. Crosby Twp.)
KNOLLMAN, Byron L. 1910 ---- s/o Henry & Elsie; Emblem on stone: triangle with double eagles, "32" in a smaller triangle within the triangle, and "spesmea in ded est" on scroll below. "Parents of William & Norman, Melvin & Carol Ann"
" ssa , Alma D(EAN) 1909 1962 d/o Henry & Nettie HAAS; O.E.S. emblem (w/o Byron, Res. Crosby Twp.)
KNOLLMAN, Milton (Eugene) 1912 1982 F & AM emblem (h/o Irene, Res. Harrison, OH)
" ssa , Irene (LOFFINK) 1910 ---- O.E.S. emblem
HOLTON, Chauncey - Father 1894 1968 46 2 (h/o Vera, Res. Hamilton, OH)
" ssa , Vera L.- Mother 1897 1984 (w/o Chauncey)
SAMMONS, Otto - husband & father 1899 1966 (h/o Helen,Res.Blue Jay)
KNOSE, John W.-Father 1877 1968 47 2 (h/o Florence)
KNOSE, Florence E. (HAEHURST) 1881 1948 Mother (w/o John, Res. New Haven, OH)
BRYANT, Ruth K.(KNOSE) R.N. 1909 1981 (Res.Cincinnati, OH)
HAEHURST, Leroy 4- 4-1908 7-12-1964 (h/o Jane SNYDER HAEHURST, d. Cincinnati, OH)
HAEHURST, David W.-husband 1879 1943 (h/o Florence N.(KNOSE) Res. Fernald, Crosby Twp.)
HAEHURST, Florence N.(KNOSE) 1883 1956 (w/o David W.)
HAEHURST, Cecil W. 9-30-1906 5- 7-1975 Sgt. Army Air Force (b/o Leroy, Res. Fernald, Crosby Twp.)
KELHOFFER, Raymond (Atwood) 1909 1977 48 2 (h/o Vesta, Res. Cincinnati, OH)
" ssa , Vesta (Mae) nee 1905 1977 KNOSE (w/o Raymond)
JOHNSON, Rachel (MOORE) 1919 1961 (w/o Floyd, Res. Dearborn Co. IN)
JOHNSON, Floyd C. 60y 1975*48* 2 (h/o Rachel)
UNDERWOOD, John W. (h/o Dovie) 1885 1970 (Res. Cheviot, OH)
" ssa , Dovie H. (THOMAS) 1893 1970 (Nurse, w/o John)
TAYLOR, Benjamin F. 1898 ---- 49 2
" ssa , Lina M(ay) (PR---) 1901 1972 (w/o Benjamin, Res. Harrison, OH)
" ssa , Loretta May 1920 1978 (d/o Benjamin & Lina)
REHG, William H.(h/o Edith) 1902 1984 50 2 (Res. Anderson Twp.)
SCHEERING, Gottlieb B.(h/o Lena)1869 1952 (Res. Shandon, OH)

NAME BD or AE DD Lot Sec.

SCHEERING, Lena (HOOK) 1875 1966 50 2 (w/o G.B.
REHG, Edith B. nee SCHEERING 1905 ----
CAMPBELL, Elbert (h/o Della) 1910 1966 51 2 (Res. New Haven, OH)
" ssa , Della (COX) 1913 ----
ISAACS, Hubert 1-10-1914 ---- Married 28 Feb. 1941
" ssa , Gladys I.(BADER) 1- 5-1920 8- 9-1986 (w/o Hubert, Res. Hamilton, OH)
BAILEY, Michele Renee 9-10-1968 5-13-1969 (d/o Harry R.)
BAILEY, Barbara A. 31y 1978*51* 2 (w/o Harry R., Res. Cincinnati, OH)
SCHARDINE, Stanley C(harles) 1881 1971 52 2 (h/o Ella, Res. New Haven, OH)
SCHARDINE, Ella B.(SIMONSON) 1885 1971 (w/o Stanley)
SCHARDINE, Hazel M. (d/o 1903 1984 (d/o Stanley & Ella)
FUCHS, Albert T., Sr. 1906 1971 (h/o Dolores, Res. New Baltimore, OH)
VOGT, E(lmore) George-Father 1893 ----
" ssa, Mabel M(arie) nee 1906 1972 52NE -SCHREIER- Mother (Res. Miller Twp., Dearborn Co. IN)
WRIGHT, Ellen 1923 1987 53? 2
SCHREIER, Frances A. (LAUER) 1907 1987 53 2 (w/o John J., Res. New Baltimore, OH)
" ssa , John J. - emblem, 1903 ---- F.C.B. in triangle
JONES, Annie - Mother 1880 1972 54 2 (m/o Vera KETTERMAN, Res. Crosby Twp.)
SCHWING, Mae B. (BOGART)11-13-1892 10-14-1972 55 2 (w/o Homer, Res. Crosby Twp.)
" ssa , Homer (h/o Mae) 6-11-1894 10-15-1975 (Res.Harrison, OH)
TEKULVE, Troy Lee 9-26-1972 10- 7-1972 56 2 (s/o Ronald, Res. Harrison Twp.)

Lot 57, Section 2 - no burials indicated.

NAME BD or AE DD Lot Sec.

LANE, William (E.) Dad 1895 1975 58 2 (h/o Minnie, Res. Cincinnati, OH)
" ssa, Minnie - Mom 1895 1982 (w/o William, Res. Harrison, OH)
LANE, Nolan(1st h/o Lula KNOSE 1918 1975 Res. Harrison, OH)
" ssa, Fern (Lula KNOSE) 1924 ---- (2nd married to Marshall STORMS)
MYERS, Albert C. (h/o Dolores L.)1913 1967 59 2 (Res. Harrison, OH)
" ssa, Dolores L. 1916 ----
MYERS, Tillie (Catherine M.) 1892 1976 Mother (m/o Wanda LAWYER, Res. Miamitown, OH)
HAMMITT, Lillie (MYERS)Mother 1919 1980 (w/o Willis, Sr., Res. Harrison, OH)
CLARK, Marshall L. - Dad 1- 8-1906 7-12-1972 (h/o Irene, Res. Crosby Twp)
"ssa , Irene A. (BADER) 9- 7-1908 ---- Mom
UNDERWOOD, Silas Edward 1931 1973 (h/o Carol, Res. Wheaton,IL)
" ssa , Carol A. 1941 ----
STORMS, Clarence A.-Dad 1892 1973 60 2 (f/o Marshall, Res. KY)
STORMS, Paul J(acob) 2-23-1911 10- 9-1970 Ohio S2 U.S. Navy, WW II Vet. (s/o Clarence & Nannie, Res. Glasgow, KY)
BRISBIN, Charles E. 4-10-1929 6-12-1969 Ohio Pfc 1 Co. 3 Engrs. Korean War Vet. (s/o Earl & Bessie, Res. Colerain Pike)

Lot 61, Section 2 - no burials indicated.

* NIEHAUS, Mary (w/o Raymond) ----* 1982*62* 2 (Res. Harrison, OH)

SECTION 3

ENGEL, Donald - Dad 1936 ---- 1 3
" ssa, Phyllis (W. FAGALY)Mom 1938 1980 (w/o Donald, Res. Harrison, OH)
MYERS, Herbert L. (h/o Dorothy)1918 1984 2 3 1st Lt. U.S. Army WW II Vet. (Res. Harrison, OH)
MYERS, Dorothy E. 1928 ----
BYBEE, Wilburn -Father 1902 1985 (h/o Anna, Res. Harrison, OH)
" ssa, Anna Mae-Mother 1906 ---- (Married 14 Dec.1923)
MILLER, Clifford T.-Dad 3- 3-1902 11- 5-1983 3W 3 (Res. Harrison, OH)
KNOSE, Charles C. 4-23-1885 2-17-1985 4 3 Father (f/o Rosemary LAIL, Res. Harrison, OH)
ssa TAYLOR, Goldie KNOSE 9- 9-1896 9- 5-1985 Mother (Onda Mae (BYERS) KNOSE TAYLOR, 1st w/o Charles KNOSE,Res.Harrison,OH)
MITCHELL, Earl F. 5-28-1929 12-21-1983 4 3 (h/o Virginia, Res. Harrison, OH)
" ssa , Virginia C. 12-20-1929 ---- (UNDERWOOD) Married 26 Apr. 1952 w/o Earl F.
REYNOLDS, George W. 1927 ---- (Res.Harrison, OH)
" ssa , Janet L. (MYERS) 1932 1985 (w/o George)
TAYLOR, Ethel M(arie SPARKS) 1918 1976 5 3 (w/o Norris, Res. Sunman, IN)
" ssa , Norris (h/o Ethel) 1913 1979 (Res. Sunman, IN)
JENNISON, Wilma G. 1917 ----
" ssa , Elmer (h/o Wilma) 1903 1986 (Res.Harrison, OH)
HAMMITT, Ralph J. 1911 ---- 6? 3
" ssa , Ruth E. 1911 ----
AIGNER, Rita J. 1921 ---- 6 3
" ssa , Albert M.(h/o Rita) 1919 1981 (Res.Harrison, OH)

Lot 7, Section 3 - no burials indicated.

FRYMAN, Clifford E(lmo) 1914 1987 8 3 (h/o Lois, Res. Saylor Park, OH)
" ssa , Lois HATHAWAY 1915 ----
FUCHS, George (h/o Mary) 1899 1981 F & A.M. emblem
" ssa, Mary L. (CARSON) 1909 ---- O.E.S. emblem (Res. Harrison, OH)
SNYDER, Catherine H. WOLF 1920 1979 (w/o Robert F., Res. Franklin Co. IN?)
" ssa , Robert F. 1915 ----
TAYLOR, Dorothy M. 1914 ---- 8?9 3
" ssa , Shirley E. 1915 1987
MURRAY, Fredrick H. 1912 ---- 8?9 3
" ssa , Marie F. 1919 ----
KESSLER, Louis 1894 1976 9 3 (h/o Mabel, Res. Cincinnati, OH)
" ssa , Mabel (POWELL) 1893 1979 (w/o Louis)
McADAMS, Thomas Lee 6-18-1939 11- 8-1986 10 3 (h/o Mary Lou FOSTER McADAMS, Res. New Haven, OH)

TAYLOR, James A(lbert) 1920 1984 10 3 Father- U.S. Vet. Marker (Res. Harrison, OH) Married 29 Apr. 1943
" ssa , Virginia B. (BACHMAN) 1922 ---- Mother
" ssa , Robert J.- Son 1947 ----
HAWK, Dale E. 1921 ---- 10? 3 Married 6 Oct. 1944
" ssa, Marjorie J. 1925 ----
KOHLER, Rudolph 1901 ---- 11 3
" ssa , Mary (STAPLETON) 1899 1980 (w/o Rudolph)
NOES, Clarence Benjamin 1- 5-1914 7-14-1981 Daddy - GM 2 U.S. Navy WW II (Res. Harrison, OH) Married 30 Aug. 1941
" ssa, Oley (MOORE) 9-11-1915 ---- Mother
NOES, Linda Jean (Frisky) 9-30-1948 7-24-1985 Daughter (d/o Clarence & Oley)
SMITH, Maggie (TURNER) 1- 1-1920 6-13-1986 (w/o Wilson, Res. Harrison, OH)
SMITH, Wilson 10-15-1918 ---- Husband
SMITH, Steven Ray, Sr. 8-17-1961 10-28-1986 (h/o Jill, Res.Bright,IN)
GAUSMAN, John 1915 1987 12 3
" ssa , Mary 1919 ----
SAYERS, Glen A. 1910 1979 12SE 3 (Res.Harrison, OH)
" ssa , Pauline B. 1913 ----
GAUSMAN, Edward (W.) 1899 1975 (h/o Bessie)
" ssa , Bessie B.(SAYERS) 1899 1985 (Res. Harrison, OH)
SHERRILL, James R(oy) 1-24-1918 5-15-1985 13 3 Pvt U.S.Army WW II (h/o Alma, Res. Lawrenceburg, IN)
UPDIKE, Harold 3-19-1919 7-25-1986 (h/o Vinette, Res. Harrison, OH; antique cars engraved on stone) Married 24 June 1944
" ssa , Vinette (BATES) 7- 5-1925 ----
ROMA, John (Frank) 11-22-1903 12-21-1983 14 3 (h/o Hazel,Res.Harrison,OH)
" ssa, Hazel 10-30-1910 12-12-1985 (w/o John)

Lots 15-19 - no burials indicated.

HATHAWAY, Rollin Lee-Father ---- 1920 20? 3 F & A.M. emblem
" ssa , Emily L.-Mother ---- 1926 O.E.S. emblem
" ssa , Marilyn R. - Daughter 1950
WALLS, John W(esley) 8-15-1898 6-20-1979 21 3 (h/o Dorothy, Res. Cincinnati, OH)
" ssa, Dorothy (GARRISON) 2-22-1922 ----
GARRISON, Orville E. (Pappy) 1926 1978 A3C U.S. Air Force, Korean War Vet. (b/o Loren, Res. Harrison, OH)
GARRISON, Loren E. 9-14-1934 ----
" ssa , Shirley 1- 3-1937 ----
GIFFORD, Earl H. 1916 19--
" ssa , Dorotha 1921 19--
GIFFORD, Baby - No dates
THOMPSON, Lydia 45 yrs. 9-13-1849 Consort of Josiah Thompson

NEW HAVEN CEMETERY

CROSBY TOWNSHIP

*No tombstones were found for the following persons. The names and information are from the cemetery records.

NAME	AGE	DD		
*ADAMS, Emma (w/o Samuel, Res. Morgan Twp. Butler Co. OH)	49y*	1918*		
*ADAMS, John W. (Res. Indiana)	21y*	1912*	14	-
*ADAMS, Samuel (h/o Emma, Res. Westwood, Hamilton Co. OH)	---	1920*		
*BARTLETT, Hannah (Res. Harrison, Hamilton Co.OH)	84y*	1903*		
*BLACKBURN, Rebecca (s/o Hannah BLACKBURN, Res. Crosby Twp. Hamilton Co. OH)	70y*	1911*		
*CALDWELL, John CAMPBELL	79y*	1925*		
*CAMPBELL, Angeline HAMMOND (Res. Cincinnati, OH)	75y*	1909*	23	
*CAMPBELL, Infant (Res. Harrison, OH)	---	1906*	11	A
*CASE, Elizabeth J. (Res. Crosby Twp. Hamilton Co.OH)	68y*	1906*	20	
*CASE, William H. (Res. Sater, Crosby Twp. Hamilton Co. OH)	79y*	1900*	20	
*CULLUM, Edward (b/o Becky CULLUM, Res. New Haven, Crosby Twp. Hamilton Co. OH)	86y*	1921*		
*DILL, Ann C. (Res. Preston, Hamilton Co. OH)	85y*	1897*		
*DILL, Mary E. (w/o M. J., Res. Preston, Hamilton Co. OH)	57y*	1899*		
*DUNAWAY, William (Buried in Old Baptist Cemetery)	56y*	1939*		
*SCUDDER, Cora BURGESS (w/o Glenn, Res. Mt. Hope, Crosby Twp., Hamilton Co. OH)	20y*	1908*	32	
*SHEATLEY, Eliaabeth GWALTNEY (Res. Crosby Twp.)	86y*	1918*	41	
*SMITH, Catherine (Res. Harrison Twp.)	85y*	1907*	44	
*SMITH, Lizzie (Res. Harrison Twp.)	58y*	1912*	44	
*SMITH, Malinda (s/o John, Res. Harrison Twp.)	67y*	1916*		
*ZEUMER, Ella (Res. Preston, Hamilton Co. OH)	33y*	1896*	33	3?
*ZEUMER, George (h/o Laura, Res. Harrison, OH)	80y*	1934*	33	A
*ZEUMER, Laura PASSMORE (w/o George, Res. Harrison, OH)	88y*	1941*	33	A
*EASTERBROOK, Lucy (d/o William, Res.New Haven, Crosby Twp., Hamilton Co. OH)	78y*	1941*	Old Yard	
*EASTERBROOK, Sam (b/o Lucy, Res. New Haven, Crosby Twp., Hamilton Co. OH)	83y*	1940*		
*EASTERBROOKS, John (Res. Butler Co. OH)	---	1906*		
*FREEMAN, Edith (Res. Middleville, Barry Co. MI)	36y*	1898*	8	A
*FREEMAN, Francis (Res. Preston, Hamilton Co. OH)	81y*	1904*		
*FREEMAN, Herbert H. (Res. Moline, Allegan Co. MI)	50y*	1908*	8	
*HAWK, Mary A. (w/o A. T. HAWK, Res. New Haven, Crosby Twp., Hamilton Co. OH)	71y*	1918*	60	
*INGERSOLL, Elizabeth A. (Res. Preston, Hamilton Co. OH)	70y*	1897*	43	A
*KELCH, Infant s/o Samuel	---	1896*		
*KINDEL, Anna (possibly KENDALL?) (Res. Harrison, Hamilton Co. OH)	85y*	1899*	Old Yard	
*KRAUS, Peter (f/o George, Res. Preston, Hamilton Co. OH)	77y*	1895*	9A	3
*MONTGOMERY, Hugh (h/o Phoebe, Res. Preston, OH)	81y*	1902*	28	A
*MONTGOMERY, Lulu (Res. Preston, Hamilton Co. OH)	2y*	1897*		
*MONTGOMERY, Phoebe BREESE (Res. Preston, OH)	75y*	1903*	33	
*MYERS, Orian Webster (Res. Preston, OH)	41y*	1897*		
*RITTENHOUSE, Erziela	65y*	1921*	Old Yard	
*WILLIAMSON, David (Res. Preston, OH)	61y*	1895*	14	3?
*WILLIAMSON, Sarah (Res. Preston, OH)	64y*	1896*	14	3?
*WITTE, Alberta KELCH (d/o J.J. KELCH, Res. Hamilton, Butler Co. OH)	45y*	1915*	1	
*WOOD, Doris (d/o John & Nora, Res. Harrison Twp., Hamilton Co. OH)	2y*	1908*	P?	
*WRIGHT, Maggie (Res. Harrison Twp.)	---*	1904*	44	A

CROSBY TOWNSHIP CEMETERY (Wilkins Cemetery)

CROSBY TOWNSHIP

This cemetery is located in Section 7, Crosby Township, Hamilton County, Ohio on the north side of New Haven Road, 400 ft. west of the intersection with Hamilton-Cleves Road (SR 128). It is across New Haven Road from the Scott Cemetery which is in Section 18. The cemetery is fenced and maintained by the township. Several stones are broken and some loose uninscribed fragments are piled against the fence. There are some sunken areas and some tombstone foundations without headstones which would indicate other burials than those listed.

These inscriptions were copied in October, 1982 by H. L. Berry. The rows were copied from west to east and each row from north to south. Hamilton County Courthouse records indicate that this cemetery was established in the year 1834 for three tenths of an acre.

_______, ______ Fieldstone, no inscription			Row 1
HARROD, John	71y 7m25d	8- 9-1872	Row 1
HARROD, Margaret w/o John -	5- 5-1802	9- 1-1881	Row 1
VOLLMER, John - Geboren in Ofdorf Ober(amt?) Ba(li?)ngen R(?)o(n?)igreich Wurtenberg	4-21-1837	8-21-1859	Row 3
WILKINS, Peter	63y 1m24d	8-20-1844	Row 2
GREASLEY, Susannah w/o W. M. GREASLEY (Stone is broken off at the base & now leans against Peter Wilkins stone).	55y10m 4d	8-24-1853	Row 3?
_______, ______ Illegible inscription	----	----	Row 4
LEWIS, Archibald	1m	1881	Row 5
LEWIS, Phil. - Father	1856	1885	Row 5
JONES, Drusilla d/o T. & Emily JONES	3y 3m 3d	6-17-1833	Row 6
GREASLEY, Henry - Native of Leistershire, England	In 48th yr.	7- 7-1844	Row 7
_______, ______ Fieldstone, no inscription			Row 7
NOSE, David s/o J. & Elizabeth (Stone is broken off & piled with Rebecca's stone.)	5m 6d	12-21 or 24-1833	Row 8
B(?UNDLE/BUMBLE/BOMBLE, Rebecca d/o Barbary NOSE (24y 1m28d (Stone is broken off its base & leaning against a tree stump.)	5-13-1823	7-11-1847	Row 8
NOSE, Catharine w/o George NOSE	55y	10- 6-1843	Row 8
NOSE, George	67y	10- 4-1843	Row 8
NOSE, Mary Ablena w/o George NOSE-53y 9m (Stone is broken off its base & leaning against a tree stump.)	1-16-1797	10-16-1859	Row 8
FIPPS, Mary J. d/o C.C. & A. FIPPS (Top is broken off, leaning against bottom half.)	7-26-1851	5-18-1853	Row 9
FIPPS, Angeline w/o Christopher C.	4-21 or 24-1829	11-23-1851/4	Row 9
(WILK?)INS, Margaret - Rest of stone is too worn to read. There are holes worn completely through tombstone.)	illegible	illegible	Row10
WILKINS, Michael (?) Top portion is broken off & leaning against bottom part.)	89y 8m21d	12-26?-1829	Row10
WOODWARD, Samuel B. s/o Joseph S. & Mary (Top of stone is broken off & leaning against bottom.)	9m29d	10-22-1826	Row 11
GAULT, Rachel J. d/o John & Patience (Supposedly buried in this cemetery but stone was not located in 1982.)	11y 1m 3d	2-11-1866	--- -

Records for this cemetery under the title of "Abandoned Graveyard near Fernald, Hamilton County, Ohio were published in Historical & Philosophical Society of Ohio Bulletin, Vol.XXI,(Jan. 1963), pp.58,59. They listed two other stones not found in 1982: SMITH, A. G. - broken & no other information. LAYTON, Amelia Ann w/o Charles W. 23 Feb. 1822 4 May 1850

SCOTT CEMETERY

CROSBY TOWNSHIP

Scott Cemetery is located in Section 18, Crosby Township, Hamilton County, Ohio on south side of New Haven Road, 300 ft. west of intersection with Hamilton-Cleves Road (SR 128). It is across New Haven Road from Crosby Township Cemetery in Section 7. The Cemetery is fenced and maintained by the township. None of the stones are broken. The stones were copied from west to east, each row from north to south in October 1982 by H. L. Berry. Hamilton County Courthouse records indicate that this burial site was recorded on December 22, 1837 for .027 fraction of an acre.

Two small fieldstones without inscriptions

One small fieldstone without inscription---

SCOTT, Andrew - F & AM emblem on stone	44y10m14d	1-29-1861
SCOTT, Janet E. d/o James & Miranda	12-24-1829	7- 3-1849
SCOTT, Miranda FLEMING-- Consort of James SCOTT & d/o Joseph & Rebecca KILBURN, b. in Vermont, 45y10m19d	4- 2-1797	2-21-1843
SCOTT, James - Native of Roxburghshire, Scotland (Stone is worn and age uncertain; the year of death is completely gone.	In 60th yr.	illegible
SCOTT, Mary Ella d/o Andrew & Maria SCOTT	7-19-1851/4	4-25-1855

Footstones with initials: J.E.S., J.S., & M.F.S.

CLARK CEMETERY (SAND RUN) WHITEWATER TOWNSHIP

This cemetery is located in Section 17 of Whitewater Township, Hamilton County, Ohio, on the north side of Sand Run Road, and three tenths of a mile west of intersection with Lawrenceburg Road. It is situated in a woods immediately west of a field at the intersection of Lawrenceburg and Sand Run roads, on privately owned property. Vines and underbrush on the east and southeast sides make it somewhat difficult to see. Most of the tombstones are broken off or have fallen over. Of eight stones still standing, five are intact and three have broken tops (one was found and two were missing). The central area has been dug up in a few places which along with the scattering and mixing of tombstones, footstones, foundations and grave-covering boulders/stones would indicate vandalism some time in the past. The cemetery has not had any care in recent years.

There are about sixty fieldstones in this cemetery, some of which are headstone/footstone combinations, but most are single stones. The fieldstones appeared not to have been disturbed. This, along with several sunken areas would indicate many more burials than those listed.

Due to the condition of the cemetery there was no way of knowing where tombstones were originally and no definite pattern of rows. Rows were marked off arbitrarily and everything copied as found within a "row". Since most of the stones, including footstones, had been removed from the ground, their present location may or may not indicate the original site of the grave. Rows were copied from west to east and each row from south to north. They were copied in October 1982 by D. E. Wilson and H. L. Berry.

A record for this cemetery was recorded at the courthouse circa 1848 for one quarter of an acre of land. Judging by the dates of these inscriptions it was discontinued for burial purposes after a change of ownership.

CALLOWAY, Jane - Consort of Wm. CALLOWAY 4- 8-1813 2-12-1844 Row 1
d/o Samuel & Hannah BOND - aged 30y10m 4d

REESE, Elizabeth - Consort of Sameul REESE 34y 8m 1- 4-1818 Row 2

BOND, ----- ----- Eleanor 60y 6m24d 6-12-1838 Row 2
-----d, ----- born -- 19, 1877 (This tombstone is broken into four pieces. The top left quarter containing the given names, etc. is missing. A loose footstone in Row 3 with initials "S.B." may indicate this is the stone for Samuel BOND.)

BOND, Lydia d/o Samuel & Hannah BOND 12-28-1810 2- 8-1840 Row 3
Aged 28y 1m 11d

BOND, Elizabeth d/o Samuel & Hannah BOND 9-10-1815 4- 8-1838 Row 3
Aged 22y 6m 29d

BOND, Mary R. d/o Samuel & Hannah BOND 11-26-1806 7-12-1836 Row 3
Aged 29y 7m 16d

BOND, Hannah w/o Samuel BOND 11-27-1778 4-10-1819 Row 3
Aged 40y 4m 13d

CALLOWAY, Samuel B. s/o William & Jane 9-28-1838 10-26-1843 Row 3
CALLOWAY - Aged 5y & 28d

HULL, Elizabeth Ann d/o John L. & Mary HULL 11y 6m 9-16-1840 Row 3

_____, ----- (top of stone is missing) 6y 6m ??-25-1817 Row 3

BOND, Edmund s/o Samuel & Hannah BOND 5-11-1804 2- 9-1839 Row 3
Aged 34y 8m 26d

_____, ----- (only small part of stone remains ??y??m18d ---- Row 4

PAYNE, ----- s/o Thomas Y. & Ellen PAYNE 12-24-1838 3- 8-1843 Row 4
Aged 4y 2m 15d

PAYNE, Infant s/o Thomas Y. & Ellen ---- 5-??-1835 Row 4

J. R. - Initials on a loose footstone ---- ---- Row 4

H.A.W. Initials on a loose footstone ---- ---- Row 4

S. Initial on a loose footstone ---- ---- Row 4

LANCASTER, John F. - born in Virginia 10- 5-1777 10?-??-1839 Row 4
In the 63rd yr of his age.

THOMPSON, Thomas 7-??-1779 3- 9-1814 Row 4

WILLIAMS, Mary M. w/o Thos. WILLIAMS 70y 1m 11d 3-16-1848 Row 5

WILLIAMS, Thos. s/o Thos. WILLIAMS, Sr. 61y 9m 9d 6-12-1842 Row 5

BONHAM, (Jo)hn [Rev. War Vet.] 62y 10- 1-1820 Row 5

_____, Helen - rest of stone missing ---- ---- Row 5

WILLIAMS, ---- ---- (2nd name may be Ann. ---- 5-24-1823? Row 5
Stone is small, possibly that of an infant or child)

WILLIAMS, Peter C. s/o Tho. & Mary 28y 4m 2d 1-15-1841 Row 5

HULL, Sanford W. s/o John L. & Mary HULL 10m 7-27-1832 Row 5

WILLIAMS, Rev. Sanford S. (son of ?) Tho. 30y 2m13d 5-23-1841 Row 5
& Mary WILLIAMS

WILLIAMS, Thos. A. s/o Peter & Mary 3y 5m 2d 7-19-1843 Row 5
WILLIAMS

HIETT, James M. ---- 9-20-1845 Row 5

_____, (Esther?) Stone is illegible ---- ---- Row 5
(There's a loose footstone with initials E. L. that may belong here. This stone may be that of Elizabeth LAFEVER, whose stone was copied by Virgil & Margaret McINTOSH of Robinson, IL in Aug. 1976.)
It read:

LAFEVER, Elizabeth 73y 7-27-1806

_____, ----- (top of stone is missing) --y 7m 16d ---- Row 5

_____, ----- (top of stone is missing & ---- ---- Row 5
no inscription except poetry remains. Same small size & type of stone & inscription as on previous stone.)

J. W. (Initials on footstone0 ---- ---- Row 5

CLARK, Sarah d/o Thos. & Susan CLARK 16y 10m 15d 2-26-1822 Row 5
(Broken into several pieces by a fallen tree.)

CLARK, Rev. Thos. (Tree growing 40y 2m 11-10-1821 Row 5
around base, broken parts of rest of stone nearby.)

BONHAM, Aaron s/o A. R. & S. BONHAM 1y 6m 16d 2-22-1831 Row 5

BONHAM, Elijah 25y 10m ?d 8-14-1811 Row 6

LANCASTER, Hugh s/o William P. & Mary 2-12-1839 6- 5-1840 Row 7
Ann LANCASTER - Aged 1y 3m 23d

BONHAM, Elizabeth - Erected by her parents 10-13-1817 10-12-1842 Row 7
A. R. & S. BONHAM - Aged 24y 11m 29d

BONHAM, Mary w/o John BONHAM 64y 11-12-1821 Row 7

HAR-GRAVES, Jo(a?)s (Hand carved on ---- 7-13-1810 Row 7
a fieldstone & difficult to read.)

H. B. (Initials on a loose footstone) ---- ---- Row 7

_____, ----- (top of stone is missing) 10y 9m 6d 10-11-1820 Row 7
(Loose footstone with initials B.T. is nearby. Believe this stone belongs to Bazaleel THOMPSON s/o Thomas THOMPSON; also buried in this cemetery. H.L. Berry)

W. P. L. (Initials on a loose footstone, perhaps of William P. Row 8
LANCASTER? -- see stone of Hugh LANCASTER.

MITCHEL, Robert - born in Scotland 7- 9-1770 7-12-1844 Row 8
Aged 74y & 3d

KARR CEMETERY WHITEWATER TOWNSHIP

This cemetery was located in Section 9 of Whitewater Township, Hamilton County, Ohio on the west side of Kilby Road, one mile north of intersection with Dry Fork Road (or 1.5 miles south of intersection with Campbell Road.) It was adjacent to Kilby Road on a farm now owned by Lloyd Smith. A deed was recorded on February 29, 1848 by Charles and John Karr for one acre of land for this cemetery. The area is now cultivated and no tombstones are to be found. Mr. Smith verified the existence of the cemetery and stated that Karrs were the main burials in the cemetery, many dying from cholera in the 1830's. Other sources also indicated this to be the site of Karr Cemetery and it contained approximately ninety or more Karr burials with some other burials, possibly nearby neighbors. It is not known what happened to the gravestones or when burials were discontinued. Only one tombstone from this cemetery is known to exist and it is presently in the possession of Mr. Gene Woefel. It was copied by Mrs. Hazel L. Berry in September 1987.

KARR, Mariah - Consort of Jacob KARR Aged 35yrs 10mos 19days d. 26 Sept. 1834

Elizabethtown Cemetery is located in Section 19 of Whitewater Township on the north side of Stephens Road and 500 feet west of Lawrenceburg-Harrison road. A deed was recorded at the Hamilton County Courthouse on September 20, 1844 for .86 hundredths of an acre. A Presbyterian Church had been next to the cemetery but it had been abandoned for use as a church. The building was removed in 1938 and the space was added for a new section of burials. The entire cemetery is enclosed with a chain-link fence and is maintained by the township trustees. There are a number of loose, out of place, initialed former footstones and some unmarked stones. The oldest stones are deteriorating. There are some large, unmarked spaces between stones in the old section which may be of burials without markers. The gravestone inscriptions were copied in May 1973 by Lucy R. Bloomquist and in July 1991 by Dennis Simpson. This is the first time for these records to be published and no other records for this cemetery are known to exist.

NAME	BD or AE	DD	Row
ASHINEAD, Hariet w/o J.	25y 9m 25d	20 Aug. 1849	D-17,18
BACON, Jemima GARISON	2y 4m	Apr.1846 or 1849	F-18
d/o James & Mary BACON			
BOLANDER, Amos s/o R. & S.	8m	10 Sept.1836	
BOLANDER, Catharine - born in	1785	11 Aug. 1853/59	K-16
Northumberland Co. PA; wife of John			
BOLANDER, Elizabeth d/o J.B. & C.R.		1821	F-11
BOLANDER, Infant s/o A.B. & M.B.	no dates	----	D,E-10
BOLANDER, Infant s/o A.B. & M.B.	no dates	----	E-10
BOLANDER, J. Henry	11 Apr. 1844	9 Jan. 1845	E-10
s/o A.B. & M.B.			
BOLANDER, John	In 66th yr.	12 July 1841	J-16
BOLANDER, Margaret	27y	12 June 1839	?
Wife of Jacob			
BOLANDER, Margaret A.	3 Feb. 1846	9 June 1848	E-9
d/o A.B. & M.B.			
BOLANDER, Martha Ann B.	1y 3m 19d	19 Sept.1842	B-15
d/O L.B. & E.A.			
BONHAM, Aaron E.	10 Feb. 1832	21 Dec. 1862	B-6,7
s/o John L. & C.S.			
BONHAM, Charlotte S.	24 Dec. 1801	22 Apr. 1878	B-7
" ssa John L.	29 Jan. 1791	17 July 1856	B-7
BONHAM, Edward H.	12d	12 Mar. 1855	C-4
s/o J.H. & S.M.			
BONHAM, Elijah P.	34y & 23d	17 Dec. 1853	L-7
s/o Aaron R. & Sarah			
BONHAM, Eugenia	----	9 Apr. 1849	M-6
BONHAM, Jacob H.	10 Mar. 1828	20 Aug. 1859	B-4
s/o John L. & C.S.			
BONHAM, John P.	26y 6m 25d	3 Aug. 1850	M-7
s/o Aaron R. & Sarah			
BONHAM, Kittie	49yrs.	no date ----	
"Erected by the Presbyterian Church of Elizabethtown."			
BONHAM, Sarah Ann	22y 7m 24d	18 Sept.1850	M-7
Wife of J. P. BONHAM			
BONHAM, U. S. Grant	9 Mar. 1861	186?	L-6
s/o E.G. & L.N.... almost illegible			
BROWER, I. M. - Ass't Surgeon, 4th Ind. Inf.			G-17
Mexican War Veteran		no dates	
BROWN, Eliza	1y 2m 24d	24 Apr. 1853	C-18
d/o James & Sarah Brown			
BUTLER, Fannie	1856	1869	D-8
" ssa Isaac, Jr.	1845	1867	D-8
" ssa Isaac N. - Father	1805	1882	D-8
" ssa Isabella	1843	1862	D-8
" ssa Nancy GIBSON	1815	1850	D-8
Wife of Isaac N. BUTLER			
CADWELL, Mary	1 Jan. 1820	1 Apr. 1849	D-18
Wife of Albert E. Cadwell; 29y & 3m			
CALLOWAY, Jesse	2mo.	17 July 1871	B-8
Twin s/o W. & M.C.			
CALLOWAY, John L.	10m & 14d	9 July 1851	B-9
s/o Wm. & Mary C.			
CANFIELD, illegible	8 Sept.1858	16 July 1859	A-14
d/o Elizur & Angeline			
CANFIELD, Eliza T.	24 June 1864	31 Aug. 1868	K-5
CANFIELD, Flora	5 Jan. 1875	6 Sept.1881	K-4,5
CANFIELD, W. J., Jr.	17 Aug. 1866	14 Sept.1866	K-5
CANFIELD, John	----	----	K-2
" ssa Lodemia	----	----	K-3
" ssa Mary	----	----	K-2
" ssa Orie -These 4 had matching footstones to			K-2
a large surname stone, all without dates.			
CANFIELD, Judson J.	14 Apr. 1869	18 Sept.1872	K-5
CANFIELD, Newton Wm.	20 Mar. 1845	25 Sept.1865	A-14
s/o William & Matilda			
CANFIELD, Sarah C.	11 Jan. 1840	10 Aug. 1907	K-4
CANFIELD, Wm. J.	11 Feb. 1840	24 June 1903	K-4
CLARK, Elizabeth	5 Mar. 1789	23 June 1852	L-6
CLARK, Harriet M.	1 Feb. 1884	28 Dec. 1902	D-4
CLARK, John	1848	1924	O-2
CLARK, Wm.	20 Apr. 1778	2 July 1832/3	M-6

NAME	BD or AE	DD	Row
DeLAMATER, Elizabeth F.	32y & 7m	12 July 1852	H-6
Wife of Rev. I. DeLAMATER			
DEMMONS, Josephine - Mother	1908	1929	D-5
DUNN, Charles M.	21y 5m 24d	13 Sept.1840	F-16
DUNN, J.(ohn) C. - Co.A 185 Ohio Inf. - Civil War Vet.			F-17
DUNN, Lewis	Aged 70 yrs.	25 Oct. 1849	F-15-16
DUNN, Sarah	45y & 4m	1 Apr. 1834	F-15
Wife of Lewis DUNN			
ELLIOT, Thomas - Co.G 5 Ohio Cav. - Civil War Vet.			E-14
ERHARD, Jessie Etna	18 Nov. 1864	15 Oct. 1956	D-6
Wife of Michael ERHARD			
" ssa Michael	25 Dec. 1855	17 July 1913	D-6
EWING, Frances P.	12 Nov. 1813	11 Feb. 1867	G-14
Wife of John W. EWING			
GARDINER, Benjamin	35y & 24d	24 Jan. 1825	F-15
GIBSON, George W.	8 Sept.1830	30 Mar.orMay 1855	N-6
GIBSON, James J.	1863	1913	F-2
" ssa Sarah - Wife of James J.	1865	1918	F-2
GIBSON, Joshua - s/o J.G. & I.G.	----	16 Oct. 1845	N-6
(This stone has 5 unmarked stones next to it in row.)			
GIBSON, Mariah &	In 22 yr.	3 Sept.1832	F-12,13
d/o Elisha & Ruth SCOGIN			
GLAZIER, Elizabeth A.	5 Apr. 1837	25 Apr. 1931	J-3
" ssa Henry B.	4 Dec. 1835	10 Apr. 1908	J-3
GROFF, Henry	52y 1m 26d	4 July 1834	I-10
(Stone in very bad condition)			
GROFF, Rebecca	39yrs.	26 Apr. 1824	H-11
GROFF, Sophia M.	59y & 1m	1 Aug. 1831	H-9
GUARD, Flora Bell	14 Sept.1891	8 Jan. 1893	K-4
(nee CANFIELD)			
GUARD, Ruth	52y 2m 22d	30 Dec. 1839	E-13
Consort of Bailey GUARD			
HAIRE, Catherine P.	23 July 1885	5 Sept.1972	G-6
Illinois Nurse Army Nurse Corps. - WW I Veteran			
HAIRE, Eddie	12 Oct. 1855	5 July 1856	H-7
" ssa Horace - sons	27 Sept.1853	8 Feb. 1855	H-7
of Edward & Mary A. HAIRE			
HAIRE, Frances S.	24 June 1838	17 Sept.1921	G-8
Wife of George W. HAIRE			
" ssa George W. Esq.	89y 2m 2d	12 Jan. 1911	G-8
(His name & dates are at base of flagpole at entrance)			
" ssa Jacob	30 Nov. 1791	1 June 1852	H-8
" ssa Jacob H.	56y 7m 4d	6 May 1910	H-8
" ssa Kate P. &	28 Jan. 1824	30 Sept.1884	H-8
Wife of George W. HAIRE			
" ssa Mary	76y 11m 26d	26 Mar. 1906	G-8
" ssa Susan	16 Dec. 1793	5 Apr. 1871	H-8
" ssa Susan	79y 7m 22d	22 Nov. 1908	G-8
" ssa Thomas	20 Dec. 1819	1 June 1846	G-8
HAIRE, Thomas (2nd stone)	26y 5m 11d	1 June 1846	H-7
HAYES, Asahel	In 31 yr.	3 Mar. 1853	C-9
HAYES, Mary Wife of James C.	----	16 Jan. 1860	A-11
HAYHURST, Tom	----	----	G-1
HEARN, Anna - Mother	1873	1942	B-2
HEARN, James (Bolden) (WW I Vet.)	1896	(8 Oct.)1918	B-2
HEARN, Theodocia	53y 5m 25d	15 Nov. 1877	A-12
Wife of J.F. HEARN			
HUNT, Charlotte - born in Pennsylvania 5 Aug. 1764 & having survived him 40 years; in the 87th year of her age. Wife of Edward HUNT			I-13,14
HUNT, Edward - born in New Jersey 1763 and emigrated with his family to Ohio in 1806 where he resided until his death 11 May 1811, aged 58 years.			
HUNT, Ezekial H.	1y & 27d	25 Sept.1832	J-13
s/o Edward & Ann HUNT			
HUNT, Joanna BROWER	2 Feb. 1806	28 Jan. 1865	J-15
widow of Thomas HUNT; born in City of New York and died in Lawrenceburg, IN.			
HUNT, Rebecca	38 yrs.	24 Apr. 1834	J-14
d/o Edward & Charlotte S. HUNT			
HUNT, Thomas (71y6m2d)	13 Mar. 1787	15 Sept.1858	J-14,15
____, Infant	----	15 Apr. 1814	N-7

Name	AE or BD	Died	Sec.
KENDRICK, Susan J.	24y 1m 8d	11 Jan. 1859	A-17
Wife of Nathan KENDRICK			
LAWSHE, Henry	21 Feb. 1845	27 Feb. 1845	N-16
" ssa Hiram	21 Feb. 1845	21 Feb. 1845	N-16
sons of H.D. & H.A. LAWSHE			
LEWIS, Aaron H.	8 Oct. 1850	12 May 1863	F-6
s/o John & C. LEWIS			
LEWIS, Delia A.	22y 5m 10d	7 July 1839	E-18
Wife of Freeborn G. LEWIS			
LEWIS, Delia Adeline	1m 10d	4 Aug. 1839	E-17
d/o F.G. & D.A.			
LEWIS, Edward Payson	1y 8m ?d	28 Mar. 1846	E-7
s/o Joseph & Binnah LEWIS			
LEWIS, George D.	1846	1889	E-6
LEWIS, Joseph	14 Jan. 1810	3 Oct. 1866	E-7
LEWIS, Keturah H.	1803	1886	E-7
LEWIS, Statira J.	44 yrs.	16 Sept.1838	E-17
LOHMES, Lillie A.	1y (5m?)17d	29 Mar. 1869	B-18
d/o J.S. & G.A.			
McDOLE, Wm. - Co.D 52 Ind. Inf. - Civil War Vet.			B-1
McHENRY, Margaret	26 May 1776	21 June 1845	J-10
69 yrs. & 26 days - 2nd stone			
McHENRY, Margaret	26 Apr. 1776	20 June 1845	J-8,9
Consort of Samuel McHENRY			
" ssa Samuel	22 June 1778	3 Nov. 1858	J-10
McMANAMAN, Little William	14 Nov.1872	15 Oct. 1873	B-8
s/o J.F. & E.C.			
MILLER, K. - no dates	----	----	
MILLER, Wm. H. - no dates	----	----	D-1
MILLS, Charles	2 Jan. 1802	28 Oct. 1848	G-16
MILLS, Eliza	45 yrs.	31 July 1851	G-16
MILLS, Mrs. Elizabeth	70 yrs.	31 July 1852	G-15
Consort of Isaac MILLS			
MILLS, Frances PIATT	----	26 Mar. 1888	G-15
"Erected in tribute of affection by her nephew, I. MILLS"			
MILLS, Isaac (71y9m15d)	4 June 1764	19 Mar. 1835	G-15
MILLS, Isaac D.	6 Oct. 1806	8 Aug. 1860	G-16,17
s/o Isaac & Elizabeth MILLS			
MURE, Mary	In 68th yr.	13 Apr. 1853	C-18
ORSBORN, John Wesley	1848	1938	M-3
ORSBORN, Katharine	9 Oct. 1859	21 Apr. 1921	M-2
ORSBORN, Stephen A. Douglas	1 Dec.1858	21 Dec.1925	M-3
ORSBORN, Stephen W.	19 Oct. 1822	28 June 1886	M-2
ORSBORN, Elizabeth	31 Oct. 1792	26 Feb. 1860	A-12
PARIS, Ellanora	1890	1901	D-2
PARIS, Jerome - Our brother	1873	1925	
PARRIS, Ferdinand	1887	1905	D-5
PARRIS, Genevra - Mother	1848	1910	D-2
PARRIS, John - Brother (WWI Vet)	1879 [14 Apr.)	1919	D-4
PARRIS, Reddick - Co.B 59th Ind. Inf.-Civil War Vet.			D-2
PETTY, Elijah	1842	1930	Q-1
PETTY, Mamie	1878	1901	C-2
PETTY, Matilda	1845	1929	Q-1
PIATT, Abraham - Infant	1m & 8d	24 Mar. 1808	J-6,7
s/o Daniel & Elizabeth PIATT			
PIATT, E. Dumond	12 Jan. 1804	16 Sept.1872	J-6
Born in Hamilton County, Ohio			
PIATT, Mrs. Elizabeth	17 Apr. 1777	23 Nov. 1854	J-8
(77y 7m 6d)			
PIATT, Hannah	3y 10m 4d	10 Feb. 1809	J-7
d/o Daniel & Elizabeth			
PORTER, Andrew (72y)	1 Jan. 1785	30 Jan. 1857	G-5
Born in Philadelphia			
PORTER, Eliza	13 May 1794	9 Apr. 1881	G-5
d/o James PATTERSON (is on the gravestone)			
PRICE, William T.	33y 6m	27 Mar. 1841	J-10
PRICE, Wm. McHENRY	7 Sept.1836	7 Sept.1845	J-11
s/o William T. & Eliza A.G. PRICE			
PURSEL, John	15 May 1815	21 Apr. 1837	H-14
s/o John & Mary			
" ssa Lieut. John(1812 War Vet)	1784-	11 Sept.1814	H-13,14
" ssa Thomas	3 Mar. 1814	27 Sept.1819	H-14
ssa" REES, Mary	30 Nov. 1791	20 Apr. 1873	H-14
d/o Edward & Charlotte HUNT; she married 11 May 1813 John PURSEL & 29 Oct. 1818 to Samuel REES.			
ssa" REES, a son	17 July 1830	31 July 1830	H-14
ssa" REES, Charlotte	14 Aug. 1819	8 Sept.1820	H-14
ssa" REES, Ellis	.8 Nov. 1828	17 Oct. 1832	H-14
ssa" REES, Franklin	11 Jan. 1821	17 Apr. 1862	H-14

Name	AE or BD	Died	Sec.
REES, Mary Elizabeth	7 May 1823	28 Sept.1823	H-14
" ssa Samuel	2 Nov. 1781	21 Dec. 1843	H-14
Died at Connersville, Ind.			
" ssa Thomas PURSEL	16 Jan. 1827	7 Jan. 1857	H-14
" ssa William PURSELL	21 Oct. 1833	14 Dec. 1907	H-14
I.O.O.F. emb. by his name.			
ssa " RHODES, Mary REES	26 Dec. 1824	7 Mar. 1846	H-14
Buried at Connersville, Ind.; all the above are on the same stone, continuation of the others.			
REES, Ellis-s/o S. & M.-13y 11m 9d		17 Oct. 1832	H-12
PURSEL, John - Adj't. 1st Batl'n. 1 Ohio Mil.-			H-13
(2nd stone as Veteran War of 1812)			
REES, Infant s/o Samuel & Mary	11days	31 July 1830	H-12
REES, W. P.	----	----	H-15
RENNERT, F. J.	12 Feb. 1901	11 Oct. 1901	G- 1
SARVER, Mary Ann	23 June 1855	25 Oct. 1857	C-17
d/o David & Maria SARVER			
SCOGEN, Aaron	In 82 yr.	13 July 1836	F-12
SCOGIN, Rachel	Aged 91 yrs.	18 Apr. 1848	F-12
Wife of Aaron SCOGIN			
SCOGIN, Elisha-Vet.War 1812-	In 39th yr.	-6 Nov. 1821	F-13
DeMOSS, Mary SCOGIN	In 29th yr.	31 Oct. 182?	G-13
d/o Aaron & Rachel SCOGIN			
SHANK, George W.	Aged 37 yrs.	31 Mar. 1827	J-12
SHANK, George W. - Civil War Veteran/Gr. Reg.		1877	0
SMITH, Corpl. Wm. J. - Co.G 169 PA Mil.; Civil War Vet.			J-4
SNIFF, Nancy d/o Wm. & Abigail SNIFF	1825	9 Aug. 1862	A-10
SPEER, James	1832	1878	H- 1
STEVENS, George Daniel	9 Apr. 1871	23 Feb. 1875	L- 3
STEVENS, Mary Eliza	21 Apr. 1850	14 Jan. 1914	L- 2
STEPHENS, T.(homas) R. - Co.D or O 5 Ohio Cav.			L- 2
Civil War Veteran			
STEVENS, Rebecca I.	11 Jan. 1851	20 Jan. 1862	B-10
d/o Alfred & Deborah STEVENS (11y & 9d)			
STEVENS, Sarah A. HAYES, his wife	1817 -	1906	A-11
" ssa Uriah	1815	1874	A-11
TEBOW, Charles	28 Mar. 1839	22 Aug. 1839	L-10
TEBOW, Helen Ida	31 ??? 1861	20 Feb. 1862	I- 8
d/o George & Martha TEBOW			
TEBOW, Isaac	20y 11m 22d	20 Feb. 1826	L-12
TEBOW, Martha, his wife	9 Nov. 1782	15 Oct. 1868	K-13
" ssa Uriah	3 May 1782	11 Apr. 1820	L-12
TEBOW, Peter	30 Sept.1802	16 Nov. 1868	M-11
" ssa Olive, his wife	26 July 1809	24 Feb. 1885	M-11
TEBOW, Uriah	23y 11m 19d	4 Apr. 1835	L-12
TEBOW, William	16 May 1816	3 May 1848	L- 9
s/o Uriah & Martha			
THOMPSON, Hiram D.	11m 22d	25 Apr. 1848	N-15
s/o W.L. & H.S. THOMPSON			
TORRENCE, Wm. - Aged 80 yrs.	1748	?? Nov. 1828	H- 8
(Stone is broken & flat on ground...has new stone)			
TORRENCE, Wm. - Pvt. PA Militia, Revolutionary War,1748-1828			
TRUE, F. M.(arion) Co.H 1st KY Inf.-Civil War Vet.			D-18
VONDOLAH, Lucinda	52y 3m 11d	3 Aug. 1854	K- 6
Wife of Peter VONDOLAH			
VONDOLAH, Watson	5 May 1831	22 Aug. 1852	K- 6
s/o Peter & Lucinda VONDOLAH			
WALKER, Mrs. Elizabeth P.	12 Nov.1798	13 Sept.1872	J- 5
(73y 10m 1d also on stone)			
WAMSLEY, A. B. - Co.D 5th Ohio Cav.; Civil War Vet.			E- 5
WAMSLEY, Mary LEWIS	8 May 1842	23 Nov. 1927	E- 6
Mother			
WEST, Peninah M.	20 Mar. 1828	20 Aug. 1862	0
WHIPPLE, Elizabeth	----	4 July 1883	0
WHITE, Permelia (?Sp)	24 Dec. 1843	----	G- 9
WILLIAMS, Mary Jane	illegible---	24 Feb. 1849	B-16
Wife of Thomas N. WILLIAMS & d/o Jacob & Elizabeth BLASDEL			
WILLIAMS, Vance - s/o Thos. N. & Ann C. WILLIAMS	1m & 3d	28 July 1851	A-16
WOODBURY, Charles S.	24 Mar. 1806	12 Oct. 1838	L-11
s/o Jonathan & Lois WOODBURY			
WOODBURY, Sarah	21y 6m	19 Apr. 1835	L-11
Consort of Charles S. WOODBURY (nee TEBOW, not on stone)			
PIATT, Daniel	19 Nov. 1774	11 Oct. 1808	J- 7
Born in Somerset County, New Jersey; 33y 10m 22d			
____, Ch---- infant of E. & A.. 1y 9m-15 Apr. 1844 & rest is illegible.			

Burials in the new section of the cemetery:

BRETT, Etholena 9 Dec. 1917 2 Jan. 1968
" ssa Stanley Leon 20 Feb. 1912 2 Jan. 1968
BRETT, Stanley Leon (2nd stone) Indiana - Fl
U.S.N.R. - WW II Veteran
BERNHARDT, Andrew 1892 1980
BETSCHER, Alfred A. 3 Aug. 1900 6 Feb. 1972
" ssa Edith M. 25 Nov. 1899 26 Jan. 1980
CLARK, Frances G. 25 Nov. 1937 ----
" ssa Omer E. 1 Dec. 1928 11 May 1985 &
they were married 24 Sept. 1951
CRAWFORD, Richard G. 1946 1981
" ssa Anita K. 1947 1989 &
they were married 30 Dec. 1963
EDWARDS, Ralph Allen 13 July 1962 23 Sept.1988
Father - Son - Brother; A new process was used to etch his picture on the stone.
EDWARDS, Raymond L. 5 Dec. 1928 20 Mar. 1981
" ssa Bertha O. 11 Aug. 1930 ---- &
they were married 25 June 1955
FAUBUS, Lena May 1932 ----
" ssa Dewey 30 May 1916 26 Dec. 1990 &
they were married 24 Nov. 1973
FAUBUS, Dewey (2nd stone) WW II Veteran
ANDERSON, George R. 17 Jan. 1976 3 May 1983
BOWMAN, Carroll 12 Mar. 1908 6 Apr. 1988 &
Pvt. U.S. Army WW II Veteran
LOECHEL, Jessica Lynn 8 Dec. 1982 22 July 1986
LOECHEL, Jamie Leigh 21 Oct. 1981 21 Oct. 1981
TYLER, Velma I. 7 May 1920 13 Aug. 1980
"ssa R. Frank 29 Apr. 1916 1 Oct. 1979
STROUD, Wayne 18 Nov. 1947 17 Oct. 1979
CASH, Roy 1895 1982
" ssa Laura 1900 ----
STORMS, Mary A. 7 Dec. 1916 6 Nov. 1982
" ssa Marshall 17 Feb. 1917 ----
HOLLAND, Virginia B. 1934 1983
" ssa Harold E. 1931 ----
BURNS, James 2 Aug. 1918 15 Aug. 1984
"ssa Nellie M. 20 Nov. 1920 4 Oct. 1978
BURNS, James (2nd stone) Fl U.S. Navy - WW II Veteran
LOTTON, David W. 1931 1978
LOTTON, Carl L. 17 Dec. 1898 13 Aug. 1966
LOTTON, Perle 5 May 1900 4 Jan. 1974
McKINNEY, Kate P. 1870 1969 Mother
McKINNEY, Margaret WOODS 1893 1964
McKINNEY, Frank GUARD 1891 1973 Mason emb.
MENDEL, George H. 12 Dec. 1919 13 Jan. 1971
MORRIS, Marie L. 1903 1982
" ssa Jessie R. 1884 1972
RECORDS, James 8 Dec. 1884 10 May 1974
SHEETS, Alfred 1888 1963
SHEETS, Tina HAYES 1890 1964
SIMPSON, Anna Mae 26 Sept.1926 ----
" ssa Raymond S. 13 Mar. 1927 20 Apr. 1973 & 2nd stone
" Raymond S. - SSgt. U.S. Air Force - Korea, same dates.
WHITNEY, Carl S. 13 Jan. 1910 12 Nov. 1965
TURNER, Irvin 1904 1981
" ssa Emma Louise 1906 1983
WOERTHWINE, Bonnie M. 1898 1970
" ssa Edward J. 1890 1966
ROCK, Hollin-Husband & Father 1956 1979
LOECHEL, Elizabeth M. 1908 1981
" ssa Jacob J. 1908 1974
HARLACHER, Stella A. 1876 1968
" ssa Charles W. 1880 1964
Initialed stones: C.W., U.T., W.V., T.P., H.G., B.G., H.P., C.S.B. & W.Mc.

BEREA CEMETERY WHITEWATER TOWNSHIP

Berea Cemetery is located is Section 15 of Whitewater Township, Hamilton County, Ohio, on the northwest corner of Brotherhood and Adams roads in small village of Hooven, Ohio. The land originally was donated by Ezekiel Hughes in 1801. A deed recorded at the courthouse in 1822 established the cemetery for one and ten hundredths of an acre of land. In 1823 a neighborhood house of worship was built at this burying ground. Seven denominations were to preach there until 1830 when it became a Presbyterian Church. No church or building remains at the cemetery today that is maintained by the township trustees. The cemetery is enclosed with a chain link fence and the gravestones are in good condition. For a cemetery so old there probably were a number of burials made for which no grave markers exist today. These gravestone inscriptions were recorded in August 1992 by Mrs. Mary H. Remler. This is the first time for these records to be published.

ARCHER, Thomas 8 Sept.1815 1 Mar. 1877
"A native of England."
ARCHER, Jane w/o Thos. 23 Jan. 1818 20 Feb. 1865
"A native of England."
ARGO, Ebenezer 7 Feb. 1810 27 Sept.1890
ARGO, Amanda, consort of Ebenezer 18 Sept.1848
in the 24th year of her age.
ARGO, Hannah, w/o Ebenezer, in the 16 May 1867
60? year of her age.
ARGO, Louisa M.C., w/o Ebenezer, 29 Dec. 1876
aged about 70 years.
ARGO, James Edgar, s/o 1y 8m 8d 16 June 1849
Ebenezer & Amanda ARGO
ARGO, Willie, s/o W. & M. 1m 13d 1 Mar. 1870
ATHENS, George O. (?1y 6m 12d) illegible
s/o J. & M.
ATHENS, Sallie, d/o J. & M. ---- 7 Oct. 1863
BALSLEY, Rectina A. 18 Nov. 1833 31 Jan. 1872
wife of G. H. BALSLEY
BALSLEY, Joseph M. 1849 1928
" ssa , Elizabeth F. 1857 1932
BALSLEY, Mary A. d/o 11m & 11d 2 July 1876
J.M. & E.F. BALSLEY
BARLION, Thomas H. - WW I Veteran 3 Dec. 1939
Ohio Corp. 333 Inf. 84 Div. Lot 155
BENGE, John - Co.B 2nd KY Cav. - Civil War Veteran Lot 177
BEST, Jane E. d/o B. & Marie 25 Dec. 1850
HAYDEN, in the 22 year of her age.
BOUTCHER, John s/o 10y 3m 26d 10 Feb. 1839
Samuel & Sarah
BROWN, David J. 28 Dec. 1806 14 Nov. 1852
Masonic & I.O.O.F. emblems & footstones
" ssa Susannah S. 67y 5m 29d 11 Sept.1854
BROWN, Stephen W. In 30th yr. 17 Feb. 1876
BUCK, Brintha w/o Wm.S. 27 Sept.1770 14 Oct. 1827
CAINE, Edmund K. - Co.F 5th Ohio Cav. - Civil War Veteran
CAINE, Fannie d/o 27 June 1872 7 May 1887
E.K. & S.A.
CAINE, Ebey s/o 3 Apr. 1879 6 July 1879
E.K. & S.A.
CARLIN, Capt. Jas. - Co.D 83rd Ohio Inf. 1900 Lot 116
Civil War Veteran
CARLIN, Emily w/o James 37y 7m 4d 5 Feb. 1871
CARLIN, Elmer B. s/o 2y 5m 20d 12 Feb. 1866
s/o J. & E. CARLIN
CARLIN, Preston Douglas 9m 23 Aug. 1857
s/o Jas. & Emily CARLIN
CARR, Henry G. - Civil War Veteran 2 Sept.1915 No stone
but name in Courthouse Grave Registration File.
CARR, Margaret A. 10 July 1831 11 May 1867
d/o J.L. & S. WATKINS
CHAMBERLIN, Louisa A. 3 May 1827 7 Sept.1877
w/o John Y. CHAMBERLIN
_____? Broken ½ of stone next to Louisa Chamberlin, has
b. 11 Feb. 1789 d. 12 Dec. 1855 and S.W.R. on footstone
CHEEK, Anna 74 years ----
ssa PURDY, Alice 18 years
ssa PURDY, Harriet 68 years
CHIDLAW, Carrie G. 1872 1956
CHIDLAW, Edward H. 1871 1937
CHIDLAW, Harrist ---- ----
CHIDLAW, John ---- ----
CHIDLAW, Mattie I. 1876 1939
CHIDLAW, Rebecca H. 1873 1951
CHIDLAW, Henry K. - one date ---- 1868 footstone
CHIDLAW, James H. 1850 1929 footstone
CHIDLAW, Betty H. 1855 1933
CILLEY, Anna H. 1862 1931
CILLEY, Martha M. 1869 1930

CHIDLAW, Rev. B.(enjamin) W. 1811 14 July 1892
Chaplain, 39 O.V.I.-U.S.A. and 43 years missionary of the Am. Sunday School Union in Ohio and Ind. Born in Wales, G.B. - Civil War Veteran.
" ssa , Rebecca HUGHES, his wife 1826 1888
" , John 1844 1922
" ssa , Harriet HAYES, his wife 1844 1933
" ssa , side, Rebecca H. - no dates
" ssa , Mattie I. - no dates
" ssa , Edward H. - no dates
" ssa , his wife, Carrie G. - no dates
" ssa , back of stone, James H. 1850 ----
" ssa , his wife, Nancy E. 1855 ----
" ssa , Grace & footstone 1881 1901
" ssa , side, Martha 1843 1873
" ssa , Henry KERR CHIDLAW 1862 1868
CILLEY, Benj. 62 years 11 Feb. 1857
" ssa , Martha M. w/o Benj. 75 years 14 Oct. 1873
ssa , ANDERSON, Howard 13 years 8 Apr. 1873
their grandson
" ssa , Joseph & footstone 23 Jan. 1831 30 Nov. 1908
" ssa , Mary HUGHES 28 Oct. 1834 25 Nov. 1856
w/o Jos. CILLEY & footstone
" ssa , Mary H. HUNT, w/o 14 June 1836 20 June 1890
Jos. CILLEY & footstone
DATES, Corridon ---- 12 Feb. 1869
" ssa Abbey G. 19 Feb. 1813 21 Apr. 1906
DAVIS, Mary w/o D.E. DAVIS In 43 year 20 Aug. 1851
DAVIS, Samuel 25y & 17days 18 Apr. 1862
Civil War Veteran - Lot 89 & Robt. Lot 88
DAVIS, Robt. E. - Co.K 5th Ohio Inf. - Civil War Veteran
DAVIS, Mattie 1850 1871
DAVIS, Baxter - Civil War Vet., Lot 90-1847 1871
DAVIS, Joseph - Civil War Veteran - Co.H 52nd Ind. Inf.-Lot 87
EWING, John 71y 11m 12d 20 June18(?4)3
EWING, Thos. - PA Mil. Rev. 1745 1823
War Veteran; Plaque placed by Cincinnati Chapter D.A.R.
EWING, Mercy w/o Wilson EWING 27y & 3m 20 Sept.1848
EWING, John W.K. s/o W.C. & 28 days 23 Feb. 1851
Sallie A. EWING
ELDER, Benjamin CILLEY 1y 5m 21d 16 Dec. 1843
ELDER, Mary consort of -62y 11 Nov. 1838
John of PA
ELDER, Jane d/o J. & M. 28 years 6 Oct. 1833
EDMONDS, Jane Ann d/o 6y 8m 25d 19 Dec. 1845
Aaron & Lydia EDMONDS
EDMONDS, William s/o A. & L.-illegible 23 July 1850
ESSERT, Henry 1891 1920
ECKEL, George H. 1859 1953
" ssa Dora A. 1880 1949
ECKEL, George J. 1920 1928
"ssa , Ruby M. 1916 1917
FULCHER, George W. In his 34th yr. 17 Dec. 1825
GRAY, Matilda w/o A.M. 29y 2m 28 Feb. 1839
GROEMDYKE, Thannie, only 9y & 21d 27 Feb. 1862
son of Enoch & M.A.
FRAZEE, Jonas, Militia Revolutionary 1759 7 Oct. 1858
War - (stone appears to be new although he is named in history of Hamilton County, OH)
HALL, Abigail M. w/o M.N. 24 Dec. 1805 17 Apr. 1871
HALL & d/o Joseph & Susannah BROWN
HALL, Henry J. s/o Merritt 5 Sept.1836 3 Sept.1837
N. & Abigail M. HALL
HARRELL, Julia w/o B.S. 27 Sept.1822 31 May 1889
" ssa , B.S. 17 Apr. 1809 8 July 1899
HARRELL, Edward s/o B.S. & Julia 3m 10d 9 July 1852
HARRELL, Abigail w/o B.S. 33y 11m 3d 1? Apr. 1848
HARRELL, Cornelia d/o B.S. 18 days 22 June 1843
& Abigail
HARRELL, Abbey d/o Harrison 2y 6m 2d 5 May 1842
& Mary Ann
HARRELL, Mary Ann, consort 20 Sept.1814 6 Feb. 1846
of Harrison _ 31y 4m 17d
HARRELL, Bailey SMITH s/o Harrison & Mary Ann HARRELL
& dates were in concrete where stone was repaired.
HALL, Merrit N. 34y & 4m 24 June 1841
HARRELL, Jane d/o B.S. & Abigail - dates broken off ----
HAYDEN, Belemus & 69y 6m 10d 5 Feb. 1872
Mason emb. on stone
HAYDEN, Maria w/o Belemus In 42yr. of age 25 June 1851
HAYDEN, Alice Maria d/o B. & Maria ?y 11m 21 Apr. 1853
HAYES, Mary 10 Dec. 1815 18 Jan. 1900
HAYES, Job C. 7 Sept.1812 25 July 1887
HAYES, Job H. s/o Job C. ---- ----
HAYES, Harrist C. 29 Feb. 1876 27 Jan. 1881
HAYES, Hattie May d/o A.W. & 22 June 1884 13/18 Mar.1885
E. HAYES
Iron fence and gate to enclosure, marked D.G. HOWELL 1868: HOWELL, Daniel G.(ideon) first white child born between the Little and Great Miami Rivers; born in the blockhouse at Northbend 23 Aug. 1790 d. 16 Apr. 1866
HOWELL, Jean Elizabeth, born 17 Apr. 1801 Charleston, SC
and died in Cleves, OH 23 Nov. 1880.
Footstones: C.L.H., H.L.H., E.A.H., M.J.H.
HOWELL, Catherine LYALL 25 Nov. 1827 14 Feb. 1895
HOWELL, Henry LYALL 16 June 1821 1 July 1871
HOWELL, Libbie ---- 25 July 1865
HOWELL, Mary ---- 16 Feb. 1865
HELMICK, Mary J. 31 Oct. 1859 30 Apr. 1902
HUGHES, James ---- 17 Sept.1840
HUGHES, John Willard 3 Oct. 1879 26 Dec. 1879
HUGHES, Jeannie LYALL 17 Mar. 1874 13 Apr. 1874
HUGHES, Dr. William Clark 15 Feb. 1848 14 May 1908
" ssa , Anna E. 10 Dec. 1853 30 Jan. 1928
" ssa Jeannie L. 17 Mar. 1874 15 Apr. 1874
" ssa John W. 2 Oct. 1879 26 Dec. 1879
" ssa , Edna P. 25 May 1876 27 Nov. 1880
HUGHES, Euselina 11y 2m 24d 11 Jan. 1868
HUGHES, Edward B. 1820 1890
" ssa Mary E. 1830 1904
" ssa , Josie & footstone 1864 1867
" ssa , Jessie & footstone 1866 1867
HUGHES, Edward Everett 1870 19--
HUGHES, William Baxter ---- ----
HUGHES, Richard 42 yrs. 25 Aug. 1850
" ssa , Elizabeth ELDER 63 yrs. 6 Sept.1870
HUGHES, Ezekiel & footstone 23 Dec. 1842 9 Feb. 1897
HUGHES, John Milton s/o broken off 3 Sept.1835
Richard & Elizabeth
HUGHES, Ezekiel, a native of Wales,G.B.1776 1849
ssa , Jane HUGHES WAKEFIELD 1810 1890
" ssa , Mary EWING w/o Ezekiel 1785 1857
born in Penn.
" ssa , Margaret BEBB, w/o Ezekiel 1776 1804
born in Wales... 1st interrment in this cemetery.
" ssa , James s/o Ezekiel & Mary 1823 1840
" ssa , Martha d/o Ezekiel & Mary - dates illegible
Footstones: M.E.H., H.J.H.- 2y 10m; M.B.H., R.H., H.L.
HUGHES, Dr. John 21 Sept.1816 23 FEb. 1880
Mexican War Veteran
" ssa , Mary B. w/o Dr. John 6 Dec. 1819 29 Feb. 1864
" ssa , Lida L., their dau. 16 Jan. 1864 8 Oct. 1864
" ssa , Elizabeth J.B. 7 Dec. 1850 7 Nov. 1892
& footstones
HUGHES, Edna Pearl & stone 25 May 1876 27 Nov. 1880
by C. SCHERING
HUNT, Edward 1799 1883
HUNT, Ann HUGHES 1806 1885
HUNT, Ezekiel H. & footstone 28 Aug. 1831 30 Sept.1832
"ssa, Charlotte H. & footstone 24 July 1842 15 Apr. 1844
Children of Edward & Ann HUNT
HUNT, 1st Sgt. Thos. H. - Co.A 5th Ohio Cav.-Civil War Vet.
HUNT, Esther F. 23 June 1848 9 June 1936
HUNT, Gertrude E. d/o T.H. & E.F. 1 Aug.1870 4 Apr. 1873
HUNT, Lucius Curtiss s/o T.H.& E.F. 18 Dec.1876 11 Apr.1877
HUGHES, Charlie 5 yr. 24 Jan. 1862
JOHNSON, Ruth - No dates ---- ----
KARR, John & footstone 1835 1894
"ssa Fannie HUGHES & footstone 1844 1912
KARR, Martha CHIDLAW w/o John KARR 1843 1873
KARR, Charles Harvey 23 yrs. 21 Sept.1897
KARR, Willie R. s/o J. & F.H. KARR - No dates
KARR, Libbie D. d/o J. & F.H. 20 Sept.1878 29 Sept.1878
KNOBLOUGH, Mary Austin w/o 23 July 1828 24 May 1862
H.E. KNOBLOUGH, born in Lebanon, OH - 33y 8m 7d.
KESSNER, Willie C.or G. s/o 25 Oct. 1875 28 June 1876
J.B. & M.E. KESSNER
LEWEDAY, Charles s/o ?H. & M. 12 days 28 Jan. 1873
LAIRD, Jennie M. w/o James H. 29y 5m 12d 2 July 1878
LAIRD, Mary nee SMITH 1815 1891
" ssa, John, born in Ireland 1813 1891
LAIRD, John L. 19y 7m 29d 29 Apr. 1874
LYNCH, Esther C. 1911 1943
LIND, Jane Amanda, consort of 21 yrs. 13 Sept.1838
Thomas N. LIND
LIND, Thomas N. - Mason emb. 62y 1m 20d 8 Oct. 1875
LACY, Stephen h/o Louisa - Father 1811 1901

LACY, Luisa - Mother - No dates
LACY, Wm. S. - No dates
LEEPER, Catherine, w/o Rob't ---- 16 Aug. 1834
LOVE, Jos. - Co.D 83 Ohio Vet. Inf. ---- 13 June 1917
Civil War Vet.
LACY, Alice - No dates ---- ----
LACY, Hazzel - No dates ---- ----
LACY, Bessie - No dates ---- ----
LACY, Harry - No dates ---- ----
MAHAFFEY, Halsey s/o T. & H. 21 Dec. 1852 27 Mar. 1853
MAHAFFEY, William Thomas 19 Oct. 1846 17 Sept.1847
s/o Thomas & Hannah MAHAFFEY
MAHAFFEY, Phebe 6y 6m 10d 25 Jan. 1867
McCLAINE, John - Co.M 5th Ohio Cav. ---- ----
Civil War Veteran - Lot 145
McCLAIN, Rebecca d/o John & Elizabeth -15 yrs.31 May 1873
MILLER, Lewis s/o Henry & 3y 8m 12d 19 Feb. 1844
Elizabeth MILLER
MIX, Sumner DeESTAING 27y 9m 24d 18 June 1874
Mason emb. on stone; also footstone
MOAK, Eliza Katharine d/o 6 weeks 2 days 1 Oct. 1838
Philip & Eliza MOAK
MOAK, Eliza w/o Philip In 23rd yr. 17 Sept.1838
NOBLE, Rhoda BONHAM w/o 29 Oct. 1794 5 Aug. 1883
Uz NOBLE
NOBIL, Uz 21 Sept.1791 25 Mar. 1864
NOBLE, Harriet R. 28 yrs. 13 or 19 Oct. 1861
PERHAM, Jesse - Co.B 2nd KY Cav. - Civil War Vet. ----
PERRY, D.H.; Ass't Surg'n 114 U.S.C.T. - Civil War Vet.
OGDEN, Benjamin S. 8 Aug. 1767 5 Feb. 1849
Born in Fairton, Cumberland Co., N. Jersey, 81y 6m
OGDEN, Nancy w/o B.S. In 79th yr.of ae 27 May 1847
OGDEN, Hiram 13 Dec. 1791 14 Mar. 1863
Born in NJ; War of 1812 Veteran; Lot 39
OGDEN, Sarah A. 54 yrs. 7 Dec. 1862
OSTRANDER, M.(artin) Co.A 5 Ohio Cav.; Civil War Veteran
RICE, Eva Zelia - One date 1870 ----
RICE, Alice Jane 1852 1920
RICE, Alva ---- 1910
RICE, Don ---- 1907
TORRENCE, Sarah w/o James M. 22y 4m 11d 28 July 1835

RICE, Eunice 63y 7m 23d 28 Jan. 1875
RITTENHOUSE, Joseph 25 Feb. 1808 3 Dec. 1822
_____, Allen - all that on stone near the above.
RITTENHOUSE, Susan A. w/o 4 Dec. 1815 26 Sept.1871
Stephen WOOD RITTENHOUSE
ROBINSON, Infant s/o M.N. & M.J. illegible 30 ---? 1879
ROBINSON, Jane E. d/o M.N. & M.J. " illegible
ROESCH, Louise, tochter von Philippu Heinrich ROESCH, Geb.
24 Juni 1857; gest. 28 Sept. 1859.
ROSECRANS, Parmenus W. 24y 5m 9d 20 Nov. 1882
" ssa , William W., killed in Battle of Tuka, Miss.
20 Sept. 1862, 33y 7m 13d; Civil War Veteran; Lot 164
" ssa , Sarah A. 17 Nov. 1831 11 Jan. 1898
SEIBEL, William H. s/o John 1y 4m 2d 31 Aug. 1872
and Evaline SEIBEL
SCOTT, Martha Maria, w/o Wm. In her 21st yr. 10 July 1844
TOMLINSON, _ broken stone..."children of J.H. & J.E.
TRIBBLE, Russell - Civil War Vet. ---- 28 Feb. 1924
WADE, H.M. - Co.M 5th Ohio Cav.; Civil War Vet.; Lot 17
WADE, Anna Maria, w/o Hezzekiah 12 Jan.1840 31 Aug. 1886
In Memory of dear Mother by her bereaved children.
WADE, John Edward s/o H.M. & A.M.- 1y ?m 2d -- Jan. 1880
WAMSLEY, A.C. - Co.D 5th Ohio Cav.; Civil War Vet.; Lot 71
WAMSLEY, Mary Ellen, infant 8m 10d 24 Feb. 1850
d/o Samuel & Catherine WAMSLEY
WAMSLEY, Capt. Samuel - Co.D 5th Ohio Cav.; Civil War Vet.
WHITNEY, Artimicia w/o In 26th yr. 4 June 1871
Wm. W. WHITNEY & d/o E.H. & M. CHAMBERS
WHITNEY, William N. s/o 1y 10m 6d 7 Apr. 1870
Wm. W. & A. WHITNEY
WILLIAMS, John, a native of N. Wales; 25y 19 Mar. 1849
WILLIAMS, John s/o John & 1y 7m 7 Aug. 1850
Hanah WILLIAMS
WILLIAMS, Eusebiah 37y 2m 24d 30 Jan. 1868
WOOD, Clarinda B. 1820 1888
WOOD, Susie A. 1847 1869
WOOD, Charles A. - Civil War Vet. 1845 1913
WATKINS, Susan B. d/o J.L. & Susan - 15 yrs. 9 Apr. 1842
WOOD, Mary ---- ----
YOUNG, Peter & footstone 66 yrs. 10 Nov. 1829
RITTENHOUSE, Stephen WOOD 1 Oct. 1805 21 Nov. 1848

COLLINS Family Burial Site

The present owner of property at 5935 State Route 128, south of Miamitown, Ohio has placed a marker at an area measuring thirty-three feet by nine feet on his property. Gravestones were removed from this area many years ago and used as a sidewalk. Approximately twelve burials had been placed on this hillside, the ancestors of a James Collins who died in 1924. James was buried in Miami (Miamitown) Cemetery.

This cemetery is located in Section 9 of Whitewater Township, Hamilton County, Ohio, east of Kilby Road and two tenths of a mile north of intersection with Dry Fork Road. It is located on a knoll behind buildings now housing a truck repair shop, formerly a farm. The cemetery is enclosed with a fence and maintained by the township. There are some broken tombstones and some piles of uninscribed pieces of tombstones. Several sunken places without stones marking them would indicate more burials in this cemetery than those listed below. The local newspaper referred to this cemetery as the old "OWRY" Cemetery at Hunt's Grove. The published list of cemeteries for Hamilton County, Ohio calls this the Karr Cemetery. However, Karr Cemetery appears to have been located further north on Kilby Road on the farm now owned by Lloyd Smith.

The gravestone inscriptions were copied in October 1982 by H. L. Berry and the list was expanded with the kind help of Mr. Gene Woefel of the Harrison Historical Society. Mr. Woefel had copied the inscriptions previously and his list contained 25 more burials (indicated with a * below).

[Rows were copied from west to east and each row from north to south.]

KITCHEN*, Lavinia w/o Farthing ---- 1847 Row 1
Stone was found in a gully in the NW corner of cemetery. Probably belongs in Row 6.

Following three burials were over the brow of the hill in SW corner of cemetery.

____, ____ * unknown ---- ---- Row 1
____, ____ * unknown ---- ---- Row 1
____, ____ * unknown ---- ---- Row 1
SHULL, Peter 55y 5- 5-1828 Row 2
SHULL, Catharine w/o Peter SHULL 54y 7m26d 10-28-1831 Row 2
CAMPBELL*, John [stone broken Vertically, 17-- 18-- Row 3
part missing, possibly Rev. War Vet. who d. 1839]
CAMPBELL*, Barton h/o Emiza BENNETT ---- 1848/9? Row 3
SHUP?, Eliza (beth?) ?1814 ??-19-1828 Row 3
Fieldstone, hand carved, badly deteriorated, b. date carved above name.
SHUP, Mary - fieldstone, worn ---- 8-29-1821 Row 3
SHUPP*, John - fieldstone, broken off ---- 1833 Row 3
WRIGHT, Infant s/o James & Letita ---- 4-20-1830 Row 4
FENTON, Harrison C.? or G.? s/o Jacob 17y? 7- 2---- Row 4
FENTON BA & S. ?. F(ENTON?) Some latin words on stone. Stone is flaking off and illegible in places.
FENTON, Sarah W. - Consort of Jacob FENTON 56y 5-24-1834 Row 4
B.A. Gentleman (Stone has fallen over & almost covered with dirt.)
WRIGHT, Lewis s/o James & Letitie WRIGHT In 6th yr. 12-30-1841 Row 4
FENTON, Jacob - (Stone broken into three 68y 2m 3-21-1845? Row 4
pieces.)
KENDRICK, James - Father 1818 1901 Row 4
" ssa , ---- Wife 1824 1881 Row 4
" ssa , Thomas - Son ---- ---- Row 4
____, ____ (Fieldstone, no inscription ---- ---- Row 4
WALSH, Infant s/o of Rd. & Ca. WALSH ---- 1841 Row 4
SKIDMORE, Charles W. 64y11m28d 11- 6-1890 Row 5
FREDRICK, Alice E. d/o C. W. & M. J. 21y & 7d 10- 7-1875 Row 5
SKIDMORE
SKIDMORE, Mary Jane w/o C.W. SKIDMORE 42y 1m20d 5-28-1877 Row 5
CALAWAY*, Charlotte w/o William (Only 37y 182 (2 or 7?) Row 5
one date on stone, could be birth or death, stone broken & difficult to read.)
KITCHEN, Thomas (Stone is in pieces, 50y 5-22-1828 Row 6
piled with other uninscribed pieces)
KITCHEN, Leonica w/o Thomas KITCHEN 65y? 6-10-185?7 Row 6
(Age could be 63 yrs & death date could be 1837)
MORGAN, Elizabeth d/o E. M. & J. M. 18y 3m 5d 2-29-1848 Row 6
MORGAN, Joannah In 14th yr. 12-13-1839 Row 6
MORGAN, Rebecca In 14th yr. 8-31-1836 Row 6
MORGAN, Miles s/o J. & Julia A. MORGAN 1y 2m 8-29-1851 Row 6
MORGAN, Thomas "My Husband's Grave" In 34th yr. 11-25-1851 Row 6

Following four stones were in a square plot, possibly surrounded at one time by a fence; handmade & illegible.

OWRY*, ------ ---- ---- Row 6
OWRY*, ------ ---- ---- Row 6
OWRY*, ------
OWRY*, ------
RADCLIFF, Mary w/o S. RADCLIFF 5-22-1786 10- 9-1849 Row 7
HARVEY, Charles - aged 53y 2- 7-1797 8- 4-1850 Row 7
" ssa, Nancy - aged 7y 2-12-1837 8-24-1844 Row 7
" ssa, Rebecca - aged 33y (?In 33rd yr.) 8- 6-1806 5-14-1839 Row 7
SCHUETZ, Emma ---- ---- Row 7
SCHUETZ, Wm. J., Jr. ---- ---- Row 7

SMITH, Nancy G. w/o Anthony SMITH - Auntie 1845 1917 Row 8
KARR, Lewis C. 1848 1912 Row 8
KARR, Thomas H. 1851 1908 Row 8
KARR, Jerusha - Mother 1811 1885 Row 8
KARR, Charles - aged 46y 7m 19d 9- 8-1806 4-27-1853 Row 8
(Iron tombstone, some Latin words on stone.)
KARR, Mary - Little d/o Char. & Erusha 7-22-1833 10-13-1834 Row 8
KARR - aged 1y 3m 20d (Iron tombstone, loosely attached to its base.)
CARR*, Erusha infant of Nancy & Michael ---- 1865 Row 8
MATISON*, Martha Jane ---- 1822 Row 8
MALONEY*, Molly 12y 1845 Row 8
HOPPING*, Estonia w/o Jeremiah ---- 1868 Row 8
(Stone beside south fence.)
LEWIS*, David ?/o Conway (Welsh) 32y 1824 Row 8
(Stone outside fence, east of entrance.)
BENTON*, Lettie May ---- 1838 Row 8
(Stone outside fence, east of entrance.)
JESSUP, Chloe E. d/o Wm. & C. JESSUP 1y 7m27d 4- 4-1847 Row 9
JESSUP, Daniel In 64th yr. 11-12-1855 Row 9
WILSON, Sarah w/o John J. WILSON 22y 3m21d 6-13-1856 Row 9
JESSUP, Alethia A. d/o Wm. & Christiania In 19th yr. 1- 1-1858 Row 9
SKIDMORE, Mary Jane w/o Marteny SKIDMORE In 28th yr. 3- 4-1858 Row 9
(d/o William JESSUP)
SKIDMORE, Infant s/o Marteny & Mary J. ---- 12-??-1851 Row 9
(Stone is broken off & leaning against Wm. TAYLOR'S stone in Row 10.)
JESSUP, Christiana RIGGS w/o William 5-16-1818 1-11-1889 Row 9
JESSUP - Mother
" ssa , William - Father 12- 7-1797 5-14-1876 Row 9
RALF?, Willie s/o G. & N.? RALF? 5- 1?-1866 7-10-1866 Row 9
RALF?, Johnnie s/o _?_ & N. RALF? 11?-15-186? ??-18-???? Row 9
(Stone is broken off the base.)
KENDRICK, Sarah M. d/o Nathan & Susan J. 5m27d 9-11-1858 Row 9
PRINDIVILLE, John 5- 2-1862 5-30-1862 Row 9
TAYLOR, Lydia w/o Griffin TAYLOR In 88th yr. 1- 8-1844 Row 10
TAYLOR, Sarah w/o William TAYLOR 49y 2m17d 1-19-1854 Row 10
TAYLOR, William 56y 9m24d 2-24-1854 Row 10
TAYLOR*, Peter h/o Josephine SATER ---- 1840 Row 10
KARR, Hu---- (Hugh?) In 67th yr. 8-30-1839 Row 11
McCLAIN, Jacob 4- 9-1844 2- 2-1868 Row 11
O____*, ----- (Four small fieldstones ---- ---- Row 11
& a taller tombstone with an "O" at the top, located between two cedar trees near the center of the east fence.)
TAYLOR, John D. s/o William & Sarah 20y 4m 9-23-1842 Row 12
TAYLOR, Mary Ellen d/o William & Sarah 12y 6m 3d 3-17-1841 Row 12
PERRINE, Beulah w/o J. PERRINE In 80th yr. 1845 Row 12
PERINE, John (different spelling) In 59th yr. 10-25-1831 Row 12
PERRINE, Barbary d/o P. & Sarah PERRINE 1y 6m 2- 1-1824 Row 12
PERRINE, Anna d/o P. & Sarah PERRINE Illegible 5-??-1828 Row 12
RIGGS*, Robert ---- 1842 Row 12
PERRINE, Sarah w/o Peter PERRINE In 34th yr. 7-19-1840 Row 12
PERRINE, Peter- aged 52y 6m27d 6-22-1805 1-19-1858 Row 12
PERRINE, Mary d/o P. & Sarah PERRINE 13y 7-20-1840 Row 12
(Stone is broken off the base.)
RADCLIFF, Sarah d/o P. & S. PERRINE 4-24-1830 4- 6-1856 Row 12
(aged 25y11m12d)
BENTON*, Jacob J.- Civil War Vet. ---- 1878 Row 12
(Only upper part of stone is by large tree at center of east fence.)
O'BRIEN*, KItty w/o Thomas ---- 1871 Row 12
(Stone is beside east fence.)
WEST, Johnathan (Broken into two pieces) 25y 2m19d 4-22-1862 Row 12
KARR*, Mary L. w/o Samuel (Stone is ---- 1827 Row 12
beside tree base, east fence.)
GALLAGHER*, Dan s/o Thomas & M. L. 27y 1822 Row 12
GALLAGHER*, Thomas-WW I U.S.Army Vet. 1894 1917 Row 12
JONES*, Owen from Wales (Stone in SE Corner) ---- 1842 Row 12

This cemetery is located in Section 6 of Whitewater Township, Hamilton County, Ohio, west of SR 128 on the south side of Miamitown, Ohio, consisting of approximately ten acres. Mrs. Hazel L. Berry completed this compilation of records in March 1989. Miami is still an active cemetery for burials.

Available records are contained in three books kept by the custodian, but they are incomplete. Book #1 contains a "Record of Deaths and Interments", dated from June 1855 through November 1881. There are no entries from December 1881 through June 1904. From July 1904 through December 1905 interments are again recorded. Also recorded in this book are "Removals from "Old Burial Grounds", "Proprietors Names", and "Record of Interments Showing What Part of Lot Interred On" (Plats of Lots). Book #2 contains "Transfers and Sales of Lots from 1943 through 1982". Book #3 contains burials recorded from 1976 to present date (March 1989). On pages 102 through 129 in Book #3 are "Records from Book 1" (referring to the sale of lots).

The cemetery contains burials of persons who died before 1855 but they were removed from other places and reinterred here after the cemetery opened in June 1855. The first burial was supposedly that of Rev. Jethro TABER who died in June, 1855 and was buried in the cemetery while it was yet a corn-field. During the span from 1855 to 1982 (127yrs) records are available for only 34 years. These are: From June 1855 thru November 1881
Missing years for records are: December 1881 thru July 1904 (22½ yrs) From July 1904 thru December 1905
January 1906 thru Jan. 1976 (70 yrs) From Jan. 1976 thru present (July 1982)

In Book #1 the section, "Record of Interments Showing What Part of Lot Interred On", did not contain dates but indicated burials of persons not listed anywhere else.

The following burial list has been compiled basically from tombstone inscriptions with data added from cemetery records. Names and data of persons appearing in "Records of Deaths and Interments" and in "Record of Interments Showing What Part of Lot Buried On" that did not give the lot and section number and/or did not have tombstones on lots will be listed separately at the end under "Burials On Unknown Lots/Section".

There are six sections in the cemetery, Section 1, Section 2, Section 3, South Section, Southwest Section and Memorial Section. Section 2 has an addition called "1st Subdivision-2nd Addition", were used interchangeably. For simplicity, Section 3 is used to describe both areas. The original plan of 1st Subdivision-2nd Addition and Section 3 has been changed causing some difficulty in locating lot markers, some of which were not found.

Originally each square lot was fifteen feet on each side and contained space for eight burials, although some had more than that. Odd-shaped lots had any number of burials. There are some burials in the aisleways between lots. Lots in the Memorial Section are ten feet square.

Tombstone inscriptions are listed as they were copied in a counter-clockwise direction beginning with the northwest corner. Burial positions, where listed, are given for those burials shown on the "Plat of Lots" which do not have a tombstone on the lot. Location of these burials will be designated by W1, W2, W3, W4, E5, E6, E7, & E8, indicating the four burials on each side; eight total. Irregular burials will be indicated as between two of the usual places. Generally the listing of burials will follow this pattern except in cases where a monument or stone lists all of the names and there's no indication in the book of the arrangement of burials.

Some tombstone inscriptions may be listed on the incorrect lot due to the lack of complete records and the inability to locate lot markers.

ABBREVIATIONS & SYMBOLS USED ONLY FOR RECORDS OF THIS CEMETERY; OTHERS ARE LISTED ON PAGE IN FRONT OF THIS BOOK.

* means no tombstone is presently on the lot. Name and date was obtained from "Record of Deaths & Interments" in Book #1. Burial was recorded with lot and section number.

x means tombstone on lot, missing name and/or date found in cemetery records.

\+ means no tombstone is presently on the lot but name is listed in the "Record of Interments Showing What Part of Lot Buried On" in Book #1. This section of Book #1 showed the burial site of persons on lots and gave the name of each deceased. In some instances this is the only place the name of the deceased was recorded and no other data was given.

Some of these burial entries were designated only as someone's child. Since there was no way to determine which child the entry may refer to, the entry (designated with a +) was added to the lot. For example, there are stones on a lot for two children, Mary and Sarah. The plat of lots shows four entries for "Child of B's" buried there. The burial list will show six burials on that lot because there is no indication that Mary and Sarah are B's children. However, both may be and there may actually be only four children buried on that lot.

( ) mean additional data obtained from cemetery records. If lot and section number was not recorded, the data matched tombstone inscription on the lot or was a child of parents buried on that lot. Burials without a lot/section number and no match with a tombstone are listed separately.

On pages 45 & 46, Book 1, twenty one persons are named in the "Remarks in Respect to the Condition of Coffins and of Deceased Persons Removed from Old Burial Grounds". No other data was given as to the location of these "Old Burial Ground". The time given in the remarks refers to the length of time between date of death and date removed from the old grounds.

Comments or additional information not on stones or in the books.

c/o for child of; chn/o for children of; bet for between; emb for emblem engraved on tombstone; kin for kindred; LO for lot owner (If name appears without birth or death dates, and is indented two spaces, it means there is no indication the lot owner is buried on the lot.) Following "LO" is the year the lot was purchased or transferred from the previous owner. If no year is shown, the year of transfer was not recorded or was made after 1942. mkr is for moveable marker placed near a stone; res means residence at time of death.

NAMES of organization whose emblems appear on tombstones or markers:

Amer Lgn	American Legion	DAR	Daughters of American Revolution	VFW	Veterans of Foreign Wars
BSA	Boy Scouts of America	D of A	Daughters of America, besides D of A, emb may have an open book on a shield or circle.		

F & AM Free & Accepted Masons (Emb has a compass & square, with the letter "G" or sometimes with a pyramid containing an eye) 32nd degree Masons may have an emb with two eagles and "Spes mea in ded est". Sometimes emb has only a compass & square without any other symbols or letters.

G.A.R. Grand Army of the Republic

IOOF International Order of Odd Fellows - Emblem (emb) has three overlapping ovals with "F-L-T" with one letter in each oval.

Jr. Ord. National Council Junior Order of United American Mechanics - Emblem (emb) has a compass, a square and an upraised arm with a hammer.

K of P Knights of Pythias - Emblem (emb) has the letters "F-C-B" by themselves or on a shield, sometimes with a knight's helmet.

O.E.S. Order of Eastern Star - Emblem (emb) has a star with or without the letters "OES", or a star with symbols on each ray. Sometimes the letters "F-A-T-A-L" are found on or around the star.

PS Pythian Sisters - Emblem (emb) has a sword, a star? and the letters "P-F-L-E".

SECTION 1

NAME	BD or AGE	DD(or DI)	Lot-Sec.
SCOGIN, Mary Ann d/o L. & C.(b.3-29-1838, d. of scrofula; b. & res Hamilton Co. OH, d/o Lewis & Christena)	25y 5m17d	9-16-1863	1 1
ssa MINGES, Catharine (Kate) w/o Nicholas d/o L. & C. SCOGIN (b.5-19-1840 Hamilton Co. OH - of consumption, res Miamitown, OH, d/o Lewis & Christena SCOGIN)	27y 8m20d	2-10-1868	
ssa SCOGIN, Christena	1813	1886	
" " , Lewis - LO 1864 (res Whitewater Twp., early resident of Miamitown, OH)	65y 1m 5d	1-24-1876	
" SCOGIN, Ruben s/o L. & C. (b. 11-12-1842 of consumption, res Miamitown, OH, s/o Lewis & Christena	30y 5m 7d	4-19-1874	
" SCOGIN, John s/o L. & C. (b. & res Whitewater Twp., OH of consumption)	31y 6m23d	6-25-1876	
SENIOR, Edwin LO 1863	1829	1914	2 1
+ ____,Unnamed bur pos W2 (Probably Edwin)	----	----	
SENIOR, Ida V. (Virginia) d/o Edwin & Rebecca (b. Cincinati, OH of typhus form of flux, res Lawrenceburg, IN & removed from Lawrenceburg, IN 4-30-1863)	1-28-1853[x]	7- 3-1858[x]	
SENIOR, Frances (I.) (b. & res Evansville, IN, of pneumonia, d/o Edwin & Rebecca)	7-23-1866	1- 6-1870	
SENIOR, Rebecca L. w/o Edwin	1831	1907	
SENIOR, Edwin, Jr.	1870	1915	
*JACKSON, Goldie - In aisle bet lots 2 & 11	----	7- 1-1976*A2&11	
BIGGS, Edith B. nee LAW w/o Chas. A.	12- 6-1874	10-31-1896	3 1

NAME	BD or AGE	DD(or DI)	Lot	Sec.
LAW, William - Father =LO 9-26-1857=	3- 1-1832	5-11-1908	3	1
"ssa, Tryphena - W/o William - Mother	6- 6-1832	4- 4-1885		
"LAW, *+ John bur pos W4 (b. Hamilton Co. OH, of typhoid fever, res Colerain Twp. Hamilton Co. OH, farmer s/o Benjamin & Mary)	5- 6-1842*	8-14-1864*		
"ssa, Susan d/o William & Tryphena (b. Colerain Twp. Hamilton Co. OH, d. of erysipelas)	10-28-1856	6- 5-1857		
"ssa, Joseph (B.) s/o Wm. & Tryphena (Joseph (H?) b. & res Colerain Twp. Hamilton Co. OH of erysipelas)	10- 1-1860	7-26-1862		
"ssa, Lewis (R.) s/o William & Tryphena (b. Hamilton Co. OH, of diphtheria, res Colerain Twp.)	3-23-1863	10-15-1873		
"ssa, Ella (P.) d/o William & Tryphena (b.Hamilton Co. OH, of diphtheria, res Colerain Twp.)	5-26-1865	10-25-1873		
"ssa, Samuel F.C. s/o Wm. & Tryphena (b.Hamilton Co. OH, of diphtheria, res Colerain Twp.)	7-16-1867	11- 1-1873		
"LAW, +Joseph J. bur pos E6 (Jos B?)	----	----		
JONES, Joseph [LO 5-4-1858]	----	----	4	1
JONES*+, Flora bur pos W4 (b. & res Colerain Twp., d/o Joseph & Fanny Jane, grd d/o Samuel L. & Deborah JONES)	2-27-1861*	3-20-1861*		
CARDEN*+, Mrs. Rhoda bur pos E5 (b. Colerain Twp., d.Cincinnati, OH of consumption; res McLaskey Co. IA, d/o Samuel L. & Deborah JONES)	12-29-1832*	1-11-1860*		
BARNES*+, Mrs. Elizabeth bur pos E6 (b. & res Colerain Twp., d. of consumption, d/o Samuel L. & Deborah JONES)	4-26-1830*	10-27-1860*		
MYERS, Albert C.	1895	1911		
REESE, Anna	1851	1920	5	1
REESE, Jane w/o Robert - Mother	3- 7-1822	8- 9-1900		
" ssa, Robert - Father [LO 3-3-1859]	52y	10- 5-1872		
_____, Valleta - name on stone with Clifford	----	----		
_____, Clifford	----	----		
WILKINSON, Lanson [LO - 1859]	----	----	6	1
LOCKWOOD, Oliver - Father [LO]	1-28-1814	5-25-1885		
" ssa , Allie - Mother	6- 1-1815	9-11-1901		
GRECO, Nicholas J.	1912	8-18-1984X		
WILKINSON*+, ----- bur pos E5 (ch/o Lanson WILKINSON)		DI-11-15-1859*		
HEDGER, Jesse E., Jr. "Bud" VFW mkr U. S. Air Force Vet.	9-30-1946	7-31-1984		
" ssa , Marcella - Mom	1926	----		
" ssa , Jesse E. - Dad	1924	----		
SIMMONDS, James S.	1914	----		
" ssa , Maxine Rea	1918	1- 2-1985X		
FRIANT, John W. [LO 5-4-1858] F & AM emb (b. 1807 NJ d. of consumption, res Colerain Twp., miller & farmer, s/o James & Margaret)	56y	11-31-1863	7	1
" ssa , John H. - Civil War Vet. Co. D 60 OVI (killed at City Point, VA)	17y	4- 6-1865		
FRIANT+, Child of James bur pos E5	----	----		
STUDY*+, Mrs. ____ bur pos E6 (res Cincinnati,OH)		DI-8-14?-1865*		
HILL*, -----(parents Taber & Margerete)		DI 9- 7-1866*		
HILL*, Mrs. Margaret (Parents John & Margaret FRIANT)		DI-11-26-1866*		
BREEZE, John L. [LO 4-24-1857] (Native of Montgomeryshire, North Wales, England, res Crosby Twp.)	9-24-1794	6- 6-1875	8	1
" ssa , Ann w/o John L. (Native of Montgomeryshire, North Wales, England; of consumption, res Crosby Twp. d/o Thomas & Jane ROWLANDS, metallic coffin)	12-25-1788	6- 1-1862		
NUGENT, Willie J. s/o Wm. S. & Elizabeth F. (12-23-1855) (b.& res Whitewater Twp.; grd s/o Andrew NUGENT)	3- 3-1856		9	1
NUGENT, Mary w/o Andrew (b. 1790 PA, of heart disease, res Hamilton Co. OH, d/o John & Sophia HILL)	In 75th yr	8- 3-1865		
" ssa , Andrew [LO 1-30-1857] (b.Washington(10-18-1787) Co. PA, res Whitewater Twp., of dropsy; s/o James & Christiena)		11-14-1872		
BARTHOLOMEW, Mary E. B. d/o T.B. & M.N.	1-24-1880	8-14-1880		
TABER, Esther (Mrs.) [LO 3-10-1856]	----	----	10	1
TABER, Wm. [LO]				
TABER, Rev. Jethro W. (b. Potters Hollow, Albany Co., NY; of diarrhea; res Miamitown, OH, merchant; b/o Gilbert TABER, Racine Co., WI; metallic coffin.) [First burial in this cemetery while it was yet a cornfield.]	7- 2-1813X	6-15-1855X		
SEAL, Wm. [LO 5-20-1856]	----	----	11	1
SEAL*, Mary (Mrs.) [LO 5-9-1863]		DI 12- 2-1866*		
SEAL, Joseph F & A.M. emb (b. Chester Co. PA; of cholera; res Colerain Twp.; stonemason; removed from Public Burying Ground adjoining cemetery 3-11-1857 to Wm. SEAL lot)	52y 9m 5d	8-12-1852		
SEAL, John T. (b. Hamilton Co. OH; of consumption; res Colerain Twp.; farmer; s/o Joseph & Mary)	10- 5-1838	4-29-1861		
BARNS, John H. (b.10-13-1850 Colerain Twp.; of typhoid pneumonia; res Miami Twp.; s/o Abram F. & Ann M.)	21y 4m 3d	2-16-1872		
SEAL, Ellen d/o Wm. M. & Catharine (b. 5-12-1859 & res Colerain Twp; grd d/o Jacob & Mary Ann CHAMBERS)	1y 8m18d	1-30-1861		

NAME	BD or AGE	DD(or DI)	Lot	Sec.
BARNES+, Abe bur pos E7 (Forest A.?)	----	----	11	1
BARNS, Forest A. (b. 6-9-1858 Colerain Twp.; res Hamilton Co. OH; s/o Abram & Ann)	16y 1m14d	7-24-1874		
NOES, Wm. [LO 2-8-1897]	----	----	12	1
NOES, James - Father [LO 1863]	1807	1898		
NOES*+, Martha Elizabeth bur pos E5 (b. Whitewater Twp.; of measles; d/o James & Martha)	11-24-1858*	3-13-1863*		
NOES, Martha - Mother	1826	1887		
LORD, Ann LEFEVER w/o Wm. 81y & 23d	10- 3-1812	10-26-1893	13	1
HOUTS, Joseph P. [LO 1862]	43y 1m 5d	9-27-1870		
MOORE, Frances A. w/o John	30y 8m26d	10- 5-1869		
HOUTS*+, Mary bur pos E5 (b. & res Cincinnati, OH; of inflammation of brain; d/o Joseph & Sarah)	2-17-1861*	9- 9-1861*		
HOUTS, Joseph s/o J.P. & S.	9m	4-21-1867		
BENSON, Zaccheus W. [LO 3-10-1858]	----	----	14	1
BENSON, Zaccheus (W.) s/o Arthur W. & Nancy (b. 3-8-1856 Colerain Twp.; of abscess of thigh; res New Baltimore, Crosby Twp.; bur on Zaccheus W. BENSON lot-grandfather)	9m13d	12-21-1856		
BENSON*+, Rhoda (?) bur pos W4 (b. June; of consumption; res Whitewater Twp.; w/o Z? W)	6-??-? *	6- 3-1857*		
BENSON*+, Wm. bur pos E5 (b. Sussex Co. DE; of brain disease; Harrison Twp.; farmer; b/o James & Z.W. BENSON of this Co)	1801*	8- 7-1858*		
BENSON*+, Katie bur pos E5-6 (b. America; of typhoid fever; res Cincinnati, OH; d/o A.W. & Nancy)	4- 7-1863*	11-29-1873*		
BENSON*+, William L. bur pos E6 (b. Ohio; of whooping cough; res Dent, Green Twp.; s/o A.W. & Nancy)	3-17-1878*	5-28-1878*		
BENSON, Arthur W.	1835	1910		
" ssa , Nancy	1837	1916		
WHITNEY+, W's child bur pos W1	----	----	15	1
CHAMBERS, Mary Ann 85y11m22d	7- 9-1806	7- 1-1892		
CHAMBERS, Jacob [LO 3-31-1856] 80y11m10d	3- 2-1800	2-12-1881		
CHAMBERS+, Jno. bur pos W4	----	----		
CHAMBERS+, D's child bur pos E5	----	----		
CHAMBERS+, Wm. Chambers' 2 children bur pos E5 & E5-6		----		
CHAMBERS*, Oliver VALEMDINGHAM [?] (b. Whitewater Twp.; of summer complaint; res Miamitown; s/o Wm. & Susanna)	9-27-1863*	8- 9-1865*		
CHAMBERS*, ----- parents Wm. & Susan		DI 12-28-1866*		
CHAMBERS+, B's child bur pos E6-7	----	----		
CHAMBERS+, B's child bur pos E7	----	----		
BRAMERS+, [?] H's child bur pos E8				
DUDLEY, William - Father	1870	1940	16	1
BAUGHMAN, Rosannah (Mrs. Rosa)	1802	1887		
BAUGHMAN, Samuel [LO 3-10-1856]	1800	1888		
BAUGHMAN, Samuel s/o S. & Rosannah (b. 3-24-1843 Crosby Twp.; of typhoid fever; res Crosby Twp.; s/o Samuel & Rosanna; removed from Public Burying Ground adjoining cemetery 3-12-1857)	7y 18d	4-11-1850		
BAUGHMAN*+, Bruce bur pos E5 (b. & res Miamitown,OH)	----	4- 2-1880*		
BAUGHMAN+, Samuel, Jr. bur pos E6	----	----		
JONES*+, Samuel L., Sr. bur pos W3 [LO 1860] (b. NY City; res Hamilton Co. OH; of consumption)	9- 6-1795*	8- 8-1868*	17	1
JONES, Henrietta B.	In 51st yr.	12-14-1901		
JONES+, Infant bur pos E5 (beside Martha)	----	----		
JONES+, Martha bur pos E5-6	----	----		
JONES*+, Frances (Miss) bur pos E6(d/o Samuel L.)		DI 9-15-1866*		
JONES*+, James bur pos E6-7 (date of death not recorded but name is recorded between May & July 1867)	----	1867*		
JONES*+, John bur pos E7 (s/o Samuel L.)		DI 10-13-1866*		
JONES+, Fletcher bur pos E8	----	----		
JONES*, ----- (d/o Samuel L. & Elizabeth)		DI 6- 3-1863*		
HILL, William C.	11-13-1861	11- 6-1891	18	1
" ssa, Elizabeth COLUMBIA w/o William Mother [LO 1-16-1908]	12- 6-1834	5-18-1915		
" ssa, William - Father- Civil War Vet.[LO1861]	4- 5-1831	2-29-1904		
ssa COLUMBIA, William	1-24-1846	4-23-1922		
ssa COLUMBIA, John A.	8-26-1848	5- 2-1893		
WERTS, Sarah w/o M. b. East Tennessee-Mother	5-26-1799	4- 1-1884	19	1
" ssa, M. (Martin) [LO 3-4-1859] Father b.N.PA	1-26-1807	11- 5-1881		
" ssa, C.M. (Kate) w/o J.J.; res Whitewater Twp	1-4-1844	8- 6-1881		
" ssa, John J. - Civil War Vet. [LO 5-17-1875]	12- 1-1837	7- 4-1884		
ssa REESE, John B. - Father	7-19-1854	9- 2-1931		
ssa WERTS, E. A. d/o J.J. & C.M. (Elizabeth Ann, b. 9-28-1865; of scrofula of head; b. & res Whitewater Twp.; d/o John J. & Catherine M.)	8-27-1865	2-13-1867		
ssa REESE, Ida A. WERTS - Mother w/o J.B.	4-20-1862	8-26-1929		
INGERSOLL, Elizabeth	1854	1942	20	1
INGERSOLL, Mary Ann	1816	1898		
INGERSOLL, Isaac [LO 1860]	1817	1902		
MANN, Nancy	1850	1937		
INGERSOLL, Abel	65y 9m	12-20-1850		
INGERSOLL, Elizabeth w/o Abel	In 68th yr.	4- 9-1857		
INGERSOLL, Robert G.	1887	1914		
MANN, Perry L.	1864	1933		

NAME | BD or AGE | DD | Lot-Sec.

INGERSOLL, Florence (Flora) 1858 1884 20 1
CONE, Ashel [LO 10-16-1858] ---- ---- 21 1
ATHERTON, Eliza d/o John & Hannah FOSTER 7-15-1827 3- 1-1884
FOSTER, Hannah w/o John (res near Mt. Carmel, IN) 72y11m 1d 11-14-1875
FOSTER, John [LO 6-19?-1865] (b.5-26-1799 66y 23d 6-18-1865 MD; of supposed apoplectic fit; res Hamilton Co. OH; farmer; s/o Absolom & Agnes
SEIGLE+? or SEICLE?, George W. bur pos E5 ---- ----
LAW, Anna 1851 1926 22 1
HILL, Priscilla - Mother 1829 1906
"ssa, Andrew - Father [LO 1-30-1857] (b. & res 1827 11- 7-1904x Miamitown, OH; of rheumatism & heart failure; farmer)
LAW, Viola ---- ----
LAW, Meta P. d/o A. & P. HILL 9- 7-1892 7- 8-1893
HILL*, ----- ch/o Andrew ---- 9- ?-1850*
FARMER*+, Phebe M. bur pos W1-2 (b. & res 7- 8-1850*10- 7-1852* 23 1 Miamitown, OH; of erysipelas; d/o Emily & Henry W. FARMER. Placed on top of box with remains of Mrs. E. H. FARMER. Removed from Public Burying Ground adjoining cemetery Mar. 12, 1857 #9, after 4y 5m.)
FARMER*+, Emily H. bur pos W2-3 (b. & res 1-19-1819* 9- 7-1852* Miamitown, OH; of confinement/inflammation; d/o Benjamin & Ann Magdelain THOMPSON. Removed from Public Burying Ground adjoining cemetery Mar. 12, 1857 #10.)
FARMER, Mary L. d/o Henry W. & Emily H. 5m23d 11-10-1841 (Mary Louezie b. 5-17-1841 Miamitown, OH & res; placed in same grave with Mrs. FARMER at her side. Removed from Public Burying Ground adjoining cemetery Mar. 12, 1857 #11.)
THOMPSON*+, Daniel bur pos W4 with Benj. 18y* 9-20-1820* (b. PA; of typhus fever; res Miamitown, OH; s/o Jessee THOMPSON;
THOMPSON, Benjamin s/o Jessee & T;h/o Ann M. 7-20-1793 9-10-1820 Removed from Public Burying Ground adjoining cemetery Mar. 12, 1857. #16 Daniel THOMPSON in the same grave with Benj. THOMPSON & was formerly removed from hill side above Miamitown.)
FARMER* , Henry W. [LO 5-7-1857] 7-27-1814* 5-24-1875* (b. Hamilton Co. OH; of fever; res Mt. Pleasant, OH; s/o R. & Mrs.)
JONES, Jefferson [LO 1863] ---- ---- 24 1
GILLESPIE, CLarence 1872 1955
" ssa , Edith 1880 1949
BAUGHMAN, Frank M. [LO 9-12-1934] 1848 1937
" ssa , Fannie 1852 1939
JONES, Harry T. (Thos.) (b. 1-10-1863 Crosby 10d 1-19-1863 Twp.; of affection of heart; s/o Jefferson & Catharine; grd s/o Samuel BAUGHMAN.)
JONES, Sammie L. (s/o Jefferson & Catharine) 1y11m 1d 2- 3-1863
ROTH, Jack - Son 1929 1934
McCORMIC, Michael [LO 1862] ---- ---- 25 1
McCORMICK, Cora B. - D of A emb 1859 1959
McCORMICK, Lucretia D. 1856 1940
MITCHELL, Jennie L. 1853 1935
McCORMICK, Elizabeth - Mother 1832 1924
McCORMICK*+, Michael bur pos E8 (b. & res 12-11-1861* 2-15-1862* Miamitown, OH; of inflammation of lungs; s/o Michael & Elizabeth.)
WHITEHEAD, Daniel H. [LO 3-18-1856] ---- ---- 26 1
VANTREESE+, Rachel A. bur pos W1-2 ---- ----
WHITEHEAD, Mary [bottom of stone is in concrete & ---- 4-28-1841 can't read age] (b. 12-14-1800 Crosby Twp., Hamilton Co. OH; of inflammation of bowels; res near Miamitown, OH; d/o Conrad & Catharine VANTREESE. Removed from Public Burying Ground adjoining cemetery Mar. 12, 1857 #12.)
WHITEHEAD, William (b. 7-10-1795 PA; of 47y 2d 7-12-1841 inflammation of bowels; res near Miamitown, OH; cabinetmaker. Removed from Public Burying Ground adjoining cemetery Mar. 12, 1857.)
HAISCH, George W. [LO 4-25-1856] ---- ---- 27 1
BLAIR, Rebecca [LO 6-13-1888]
ARNOLD, Mattie [LO 8-5-1895]
FLOWERS, Jeff [LO 7- 3-1919]
FLOWERS, Emma L. - Mother 4-18-1863 12-25-1927
" ssa , Thomas J. - Father 3- 2-1860 2-26-1957
HAISCH, Emma L. w/o George W. (b.1-26-1825 30y 9m27d 11-22-1855 Springfield Twp. near Lockland, OH; of parturition/confinement; res near Miamitown, OH; d/o Mrs. BLAIR; infant buried with her in same coffin.)
HAISCH*, Infant of George & Emma ---- ----
HAISCH*+, Samuel bur pos W4-E5 (b. & res 3-17-1860* 7- 4-1860* Colerain Twp.; s/o George W. & Betsa; grd s/o Mrs. Sally LIND.)
FLOWERS, Stanley s/o Elizabeth & Stacey 11- 7-1923 7-16-1981
FLOWERS, Elizabeth Marie 8- 2-1896 11-26-1965
FLOWERS, Stacy R. (Ohio Engineman 2/CL 2-23-1897 3-11-1946 U.S. Navy)
FLOWERS, Eugene L. - Baby 6-21-1922 8-12-1922
MILLER, Sarah nee FLOWERS 1904 1931
LEMMON, Margaret w/o David 78y 6m 7d 3-15-1885 28 1
"ssa , David-Father [LO 3-18-1856] F & AM emb 61y 6m 12-25-1871

LEMMON+, Child of H. bur pos E5 ---- ---- 28 1
WALKER, Edw. B. [LO 2-2-1859] 29 1
WALKER*+, John Foster bur pos W3-4 (b.Mill- 5-31-1833* 7- 3-1859* creek Twp.; of Consumption; res Colerain Twp.; s/o Edward B. & Anna.)
WALKER*+, Edward P. bur pos center of lot 1874*DI 12-27-1904* bet W2-3 & E5-6 (b. American; of tuberculosis; res Hamilton, Butler Co. OH; s/o Christofer & Flora.)
HUNGERFORD*+, Sarah Jane bur pos E5 10- 7-1858* 2- 1-1859* (b. & res Colerain Twp.; of inflammation of brain; d/o Plinn A. & Lovinia A.; grd d/o Edward B. & Anna WALKER.)
WERTS, Martin [LO 1860] ---- ---- 30 1
FLOWERS, John [LO 11-29-1865]
NUGENT, Wm. S. [LO 2-11-1887]
BARTHOLOMEW, William N.B. s/o T.B. & M.N. 2-25-1883 6-23-1902
NUGENT, Jacob A. (Andrew) s/o W.S. & E.F. 15y10m23d 8- 7-1873 31 1 (b. 9-11-1857 Hamilton Co. OH; of lockjaw; res Crosby Twp.)
NUGENT, John C. s/o W.S. & E.F. 18y 3m 26d 5-29-1877 (b. 2-3-1859 & res Crosby Twp.; of concussion; murdered by John REESE & Evan BREESE
" ssa , Elizabeth F. w/o W. S. 42y11m15d 11-10-1877 (b. 12-25-1834 & res Crosby Twp.; of mental troubles; d/o Thos. & Ann H. LACY.)
NUGENT, Lydia L. d/o W. S. & E. F. 9m15d 7-11-1872 (b. 9-26-1871 Hamilton Co. OH; of cholera; res Crosby Twp.)
NUGENT, FLora A. d/o W. S. & E. F. 4y 16d 7-11-1872 (b. 6-25-1868 & res Crosby Twp.; of cholera.)
NUGENT, Clarinda M. d/o W. S. & E. F. 2y 9m24d 9-13-1875
NUGENT, William S. s/o A.J. & M. [LO 1862] 2-23-1828 9-24-1894
KELLER, Kate C. N. 1862 1896
BARTHOLOMEW, Mary N. d/o W.S. & E.F. NUGENT 5-28-1860 5-22-1897
HAISCH, John [LO 1859] ---- ---- 32 1
HAISCH, Mary w/o John (Poley/Polly Hash 67y11m28d 4- 9-1876 d. 4-8-1876, b. & res Colerain Twp.)
HAISCH, Johney s/o Christopher F. & Caroline 1y 5m28d 11-15-1860 (b. 5-18-1859 & res Colerain Twp.; of croup)
HAISCH, Christopher ---- 10- 9-1875x Co. D 70th Ohio Inf (b. & res Colerain Twp.)
HAISCH, Christopher F. - Civil War Vet. 3- 7-1834 9-22-1882
" ssa, Caroline 10-17-1835 10-18-1895
GLASS, Kate (Mrs. res Whitewater Twp.) ---- 5-15-1861x 33 1
"ssa , Robie (Robert?) (res Hamilton Co.OH, 3-22-1781 7-31-1865x farmer; s/o James & Mary)
ssa HUFFORD, Katie ---- ----
ssa INGERSOLL, Betsy (GLASS?) 8- 2-1819 12-31-1893
ssa INGERSOLL, Joseph L. [LO 6-24-1856] 9- 5-1803 9-27-1862 (b. Dutchess Co. NY; of bilious fever; res Miamitown, OH; s/o Ezra & Elizabeth; bridge builder & undertaker; at time of his death was a trustee of this cemetery.)
ssa INGERSOLL, Joey E. s/o J.L. & B.S.G. 8-23-1857x 2-18-1859x (Joseph E. b. & res Whitewater Twp.; of inflammation of lungs; s/o Joseph & Betsy G.; grd s/o Robert & Catharine GLASS.)
ssa CUNNINGHAM, Betsy - Aunt (Miss Elizabeth 70 or 75y 1-10-1863x b. Wooster Co. MA; of consumption; res Whitewater Twp.; d/o Johnathan & Sophia; lived with Robert GLASS family since about 8-19-1819 until died
ssa INGERSOLL, Children of J. L. & B.S.G. ---- ----
Following 3 names are not inscribed on the above stone but the inscription "Children of J.L. & B.S.G. INGERSOLL" may mean the following 3 who were reinterred from the Public Burying Ground:
INGERSOLL*+, Catherine G. bur pos E5 7-.5-1846* 3-18-1849* (b. & res. Miamitown, OH; d/o Jos. & Betsy S.G.; removed from Public Burying Ground adjoining cemetery 3-11-1857 #6.)
INGERSOLL*+, Catherine bur pos E5-6 2-15-1851* 4-15-1851* (b. & res Miamitown, OH; d/o Jos. & Betsy S.G.; removed from Public Burying Ground adjoining cemetery 3-11-1857 #8 ? time 5y 11m)
INGERSOLL*+, Robert G. bur pos E6 6-21-1848* 7-15-1848* (b. & res Miamitown, OH; s/o Jos. & Betsy S.G.; removed from Public Burying Ground adjoining cemetery 3-11-1857 #7, ? time 8y 8m.)
INGERSOLL*, Infant of Jos., Jr. (b. White- 1-19-1861* 1-19-1861* water Twp.; stillborn; res. Miamitown, OH; d/o Joseph & Lucetta)
HERIDER, Wm. C. [LO 1856] ---- ---- 34 1 F & A.M. emb on monument with "LEMMON"
LEMMON, Frances L. 1868 1942
LEMMON, Harry H. 1867 1934
LEMMON, Henry [LO 11-27-1900] 1839 1909
LEMMON, Sarah J. 1840 1914
LEMMON, Genevieve 1898 1961
LEMMON, Ellsworth H. 1912 1920
LEMMON, Genette 1898 4-27-1979x
HERIDER, Wm. C. [LO 4-25-1856] 35N 1
HERIDER*, Nancy bur pos W1-2 (bur tog 6- 6-1794 3-18-1824* with Caroline; b. near Lexington, KY; of confinement; res Miamitown, OH; d/o Conrad & Catharine VANTREESE, 1st w/o Jacob HERIDER. Removed from Public Burying Ground at the CORNICK, now NUGENT farm, Crosby Twp.to here

NAME BD or AGE DD Lot-Sec.

HERIDER*, Nancy - continued: removed on Mar. 12, 1857, #18; Some of the hair I have cut off for the purpose of retaining it to put in a pin - & it was signed by Wm. C. HERIDER.)

HERIDER*+, Caroline bur pos W1-2 with Mrs. ---- ---- 35N 1
Nancy HERIDER (b. Miamitown, OH; of whooping cough; d/o Nancy & Jacob. Removed from hillside, west above Miamitown at time of Mrs. Nancy Herider's death & deposited with her at Cornick's & removed at the time & placed in the same box with her mother at the cemetery at Miamitown, OH, Mar. 12, 1857, #19. 'Caroline originally was buried on the hillside above Miamitown at the west end of Ferry St. but removed at the time & buried with her mother, Nancy HERIDER, & also taken up at the same time.'

The following 2 burials are listed as being on Lot 34, Sec. 1 in the NE qtr, but probably are on the NE qtr of Lot 35N.

HERIDER*+, Mary S. (b. Miamitown, OH; of 11- 2-1864* 8- 2-1865* 35NE 1
inflammation of bowels & head; res Hamilton Co. OH; d/o Wm. P. & Sarah P.)

HERIDER*+, Sarah F. (Frances) (b. & res 7-19-1858* 9-24-1858*
Miamitown, OH; of inflammation of bowels; d/o Wm. C. & Sarah P.)

HERIDER+, Mrs. ___ bur pos E5 (2nd wife) ---- ---- 35S 1
HERIDER+, Jacob bur pos E6 [LO 12-29-1876] ---- ----
SNYDER, Geo. W. [LO 3-20-1857] 36 1
SNYDER, Samuel (b. 2-1793 Lancaster Co. PA; In 48th yr. 9-10-1940
of bilious fever; res Miamitown, OH; miller; b/o John SNYDER of Harrison, IN; removed from Public Burying Ground adjoining cemetery, Mar.12, 1857, #15)

FAGALY, James H. [LO] 1834 1907 37 1
FAGALY, Maria DAVIS - His wife 1837 1925
BOGART, Rosalie Evaline 1835 1917 37 1
BOGART, Elbert Sgt. Co. D 70 Ohio Inf. ---- ----
Civil War Vet.

Monument on lot with only the following: 38 1

SCOFIELD, Cornelius & family

Following 2 entries, unnamed, same date of death but two different lot & section numbers, first entry may be incorrect:

SCOFIELD*, Unnamed (Lot 20 Sec.2) ---- 6-26-1863*
SCOFIELD*, Unnamed (Lot 20 Sec.1) ---- 6-26-1963*
SCOFIELD*, Cornelius [LO 1864] DI 4- 3-1865*

BORDEN*+, Naomi bur pos W1 (b. NJ; of bilious 1-10-1801*11-16-1827*
& typhoid fever; res Cincinnati, OH; d/o Joel & Susannah STEWART. Removed from Cincinnati, OH 4-21-1863 & deposited this cem. 4-24-1863.)

BORDEN*+, Susannah S. bur pos W1-2 (b. NJ; 3-20-1827*12- ?-1827*
of croup; res Cincinnati, OH; d/o John & Naomi. Removed from Cincinnati, OH 4-21-1863 & [DI 4-25-1863]in Miamitown Cemetery.)

___+, unnamed bur pos W2-3 ---- ----
SCOFIELD+, Matilda bur pos W3 ---- ----
SCOFIELD+, Unnamed bur pos W4 ---- ----
SCOFIELD*+, Harriet bur pos E5 (b. & res 9-13-1842*11-18-1866*
Green Twp.; of P.I. rheumatism; d/o Cornelius & Sarah)

HART, Alfred - Father [LO 1864] 1810 1884 39 1
"ssa, William - Son 1861 1946
"ssa, Caroline - Mother 1812 1882
"ssa, Mary - Daughter 1859 1901
HART*+, Harriet bur pos W4 (b. Hamilton Co. 9-27-1847* 4- 2-1879
OH; of consumption; res Dent, OH; d/o Alfred & Caroline)

CADY, Naham [LO 1867] ---- ---- 40 1
CADY, John [LO] (b. 6-4-1846 Hamilton Co. 26y & 26d 6-30-1872 40N 1
OH; of consumption; res Miami Twp.; s/o Naham & Frances) Civil War Vet.

ANTHONY, Edw'd [LO] Civil War Vet. Co. D 5 Cav.-[Ashes-10-29-1923] 40S 1
SPINNING, William D. - Dad [LO 1886] 1882 1953 41 1
SPINNING, Kate B. 1857 1886
PRINCE, Thomas [LO] 1913 4-20-1981x 42 1
" ssa, Lucy [LO] 1916 ---- NW
KRIMMER, Peter - Father [LO] 1905 5-30-1980x 42 1
" ssa , Anna - Mother [LO] 1907 ---- SW
RAMSEY, R. & J. [LOs] 42SE 1
WRIGHT, Howard L. [LO] Amer Lgn mkr 1913 2-12-1983x 42NE 1
" ssa, Hazel H. 1918 5-22-1981x
ANTHONY, John [LO 1865] ---- ---- 43 1
MILLER, Harry J. - Pop 1871 1951 43 1
COX, Geo. W. - Civil War Vet. Co.K 72 Ohio Inf. ---- ---- 43 1
COX, Hannah - Mother 63y 2- 4-1888 43 1
COX, Andrew J. Civil War Vet. Co.K 72 Ohio Inf. ----[20 Mar.1926]43 1
[LO 5- 2-1873] 43 1
COX, Nancy - Mother 4- 7-1852 10-28-1932 43 1
COX, Sherman T. - Brother 5-27-1888 6-27-1943 43 1
COLEMAN, Jacob 5-22-1844 5-18-1902 44 1
" ssa , Mary Ann (b. & res Miami Twp.; 3-17-1846 9-10-1848
of Scarlet Fever; kin Benjamin & Sarah Ann. Removed from farm of Benj. COLEMAN, Miami Twp. Mar 23, 1864)
" ssa , Benjamin - Father [LO 1864] 2- 8-1814 6-18-1895

NAME BD or AGE DD Lot Sec.

COLEMAN, Sarah Ann - Mother - on same 11- 8-1819 3-17-1912 44 1
stone as others in Lot 44 Sec. 1
ssa SCULL, Francelia COLEMAN 3-10-1856 6- 5-1893
ssa STEVENSON, Rebecca (b. Indiana; of 1843 11- ?-1905x
heart failure; res Miamitown, OH; d/o Benj. & Sarah COLEMAN)
____, Elizabeth ---- ----
McHENRY, Evaline 1831 1921 45 1
McHENRY, Samuel P. 41y 1m17d 10-22-1868
McHENRY, Joseph H. (b.11-22-1798; of In 66th yr. 8-26-1864
chronic stomach inflammation; res Colerain Twp.; farmer; s/o Van & Catharine)
McHENRY, Nancy w/o Joseph H. [LO 1866] 71y10m23d 10-13-1874
(b.11-20-1802 Butler Co. OH; of chronic disease; res Colerain Twp.; d/o Samuel & S. POTTINGER)
McHENRY, Joseph F. s/o Van & Charlotte 7-13-1858 11-27-1876
18y4m14d (d. of consumption, res Colerain Twp.)
FAGALY, Mary [LO 1863] 46 1
FAGALY, Emanuel [LO]
FAGALY, John (b. MD; of typhoid pneumonia; 9-25-1806 2-24-1863
res Hamilton Co.OH; farmer; s/o George M. & Rosalia E.)
FAGALY, Sarah Caroline d/o J. & M.T. 1- 8-1840 8- 7-1841
(b. & res Green Twp.; of inflammation of brain; d/o John & Mary T. removed from Old Ground at Miamitown, OH Mar.30, 1863)
____, ----- [top of stone is broken off] 6m25d 1-22-1873
FAGALY, Robi(e?) s/o John L. & Eliza J. 7m15d 10-20-1874
BOGART, Frankie (Francis) s/o E. & R.E. 6- 7-1867 11-20-1869
(b. & res Green Twp.; of chronic diarrhea; s/o Elbert & R.E.
MILLER, John F. [LO 1864] 47 1
MILLER*+, Indiana R. bur pos E6-7 (b. & res 9- 9-1868* 4- 8-?1870?*
Dry Ridge, Hamilton Co. OH; of inflammation of lungs & bowels; ch/o John F. & Eliza Jane)
COLLINS*+, Hester bur pos W1 (b. & res 1-28-1842*12-31-1865* 48 1
Whitewater Twp.; of consumption; d/o Robert & Susannah)
COLLINS, Robert - Father [LO 1862] 76y 8m15d 2-27-1881
(b. 6-12-1804 PA; of apoplexy; res Whitewater Twp.; farmer; s/o Ephraim & Catharine)
COLLINS, Susan w/o Robert - Mother 38y 6m27d 3- 3-1852
COLLINS, James - Husband - Civil War Vet. 1846 1928
"ssa , Tillie - Wife 1855 1924

Following 4 stones are cemented side by side in a row & may not be in correct order of burial:

COLLINS, Sarah C. bur pos E5 (b. 9-19-1848 14y & 19d 10-18-1862
& res Whitewater Twp.; of consumption; d/o Robert & Susannah)
COLLINS, Winfield S. 2y 7m16d 4-19-1853
COLLINS, Letty M. bur pos W2 (b.5-15-1843; 20y 4m13d 9-28-1863
b. & res Hamilton Co. OH; of consumption; d/o Robert & Susannah)
COLLINS, William H. bur pos E7 2y & 15d 10- 4-1846
COLLINS*+, Unnamed bur pos E5-6 DI 6- 2-1863*
COLLINS*+, Unnamed bur pos E6-7 DI 6- 2-1863*
RYAN, C? or G? W. [LO 6-24-1856] ---- ---- 49 1
RYAN*+, Wm. Edward bur pos E5 3- 3-1860* 8-26-1861*
(b. Miamitown, OH; of whooping cough; res Cheviot, OH; s/o John B. & Mary B.)
ARNOLD, Joseph J. - Civil War Vet. 28y 1m 3d 5-12-1873
" ssa, Harrie G. - Babe 4m13d 12-26-1870
McCULLOGH, John [LO 1-8-1858] ---- ---- 50 1
STRATTON, B? S. [LO 2-11-1896]
STRATTON, Hazel I. 1888 1969
STRATTON, Mattie A. [LO 5- 3-1889] 1859 1947
" ssa , Levert S. - Civil War Vet. 1847 1915 2
McCULLOUGH*+, Edgar bur pos W4 (b.Harrison, 9-11-1828* 4-14-1845*
Co. VA; of Scarlet Fever; res Miamitown, OH; blacksmith; s/o John G. & Elizabeth B.; interred on lot of John G. McCULLOUGH. Infant of John G's & L. McCULLOGH interred in the same grave. Removed from Public Burying Ground adjoining cemetery 3-11-1857 #4.)
McCULLOUGH*+, Infant child of J.G.'s & 6-15-1851* 6-15-1851*
Lucetta McCULLOGH (stillborn); interred with Edgar S. Removed from Public Burying Ground adjoining cemetery 3-11-1857 #5)
STRATTON, Effie I. 1893 9- 7-1985x
STRATTON, Edgar S. 1890 1968
WEBB, Lucille STRATTON 1899 10- 8-1985x

In aisle between lots 50 & 55: A50 1

STRATTON, Ralph R. - Ohio Pvt U.S.Army WW II 4-23-1905 3-13-1972 &55
ARNOLD, Susan E. (Elizabeth) w/o Wm. G. 22y10m29d 8- 8-1860 51 1
(b. 9-9-1837 Butler Co. OH; of consumption; res Miamitown, OH; d/o Joseph R. & Elizabeth Ann CROWELL, niece of Joseph INGERSOLL.)
ARNOLD+, Unnamed bur pos W1-2 (Susan?) ---- ----
ARNOLD+, Unnamed bur pos W2-3 (Wm. G.?) ---- ----
ARNOLD, William G. [LO 1960] 1836 1920
ARNOLD, Mary nee BACON 1846 1883
ARNOLD*+, child of W. G.'s bur pos W4 (Wm.; ---- 3- 5-1875*
b. Colerain Twp.; res near Miamitown, OH; ch/o Wm. & Susan.)

NAME	BD or AGE	DD	Lot	Sec.
ARNOLD*+, Myrtle bur pos E5	DI	4- ?-1879*		
FLOWERS, John [LO 1863, transferred to Mrs. Sarah ARNOLD, no date)			52	1
ARNOLD, Samued F & A.M. emb	In 50th yr.	7-16-1850		
(Samuel & Child reinterred, same grave)				
"ssa , Sarah I. - His wife [LO]	In 66th yr.	8-12-1872		
"ssa , Rebecca C. d/o Samuel & Sarah	In ?4th yr	11-12-187_		
[age appears to be "4th yr" but stone is quite worn & date is not complete. Her mother would have been quite old if Rebecca was born in the 1860's.]				
"ssa , Kate S. d/o Samuel & Sarah	In 18th yr	9-29-1865		
ARNOLD+, Child of Jos. bur pos E5	----	----		
ARNOLD*, Sarah C. (b. & res Whitewater	2- 4-1848*	9-29-1865*		
Twp.; of bilious fever; d/o Samuel & Sarah)				
NUGENT, James [LO 1863]	----	----	53	1
NUGENT, Catherine d/o J. & S. (b. 4-20-1856	4y11m25d	3-15-1861		
Crosby Twp.; of flux; res Whitewater Twp.; d/o James & Susan; grd d/o Andrew NUGENT)				
NUGENT*+, Child of Jame' bur pos E6-7	1-17-1866*	12- 6-1866*		
(Royal NUGENT, b. Hamilton Co. OH; of scrofula; res. Whitewater Twp.; ch/o James & Susan)				
ROWINS, Benton V. ("Vall") F.& A.M.	1-17-1863	1- 7-1897	54	1
"ssa , Mary E. - Mother	9-12-1827	5-21-1922		
"ssa , Samuel A.- IOOF emb	12-30-1848	1- 5-1908		
"ssa , James D. - Father [LO 1862]	6-22-1819	1-13-1892		
(b. Maryland 72y6m21d)				
"ssa , William J.	6-28-1860	10-22-1927		
"ssa , Belle S.	3- 1-1852	4-16-1943		
ROWINS+, S. A.'s Child bur pos E6	----	----		
ROWINS, S. A.'s Child bur pos E7	----	----		
In aisle between lots 54 & 55:			A54	1
POTO, Ada A.	1912	7-26-1984x	&55	
JOHNSON, Ray [LO aisle Lot]	----	----	A54	1
			&48	2
HERIDER, Daniel [LO 3-31-1856]			55	1
HERIDER+, Harry's Child bur pos W2-3	----	----		
HERIDER+, Harry's Child bur pos W3	----	----		
HERIDER*+, Isadora bur pos W4 (b. & res	4-10-1852*	4-11-1853*		
Miamitown, OH; of inflammation of brain; d/o Daniel & Elizabeth. Removed from Public Burying Ground adjoining cemetery 3-12-1857 #17)				
____, Unknown child	----	----		
BUNNELL*+, Washington's Child bur pos E5	DI	2-23-1865*		
BUNNELL*+, Washington's Child bur pos E5	DI	2-24-1865*		
GANT, Nellie S.	1884	1969		
GANT, Charles F.	1886	1965		
In aisle between Lot 55, Sec. 1 & Lot 47			A55	1
Section 2			&47	2
CRUTCHLED, Goldie E. - Mother	1903	1976		
LITTLE, Chas. C. - Husband [LO 3-10-1856]	1-29-1817	6-20-1862	56	1
(b. New Haven, OH; of jaundice; res Miamitown, OH; physician; s/o Geo. & Philena)				
"ssa , Catharine	1825	1904		
SCHARDINE+, Harold bur pos E5	----	----		
CATTON, Mary - one date on stone	----	1936		
"ssa , James one date of stone	----	1935		
LITTLE, H. [LO 1863]			57	1
MILLER, S. C. [LO 7-22-1887]				
ROLF, Alma S.	1900	19--		
"ssa, Edgar H.	1891	1958		
FOWLER, John (His remains are in the same	In 6th yr.	7-20-1850	58	1
box with Margaret) (b. 3-7-1845 Hamilton Co. OH; of cholera; res Walnut Hills, Cincinnati, OH & removed from Walnut Hills 1-13-1863; s/o John & Mary Ann)				
FOWLER*+, Margaret bur pos W1 (b. Hamilton	10-22-1834*	7-23-1850*		
Co. OH; of cholera; res Walnut Hills, Cincinnati, OH & removed from Walnut Hills 1-13-1863; d/o John & Mary Ann)				
BOGART+, Mollie bur pos W2	----	----		
FOWLER, William ARBEGUST s/o John & Mary	4-27-1836	1-24-1862		
Civil War Vet. d. in service (b. Clermont Co. OH; of typhoid fever; DI 4-23-1862; res Colerain Twp.; farmer: Enlisted in Union Army & d. in VA; his remains brought to Cincinnati, OH & deposited in vault in Walnut Hills Cemetery on Jan. 28, 1862.)				
FOWLER, Mary Ann - Our Mother	1810	1901		
FOWLER, John Our Father [LO 1863]	9- 7-1795	10-18-1872		
(b. England; of paralysis, res Colerain Twp.)				
FOWLER, Thomas s/o J. & M.; Civil War Vet.	54y 2m18d	2-15-1893		
Corpl. Co. D 70th Ohio Inf.				
FOWLER, John	1850	1911		
FOWLER, Benj. Corpl. Co. K 5 Ohio Cav.	----	----		
Civil War Vet.				
FOWLER*+, Charles Richard bur pos E7-8	6-16-1853*	2- 6-1854*		
(b.Hamilton Co. OH; of inflammation; res Walnut Hills, Cincinnati, OH s/o John & Mary Ann. Removed from Walnut Hills Cemetery 1-13-1863)				
FAGALY, Peter s/o Emanuel & Anna M.	10-24-1831	2-21-1884	59	1

NAME	BD or AGE	DD	Lot	Sec.
FAGALY, Anna M. RIGHTER w/o Emanual, Sr.	9-30-1808	2-20-1884	59	1
FAGALY, Emanual, Sr.-Civil War Vet. [LO 1864]	4-30-1809	3-15-1886		
FAGALY, Rhoda May d/o Emaual & Retty (8y2d)	10- 6-1876	10- 8-1884		
FAGALY*+, Margaret bur pos E5-6	1-25-1837*	12-23-1841*		
(b. Cincinnati, OH; of putred sore throat; res Miami Twp.; d/o Lewis & Mary Ann. Removed from Old Burying Ground at Miamitown 3-30-1863)				
FAGALY, Willie A. s/o Emanual & Retty	7- 5-1879	10-19-1884		
FAGALY*+, Mary S. bur pos 8 (b. & res	2-12-1840*	12-31-1841*		
Miami Twp.; of putred sore throat; d/o Lewis & Mary Ann. Removed from Old Ground at Miamitown, OH 3-30-1863)				
McHENRY, Millison w/o T. P.	45y 9m 3d	7- 8-1889	60	1
" ssa , Thomas [LO 1866]	1836	1902		
WILSON, Margaret McHENRY w/o John A.	1868	1921		
WILSON, John A.	1-29-1861	12- 7-1931		
McHENRY*+, Child of Thomas' bur pos E7	9-29-1866*	3-23-1870*		
(David, b. Colerain Twp.; of measles & croup; res Hamilton Co. OH; s/o Thomas P. & Millisen)				
McHENRY+, Infant of Thos' bur pos E8	DI	3-29-1863*		
(b. & res Colerain Twp.; stillborn; ch/o Thos. & Milla)				
HERIDER, Wm. C. [LO 1867]			61	1
McINTYRE, Eliza [LO]				
SMITH, James J. - married Dec. 24, 1948 to	1927	12-20-1984x		
" ssa, Minnie F. (w/o James J.)	1930	----		
LYNN, Whipple [LO]			62	1
LYNN*, Aldora (?) (b. & res Miamitown, OH;	3-23-1866*	4-26-1866*		
ch/o Whipple & Nancy)				
SCHROEDER, Walter J. - Father	1903	5-24-1980x	63NW	1
" ssa , Edna L. - Mother [LO]	1914	19--		
WALTER, R. [LO]	----	----	63SW	1
ZINKHON, Wanda - [LO]	1940	19--	63SE	1
ZINKHON, Dale (Allen Dale) [LO]	1935	9-25-1980x		
ZINKHON, Paul [LO]	1910	12-28-1988x	63NE	1
"ssa , Eunice]LO]	1914	----		

Start SECTION II

NAME	BD or AGE	DD	Lot	Sec.
STRONG, Heirs of Chas. [LO 1860]			1	2
STRONG, Charles - (b. Orange Co. VT; of	10-12-1795	11- 1-1859		
consumption; res Hamilton Co. OH; farmer; kin Barnabas & Lydia STRONG)				
LUKENS, M. J. (Jane) (b.Cincinnati, OH;	9- 1-1870	3-28-1874		
of Scarlet Fever; res No.2 Dayton St., Cincinnati, OH; d/o Thos. & Lorana)				
LUKENS, Harry (b. Cincinnati, OH; of Scarlet	10- 9-1866	3-15-1874		
Fever; res No.2 Dayton St., Cincinnati, OH; s/o Thomas & Lorana)				
STRONG, Jedediah (b. 6-22-1822 Ohio; of	23y 3m	9-22-1842		
bilious fever; res Colerain Twp.; s/o Charles & Charity. Removed from Fosters Burying Ground, Colerain Twp. Sept. 4, 1860)				
STRONG*, Charity (Mrs.) (b. PA; of winter	9- 1-1799	1-19-1837*		
fever; res Colerain Twp.; kin Christian Eli & Louise MOAK. Removed from Fosters Burying Ground, Colerain Twp. Nov. 2, 1859)				
STRONG*, Wm. (b. OH; of winter fever; res	6-12-1824*	2- 5-1837*		
Colerain Twp.; s/o Charles & Charity. Removed from Fosters Burying Ground, Colerain Twp., Sept. 4, 1860)				
STRONG, Louis R. - Father [LO 9-3-1858]	8- 6-1827	10-14-1893	2	2
"ssa , Hannah - Mother	2-27-1829	7-26-1903		
STRONG, Louis (R.) (b. & res. Hamilton Co.	12-15-1868	4-13-1869		
OH; of lung fever; s/o Louis R. & Hannah)				
STRONG, Charles s/o Louis R. & Hannah	20y 4m 2d	4-27-1870		
STRONG, William E. s/o L.R. & H.S.	14y10m10d	9-13-1876		
(b. 11-3-1861 & res Colerain Twp.; of lockjaw; s/o Louis)				
STRONG*, ----- (ch/o Louis; burn't)	DI	10-22-1859*		
STRONG*, ----- (res Colerain Twp.; ch/o Louis)	DI	5-15-1864*		
SHEAR, Tobe [LO 1859]	----	----	3	2
GREINER, Jacob [LO, no date, transferred from SHEAR TO GREINER to NEIDHARD]				
NEIDHARD, E. J. [LO 10-6-1941) "E.J.NEIDHARD -Babies"		----		
SCHNELL, Infant son	one date ----	10-30-1959	A3NW	
POPE+, Jane bur pos W1	----	----		
POPE+, Joe bur pos W2	----	----		
COLEGATE, Suzanne M.	1-21-1944	1-23-1944		
SHEARER*+, Frances bur pos W4 (b. & res	12- 2-1828*	4-16-1877*		
Dearborn Co. IN; of consumption; d/o Matson & Catherine ISGRIGG)				
PETERS, CHeryl	one date ----	2-12-1948		
TILLETT, Infant Twins	one date ----	12-28-1958		
SHEAR*+, Tobe bur pos E6-7 (b. & res	4-15-1853*	6-25-1857*		
Green Twp.; of inflammation of brain; ch/o Tobe; grd ch/o Catherine & Matson ISGRIGG. Removed from Burying Ground at SHEAR'S Farm, Green Twp., Hamilton Co. OH, 11-19-1859.)				
WRIGHT, Elaine	1d	1945		
SCHLEMMER, Dale L. - Baby	one date ----	5- 6-1947		
ROSS, Thomas Jay	one date	3-11-1959	A3NE	

NAME BD or AGE DD Lot Sec.

In aisle between lots 3 & 6: A3&6 2
MAPES, Emory M. 1904 5-27-1983^x
"ssa, Catherine M. 1902 2-20-1985^x
TENKOTTE, Henry F., Sr. 1913 8- 6-1983^x E
" ssa , Billie H. 1916 ----
SHEAR, John [LO 1-27-1857] ---- ---- 4 2
SHEAR+, Mrs. John bur pos W2 ---- ----
WHEELER*+, Alice bur pos W4 (b. Hamilton 4-25-1866* 3- 3-1868*
Co. OH; of ulcerated sore throat; res Miamitown, OH; d/o
Charles C. & Martha)
SODDERS*+, Unnamed bur pos E5 8- 6-1862* 8-14-1862*
(John, s/o Frank & Mary)
SODDERS*+, Unnamed bur pos E6 (Francis, 8- 6-1862* ----
b. & res Colerain Twp.; s/o Frank & Mary)
[For following no entry for dates of death but entries recorded
between 8-19-1862 & 9-29-1862]
SHEAR+, Child of James' bur pos E6-7 ---- ----
SHEAR+, CHild of James' bur pos E7 ---- ----
SHEAR*, Child of James' (b. & res ---- 11-23-1875*
Miamitown, OH; ch/o J. & Ellen SHEAR) [could be another of ch/o
James' or one of the three shown on "Plat of Lots"]
JONES*+, Susan (nah) bur pos W1 (b 5- 2-1789*12-22-1869* 5 2
(b. Bourbon Co. KY; res Hamilton Co. OH; d/o Michael &
Barbary ISGRIGG)
ISGRIGG+, Catherine bur pos W2 [LO 1859] ---- ----
ISGRIGG, Matson, Sr. (b. Bourbon Co. KY; 9-22-1787 6-25-1855
of cholera; res Green Twp.; farmer; uncle of Daniel ISGRIGG;
Green Twp.; Removed from Burying Ground at SHEAR'S farm, Green
Twp. 11-19-1859) [unidentifiable emb on stone]
ISGRIGG, Matson, Jr. - F. & A.M. emb 5- 3-1830 6-20-1855
(b. Hamilton Co. OH; of cholera; res Green Twp.; laborer;
s/o Matson. Removed from Burying Ground at SHEAR'S farm, Green
Twp. 11-19-1859.)
STRIMPLE, Mary (b. & res Whitewater Twp. 8- 3-1849^x 7-14-1850^x 6 2
of inflammation of head; d/o Aaron & Lurania. Interred on lot
of Aaron STRIMPLE; removed from Public Burying Ground adjoining
cemetery 3-11-1857 #3.
" ssa , John 1852 1901
" ssa , Lurena - Mother 1820 1908
" ssa , Aaron - Father - F. & A.M. emb 1821 1907
[LO 6-13-1856]
ssa THOMPSON, Carrie 1882 1954
CROWELL, Clara - m/o Susie STOUT 1839 1884 7 2
CROWELL, John W. - My brother-Mexican War 47y10m17d 9-10-1873 5
Vet. (b. 10-27-1825 Green Twp.; s/o Archibald & Susannah)
" ssa , Susannah - Our Mother 77y 7m16d 12-31-1880
w/o Archibald (res Cheviot)
"ssa , Archibald - Our Father 79y 6m21d 7-31-1882
[LO 6-14-1856] (b. & res Green Twp.)
CONWAY*+, Clarra Matilda (b. Hamilton Co. 3- 6-1852*10-28-1864*
OH; of typhoid fever; res Green Twp.; d/o Thomas & Martha CONWAY;
an adopted child of Archibald CROWELL's was much beloved by the family)
CROWELL*+, Edward A. bur pos E7 (b. Green 3- 4-1855* 1-11-1861*
Twp.; of Scarlet fever; res Cincinnati, OH; s/o John.)
BUNNELL+, Washington bur pos W1 ---- ---- 8 2
BUNNELL+, ----- w/o Daniel bur pos W1-2 ---- ----
BUNNELL, Sarah J. w/o G.W. (b. 7-19-1834 30y 7m23d 3-12-1862
Dearborn Co. IN; of childbirth; res Hamilton Co. OH; d/o
Joseph & Sarah LYNESS)
" ssa , Daniel [LO 10-16-1858] (res 68y 9m28d 1-30-1864
Hamilton Co. OH; farmer)
" ssa , Elizabeth 14y 5m29d 8-26-1839
" ssa , Barten s. 1y 7m14d 8-28-1841
" ssa , Sarah 14y 3m 4d 4-18-1845
" ssa , Mary 20y 9m 2d 3-26-1855
CLEAVER*+, Margaret bur pos W4 1796*12-16-1878*
(b. PA: of senile decay; res Miamitown, OH)
BUTLER*+, Martha bur pos E5 (b. Hamilton 3- 3-1838* 4-14-1867*
Co. OH; of consumption; res Miamitown, OH; d/o Daniel & May BUNNELL.)
____+, ----- a Child bur pos E6 (Isaac ?) ---- ----
BUTLER*,Isaac N. (s/o Alfred & Emily) DI 7- 9-1866*
BUTLER+, Emma bur pos E7 (Emily?) ---- ----
BUTLER*, Emily (WALKER?) (b. & res Whitewater --DI 11- 9-1865*
Twp., Hamilton Co. OH)
BUTLER*+, John M. (Milton) bur pos E8 7-10-1863* 8-18-1863*
(b. Hamilton Co. OH; of congestion of brain; res near Elizabethtown,
Hamilton Co. OH; kin of Alfred C. & Emily B.; grd s/o E.B.WALKER)
BUNNELL+, Wm. [LO 10-16-1858] bur pos W2 ---- ---- 9 2
BUNNELL, E. F. [LO] 9W 2
FENSTERMACHER, Edna M. - Mom 1922 19--
" ssa , Edwin A. - Dad F. & A.M. emb 8-23-1923 3-28-1980
Tec 4 U.S. Army WW II
BUNNELL, Samuel [LO 10-8-1912] 1860 1930 9E 2

NAME BD or AGE DD Lot Sec.

BUNNELL, Mary E. 1867 1919 9E 2
GLEESON+, Elizabeth bur pos E8 ---- ----
COX*+, Jacob bur pos W1 (b. & res Miamitown, 5-21-1858* 7-21-1859* 10 2
OH; of cholera; s/o Oliver & Eliza)
COX*+, Mrs. Eliza bur pos W2 4-11-1818* 9-13-1858*
(b. Franklin Co. IN; of ab'd dropsy; res Miamitown, OH; d/o Jesse PYLE)
COX*+, Oliver bur pos W3 [LO 6-4-1856] ---- ----
(died of consumption; res Miamitown, OH [no date of death was given but
entry was made between 12-28-1876 & 2-10-1877]
COX+, Nettie bur pos W4 ---- ----
CHAMBERS+, Susie bur pos E5 ---- ----
CHAMBERS+, Wm. bur pos E6 ---- ----
THORNELL, Isaac [LO 6-4-1856] 11 2
WOLFE, Fannie 1868 1939
CADY, Margaret 1846 1917
CADY, Joseph - Father 1844 1928
THORNELL, Louis H. s/o Isaac & Charlotte 21y 3m 2d 9- 4-1864
A soldier Co. F 83 Reg O.V.I. wounded in the Battle of (Ark.?) Post
Civil War Vet. (b. 6-1-1843 Dent, Green Twp., Hamilton Co. OH; of
consumption; res Green Twp.; farmer; s/o Isaac S. & Charlotte)
WOLFE, Albert L. 1870 1950
WHIPPLE, Susanna POTTENGER His wife - Mother 1823 1885
" ssa , Daniel - Father [LO 1867] 1821 1888
CONE, Mary A. w/o Azel C. 64y11m 6d 12-30-1880 13 2
"ssa, Azel C. b. Rutland Co., VT 2- 7-1813 12-29-1874
61y10m22d [LO 1865]
ssa **BARTLETT**, Ursula CONE 59y 9m16d 11- 7-1901
" ssa, William S. s/o A.C. & M.A. 4-10-1838 7-21-1869
31y3m11d (b. Whitewater Twp.; of consumption; res Laurel, IN;
s/o A.C. & Mary A.)
SHAFFER*+, Oliver C., Jr. bur pos E8 9-13-1878* 7- 8-1879*
(b. & res Whitewater Twp.; of cholera morbus; s/o Oliver & Ursulie)
WILKINSON, Ira [LO 1862] ---- ---- 14W 2
WILKINSON*+, Martha bur pos W1 (b. & res 5-26-1821* 1-27-1875*
Colerain Twp.; of lung fever; d/o Charles & C. STRONG)
WILKINSON*+, Tryphena (Miss) bur pos W2 12-25-1842* 1-27-1862*
(b. & res Colerain Twp.; of hasty consumption; d/o Ira & Martha)
WILKINSON+, Child of A.'s bur pos W4 ---- ----
HINE, Rachel [LO 4-30-1900] ---- ---- 14E 2
HINE+, Child of H. HINES bur pos E7 ---- ----
HINE*+, Infant of Henry's bur pos E7-8 8-18-1862* 8-18-1862*
(b. & res Colerain Twp.; s/o Henry D. & Rachel)
HINE*+, Infant of Henry's bur pos E8 6- 5-1863* 6- 5-1863*
(res Hamilton Co. OH; ch/o Henry & Rachel)
FRUSKOUR, David [LO 5-22-1858] 15 2
FRUSKOUR*, Mary E. (b. & res Whitewater Twp. 9-23-1854*10-19-1855*
died of inflammation of lungs; ch/o David & Marthy. Removed from Public
Burying Ground at Miamitown, OH, 3-12-1857, #20)
FRUSKOUR*, David (b. & res Whitewater 1-29-1859*11-10-1860*
Twp.; s/o David & Martha Ann)
FRUSKOUR*, Elizabeth (b. & res Whitewater 4-11-1865* 1- 1-1866*
Twp.; of head & spine; d/o David & Martha)
BUNNELL, Benj. [LO 1859] 16 2
BUNNELL, Laura d/o B. 25y 3m 1d 9-22-1883
APPIARIUS, Adda - Mother 1866 1931
TABER, Aaron W. [LO 1859] 17 2
TABER*, George S. (b. & res Whitewater Twp. 9-30-1857* 3- 7-1859*
died of inflammation of brain; s/o Aaron W. & Susannah; grd s/o John
& Mary BAUGHMAN)
SIMMONDS, Earl & Florence [LOs] ---- ---- 18 2
SIMMONDS, Susannah w/o Richard 55y9m27d 9-20-1804 7-17-1860
(b. Butler Co. OH; of epileptic fit; res Whitewater Twp.; d/o Samuel
& Susannah POTTINGER, s/o John POTTINGER & of Nancy McHENRY.)
" ssa , Richard [LO 8-10-1858] 3-14-1800 ----
" ssa , James P. 9-20-1834 10-25-1884
" ssa , Lucinda C. 12- 6-1838 7-24-1901
SIMMONDS+, R. bur pos W3-4 ---- ----
____+, Father & Brother reinterred on W4 ---- ----
[?R. SIMMONDS & ?]
LEWIS*+, Delila bur pos E7 (b. KY; of lung 11-15-1794*11-12-1861*
fever; res Miamitown, oh; d/o John & Marthy TATE(?)
PURCELL, Joseph 3-15-1847 4- 3-1924
POTTENGER, Sarah w/o John 79y7m22d 10-21-1800 6-13-1880 19 2
" ssa , John [LO 1863] 74y3m23d 4- 2-1797 7-25-1871
ssa STARLIN, Elizabeth E. 1842 1914
____, -----Baby ---- ----
(May STARLIN, b. & res Crosby Twp.; 5-25-1881* 5-25-1881*
stillborn; d/o Dan'l & Eliza E.)
DENNING, Daisy R. 1875 1893
POTTENGER*+, Elizabeth H. bur pos W1 12-23-1861* 7- 9-1863* 20 2
(b. & res Crosby Twp.; of inflammation of brain; d/o James & Annie M.)
POTTENGER*+, James bur pos W2 [LO 1864] 8- 8-1831* 9-10-1910*
(b. Crosby Twp.; res Greensburg, IN; s/o John & Sarah)

NAME	BD or AGE	DD	Lot	Sec.
PLATTS, Gilman [LO 1863]	----	----	21	2
MILLER, Wm. - Civil War Vet. Co.G 5h Ohio CAV [LO 5-13-1896]	----	----		
PASELEY, Frances A. d/o Alfred T. & Carrie (Caroline) H.	1y 2m16d	10-14-1866	22	2
" ssa , John - Grandpa [LO 1862]	12-16-1812	10-29-1896		
" ssa , Hannah w/o John - Grandma	10- 8-1816	1-19-1908		
" ssa , Alfred T. - Father	1836	1913		
" ssa , C. H. - His wife - Mother	1840	1919		
SIMMONDS, James P., Sr. [LO 8-16-1858]			23	2
SIMMONDS, Earl & Florence [LOs]				
SIMMONDS, Richard E., Jr.	1888	1973		
SIMMONDS, Katherine	1883	1921		
SIMMONDS, Earl S., MD.	1882	1962		
SIMMONDS, Rev. James P.	1885	1968		
SIMMONDS, Grace S.	1889	1971		
SIMMONDS, Dr. Richard S.	2-20-1913	12-24-1945		
SIMMONDS, Amelia H.	4-24-1862	7-22-1938		
SIMMONDS, Richard E. [LO 2-11-1896]	5-16-1861	3-26-1925		
SIMMONDS, Emma M.	9-18-1905	----		
SIMONSON, Ella M.	1862	1890	24	2
STRIMPLE, Sarah (b. Whitewater Twp.; of cancer; res Miami Twp.; d/o Caleb & Mary HOPPING)	7-26-1838	11-19-1879		
HOPPING, Caleb L. [LO 1860]	1811	1897		
" ssa , Mary	1821	1902		
SIMONSON, Edgar - Ohio Cpl. HQ Co. 322 Field Arty WW I Vet.	11- 7-1889	6-24-1960		
SIMONSON, Fannie H.	1850	1938		
SIMONSON, Zarum A.	1859	1939		
HOPPING*+, Albert bur pos E7 (b. & res Whitewater Twp.; of croup; s/o Caleb L. & Mary)	9-18-1857*	9- 8-1860*		
HOPPING, Caleb, Jr.	1864	1891		
In aisle between lots 24 & 25:	----	----	A24	2
McCULLOUGH, Nancy A.	1891	1972	&25	
HOPPING, Rebecca IRELAND - His wife - Mother	1827	1917		
" ssa , George - Father [LO 1861]	1826	1908		
HOPPING, Charles A.	1866	1945		
FOX, Hattie	1867	1957		
"ssa, John N.	1866	1944		
HOPPING, Nancy Ann WEST	1869	1943		
" ssa , Benjamin Franklin	1863	1948		
CREMAR, Mahlon B. [LO 1859]			26	2
CREMAR, Rebecca w/o M.B. (b. 7-17-1816 at Hunterdon Co. NJ; of apopletic fit; res Hamilton Co. OH; kin of John & Margaret WARMAN (?)	47y 5m17d	1- 4-1864		
CREMAR*, Henry S. (b. Whitewater Twp.; of spinal meningitis; res Butler Co. OH; s/o Mahlin B. & Rebecca)	9- 9-1860*	3-27-1872*		
BRITTON*, Mary Ellen (b. & res Whitewater Twp.; of flux; d/o Wm. & Sarah C.; grd d/o Mahlon CRAMER)	2-28-1859*	8- 4-1859*		
BRITTON*, Charles A. (b. Hamilton Co. OH; of diarrhea; res Harrison, OH; s/o Asa & Lydia)	6-28-1867*	7-27-1868*		
STEVENSON, Andrew H. - Father	6- 4-1804	11-10-1889		
STEVENSON, Sarah J. - Mother (b. Hunterdon Co., NJ; of disease of brain; res Cleves, OH; d/o Caspar & Catharine CREAMER)	6-14-1805	2-27-1866		
STEVENSON, William H.	1868	1919		
SEAL, John	1862	1931	27	2
SEAL, Catherine nee HOUTZ	1832	1912		
SEAL, W (m). M. - Civil War Vet. Co. K 5 Reg. O.V.C. -IOOF emb. [LO 1862] (b. Taylor's Creek, near Miamitown, OH; of consumption; res Colerain Twp.; s/o Jos. & Mary)	10-30-18--*	7-20-1875*		
SEAL, Edward	1875	1924		
____, Madge (Madge SEAL; b. Colerain Twp.; res Colerain Twp.; d/o Wm. & Cate)	11-15-1873x	7-25-1875x		
RICHARDSON, John [LO 1863]	----	----	28	2
BARNES, Uriah [LO 1863]			29	2
BARNES, Charlotte w/o U.H. - Mother	9-14-1840	6- 8-1888		
" ssa , Willie G. s/o U.H. & C.A. (b. & res Hamilton Co. OH; s/o Uriah & Charlotte)	7- 9-1863	8-27-1863		
HOWARD, Chas. [LO 1863]			30	2
+Three bodies reinterred, bur pos W1, W2, W3	----	----		
[Plat of Lots shows three burials (names not recorded) on the lot of Charles H. HOWARD but no lot # is recorded. He owned lot 30, sec. 2 & lot 66 Sec. 2. Perhaps the three burials on lot 66, Sec.2 were reinterred from lot 30 to lot 66?)				
HYLAND, Charles Howard s/o Francis & Mary (b. 7-31-1859 Cincinnati, OH; of congestion of brain; res Colerain Twp.; s/o Matthew F. & Mary Ann; grd s/o Chas. HOWARD)	3y 4m 8d	11- 8-1862		
HYLAND, Mary Belle d/o F. & M. (Mary Isabell b. 9-7-1865; b. & res Cincinnati, OH; of diphtheria; d/o Mathew F. & Mary Ann)	1y 6m 7d	3-16-1867		
WILKSON(?)+, Unnamed bur pos E8	----	----		
MANNING, Baby	One date	12-11-1919	31	2

NAME	BD or AGE	DD	Lot	Sec.
ORR, Arthur C.	9-21-1874	2- 9-1900	31	2
"ssa, Hervey	4-19-1837	4-11-1917		
"ssa, Rebecca M.	6- 2-1838	10-26-1914		
"ssa, Wm. M. [LO 11- 4-1858]	10-10-1795	9- 4-1884		
"ssa, Elizabeth (Mrs. Wm.) (b. Butler Co.OH; res Twylor's Creek, Hamilton Co. OH; d/o John & Nancy DIXON)	6-16-1796	12-18-1880		
"ssa, Edwin (b. & res Hamilton Co. OH; of diphtheria; s/o Harvey & Rebecca M.)	5-30-1864	1-13-1865		
"ssa, Alice Ann (b. & res Green Twp.; of fever; d/o Wm. M. & Eliza; grd d/o Arthur & Alice ORR. Removed from Burying Ground on farm of Wm. M. ORR, Mar 24, 1859.)	8-29-1829	12- 1-1837		
"ssa, John D.	1-10-1835	6-17-1884		
"ssa, Arthur (b. Morris Co., NJ; of disease of kidneys; res Green Twp.; farmer & miller; f/o Wm. Melvil ORR. Removed from Burying Ground on farm of Wm. M. ORR, Mar. 23,1859)	2-14-1772	9-11-1851		
"ssa, Alice (b. Scotland, Great Britan; res Green Twp.; d/o Wm. MUNGAL of NJ. Removed from Burying Ground on farm of Wm. M. ORR, Mar. 23, 1859.)	8-22-1775	9-15-1858		
ORR, Wm. M. [LO 1859]			**32**	2
GANT, Stanley E. s/o Wilbur & Mary	1896	1898		
MUNGAL, Alex. (Alexander) 87y8m3d (b. Scotland, Great Britan; res Green Twp.; farmer; s/o Wm. of NJ. Removed from Burying Ground on farm of Wm. M. ORR, Mar. 23, 1859.)	5- 4-1769	1- 7-1857		
ORR, Alfred J. (Julian) s/o Henry L. & Anna (b. Chicago, IL; res Green Twp.; grd s/o Wm. M. & Eliza ORR. Removed from Burying Ground on farm of Wm. ORR, Mar. 24, 1859.)	6-13-1851	11-29-1852		
____, Arthur	----	----		
ORR*, Scott (b. & res Cincinnati, OH; s/o Henry L. & Anna; grd s/o Wm. M. & Eliza ORR. Removed from Burying Ground on farm of Wm. ORR, Mar. 24, 1859.)	6-21-1846*	6-24-1846*		
ORR*, George C. (b. Hamilton Co. OH; of Diphtheria; Res Bridgetown, Green Twp.; s/o Joshua W. & Frances)	11-20-1862*	11-13-1864*		
ORR*, Edward (b. & res Hamilton Co. OH; of diphtheria, s/o Joshua & Frances)	11-25-1864*	2-14-1865*		
ORR*, Katerine (b. OH; of measles; res Cincinnati, OH; d/o James E. & Nancy)	1- 9-1865*	2- 9-1866*		
BODE, Wm. [LO 1868]			33	2
LEIGHTWEISZ, Mary [LO 1872]			34	2
LEIGHTWEISZ, George (b.?2-20-1836 Germany; of consumption; res Colerain Twp.; s/o Mary LEICHWEIZ)	2- 8-1834	4-15-1872		
MOAK, Daniel B. (BUSHNELL) F. & A.M. emb (b. Mt. Nebo, OH; d. Westwood, OH; erected by the Hamilton Co. Teacher's Association; of consumption; teacher)	10- 6-1842	6-10-1881	35	2
"ssa, Adelaide A. [LO 1873]	1851	1910		
BLEDSOE, A. T. [LO 1872]	----	----	36	2
FAGALY, Mary [LO 1864]	----	----	37	2
DELANEY, R. G. (Mrs.) [LO 1881]	----	----	38	2
SHELDON, George W. - Husband	1854	1929		
" ssa . Emily S. - Wife	1853	1932		
PAYTON, Hannah - Our Mother (b. 4-8-1804 United States; of palsy; res Green Twp.; d/o John & Mary HOLLIDAY)	77y 3m 9d	7-17-1881		
HOPPING, Lucy (b. & res Whitewater Twp.; of spotted fever; d/o Henry & Mary)	1874	10-20-1876x	39	2
" ssa , Margaret OES emb	1871	1953		
" ssa , John F. & A.M. emb	1869	1933		
" ssa , Henry C. - Father [LO 1876]Civil War Vet.	1841	[3-15]1922		
" ssa . Mary A. - His wife - Mother	1845	1910		
HOPPING, Banning F. & A.M. emb	4-26-1881	12-20-1951		
" ssa , Jessie [On a bench facing the above stone, "In Memory Of Our Parents by Harold & Hilda HOPPING 1961"]	11-25-1883	12-22-1958		
HOPPING, Wm. [LO 1876]	----	----	40	2
HOPPING, Mary A. d/o Wm.& Sarah (b. & res Whitewater Twp.)	1y11m 3d	8-13-1876		
____, ----- Grandma	1835	1908		
____, ----- Mother	1852	1923		
____, ----- Father	----	----		
[HOPPING, William H. - Civil War Vet.]		----		
HINE, William - Father	1881	1968		
HINE, Sally - Mother	1885	1958		
HOPPING, Theodore G. [WW I Vet.]	1888	1930		
GIBSON, Wm. [LO 1868]	----	----	41	2
GIBSON, Euphema w/o Wm. M.	26y 6m24d	3-10-1866		
POOL, Mrs. Mary [LO 1865]	----	----	42	2
GREEN, Hettie A. w/o George L.(Hattie A. b.12-31-1852; b. & res Colerain Twp.; of consumption; d/o Peter & Mary POOLE)	20y11m 7d	12- 7-1873		
____+, Unnamed bur pos W2	----	----		
____+, **Unnamed bur pos** W2-3	----	----		
POOL, Peter F. & A.M.? emb - Civil War Vet. d. at N. Cherry Creek Inlet, PA (b. & res Hamilton Co. OH, DI - 1-8-1865)	42y 5m 8d	8-10-1864		
"ssa, Marion s/o Peter & Mary J. (Francis Marion, b.1-26-1847, b. & res Colerain Twp.; of typhoid fever)	17y 8m 9d	9-24-1864		

NAME | BD or AGE | DD | Lot | Sec.

_____+, Unnamed bur pos E5 ---- ---- 42 2
CUTTER*+, Susie R. bur pos E5-6 12-27-1876* 8-20-1878*
(b. & res Colerain Twp.; of whooping cough; d/o A.W. & Amanda)
_____+, Unnamed bur pos E6 [Perlie?] ---- ----
_____+, Unnamed bur pos E6-7 [Mary?] ---- ----
GREEN, Perlie d/o George L. & Hettie A. 1y & 9d 9- 7-1873
(b. 8-25-1872 Hamilton Co. OH; of dysentery; res Taylor's Creek, OH)
DUNN, Mary R. (Rachel) d/o Timothy & 9m27d 3-17-1869
Rebecca (b. 5-20-1868 & res Colerain Twp.; of congestion of lungs)
STOWGHTON, Edward [LO 1863] 1- 8-1788 8-14-1863 43 2
DEAN+, John bur pos E8 ---- ----
FOWLER, John [LO 1863] ---- ---- 44 2
BOGART, Mary d/o J.H. & E.E. 8-12-1868 3- 1-1870
BOGART, Ellen - Mother [LO 10-11-1889] 1843 1925
" ssa , John - Father 1844 1920
GREAR, David W. 1867 1921
GREAR, Ella E. 1872 1935
HOLLIDAY, Lott [LO 1863] ---- ---- 45 2
SHELDON*+, ----- bur pos W@-3 (Scott, b. 12- 3-1846*11-24-1866*
& res Green Twp.; of consumption; farmer; s/o Nathaniel & Hester)
SHIELD+, Scott (Scott SHELDON?) bur pos W3 ---- ----
SHELDON*+, Miss bur pos W4 (Annetta, b. 11-21-1844* 7-20-1865*
Green Twp.; of consumption; d/o Nathaniel & Hester A.)
HOLLIDAY*+, Bell (Belle E.) bur pos E6 2-21-1859* 1-13-1864*
(b. & res Hamilton Co. OH; d/o Lott & Rachel)
HOLLIDAY*+, Daniel W. (Webster) bur pos E7 12-15-1854* 5-24-1862*
(b. Miamitown, oh; of spotted fever; res Green Twp.; s/o Lott & Rachel)
Mc___ +, D.B. bur pos E8 (possibly Dellie McMINN?---- ----
see undetermined Section)
PORTER, Richard L. [LO 1863] ---- ---- 46 2
PORTER*+, Wm. Herider bur pos W3-E6 in 10-31-1856* 3-22-1859*
center of lot (b. & res Whitewater Twp.; s/o Richard & Catharine;
grd s/o John BARNES)
PORTER, George W. s/o Richard & Catharine 1y & 25d 12-29-1847
(b. 12-4-1846 & res Colerain Twp.; of scarlet fever; grd s/o John
BARNES. Removed from Public Burying Ground at Miamitown, Mar.23,1859)
[Following two entries in the cemetery records may be for same person.]
_____+, Unnamed bur pos E5 ---- ----
PORTER+, Unnamed ch/o Richard & Catherine DI 3-30-1865*
BAXTER, Oliver P. [LO, no date of transfer 1841 1871 47 2
from H.H. SMITH]
BAXTER, Clara T. 1846 1924
_____, Perry (Perry BAXTER, b. & res 1871 9-12-1876x
Miamitown, OH; of tabes mesenterica; s/o Perry & Clary)
SMITH*+, Wm. H.H. (Wm Henry Harrison) 8-12-1830* 9-13-1861*
bur pos W3-E6 center of lot [LO 1861] (b. mouth of Big Miami, Hamilton
Co. OH; of consumption; res Lawrenceburg, IN; auditor of Dearborn Co.
IN by appointment; s/o Honorable Judge Patrick & Ann Eliza)
ROWINS, James [LO 2-15-1892] ---- ---- 48N 2
ROWINS, Mary 1859 1956
_____, Samuel ---- ----
ARNOLD, George [LO 1861] ---- ---- 48S 2
ARNOLD+, Child of Geo. bur pos W3 ---- ----
NUGENT, Jackson [LO 1864] ---- ---- 49 2
LEMMON, David, Jr. [LO 1869] ---- ---- 50 2
LIST, Elizabeth 1870 1946
LEWIS, Watson [LO 12-1-1892] Civil War Vet. 1834 1892
LEWIS, Edward 1859 1881
LEWIS, Hannah 1868 1881
LEWIS, Frank - Father 1868 19--
TEAGUE, Ralph L. - Indiana Cpl. U.S.A.- WWI 2- 5-1896 11-11-1968
TEAGUE, Dollie 1896 1959
KIEHBORTH, Mamie [LO no date of transfer from Teter CROWELL) ---- 51 2
CHAMBERS*+, Susanna bur pos W1 (b. OH; of 7- 6-1843*11-21-1868*
dropsy; res Green Twp.; d/o Peter & Julia Ann CROWELL)
CROWELL, Theodore - Civil War Vet. 12- 1-1831 2- 5-1883
CROWELL*+, July (Julia Ann) bur pos W3 5-11-1802* 1-25-18??*
(b. Orange Co. NY; of enteritis; res Green Twp.; d/o Joseph B. &
Mary SMITH) [Year of death was blank & surrounding entries were
mixed years from 1868-1871]
CROWELL, Teter [LO 1863] (b.10-29-1800 NC; 73y 1m 8d 12- 6-1873
of paralysis; res Hamilton Co. OH; s/o John & Margaret)
CHAMBERS*+, Anna E. bur pos E5 10-20-1877*10-19-1879*
(b. Miamitown; of scarlet fever; res 39 Pearson St., Cincinnati, OH;
d/o Annie E. & David)
CROWELL+, Child of Theodore's bur pos E8 ---- ----
TAYLOR, Nancy M. 1842 1903 52 2
" ssa , William E. 1846 1923
TAYLOR, Nancy Jane - Mother 1817 1889
TAYLOR, William - Father [LO 1865] 9-23-1797x 3- 1-1876x
(b. PA; of typhoid fever; res Dent, OH)
TAYLOR, Oscar 1876 1910
TAYLOR+, Charles bur pos E5 ---- ----

NAME | BD or AGE | DD | Lot | Sec.

TAYLOR, Edith - Daughter 1882 1887 52 2
_____, ----- - Father ---- ----
In aisle between lots 52 & 55: A52 2
HORNING, Rita M. Ladies Aux. VFW mkr 5- 7-1919 4-18-1974 &55
PALMER*+, Wm. [LO 1-16---- yr. of transfer from 53 2
James PALMER not recorded)
PALMER*+, Elizabeth E. bur pos W2-3 9-22-1848* 3-28-1864*
(b. Colerain Twp.; of quinsey; res Miamitown, OH; d/o James & Mary Ann
PALMER)
PALMER, James - Civil War Vet. Co. G 39th Ohio Inf ---- ----
[LO 1863]
PALMER+, Child of W.'s bur pos W4 ---- ----
PALMER*+, Archie bur pos SE corner 11-19-1873* 8-16-1875*
(b. Matson Mill; of flux; s/o Wm. & Isabell)
STRONG, Chas. [LO 1864] ---- ---- 54 2
STRONG, Katherine (Maria) (b.10-21-1835, 1836 4- 4-1864x
Miamitown, OH; of typhoid pneumonia; res Colerain Twp.; d/o David
Mary PALMER, leaves four small children.)
CHAMBERS, Mary 5- 8-1801 1- 2-1891 55 2
CHAMBERS, James, Sr. F. & A.M. emb 4-23-1798 7-16-1850
(reinterred; b. Boon Co. NY; of cholera; res Miamitown, OH; s/o
Benjamin & Lydia. Removed from Old Burial Ground & interred in same
grave with James S.)
CHAMBERS, James S., Jr. - Civil War Vet. 4-25-1833 8-28-1864
(reinterred; b. & res Miamitown, OH; of consumption; cooper; s/o
James & Mary)
CHAMBERS, Margaret 1837 3-14-1901
" ssa , Isaac V. - Civil War Vet.[LO 1864] 9-28-1835 1-10-1911 9
" ssa , Sarah Frances w/o Isaac 6-19-1843 4-16-1871
WEST, Alice A. - Wife-OES emb 1854 1935 56W 2
"ssa, J. H. - Husband - F. & A.M. emb [LO] 1859 1931
COCHRAN, Boswell [LO 1863] ---- ---- 56 2
CROWELL, T. [LO 10-17-1870] ---- ----
SHEPPARD, Charles H. 1820 1892
" ssa , Mary J. - His Wife (b. & res 1-31-1830x 1-21-1873x
Dent, OH; of consumption; d/o Samuel & Parmelia STAUTON? or
STANTON?)
" ssa , "Their Children" (the following two):
" ssa , Joseph (Henry) (b. & res Dent, 10- 7-1846* 1- 8-1873*
OH; of consumption; s/o Charles & Mary)
" ssa , James ---- ----
SHANNON, Edward J. 1871 1916
SHANNON, Jennie W. - His Wife 1869 1936
FLINCHPAUGH, Susan BURTON - Mother 1867 1949 57 2
FLINCHPAUGH, Anderson E. - Father 1866 1951
BURTON, Susan 1824 1919
BURTON, George W. [LO 1861] (b. Butler Co. 12-15-1825x 7-13-1904x
OH; of suicide; res Sater, Crosby Twp.; farmer)
FLINCHPAUGH, Reece 1938 1967
SCHNEIDER, Charles G. 1902 3-27-1977x
SCHNEIDER, Alice F. 1906 1973
FLINCHPAUGH, James E.- Son & brother 1904 1945
(Sgt.) emb: 2 wings, a star & a "9" within a circle, all on a shield.
MABREY, Carrie P. 1837 1917 58 2
TOMLINSON, Nancy M. w/o G.L. 1841 1903
" ssa , G. (Gershom or Gershem) L. 1-12-1832 9-11-1866
(b. Hunterdon Co., NJ; d. Miamitown, OH; Civil War Vet.;
[LO 1863] merchant; united with M.E. Church, Mar. 1866)
" ssa , Charlie T. (b. Hamilton Co. OH; 6- 4-1862 12-29-1862
of bilious colic; res Green Twp.; s/o Gershom L. & Nancy M.
Deposited in Wesleyan Cemetery Vault & removed here.)
" ssa , John L. (s/o G. L. & Nancy) 7-11-1865 8-26-1866
HAGGARD, R. & E. [LO's] ---- ---- 58E 2
HAGGARD, Theresa Anne - Daughter 6- 4-1979 9-12-1980
[No lot owner listed] 59W 2
JAMISON, Alexander [LO 1864] 59 2
JAMISON+, Matie bur pos W1-2 ---- ---- 59 2
INGERSOLL, Lucetta [LO 1863] ---- ---- 60 2
_____, ----- (Stone with lamb on top) ---- ----
INGERSOLL, Jos. H. - Civil War Vet. 1836 [9-19-1862]
STAPLES, Rebecca one date 1907
LIND, Sarah M. 8-21-1801 9- 2-1884
ssa , RUNK, Samuel 12- 9-1820 9-16-1892
ssa , RUNK, Lucy M. - His Wife 5-13-1841 11- 2-1900
WESCOTT, Josey (Joseph) (b. NJ; res ---- 9-19-1863
Hamilton Co., OH)
SAND?, Edward [LO 1863] ---- ---- 61 2
GREASLEY, Elizabeth 1838 1913
ssa UNDERWOOD, Hiram 1851 1896
ssa UNDERWOOD, Sarah Ann [LO 2-17-1896] 1853 1934
_____, Ruth one date 1901
UNDERWOOD, Frank [LO 2-17-1896] 1853 1919
UNDERWOOD, Alice 1863 1925

NAME	BD or AGE	DD	Lot	Sec.
BACON*+, Child of John's bur pos W1	7-20-1865*	9-18-1866*	62W	2
(Willy H., b. & res Green Twp.; of flux & inflammation of lungs; s/o John H. & Lucinda A.)				
BACON, J. (John) H. [LO 1867]	11-30-1836	1-17-1899		
"ssa , Lucinda	4-22-1843	1- 9-1926		
FRANKHOUSE, Wm. [LO 1867]	----	----	62E	2
FRANKHOUSE+, Child of W.'s bur pos E5	----	----		
____, George	----	----		
____, Edna	----	----		
FRANKHOUSE, George O.	12-17-1859	11- 2-1899		
PERRY, Blume [LO 1875]	----	----	63	2
HOFFMAN, Frank W.	1891	1907		
HOFFMAN, Joseph [LO 10-12-1907]	1856	1949		
HOFFMAN, Joseph J. (Ohio Sgt. Air Service WW I Vet.	6- 3-1895	7-29-1967		
LOHREY, John	1863	1922	64	2
LOHREY, Margareth - Mother [LO 1873]	7-26-1818	10-23-1896		
" ssa , Henry - Father (b.?10-10-1813	11-15-1813	8- 8-1873		
Hess, Germany; of consumption; res Whitewater Twp.; s/o Jacob & Elizabeth LOHREI)				
GIERINGER, Lawrence	----	----	65	2
GIERINGER, Peter	----	----		
GIERINGER, Rachel - Mother	1849	1939		
GIERINGER, Joseph - Father [LO 1875] G.A.R. emb	1846	[5-15-1931]		10
Civil War Vet.				
GIERINGER, Cliff (In aisle S of lot)	----	----		
GIERINGER, George (b. & res Miamitown, OH	1-22-1873x	2-18-1875x		
of burns; s/o Joseph & R.)				
GIERINGER, Mary	----	----		
GIERINGER, William	----	----		
GIERINGER, Rosa	----	----		
GIERINGER*, Infant (b. & res Miamitown, OH;	9- 1-1877*	9- 1-1877*		
stillborn; ch/o Joe)				
HOWARD*+, Lotta B. bur pos W1 (b. & res	8- 1-1878*	9- 7-1878*	66	2
Colerain Twp.; of inflammation of bowels; ch/o Chas. A. & Susan B.) [Plat of lots also show her buried on lot 30, Sec. 2]				
HOWARD,Sarah - His Wife- Mother	2-14-1809	10- 2-1882		
"ssa , Charles H. - Father [LO 1870]	11-16-1804	1-23-1885		
HINE, Johnie s/o C.D. & B.	6-22-1867	3- 4-1870		
"ssa, Anna Mary d/o C.D. & B. (b. & res	10- 9-1871	12-26-1874		
Whitewater Twp.; of burns; d/o Chas. & Barbara)				
"ssa, Mary B. d/o C.D. & B.	12-25-1863	7-27-1864		
"ssa, Barbara w/o Charles D. - Mother	11- 8-1845	4-23-1894		
"ssa, Charles D. - Father [LO 1870]	6- 1-1841	10-26-1912		
ROHLFING, John	1869	1952		
"ssa , Margaret nee HINE	1873	1954		
HINE, Leonore - OES emb	1877	1972		
POPE+,Child of Adam's bur pos E8	----	----		
HOPPING, Chas. [LO 1869]	----	----	68	2
HOPPING+, Benj. bur pos W1	----	----		
JOHNSON, Phoebe L. HOPPING w/o J.W.	9-22-1822	3-19-1892		
JOHNSON, Wm. -Civil War Vet. Co.G 5th Ohio Cav.	----	----		
HALSTED, John (b. 7-12-1754 NJ; Militia of	86y 8m 5d	3-17-1841		
Rev. War Vet.; Battle of Monmouth; descendant of King Edward I of England.				
ssa HOPPING, Edmond s/o L. & S.	45y 3m27d	11-12-1852		
ssa HOPPING, Luther s/o L. & S.	2y 6m15d	8-15-1820		
ssa HOPPING, Luther	68y 1m22d	5-18-1851		
ssa HOPPING, Sarah w/o Luther (b. 3-11-1788	78y 6m 1d	9-12-1866		
Morris Co., NJ; res Whitewater Twp.; d/o John HALSTED)				
ssa HOPPING, David H. s/o L. & S.	30y 7m 8d	10- 3-1839		
ssa HOPPING, Jane d/o L. & S.	14y 7m 2d	9-19-1844		
KUPFER, John [LO 1868]	----	----	69	2
DAVIS, John A. 32nd F. & A.M. emb [LO, no	63y	11- 6-1870		
date of transfer from John KUPFER)				
ssa SEAL, Mary A. DAVIS w/o James H.	30y	11- 3-1871		
ssa DAVIS, Ann Eliza (b. 2-17-1845 Walnut	23y	4-12-1868		
Hills, Hamilton Co., OH; of consumption; res Cheviot, OH; d/o John A. & Rachel)				
DAVIS*+, John H. bur pos E5 (b. America;	10-14-1848*	2-21-1877*		
of phthisis(?); res Cheviot, OH; s/o John A. & Rachel)				
BOGART,Matilda Virginia d/o Helmus & Mary	20y 3m21d	9-26-1866	70	2
(b. 6- 5-1846; of flux; b. & res Miami Twp.)				
BOGART, Alice d/o Helmus & Mary	20y10m20d	3- 5-1885		
BOGART, Helmus - Father [LO]	3-16-1818	3-16-1896		
" ssa , Mary NOBLE - His Wife - Mother	2-11-1823	4-23-1898		
BOGART+, Infant bur pos E8	----	----		
CAMPBELL, John S. [LO 1876]	9-26-1850	7-22-1883	71	2
CAMPBELL, Fanny H. w/o J.S. 25y6m13d	1-12-1851	7-25-1876		
(b. Miamitown, OH; d/o J. & Maria VANCLEVE)				
CAMPBELL, Stella d/o J.S. & F. H.	4-30-1876	6-18-1876		
(b. & res Harrison, OH)				
[LO not listed]			72E	2

NAME	BD or AGE	DD	Lot	Sec.
KNOSE, Edgar Lee	1892	1946	72E	2
METZGER, Margaret [LO 1900]	----	----	72	2
GERBUS, Gerald J.	11-16-1961	8-26-1974		
METZGER, Ethel M.	9d	----		
METZGER, Samuel L.	11m	----		
MOAK, Nancy	1898	1-17-1985x	72R	2
"ssa, Lester D. [LO]	1900	2-21-1985x		
ReVORE, Mary Alice w/o Henry Clinton ReVORE	1860	1952		
COLEGATE, Albert E. (Jr., "Bud")	1911	4- 1-1985x		
" ssa . Marcella B.	----	----		
DEAN, Ethel [LO]	1883	1972	73R	2
"ssa, Everett [LO]	1879	1948		
GANSE, A. (Andrew) J. [LO 1866]	----	----	73	2
NEIDHARD, E. J. [LO 9-11-1933]	----	----		
GANSE, Wm. Eddie s/o Andrew J. & M(ary) J.	2y11m17d	11-30-1863		
(b.12-13-1862 Whitewater Twp.; of croup; res Harrison, OH)				
VEST, Anna - Mother	1873	1934		
DOERING, John H. - Father	1887	1933		
BRUNSWICK, Flossie - Wife	----	----		
" ssa , Clifford - Husband	1912	1934		
SPER, & Following 4 names on one stone:				
" , Catherine	1884	1936		
" , Andrew	1884	1937		
" , Arthur	1924	1941		
" , Edwin	1927	1927		
GEEDING, Isaac & Simon [LOs 1864]	----	----	74	2
GEEDING, Charlotte w/o Simon 79y3m19d	3-19-1787	7- 8-1866		
JOHNSON*+, 2 children of Samuel's bur pos E5	DI	10-16-1866*		
(Remains removed to Lot 74, Sec.2; ch/o Samuel JOHNSTON [JOHNSON]; remarks: lot near tool house no(t) on plat; lost until new one is made.)				
PROSSER*+, Rebecca bur pos E8 (b.Green Twp.;	12-10-1832*	2- 9-1864*		
of consumption & stomach congestion; res Cincinnati, OH; kin Simon & Charlotte GEEDING)				
BOYER, W. W. or G.W. [LO 1864]	----	----	75	2
SCHWEIZERHOF, Simon [LO 1919]	----	----		
BOYER*, Unnamed	DI	4-30-1864*		
SCHWEIZERHOF, Fred	1871	1938		
" ssa , Rose	1884	1965		
ROHR, George R.	1911	12-24-1985x		
"ssa, Ruth E.	1912	6-28-1983x		
SCHWING,----- [LO]	----	----	75.5	2
PALMER, Angeline [LO 1864]	----	----	76	2
WEIL, Theresa	1829	1923		
WEIL, Joseph [LO 1889]	1825	1914		
WEIL, Minnie - D of A emb	1864	1950		
"ssa, Henry - Jr. ord & K of P embs	1863	1917		
____, Edward	----	----		
____, William	----	----		
____, Carl	----	----		
____, Infant	----	----		
WEIL, Joseph, Jr. - Husband	1858	1955		
"ssa, Kuney - Wife	1865	1949		
KARETH, Paul [LO 1919]	1852	1930	76.5	2
" ssa , Lenora - His Wife	1855	1930		
SHIVELY, Charles E. - Father [LO]	1871	1944	76R	2
SHIVELY, Laura T. - Mother	1890	9-19-1984x		
JOHNSON, Samuel's Heirs [LO before 1899]	----	----	77	2
METZGER, Margaret - His Wife - Mother[LO 1899]	1838	1908		
" ssa , George - Father [LO 1899]	1835	1916		
METZGER, Karl G.	1899	1908		
METZGER, Pearl E.	1884	1960		
" ssa , Charles L.	1880	1962		
METZGER, George [LO 1899]	----	----	77.5	2
METZGER, Anna B. - Mother	1871	1954		N
METZGER, John - Father	1871	1934		
METZGER, Stanley (L.) [LO]	1902	11-12-1981x		
" ssa , Hallie [LO]	1910	7-2?-1986x		
METZGER, George [LO 1911]	----	----	77.5	2
FLINCHPAUGH, Josephine METZGER	1865	1947		
FLINCHPAUGH, Jacob S.	1860	1940		
FLINCHPAUGH, Elmer M. [LO]	1886	1926		
FLINCHPAUGH, Stella	1888	1925		
[No LO listed]			77R	2
KNOSE+, M. bur pos W2-3	----	----	78	2
KNOSE, Alfred D. [LO 1904]	11-18-1872	9-26-1952		
COLEGATE, J. & R. [LOs]	----	----	78.5	2
MELTON, Wilma June	11-18-1931	8-26-1977		W
COLEGATE, Ruth L.	3-22-1912	1-11-1980		
SCHALK, Dorothy M. [LO] "Married Aug. 15,1931"	1910	9-12-1977x	78.5	2
" ssa , Peter J. [LO]	1908	----		E
GORDON, Thomas [LO 1866]	----	----	79	2
MANN*+, Jacob bur pos W3	----- DI	12- 8-1866*		
MANN+, Mrs. __ bur pos W4	----	----		

NAME	BD or AGE	DD	Lot	Sec.
MANN, Mina - Dear Little	----	----	79	2
"ssa, David R. [LO date not recorded]	27y11m29d	5-20-1865		
Civil War Vet. Co. D 39 O.V.I. died from a wound received in defense of his country.				
MANN*+, Emma bur pos E6-7 (d. of gastritis;	----	1878*		
res Miamitown, OH) [No date of death but entry was recorded between 4-18-1878 & 5-29-1878)				
MANN*, Unnamed (b. & res Hamilton Co. OH; of diphtheria)	----	DI 1-18-1865*		
MANN*, Wm. (?)	----	DI 6- 8-1865*		
SCHALK, A. & B. [LOs]	----		W 79.5	2
JOHNSON, C. [LO]	----		SE 79.5	2
JOHNSON, W.	----		NE 79.5	2
FOSTER, George [LO]		----	80	2
FOSTER, S. (Solomon) N. Civil War Vet.	----	----		
Co. G 39th Ohio Inf.				
WILLIAMS, Samuel G. s/o Geo. & Martha J.	9y 7m15d	9-29-1864		
(George S., b.2-14-1855 Indianapolis, IN; of typhoid fever; res. Hamilton Co. OH; s/o George W. & Martha)				
JACKSON, Katharyn R. - Mother	1900	1967	80?	2
SOUTHER, Luretta - Mother	1866	1932	80E?	
RUNCK, ----- [LO]			80E	2
RUNCK, Thelma - Infant	one date	1924		
The 3 following stones were placed in an area between 80E & roadway after being found in the pile beside cemetery fence. Actual site of burial is unknown:				
VANCLEVE, Rebecca T. - Infant	2y ----	----	80X	2
VANCLEVE, Mrs. Mary G.	2-21-1806	2- 6-1840		
VANCLEVE, Asher - Who was killed by his horses running away.	7-17-1796	5-19-1840		
HUDNUT?, Catharine d/o M. & S.-burial site unknown - stone found on this lot.	3m28d	8-26-1846		
HILDRETH, Ethel [LO 1906]	----	----	80.5	2
HILDRETH, Jacob - Corp'l Co. B 5 Ohio Cav.	----	----		
Civil War Vet.				
Following lot is numbered 5½ on cem. map but is located between lot 80.5 & cemetery road.			E. of 80.5	2
SCHUBERT, Margaret A. - Daughter	1872	1933	5.5	2
SCHUBERT, Margaret - Mother	1838	1922		
SNYDER, Robert B. - Father - F. & A.M. emb & Jr. Ord U.A.M. #26 emb	1871	1906		
SNYDER, Ottilia - Mother [LO 1906]	1875	1923		
[DO not listed]			81W	2
CATT*, George (res Green Twp.) [LO 1863]	----	10-23-1875*	81	2
_____, ----- Mother	----	----		
_____, ----- Father	----	----		
CATT, Frank (John Franklin) (b. Green Twp.; of inflammation of bowels; res Cincinnati, OH; kin of Josephus J. & Lavina)	6-18-1861*	10-19-1864*		
BOGGS, Carrie (b. Green Twp.; res Cincinnati, OH; d/o Wm. C. & M. Jennie BOGGS; grd d/o George CATT)	10-27-1862*	10-10-1863*		
BOGGS, Jennie	----	----		
Following lot is numbered 6½ on cem map but is located between lot 81.5 & road:			W. of 81.5	2
FLINCHPAUGH, Chas. [LO 1908]	----	----	6.5	2
NEIDHARD, E. J. [LO 3-26-1928]				
WALTERS, Anna - Mother [LO]	1862	1928	6.5W	2
WHITEHEAD, Agnes L. - Wife - [LO]	1882	1- 9-1976x	6.5E	2
" ssa , Samuel J. - Husband - Jr. Ord mkr	1880	1928		
DISSER, Dennis M. - Son	one date	1946	81.5	2
DISSER, Jennie - Sister	1894	1906		
DISSER, May E. - Mother	1861	1932		
DISSER, Samuel M. - Father [LO 1908]	1865	1932		
DISSER, Samuel M. - Husband	1895	1-27-1980x		
DISSER, Elizabeth M. - Wife	1910	----		
DISSER, David S. - Son	1939	1961		
FOSS, Henry [LO 1864]	----	----	82	2
FOSS*, Mary (b. Hanover, Germany; of consumption; res Whitewater Twp.; kin Armick(?) MIRE)	3- 8-1800*	9- 6-1864*		
NEIDHARD, Ed. [LO 3-28-1913]	----	----	82W	2
SATTERS, [M?)ary - Mother	1844	1914		
RANZ, Anthony F. s/o late John & Mary	----	2- 2-1914		
HAYS, William B.	1880	1942	82E	2
HAYS, Zitella [LO, E½, 11-29-1913]	1881	1961		
HAYS, Robert M. - Husband	1906	9- 3-1980x		
HAYS, Helen E. - Wife	1906	1970		
JACKSON, John E., Sr. - Father	1851	1907	82.5	2
" ssa , Mary - Mother	1850	1922		
JACKSON, Mary E. (Elizabeth) Daughter [LO 1907]	1889	12-26-1976x		
JACKSON, John E.-Ohio Pvt.Co. I 104 Inf. WW I	9-25-1887	5- 8-1967		
JACKSON, Edward a. - Son	1884	1964		
JACKSON, Frank C. - Son	1891	1968		
SEAL, Miss Sarah [LO 1867]	----	----	83	2

NAME	BD or AGE	DD	Lot	Sec.
SNYDER, John	1877	1951	83	2
SEAL*+, Ben [LO] bur pos W3 (b. Franklin Co. IN; of inflammation of bowels; res Colerain Twp.; stonemason; s/o Joseph & Martha)	9-21-1806*	4- 5-1866*		
SNYDER, May - Mother	1875	1940		
SNYDER, John - Father	1834	1913		
" ssa , Sarah - Mother	1842	1923		
IRELAND, Audrey Opal	1911	1963	83.5	2
HINE, Ira W. - Son	1868	1943		
HINE, Rachel - Mother	1844	1903		
HINE, Henry - Father [LO 1903]	1839	1908		
DUNAWAY, Oscar	1885	1973		
DUNAWAY, Clara B.	1881	1950		
HURLEY, B. F. [LO 1866?]	----	----	84	2
GREEN, Geo. L. [LO 1879]	----	----		
HURLEY+, Child of Frank's bur pos W4 (b. & res Miamitown, Oh)		DI 8-14-1866*		
GREEN*+, Mrs. Ellen bur pos W1 (b. & res Miamitown, OH; of consumption)		DI 10-21-1879*		
GREEN*+, Josiah, Jr. bur pos E8 (b. & res Cheviot, OH; of marasmus; s/o Ella & Geo. L.O	9- 1-1879*	11-16-1879*		
FRANKHOUSE, Wm. - Father [LO 1906]	1833	1927	84.5	2
" ssa , Mary - His Wife - Mother	1835	1912		
_____, Sherman	1874	1941		
FRANKHOUSE, Edw.	1863	1918		
FRANKHOUSE, Birdie	1871	1947		
FRANKHOUSE, Grant	1869	19--		
RIARDEN*, J.M. (b. & res Green Twp.) [LO 1875]	----	9-25-1875*	85	2
RIARDEN+, Jennie bur pos W2 (J.M.?)	----	----		
RIARDEN*, Infant bur pos W4	----	----		
MILLER, Mrs. [LO 1908, transferred to Claude MILLER, no date			85.5	2
MILLER, Margaret [LO 1942]	----	----		
HOLROYD, Peter	1830	1908		
MILLER, Jacob L.-Civil War Vet. Co.C 16 KY Inf	----	----		
HOLDERER, Edwin	1901	1-23-1987x		
" ssa , Sylvia	1919	10-22-1976x		
MILLER, Claude L.- [LO, no date, transferred 1942?]	1892	10-14-1985x		
MILLER, Minnie C.	1892	1967		
WILSON, Mary [LO 1870]	----	----	86	2
WILSON+, Unnamed bur pos W2	----	----		
WILSON, Chas.-Sgt. Co.B 5th Ohio Cav. Civil War Vet.	----	----		
BELL, William H. [LO 1908]	1862	1932	86.5	2
"ssa, Ida C. nee EDWARDS	1862	1931		
MOFFETT, Harley L. - Son	2- 4-1920	11- 7-1929		
WOERTHWEIN, Jacob H.-Civil War Vet. Co. H 187th O.V.I. (res Whitewater Twp.; of consumption)	3-21-1824	9-20-1876	87	2
" ssa , Christiana Margaretha	10-29-1826	5-31-1903		
WOERTHWINE, John	1858	1936		
WOERTHWINE, Nancy E. [LO 1876]	1853	1935		
STEVENSON, Louise - D of A emb	1-19-1875	12- 2-1947	87.5	2
KUPFER, Johanna	1852	1897		
KUPFER, John [LO 1897] Civil War Vet.	1842	[3-30-1910]		
KUPFER, Louis - Jr. Order U.A.M. emb	1871	1930		
KUPFER, George E.	1872	1934		
SMITH, Henry [LO 1869]	----	----	88W	2
SCHMIDT+, Hattie bur pos W3	----	----		
SMITH*+ /SCHMIT, Catherine bur pos W4 (b. & res Colerain Twp.; of diphtheria; d/o Henry & Catherine)	12-15-1867*	3-19-1869*		
SMITH, Henry [LO 1869]	----	----	88E	2
FERRY, M. [LO]	----	----		
SMITH, John C. - Father	1879	1951		
SMITH, Elizabeth	1860	1942		
FERRY, William J.-Pfc. U.S.Marine Corps.WW II	5- 8-1910	5-16-1980		
SMITH, Ida	1896	1898	88.5	2
SMITH, Henry A.-Father [LO 1898] "Married Sept. 23, 1886"	1862	1940		
" ssa, Cornelia - Mother	1860	1939		
SMITH, William	1900	4-20-1980x		
"ssa , May A.(nn)	1901	8-18-1980x		
SMITH, John H.	2- 2-1890	7-10-1969		
SMITH, Edward C. - F. & A.M. emb	9-15-1887	5-12-1968		
HUGENTOBLER, Mary E. nee HESTER	1865	1913	89	2
HESTER, William [LO 1868]	1839	1881		
" ssa , Margaret - His Wife	1839	1914		
HESTER*+, Child bur pos W4 (William S., b. & res Hamilton Co. OH; of inflammation of lungs; ch/o Wm. & Margretta)	1-29-1868*	3- 9-1868*		
SCHARDDEIN, Mary W. frau of (w/o) F. (b. Colerain Twp.; of dropsy, res Blue Jay, Whitewater Twp.; d/o John & Wilhelminia SOAGEL (?)	12-26-1849	12-23-1872		
SCHARADINE, Barbara	1847	1895		
SCHARDDINE+, Daisy bur pos E6-7	----	----		
SCHARDDINE+, Child of G's bur pos E7	----	----		
SCHARDDINE+, Child of G's bur pos E8	----	----		

NAME	BD or AGE	DD	Lot	Sec.
FAGALY, Emanuel [LO 1903]	1865	1942	89.5	2
" ssa , Clara	1869	1943		
FAGALY, Elvyn E. - KIA in France, Ssgt. Co. F 276th Inf Regt Amer Legion mkr [WW II Vet]	1913	1945		
FAGALY, Raymond M. [LO]	1901	7-23-1988x		
" ssa , Millie S. [LO]	1902	----		
SHEAR, Anna B. [LO 1868]	----	----	90	2
SCHAR, Familien Monument Von Jacob & A.B.	----	----		
"ssa , Jacob	12-25-1821	12-10-1868		
McINTYRE, Sarah	1878	1907	90.5	2
McINTYRE, John [LO 1908]	1865	1954	NW	
McINTYRE, John [LO 1908]	----	----	90.5	2
ROWE, Ben J.	1919	6-13-1986x	E	
ROWE, Clifford M. Tec 5 U.S.Army WW II Vet.	1916	5- 3-1984x		
BERRY*, Bernice	----	3- 2-1984*		
NOSE, Francis [LO 1875]	----	----	91	2
NOSE, Fredrick M. aged 7m10d (b. Whitewater Twp.; of inflammation; res near Miamitown, OH; s/o Francis & Mary Ann)	11- 7-1874	6-17-1875		
BENDER, Opal [LO]	----	----	91W	2
BENDER, Ervin H. Ohio Ssgt Co. E 351 Inf WW II SS-BSM	**8-26-1919**	4-24-1954		
WERGER, John H. - Husband [LO]	1876	1956	91SE	2
WERGER, Elizabeth H.- Wife	1881	1961		
McPEEK, Leonard - Dad (d. bet Feb.28 & Mar.23)	1913	1980	91NE	2
"ssa , Hazel - Mom [LO]	1910	----		
BATES, Thomas J. [LO]	1835	1908	91.5	2
"ssa , Catherine - His Wife	1840	1918		
FULTON, C.C. [LO 1879]	----	----	92	2
FULTON*+, Infant bur pos W1 (b. & res Whitewater Twp.; ch/o C.C. & Ella H.)	9-26-1879*	9-30-1879*		
GANT, Ann [LO]	----	----	92.5	2
GANT, John [LO 1905]	1862	1906		
_____, ----- Mother	----	----		
[No LO listed]			93	2
[No LO listed]			93.5	2
[No LO listed]			94	2
[No LO listed]			94.5	2
[No LO listed]			95	2
[No LO listed]			95.5	2
MEDL, Rosa [LO 1925, transferred south 6 graves to Charles OATS, no date]			96NW	2
MEDL, Josef	1882	1925		
MEDL, Barbara	1913	1928		
THALER, Jesse G. - Husband	8-16-1884	9-26-1958	96.5	2
THALER, Bessie M. - Wife [LO]	12-13-1901	----	&SW	
WESTRICH, Katherine	**1916**	**1968**	96.5	2
WESTRICH, Edward	1913	1974		
SCHAEFER, Bertha	**1886**	1954		
OATS, Edna - Mother	1884	1952		
"ssa, Charles - Father [LO no date]	1888	1958		
_____, ----- (foundation, but no stone)	----	----		
In aisle between lot 97 & 104:			A97&	2
MUELLER, Wilbur M. Ohio Tec 5 Co.B 660 Engineers WW II - VFW mkr	3- 2-1910	8-27-1961	104	
MORGAN, Fred D., Jr.	1903	1971		
KRAUS, Edward W. [LO 1920]	1888	1937	97	2
"ssa , Susan K.	1889	1930		
SCHWING, Charles F. - Son	1913	1967	98	2
KINCAID, Alice S.	1911	1971		
SCHWING, Arthur E. [LO 1920] Sgt. 1Cl 1 Ohio Inf NG WW I Vet.	12-30-1887	9-12-1948		
SCHWING, Kathryn - Mother	1886	1967		
SCHWING, William L. Tec 5 U.S.Army WW II	5- 9-1907	4-12-1976		
DELL, Frank [LO 1925]	----	----	99	2
DELL, Carl F. Tec 5 U.S.Army WW II VFW mkr	1919	5-26-1976x		
SILVERS, John [LO]	----	----	100	2
SILVER, Stanley D. Ohio Pvt 12 Co.158 Depot Brigade WW I [LO 1930]	11-22-1896	6-20-1960		
MOAK, Arthur E. [LO 1921]	----	----	101W	2
PEACOCK*, Nancy	----	12-27-1987*		
MOAK, Mae TAYLOR	1871	1946	101E	2
"ssa, Leslie G. [LO 1921]	1871	1948		
PEACOCK, Edward F. Ohio RDM 2 USNR WW II	5-11-1908	2-18-1961		
MOAK, Margaret WHITE	----	9- 8-1944	102	2
MOAK, Arthur E.	**1868**	1934		
MIRE, David Thomas-Pvt US Marines WWI;LO-1927	2-28-1895	8-27-1976		
MIRE, Agnes M.	1918	1927		
SEITZ, Mollie - Mother	3-15-1886	5-22-1961	103	2
SCULL, Elizabeth - Mother [LO 1918]	7- 4-1859	10-18-1920		
SCULL, Martin - Father	3-14-1858	11-20-1917		
SEITZ, Joseph J. - Daddy	3- 9-1882	5-15-1927		
SCULL, George Ohio Cook 2 Inf 1 Div	----	8-31-1941		
SNYDER, Herbert H. -Ohio Pvt Co.C 68 Inf WW I	4-21-1894	11-15-1964		
SNYDER, Emma A. - Wife	5-10-1888	10-30-1967		

NAME	BD or AGE	DD	Lot	Sec.
In aisle between lots 104 & 105	----	----	A104	2
SHARP, Timothy R., Sr.	5-16-1951	5-28-1972	&105	
SMITH, Dale Foster - Ohio Cpl Co.K 273 Inf WW II Vet.	6-13-1916	10-10-1972		
PLATTS, Eva A. - Daughter	1884	1967	104	2
PLATTS, Agnes M. - Mother	1844	1908		
PLATTS, David E. - Father - Civil War Vet.[LO 1903]	1845	[4-28]1928		
PLATTS, E. Leroy - Son	1882	1902		
PLATTS, George E.-Ohio Sgt 8 Co. Coast Arty	11- 2-1877	12-17-1947		
PLATTS, Ida M. - Daughter	1880	1950		
SCHARDDINE, Harry [LO, duplicate deed,1898]	----	----	105	2
SCHARDDINE, Maggie	1866	1898		
" ssa . George [LO, duplicate deed,1898]	1837	1903		
SCHARDDINE, Michael	1854	1917		
SCHARDI**NE**, Joseph	1875	1951		
SCHARDINE, Mayme	**1887**	1967		
WOOD, Elsie [LO 1912]	----	----	106	2
SCHARDINE, Benjamin F.	**1868**	1938		
" ssa , Katherine	1870	1945		
SCHARDINE, Infant	one date	12-11-1965		
SCHARDINE, Matthew	one date	3-27-1966		
SCHARDINE, Charles C. - Father	4-28-1905	1-22-1960		
KELLY, Alma SCHARDINE - Wife & Mother	3- 9-1917	6-14-1978		
SCHARDINE, Janet MIRUS - Daughter & Mother	1946	1972		
SCHARDINE, Edward	4-15-1900	9-15-1949		
HAMMITT, Carl Owen	1-26-1911	7-27-1987	107	2
VEST, Geneva G. - Wife	1909	1969		
VEST, Herold C. - Husband	1898	1957		
HAMMITT, Edward E. - "Married Feb. 5, 1949"	1927	----		
" ssa , Marian M.	1931	----		
HAMMITT, Jessie M.	1888	1966		
HAMMITT, Edward R. [LO 1922]	1887	1968		
HAMMITT, Cecelia D. - Daughter - D of A emb	1920	1934		
HAMMITT*, Bertha	----	7-16-1982*		
[No lot owner listed]			108	2
BECKETT, Opal - Wife	1909	----	109	2
BECKETT, Jewell - Husband Cpl U.S.Army WW II	5-17-1908	10- 3-1983		
BECKETT, Mary E. - Mother	1887	1932		
"ssa , Richard E. - Father [LO 1932]	1880	1952		
BECKETT, Raymond L. - Son	1906	1932		
BECKETT, Lyman R.	4-16-1920	----		
BECKETT, Rosella **C.**	12-29-1922	8-28-1984		
SNYDER, Henry [LO 1921]	----	----	110W	2
SNYDER, Gertrude - Mother	1919	----		
SNYDER, Clarence - Father	1907	1960		
SNYDER, Ida K.	1879	1943		
"ssa , William G.	1875	1967		
McFARLAND, Mary	7-31-1969	8- 7-1969		
BAGEL, Mary SNYDER	1843	1921		
SNYDER, Ella Olevia	1849	1921	110E	2
SNYDER, Andrew [LO 1921]	1848	1926		
SNYDER, Owen A. - Husband - [LO 3-29-1930]	1872	1935		
" ssa , Lottie A. - Wife [LO 3-29-1930]	1873	1964		
GRAY, Frank E.	1869	1923	111	2
GREAR, Lizzie	----	----		
GREAR, David [LO]	----	----		
_____, ----- - Mother	----	----		
HEARN, Albyn H.	1872	1902	112	2
HEARN, Alice C.	1849	1932		
HEARN, John P. [LO 1902] Civil War Vet.	1843	1920		
HICKS, Kate	1851	1940		
HEARN, Albert M.	1848	1924		
McGEE, Edward F. - F. & A.M. emb	1877	1944		
McGEE, Ella R.	1875	1959		
FAGALY, Benjamin F.	10-20-1839	----	113	2
" ssa , Caroline - His Wife [LO 1896]	10-14-1841	3- 4-1898		
ssa **LINGO**, Lida	12- 1-1892	10-16-1896		
RUTZ, Elizabeth A.	1866	1948	114	2
"ssa, Jacob [LO 1919]	1865	1943		
RUTZ, Harold	1900	1951		
RUTZ, Charles P. - Pvt U.S.Army WW I	10-14-1895	2-10-1977		
RUTZ, Anna May - Mom	5-10-1912	----		
"ssa, Howard H. - Dad "Pete"	4-15-1909	11-26-1978		
HENRIE, Helen (Mrs.) [LO L921]	----	----	115W	2
HENRIE, Raymond - WW I Vet.	1893	[8-21-1921]		
HENRIE, Ora Ray	8-24-1920	7-10-1938		
CLARK, Helen B.	1902	19--		
CLARK, Fred E.	1887	1964		
TAYLOR, R. [LO]	----	----	115E	2
TAYLOR, Jane - Mother	1852	1936		
" ssa , Robert - Father - Civil War Vet.	1849	[8-25] 1921		
TAYLOR, Robert J. - Son	1906	1945		

NAME	BD or AGE	DD	Lot	Sec.
HENRIE, Wm. [LO 1923]	----	----	116	2
HENRIE, Goldie G.	1905	1969		
HENRIE, Atchel W.	1895	6-19-1988x		
HENRIE, Diana	1857	1956		
HENRIE, Napoleon	1861	1933		
MARTIN, Joseph	1870	1945	117	2
MARTIN, EMma	1861	1927		
MARTIN, Jacob - 5 Ohio L.A. - Civil War Vet.	----	----		
MARTIN, Mary - Grandmother [LO 1906]	1848	1927		
In aisle between lots 115 & 118:			A115	2
AGEE, Calvin - Ohio Pvt U.S.Army WW II	1-15-1912	1-25-1972	&118	
AGEE, Everett [LO]	1888	1954	118E	2
"ssa, Melissa	1884	1951	&NW	
LISTERMAN, Anna	1854	1920	118	2
" ssa , Christopher [LO 1920]	1858	1925	SW	
SHINKLE*, Mary R.	----	10- 4-1986*	118W	2
RUDOLF, C. [LO]	----	----	119	2
RUDOLF, Betty L. - Mother	1910	1957	MW	
LAW, R. [LO]	----	----	119	2
LAW, Edna	1888	1957	SW	
"ssa, Andrew	1891	1961		
SNYDER, Edward - Husband - Jr. Ord emb [LO 1914]	1875	1963	119E	2
SNYDER, Minnie c. - Wife - D of A emb	1883	1964		
RIANER, Calvin [LO 1895]	----	----	120	2
REINIER*, Andrew)NW Corner)	----	4-23-1984*		
REHFUES, Ernest - Father	1881	1945		
REHFUES, Patricia "SCHRIER" - Daughter	1919	----		
SCHRIER, R. Earl - Husband	1918	----		
REHFUES, Dora R.	1883	1970		
In aisle south of lot:				
REHFUES, Charles E. - Ssgt U.S.Marines WW II	3-19-1912	12- 1-1983		
REHFUES*, Edith	----	7- 9-1986*		
DRESCH, A. [LO 1895]	----	----	121	2
DRESCH, Christina - Mother	9- 8-1843	5- 7-1895	NW	2
HAUCK*, Hilda Mae	----	9- 7-1984*	SW	
[No LO listed]			SE121	2
TAYLOR, Emma -Mom - OES emb [No LO listed]	1873	1955	NE121	2
BERTLINE, Anthony [LO 1912]	----	----	122	2
WRIGHT, Sasie V. _ OES emb	1903	10- 8-1981x	122	2
" ssa , Andrew J. - Amer Legion mkr - Ohio Cpl Co.F 30 Inf WW I SS [LO]	1-19-1896	3-16-1960	W	
BERTLINE, Anthony [LO 1912]	1880	1963	122E	2
" ssa , Maggie	1884	19--		
BORTLEIN, Jacob S.	1908	1912		
SNYDER, George	1868	1941	123	2
WEAVER, George	1883	1920		
"ssa , Edith [LO 1920]	1888	1972		
STITLE, Arthur	1884	1971		
HENRIE, Harvey	1886	3-22-1979x		
BORTLEIN, Amelia	1857	1934	124	2
" ssa , Philip [LO 1895]	1852	1934		
GEIGER, Maggie	11-22-1872	12-30-1897		
BORTLEIN, Mary	2-19-1881	3- 2-1895		
CHAMBERS, Benjamin - Father	3-25-1838	10-15-1900	125	2
CHAMBERS, Adaline HAY - Mother [LO 1900]	5- 5-1842	12- 3-1926		
WHITNEY, Charlotte	8- 7-1865	1-17-1917		
WHITNEY, Wilford E.	1864	1929		
WILLSEY, Anna - Mother	1855	1916	126	
" ssa , Thomas - Father [LO 1916]	1854	1942		
LICKLITER, Delva W.	1895	1963		
OTTO, Edgar	7-20-1916	9- 9-1916		
HENRIE, Benj. F. [LO 1911]	[4-13-1858	6-21-1926]	127	2
HENRIE, Bessie Mae	82y 1m25d	10-26-1975		
MEACHAM, Ira M.	1909	1911		
WHITNEY, Wm. [LO 1910]	----	----	128	2
ELBLE, Elizabeth A. nee WHITNEY - Mother	1883	1920		
ELBLE, Clement F. (Frank) - Father [LO 4-28-1923]	1884	3- 5-1976x		
ELBLE, Jeanette - Mother	1886	1954		
ELBLE, Betty Jane	1922	1923		
SCHARDDINE, Roscoe V. - KIA France Co.H 127 Inf WW I Vet.- Amer Legion mkr	1895	[10-26]1918	129	2
SCHARDDINE, Lena Jane nee LITTLE - D of A emb	1858	1916		
SCHARDDINE, Peter [LO 1899] K of P emb & D of A?	1857	1944		
JACOBS, Robert E.	1881	1938		
SCHARDINE, Ruth D. OES emb	1892	7-15-1981x		
SCHARDDINE, Ralph L. F. & A.M. emb	1894	1931		
In aisle between lots 130 & 135:			A130	2
, ----- [Burial indicated - no stone]	----	----	&135	
WEBER, Peter [LO 1911]	1863	1917	130W	2
COLEGATE, George M. [LO 1911]	1879	1932	130E	2
HENRIE, Thomas James - Ohio Tec 4 U.S.Army	7-31-1922	4-20-1967	131	2
HENRIE, Sarah A.	1909	3- 4-1989x		
" ssa , Thomas [LO 1922]	1895	1953		
HENRIE, Mary A.	1864	1943	132	2

NAME	BD or AGE	DD	Lot	Sec.
HENRIE, Wm., Sr. - [LO]	1844	1924	132	2
SEBLEY, John [LO]			133	2
STATES, E. Nee TRITSCHLER	1932	1954		
TRITSCHLER, Evelyn - Mother	1904	7-23-1979x		
" ssa . Frank - Father	1903	1966		
LEBHERZ, John	1873	1955		
" ssa , Elizabeth	1872	1953		
COLEGATE, John T. - Father	1842	1923	134W	2
" ssa , Dana WILLSEY - His Wife - Mother[LO 1923]	1847	1928		
COLEGATE, Albert E. [LO 12-7-1928]	1886	1971	134E	2
" ssa , Flossie E.	1890	1971		
GREGG?, Harry [LO 1913]	----	----	135	2
MUELLER, Michael F.	1881	1957		
" ssa , Anice V.	1893	1955		
McCLANAHAN, Margaret D.	1860	1950		
" ssa , J.(James?) Marcus [LO 1922]	1867	1941		
MUELLER, Earl G.	1910	1920		
MUELLER, Velma M.	1914	1922		
WHITNEY, Bismarck F & A.M. emb [LO 1908]	1878	1931	136	2
" ssa , Sarah HOPKINS - His Wife - OES emb	1876	1952		
____, Hazel Marie	1912	1916		
WHITNEY, Howard H.	1905	1908		
WHITNEY, Franklin r.	1924	1926		
DEAN, Curtis Mrs. [LO 1921]	----	----	137	2
TAYLOR, Everett - Father	1894	1963		
" ssa , Bessie B. - Mother	1892	1960		
TAYLOR, Fannie	1868	1944		
" ssa , Thomas J.	1862	1939		
DUNAWAY, Laura B.	1857	1932	138	2
DUNAWAY, Rosemary	1918	1972		
" ssa , Lenard	1915	----		
DUNAWAY, Pearl E.	1919	1922		
" ssa , Norma L.	one date	1930		
BLANTON, Millie Kay (stillborn; bur at foot of Cleve DUNAWAY)	11-21-1977x	11-21-1977x		
DUNAWAY, Irene	1896	1972		
" ssa , Cleve, Sr. [LO 1922]	1892	1975		
NEIDHARD, E. J. [LO 1923, transferred east half to Nancy TAYLOR, no date]	----	----	139	2
HINE, Joseph C.	1884	1924	139W	2
MARTIN, John R.- Brother	1925	1940		
TAYLOR, Nancy [LO not date]			139E	2
ECKEL, William Penn	1836	1923		
HINE, Walter L.	1906	1924		
[No LO listed]			140	2

The following burials are in the Veterans Circle are of Section 2:

NAME	BD or AGE	DD	Lot	Sec.
PASELEY, Raymond E. - Ohio Pfc 24 Marines 4 Marine Div WW II	5- 4-1922	3- 3-1945	Cir.	2
GABBARD, Theodore R.-Ohio Cpl 13 Armd Inf Bn 3 Armd Div..	7-28-1929	1-24-1953	Cir.	2
MILTON, Raymond E.-Ohio Sgt 2140 Base Unit AAF WW II	3-15-1924	6-20-1956	Cir.	2
WALLACE, Ben(ton) Ohio Fireman 1Cl U.S.Navy Civil War Vet.	one date	2-28-1930	Cir.	2
ESCHENBRENER, Tiebold - 9th O.V.I. Civil War	2-27-1837	7- 3-1925	Cir.	2
BOOK, Lewis.- Co.K 18 Ohio Inf-Civil War Vet.	----	----	Cir.	2
FUCHS, George H.- Corp'l 102 Inf Machine Gun Co. 26 Div. A.E.F.-KIA Argonne, France; Still leading his men 3 miles after being wounded; WW I Vet.	----	10-29-1918	Cir.	2
DUNAWAY, Omer Scott - Ohio Pvt Mil Police Corp.	----	6-22-1943	Cir.	2

Start SECTION 3

There are 18 lots in the circle are of Section 3, numbered from 1 through 8, 11 through 19, and 23. There are only eight lots on the west side of the circle. There were supposed to be ten, but the first eight were made larger to accomodate eight graves for each and to make the lots square. These lots are numbered from 1 through 8. Lots 9 and 10 were eliminated. Lots 11, 12, and 13 were to be used to bury singles only and not to be sold otherwise. Lots 14,15,16,17,18,19, and 23 on the east side were made large enough to bury eight. Therefore lots 20,21,22 and 24 were eliminated. The following eighteen lots are in the circle area only:

Lot 1 is divided into 5 parts. The west half is divided into 3 lots and the east half is divided into 2 lots.

NAME	BD or AGE	DD	Lot	Sec.
ARNOLD, Mrs. F. [LO 1938]		----	Cir.1	3
ARNOLD, Pearl	1900	----	NW	
" ssa , Margaret	1900			
HORNER, Charles	1893	1969	Cir.1W	3
" ssa , Myrtle M.	1895	1948		
ARNOLD, Virgil L. (Lee)	1918	5-20-1982x	Cir 1	3
" ssa , Alice H.	1914	6- 2-1980x		
ASHER, Marvin N. [LO]	2-11-1919	10-25-1985	Cir 1	3
ASHER*, Ester	----	3-10-1989*	SE	

NAME	BD or AGE	DD	Lot	Sec.
ARNOLD, Frank	1873	1936	Cir 1	3
ARNOLD, Sarah	1879	1960	NE	
COLEGATE, Myrtle, Home & Gladys [LOs[			Cir 2	3
BLACK, Denise Renee	9-25-1969	11-12-1969		
COLEGATE, William C. "Married Oct. 26,1933"	1908	1-14-1988x		
" ssa , Gladys E.	1917	----		
BUELL, Raymond	1905	1-25-1976x	Cir 3	3
" ssa, Emma D.	1910	----		
BUELL, Matilda - Mother - D of A emb	2-23-1883	1971		
BUELL, Maxwell - Father [LO]	6- 1-1879	3-30-1960		
BUELL, Ted - Father	1902	1977		
" ssa, Helen - Mother	1919	----		
BUELL*, Granville [Ted?]	----	5- 8-1977*		
WILLS, Arthur J. [LO]	1-14-1904	1-22-1982	Cir 4	3
"ssa , Lulu C.	7-28-1905	----		
BOHNING, Pearl	1889	9-26-1983x		
"ssa , Fred	1876	1966		
CADY, W. & J. [LOs]			Cir 5	3
CADY, William - Father	1882	1946	W	
CADY, Josephine	----	2- 5-1989x		
McMURRAY, Oscar D. [LO]	1908	7-22-1984x	Cir 5	3
" ssa , Helen V. [LO]	1911	3-26-1989x	E	
McMURRAY, Donna J. -Baby	one date	8-19-1945		
GIERINGER, Mabel nee INGERSOLL [LO] OES emb	1885	1964	Cir 6	3
GIERINGER, Charles P. - Husband [LO] F & A.M.emb	1882	1973		
HUTCHENS, Raymond P. - Ssgt U.S.Army WW II	1913	5-26-1984x	Cir 6	3
Lt. USNR			SW	
FLINCHPAUGH, Viola [LO] OES emb	1908	8-31-1987x	Cir 7	3
" ssa , Swain [LO]	1907	4-18-1979x		
ssa, **KOPP**, John - F. & A.M. emb	1885	1951		
ssa, " , Marie A. GROLL - OES emb	1886	1972		
DITTOE, George E. - KY Pfc U.S. Army WW I	10-28-1891	9- 5-1971	Cir 8	3
DITTOE, Evelyn nee STONE	1894	1960		
STONE, Walter [LO 1941]	1862	1946		
" ssa, Virginia	1869	1952		
WAYNE, Emmett W. "Married Dec. 31, 1919"	11-20-1898	4-26-1951	Cir11	3
"ssa , Lois	1902	----		
THIEMAN, William	1882	1961		
WILSON, Perry Thomas - Ohio Cpl Co.L 362	4-16-1896	4-28-1963		
Inf WW I				
HOWARD, James - Alabama Pvt 120 Engineers WW I	2-17-1894	12-6-1950		
BROXTERMAN, Howard L.	6- 6-1932	12-27-1950		
SCHULTE, Harry B.	1894	1961		
" ssa , Hazel I.	1893	1967		
ADAMS, Lida - Wife [LO]	1876	1963	Cir12	3
ADAMS, William - Husband	1874	1949		
TAYLOR, Harold c. - Father	1905	1961		
TAYLOR, William R.	1-11-1860	9-24-1948		
"ssa , Lulu B.	10-15-1877	10-17-1969		
WILLIAMSON, David H.	1883	1948	Cir13	3
" ssa , Anna M.	1878	1950		
HAYES, Paul D. s/o Earl & Marjorie (?which lot)	one date	1948		
HAUSER, Edna	1898	----	Cir14	3
HAUSER, Arthur [LO]	1897	1963		
JUTZI, Katherine HAUSER	1901	1- 1-1989x		
DUNTON, Dr. Allen H.	1887	1958	Cir15	3
DUNTON, Gladys J.	1899	1959		
ROWINS, Margaret A. - Wife	1910	1949		
ROWINS, Samuel J.	1902	2-13-1985x		
ROWINS, Charles J. - Father	1867	1946		
ROWINS, Minnie - Mother [LO]	1877	1961		
BROCKHOFF, William J. - Father [LO] F. & A.M.emb	1884	1972	Cir16	3
BROCKHOFF, Mollie K. - Mother - D of A emb	1889	1956		
In aisle NW of lot 17			Cir	3
STEINER, Warren A. - F. & A.M. emb	1912	----	A17NW	
" ssa , Loraine A.	1912	1-25-1987x		
SMITH, Marcella M. - Wife	11-13-1916	3-20-1982	Cir17	3
SMITH, Howard W.-Sgt U.S.Army WW II	12- 2-1918	5-24-1975		
F. & A.M. emb				
NEIDHARD, Pfc Charles E. - Husband	12-29-1918	5- 6-1945		
NEIDHARD, Loraine B.- Wife	11-28-1924	5- 6-1945		
NEIDHARD, Ed. - Father [LO]	12-14-1888	3-29-1980		
NEIDHARD, Katie - Mother	4-19-1893	9-20-1975		
The following aisleway lots are located east of Circle lot 17:				
LIPPERT, Charles W. - Father [LO]	1- 3-1906	----	17A	3
" ssa , Nina D. - Mother	7-29-1909	11-12-1979		
[LO not listed]			17B	3
HARMS, Wanda M.	12-27-1920	10- 6-1984	17C	3
SCHAEFFER, S. & R. [LOs]	----	----	17D	3
HUGENTOBLER, Irene	1921	1944	Cir18	3
HUGENTOBLER, Robert J. - Killed in Germany	1923	1944	W	
HUGENTOBLER, Robert	1888	1958		
" ssa , Madge [LO]	1888	1958		
HUGENTOBLER, Robert K.-Cook U.S.Army WW I	11-15-1887	10- 6-1978		

NAME	BD or AGE	DD	Lot	Sec.
LAPE, ----- [LO]	----	----	Cir18	3
LAPE, Charles J.	1912	----	E	
"ssa, Bertha M.	1915	1-30-1979X		
LAPE, Philip M. - Father	1881	1968		
"ssa, Pearl M. - Mother	1883	1957		
FELTER, Charles H.	1878	1949	Cir19	3
FELTER, May A. [LO]	1878	1968		
WESSELER, Curtis-mkr "Boy Scouts of America.	11- 5-1925	6-27-1938	Cir23	3
res Mack, OH, Troop 294 Tenderfoot."			W	
WESSELER, Albert F. [LO 9-1837]	1894	19--		
" ssa , Edith M.	1892	1960		
WESSELER, Hilda HEGEMEIER - Mother	5-23-1904	10-26-1979		
HUGENTOBLER, Harry W. - Ohio Pvt. U.S.Army WW I	1890	1961	Cir23	3
" ssa , Florence H. [LO 1938, transferred	1907	19--		
west half to Albert F. WESSELER]				
SEILER, Louis	1882	1938		
"ssa , Anna MASON	1885	1966		
MASON, William - Ohio Wagoner 325 Fld Arty	3-23-1887	5-15-1954		
84 Div. WW I Vet.				

SECTION 3

NAME	BD or AGE	DD	Lot	Sec.
ROESSLER, Gotlieb [LO 1890]	6-12-1843	7- 4-1894	1	3
" ssa , Marie w/o G.	7- 1-1848	4-29-1890		
COLLINS, J. J. [LO 1894]	----	----	2	3
STIEG, Fred G. [LO 1894]	1867	1953	3	3
HOFFMAN, Cora	1868	19--		
STIEG+, G. F. bur pos between W3-4	----	----		
HEARN, Cordelia [LO 1892]	----	----	4	3
WOLFE, George	1862	1892		
ssa **HEARNE**, Marie C.	1844	1907		
ssa HEARNE, Charles W.	1870	1895		
ssa HEARNE, George F.	1873	1895		
FAGALY, Emanuel [LO 1892]	1844	1912	5	3
" ssa , Loretta	1846	1940		
FAGALY+, Sophia bur pos W1-2	----	----		
DAVIS, Edward [LO 1898]	----	----	6N	3
TAYLOR, John G. [LO 1896]	----	----	6S	3
KRAMER, William - Spanish American War Vet.	1871	1900	7W	3
KRAMER, Jacob - Civil War Vet. [LO 1896]	7-24-1829	6-20-1898		
KRAMER, Katharina	8-23-1835	2-25-1902		
KRAMER, Elizabeth	20y 4m17d	3-22-1896		
KRAMER, Carrie -tochter von Jakob & Catharina-	6y 2m27d	4-14-1885		
KRAMER, Minnie	1870	1897		
APPLEGATE, Sherman [LO 1897]			7E	3
SNYDER, P. J. (Peter J.) [LO 1887]	1846	1924	8	3
" ssa , Lena SHEAR His Wife	1852	1926		
SNYDER+, Samuel - bur pos E5	----	----		
LAKE, Donna J.	9- 4-1962	9- 5-1962	8-9?	3
MILLER, Adam [LO 1887]	----	----	9	3
MILLER+, Jos. bur pos W2	----	----		
MILLER+, Jno. bur pos W3	----	----		
MILLER+, Pauline bur pos W4	----	----		
RYBOLT, Jacob [LO 1887] Civil War Vet.	----	----	10W	3
RYBOLT, Adda E. w/o J.J. _ Mother	49y 3m26d	1-11-1894		
" ssa . Ella T. d/o J.J. & A.E.	21y 1m16d	9-13-1893		
" ssa , George H. s/o J.J. & A.E.	1(6?)y 8m17d	5-19-1887		
NOES, Nancy [LO 1899]	----	----	10E	3
SHAFFER, Wm. & Martha [LO 1886]	----	----	11	3
NEIDHARD, E. J. [LO 5-12-1938]	----	----		
VANALLEN, William	1863	1940		
FEDERLE, David - Brother	1873	1942		
KAETZEL, William H. - Father	1858	1940		
KAETZEL, William F. - Brother	1898	1953		
FEDERLE, George - Brother	1879	1940		
OLDMAN, Jos. [LO 1885]	----	----	12	3
UHLMANN, Christiana M.	10- 1-1813	8-25-1889		
UHLMANN, Jakob	10-31-1811	4-22-1885		
UHLMANN, Charles	1848	1930		
UHLMANN*, Gotlieb (b. Germany; res Green	7-14-1840*	2- 8-1905*		
Twp.; of grippe; laborer; s/o Jacob)				
POOLE, Richard [LO 1886]	----	----	13	3
POOLE, Mary Jane - Mother	1821	1894		
HAUSER, Eliza - Mother	1823	1898		
HENRIE, William [LO 1906]	----	----	14	3
GIBBS, William H.	1868	1946	15	3
" ssa, Elizabeth	1881	1949		
ASH, Joe R.	1873	1951		
WEBER, Christian J. - Father/Husband	10-18-1821	8-18-1887		
[LO 1879] - Erected by their son August				
WEBER, Mary M. - Mother	5- 2-1830	5-26-1908		
WEBER, Annie M. B. (Anna Mary)(b. Hamilton	7-13-1869	4-15-1879		
Co. OH; res Colerain Twp.; d/o Christian)				
BEYER, August [LO 1937]	----	----	16	3

NAME	BD or AGE	DD	Lot	Sec.
HAMMITT, Sadie	1903	1964	17	3
HAMMITT, Joseph	1856	1915		
" ssa , Mary [LO 1915]	1861	1941		
HAMMITT, Margaret	1894	----		
HAMMITT, Bertha C.	1900	1982		
HAMMITT, Jacob - U.S.Navy WW I	1892	6- 3-1983x		
HAMMITT, Charles	1885	1958		
HAMMITT, May	1888	1961		
DIETRICH, Walter - F. & A.M. emb	1892	1939	18W	3
" ssa , Emma K. [LO 1938]	1888	1963		
ALLGEIER, John C. - Father [LO 1938]	1882	1956	18E	3
" ssa , Margaret S. - Mother	1890	1938		
MYERS, Rosalie e. [LO 1888]	----	----	19	3
Lot 20 is not on cemetery map.				
STEWART, James H. [LO 1872] Civil War Vet.	1822	1891	21	3
" ssa , Mary L.	1830	1916		
" ssa , Polly P. (b. Louisville, KY; of neuralgia; res Miamitown, OH; d/o John & Polly PHILLIPS)	1798	11-10-1879x		
" ssa , William W.	1846	1927		
" ssa , Amanda J.	1849	1930		
HENGEHOLD, M. [LO]	----	----	22NW	3
COOK, J. R. [LO]	----	----	22SW	3
RATLIFF, C. M. [LO]	----	----	22E	3
RATLIFF, William C. **(Clyde)**	5-14-1954	9-17-1978		
HENRY*+, Mattie bur pos W1 (d. of consumption; [No date of d. but name was entered in book between 10-1-1879 & 10-21-1879)	----	----	23	3
HENRY*+, Harvey - bur pos W3 [LO 1877] (b. Va; of cancer; res Hamilton Co. OH; s/o Benj. & Mary)	1803*	2- 9-1877*		
HENRY*+, Mattie bur pos E8 (No date except for name entered in book between 6-26-1880 & 7-23-1880)	----	----		
SCHREIBER, Peter [LO 1891]	1857	1935	24N	3
SCHREIBER, Anna Maria	1832	1908		
SCHREIBER, Peter	1817	1891		
SCHREIBER, Matilda	1862	1913		
SCHREIBER, Charles	1852	1929		
SCHREIBER, Barbara	1854	1935		
SCHREIBER, George - F. & A.M. emb	1856	1931		
SCHREIBER, JOhnny	5- 3-1922	4-17-1923		
SOHN, Anna Maria	1808	1892		
SCHREIBER, Josephine	1900	1902		
SCHREIBER, Mary	1884	1905		
ROWINS, Samuel [LO 1891]	----	----	24S	3
SCHREIBER, Charles [LO 2-9-1915]	----	----		
LAWYER, Ida B.	1856	1938	25	3
LAWYER, Martha A. TAYLOR His Wife - Mother	2- 5-1826	5- 9-1908		
LAWYER, Isaac P. - Father [LO 1888]	11-11-1825	6-29-1891		
LAWYER, Pet	1865	1939		
TAYLOR, Amanda	1840	1916		
LAWYER, Sarah J.	12-10-1867	7-26-1900		
LAWYER, Isaac N.	9-24-1858	9-22-1888		
HAUSER, Arthur D. [LO 1897]	----	----	26	3
HAUSER, Annie d/o W. & H. HAMMITT;w/o ArthurD.	1- 1-1867	5-16-1897		
HAUSER, Michael	1-26-1855	10-26-1899		
RIGBY, Edw. S.	1864	1916		
SNYDER, Edward [LO 1870]	----	----	27	3
SNYDER*+, Elizabeth (b. Bavaria; of hernia; res Miamitown, OH; d/o Julia & Philip SMITH)	5- 3-1820*	2-28-1877*		
HINE, Louis M.	9- 7-1892	10-23-1896	28	3
HINE, Mary E. - Mother	1866	1938		
HINE, George H. - Father [LO 1896]	1865	1951		
RUOFF, Arthur J. - Son	1885	1924	29	3
RUOFF, Helen - Mother	1858	1911		
RUOFF, Jacob - Husband [LO 1895]	1856	1930		
BECK, Cora RUOFF	1880	1956		
"ssa, Cameron	1879	1971		
HETTESHEIMER, Peter Aged 65y-Civil War Vet.	7- 4-1838	3- 4-1903		
" ssa , Eliza	9- 7-1836	4- 1-1907		
HETTESHEIMER, Dan [LO 1894]	----	----	30	3
HETESIMER+, Mrs. Matilda bur pos W1-2	----	----		
STINE, Marvel - Son	1911	1942		
STINE, Florence - Mother	1889	1965		
KOHL, John A. - Dad	1862	1933		
"ssa, Josie - Mom	1863	1920		
KOHL, Walter J.	1892	1894		
HILL, Walter R - Husband	1882	1957	31	3
McMINN, Sarah J. - Mother [LO 1892]	1848	1919		
McMINN, Edith R.	1880	1906		
McMINN, Frederick - Father - Aged 53y	3-24-1839	5- 1-1892		
ssa, HOLLIDAY, Lott	----	----		
ssa, HOLLIDAY, Rachel	----	----		
McMINN, Fred F. - Brother	1886	1959		
McM? HILL, Kathryn - Wife	1884	1970		
HOLLIDAY, Lot	1817	1897		

NAME	BD or AGE	DD	Lot	Sec.
BREESE, Evan W. - Father [LO 1879]	1852	1921	32	3
" ssa . Ida Ann - Mother	1855	1932		
BREESE*+, Carrie (Carra) bur pos W4 (b. Hamilton Co. OH; of scarlet fever; res Crosby Twp.; d/o Evan W. & Ida Ann)	12-22-1876*	4-10-1879*		
KIDNEY, William W. - F. & A.M. emb	1875	1941		
" ssa , Amanda	1880	1961		
WILLEY, Samuel	30y 8m 6d	11- 2-1858		
DAYTON, Dr. George M. [LO 1877]	1849	1917	33	3
" ssa , Lena S.	1851	1919		
" ssa , Daisy B.	1875	1885		
" ssa , Charles F. (b. & res Whitewater Twp.; of consumption of bowels; s/o G.M. & Lena)	3-16-1881x	9-21-1881x		
ssa MEERS, Pearl B.	1883	1911		
TAYLOR, Joshua P. - Father - F. & A.M.emb [LO 1903]	1855	1932	34	3
TAYLOR, Aramenta G.-His Wife-Mother	1855	1926		
TAYLOR, Edward E. - Son	1881	1925		
TAYLOR, Robert D.	1887	1943		
TAYLOR, Flossie E.	1891	1972		
BRADFORD, Anna M.	1890	1965		
BRADFORD, T. Edgar	1890	1970		
CONGER, Harriet L. - Wife	1852	1929	35	3
BACON, Fanny - Mother	1813	1887		
BACON, Joseph - Father [LO 1875]	1805	11-15-1875x		
BACON, William L.- Husband	1854	1933		
BACON, Mary J. - Wife	1856	1927		
LORETAN, Joseph M. - IOOF emb	1868	1938		
LORETAN, Cora BACON [LO 5-6-1934] Emb. with the letters "D" & "R" imposed upon each other & to the left of a dove on a cresent moon filled with stars.	1875	1951		
In aisle between lots 35 & 57;			A35 &57	3
MEURER, Wayne A. - Husband & Father	5-30-1959	10- 2-1984		
GRIFFITH, David K. - Our Father	3-16-1811	12-27-1843		
" ssa , Eliza LAWRENCE w/o David [LO 1871]	10- 4-1812	1-26-1881		
GRIFFITH, Daniel D. (David)Civil War Vet. b. Green Twp.; of consumption; res Miamitown, OH; s/o DAvid K. & Eliza F.G.)	4- 7-1843	4-11-1871		
In aisle between lots 36 & 56:			A36 &56	3
MERKLE, Guy Joseph - Son & Brother	12- 9-1933	10-28-1987		
In aisle between lots 35 & 57:			A35 &57	3
TOLLE, Elizabeth G.	12-22-1913	6-25-1985		
RITTENHOUSE, ?Lemul or ?Semul (Samuel?)[LO ca 1867-68]		----	37	3
RITTENHOUSE+, Katie bur pos W1	----	----		
RITTENHOUSE+, Mrs. bur pos W2	----	----		
RITTENHOUSE+, S? or L? bur pos W3	----	----		
MILLER, Jeanette E. nee RITTENHOUSE Lin. No.59, D of A emb	----	5-29-1934		
ssa RITTENHOUSE, Mary nee FLOWERS	----	2- 1-1920		
WEST, Lee F. - Son - Great grd s/o Mary RITTENHOUSE	----	8- 6-1920		
RITTENHOUSE+, George bur pos E7	----	----		
In aisle between lots 37 & 55:	----	----	A37 &55	3
WILLIS, Loretta - Mother	1917	10-16-1985x		
In aisle between lots 37 & 55:	----	----	A37 &55	3
ROWE, Sam H. Pvt U.S.Army WW II	4-14-1927	8-25-1985		
HERIDER, John [LO 1865]	----	----	38	3
SHAW*+, William M. bur pos W1 (b. PA; res Miamitown, OH; farmer)	----	3- 7-1869*	?39NE	3
HERIDER*+, Child of John's bur pos W4 (b. & res Hamilton Co. OH; of head fall; ch/o John & Eliza HERIDER; first interment made in the new ground)	**11-14-1864***	**11-21-1864***		
In aisle between lots 38 & 54:			A38 &54	3
SIMMOND,----- [LO]	----	----		
In aisle between lots 39 & 54:			A39 &54	3
KING, Thomas Harold - Pvt. U.S.Army WW II & Korea	1929	11- 8-1987x		
BEYER, August - Pvt U.S.Army WW I Amer Legion mkr	10- 9-1892	1- 8-1978	A39 &54	3
ISGRIG, Daniel [LO 1876]	6-30-1796	11-13-1884		
"ssa , Mary SEAL	1849	1934		
"ssa , Robert - Civil War Vet.	11-26-1844	8-15-1876		
HAYES, Stephen [LO 1911]	----	----	40	3
KING, Mary J.	1929	1969		
DEAN, Harold J.	1892	1971		
"ssa, Theresa	1888	1970		
HAYES, Russell S.	3m17d	----		
HAYES, Mattie M.	1884	1965	41	3
HAYES, Frank M. - F. & A.M. emb [LO 1919]	1883	1918		
EDWARDS, Hannah Christine nee DICKMEIER [LO 1881]	11-20-1837	2- 8-1903	42	3
POPE, Ella nee EDWARDS D of A mkr (b. Blue Jay, Hamilton Co. OH; of consumption)	5-21-1856	5- 9-1881		
EDWARDS, Jennie C. - Sister	1870	1941		
"ssa , Samuel L. - Brother	1858	1932		
BRUNSWICK, ----- [LO, N2/3 of W half]			**42.5** W	**3**
BRUNSWICK, Marygene	1946	----		

NAME	BD or AGE	DD	Lot	Sec.
BRUNSWICK, Fred W. - Ohio S2 USNR WW II	2- 9-1910	12-31-1971	42.5	3
"ssa , Margaret-(also on ssa Marygene)	1906	19--	W	
[No LO listed, S 1/3 of W half]			42.5	3
BECKMAN, ----- [LO]	----	----	42.5	3
BECKMAN, Leo	1898	1971	SE	
" ssa , Alice	1907	12- 4-1982x		
WEAVER, ----- [LO]	----	----	42.5	3
WEAVER, Mary V.	1911	3- 5-1979x	NE	
" ssa , Earl G.	1907	----		
COMBS, Lou Ayrs [LO, N third, 1933]	----	----	43N	3
SPARKS, Jonas [LO 1937]	----	----	43NW	3
SPARKS, Mamie - Mother	1888	1937		
BEYER, Rosa	1859	1937	43SW	3
BEYER, Charles, Sr. [LO]	1864	1956		
POTTSCHMIDT, V. [LO S part SE 1/3, 1937]	----	----	43SE	3
HEARN, Scott [LO?]	1867	1936	43Mid	3
" ssa, Nellie	1872	1936		
WULFHORST, Louis [LO N part SE 1/3 1937]	----	----	43SE	3
WULFHORST, Josephine	1881	1937		
Lots 44,45, & 46 are not on cemetery map.				
BUNCE,----- [LO	----	----	**47**	3
BUNCE, Griffin M. -b. Green Co. NY	7-29-1839	5- 5-1869		
F. & A.M. emb.				
_____, ----- [Foundation, but no stone,	----	----		
possibly Emily BUNCE, d. 1873, see "Unknown" section]				
WEIL,----- [LO]	----	----	48	3
BOICOURT, Elizabeth (b. & res Cincinnati,	11- ?-1905x	11-26-1905x		
OH; d/o W.L. & Sarah)				
WEIL, Jacob	8- 8-1890	7-31-1950		
"ssa, Dorothy	5- 9-1891	11-15-1950		
BRUG, ----- [LO]	----	----	49	3
BRUG, John s/o Peter	8-24-1886	1-10-1907		
BRUG, Peter	4-21-1865	11- 6-1949		
"ssa, Barbara	8-27-1865	5-26-1945		
Lots 50 & 51 are not on Cemetery map.				
DANFORD, Sarah J.	1831	1919	52	3
DANFORD, James [LO 1871] (b. IN; of	8- 1-1818x	6-16-1872x		
paralysis; res Green Twp.; s/o John & Judah)				
DANFORD, Sarah E.	----	----		
DANFORD, E. J.	----	----		
DANFORD, Abbie	----	----		
DANFORD, Daisy	----	----		
DANFORD, Stella	----	----		
ROSS, ----- [LO]	----	----	52.5	3
ROSS, Melvin M. - F. & A.M. emb	1911	----		
"ssa, Marie H. - OES emb"Married Feb.28,1934"	1910	----		
HILLEBRAND, ----- [LO, rest of lot]	----	----	52.5	3
MILLER, Allen E. - Father [LO 1870]	9-28-1818	10-25-1884	53	3
HENRIE, Cora E.	1887	1958		
MOORE, John Riley - KY Pfc MG Co 319 Inf WW I-	4-16-1895	2-10-1970		
MOORE, Sylvia M.	1892	19--		
WALDRIDGE, Sophia	1874	1896		
HENRIE, Sarah E.	1847	1901		
HENRIE, Allen E.	1882	1909		
HENRIE, Clarence	1889	1910		
HENRIE, William, Jr.	1880	1935		
MANUEL, William, Sr. [LO NW part of lot]	1900	1971	53.5	3
MANUEL, Opal D.	1905	11-16-1987x	NW	
HEISEL, ----- [LO SW part]	1900	1971	53.5	3
HEISEL, Florine - Wife	6-29-1909	----	SW	
HEISEL, James - Ohio Fl U.S.Navy WW II	5-10-1909	1-13-1971		
BEYER,----- [LO SE part of lot]	----	----	53.5	3
BEYER, Elizabeth (Pearl Elizabeth)	1910	7-10-1978x	SE	
ZEINNER*, Jared Michael (bur between great	----	7-30-1988*		
grandparents)				
BEYER, Charles, Jr.	1899	1948		
AUGUSTUS, ----- [LO Center lot, E part]	----	----	53.5	3
AUGUSTUS, Chauncey T.-Jr ord & VFW embs	7-31-1923	----	E	
" ssa , Anna M. Ladies Aux VFW emb &	12-24-1920	7-26-1978		
emb with the letters "P-Y-T-" in a square with a flame on top.				
GEINER[?], [ZEINER?], ----- [LO NE part]	----	----	53.5	3
BARNES, Hugh V. [LO 1867]	----	----	54	3
BARNES+, Unnamed bur pos W1	----	----		
BARNES+, Unnamed bur pos W2	----	----		
BARNS, Katie M. d/o H.V. & M.J. (b. & res	9- 3-1855	1- 3-1875		
Harrison, OH; of consumption; d/o Hew & Jane)				
BARNS, Grandville G. s/o H.V. & M.J.	5-29-1852	3- 9-1855		
BARNS, Forest s/o H.V. & M.J.	8-31-1850	7-27-1851		
BARNS, John (b. KY; res Hamilton Co.OH;	11-14-1796	6- 4-1874		
s/o A. & C.)				
BARNS, Araminta - Our Mother- w/o John	3-10-1796	6-22-1873		
MITCHEL, Kate [LO 9-20-1936]	----	----	55	3
WERTS, Rosa Belle d/o W. & E.	19y10m 3d	12-15-1875		

NAME	BD or AGE	DD	Lot	Sec.
WERTS, Rosa Belle-continued: Sister (b. Miamitown, OH; res Greensburg, IN;				
d/o Wm. & Elizabeth)				
" ssa, Elizabeth	8-28-1835	10-29-1909		
" ssa, Wm. J. - Father [LO 1875]	6-12-1831	9-15-1895		
" ssa, Ella	3- 8-1861	3-21-1897		
GUENTHER, Henry	1857	1948		
WOOD, Ruel B.	1884	1938		
HEID, Barbara	1851	1936		
"ssa, Jacob	1855	1938		
In aisle between lots 55 & 70			A55	3
LITTLETON, Dresulla - Mother	----	2-23-1987x	&70	
HOFFMAN, ----- Mother (Mary?)	1826	1916	56	3
HOFFMAN, ----- Father (Joseph?) (res Green	9- ?-1820x	9-15-1905x		
Twp.) LO 1870]				
HOFFMAN, Emily (Emma?) (b. OH; of typhoid	7-19-1854x	7-13-1872x		
pneumonia; res Dent, OH; d/o Joseph & Mary)				
HOFFMAN, Katie	1863	1950		
HOFFMAN, Elizabeth d/o J. & M. (b. & res	3- 1-1859	4- 1-1870		
Green Twp.; d/o Jos. & Mary)				
HOFFMAN, John	1850	1886		
HOFFMAN, Charles	1861	1937		
In aisle between lots 56 & 69:			A56	3
BAILEY, Etta - Mother	1903	7-15-1986X	&69	
In aisle between lots 56 & 69:			A56	3
EVANS, Lillian L. - Mother	1917	5-17-1986x	&69	
RITTENHOUSE, Amanda - Mother	1847	1929	57	3
" ssa , Charles [LO]	1867	1929		
RITTENHOUSE, Hugh B. - Husband	1874	1947		
RITTENHOUSE, Grace B. - Wife	1888	19--		
BACON, Ruth w/o John - Mother	73y 5m18d	1-18-1892	58	3
"ssa , John - Father [LO 1892]	----	----		
SIEGLE, Dwight - Our Son	1948	1960	59	3
SCHNEIDER, Jessie F. (Frances) Mother	2- 8-1911	6-30-1976		
SIEGLE, Roy - Brother	1900	1967		
SIEGLE, Harry - Brother	1908	1971		
HINE, Lillie M. nee ARNOLD	1871	1913		
ARNOLD, John J. - Father [LO 1903]	1- 6-1849	10-13-1903		
" ssa , Frances - His Wife - Mother	3-23-1845	7- 7-1925		
SIEGLE, George	1874	1947		
" ssa , Mattie	1876	1944		
SIEGLE*, Infant	----	7- 5-1976*		
RICHARDSON, W. B. [LO 1892]			60	3
GANT, **Wilbur** & ELDON, Frank [LOs 1904]			61	3
GANT, Mary C.	12-11-1869	5- 3-1933		
GANT, Silas Wilbur	3- 7-1866	10-17-1950		
GANT, Leslie	1900	1966		
"ssa, Anna	1903	12- 6-1976x		
ORR, Jennie E.	11- 4-1867	6-24-1926		
ELDON, Alice ORR	12- 2-1872	3- 9-1904		
GANT, Baby	one date	1-10-1929		
_____, Anna M.	1868	1911		
WILSON, George W.	1873	1939	62	3
WILSON, Thomas H.	1858	1925		
WILSON, Christopher - Father	1822	1903		
" ssa , Cecelia S. - Mother [LO 1904]	1835	1933		
WILSON, Margaret - Sister	1882	1923		
STRONG, Louis R. - Dad	1883	1942	63NW	3
STRONG, Anna - Mother - Age 36y	1860	1896		
STRONG, Peter - Father [LO 1896] Age 66y	1852	1919		
SCOGGINS, Susan - Mother (names on W side of stone)	1847	1896	63S	3
" ssa , Robert H. - Father [LO 1896]	1847	1932		
" ssa , Hattie (Harriet)	1872	1923		
BURK-SCOGGINS (names on E side of above/stone)				
-----, William A.	1864	1935		
-----, Dora S.	1874	1945		
-----, May S. DOWDELL	1879	1951		
-----, John L. - Daddy	1875	1936		
WRIGHT, Charles	1888	1942	63NE	3
" ssa , Mary B. [LO]	1890	1-18-1981x		
RUDISELL, William - emb has crossed bats over a	1886	1951		
baseball				
HAMMITT, Sarah [LO 1894]			64	3
FLOWERS, John - Civil War Vet.	1831	1913		
" ssa , Martha - His Wife	1834	1913		
HAMMITT, William S.	39y11m22d	4-29-1894		
ssa MINGES, Sadie HAMMITT His Wife	----	6-19-1926		
HAMMITT, Allie	1885	1908		
" ssa , Glenna May - Daughter	1907	1912		
HAMMITT, Wm.	1882	1953		
" ssa , Elsie - His Wife	1894	1916		
HAMMITT, Willis J.-Ohio Pvt Co A 61 Mil Police Bn WW II-	1916	1962		
BALL, Harry	1878	1918		
"ssa, Lulu FLOWERS - His Wife	1867	1913		

NAME	BD or AGE	DD	Lot	Sec.
GIERINGER, Millie [LO]	1868	1902	65	3
" ssa , Joseph M.	1869	1960		
_____, Joe Boy	1915	1915		
GIERINGER, Victor E. - Ohio Sgt U.S.Army WW I	6-26-1898	7- 3-1971		
_____, Ivory	1905	1915		
GIERINGER, Daisy - Mother	1884	1937		
WALKER, Sol [LO 1867]	----	----	65A	3
HUGENTOBLER, Alex & Robert [LOs 1909]			66	3
WILDS, Edward A. - F. & A.M. emb	1894	1969		
"ssa , Alice K.	1895	11- 2-1982x		
HUGENTOBLER, Charles - Father	1859	1935		
HUGENTOBLER, Robert C.	1862	1936		
STRIMPLE, Minnie	1854	1938		
[No lot owner listed]			67	3
In aisle between lots 57 & 68:			A68	3
FLINCHPAUGH, Gary W. - Our Son	12-28-1955	6-26-1972	&57	
FLINCHPAUGH, David [LO 1883]	----	----	68	3
FLINCHPAUGH, Robert G. Ohio Tec 4 Signal Corps WW II	7- 1-1927	12-27-1955		
FLINCHPAUGH+, Hannah bur pos W2	----	----		
FLINCHPAUGH, George E. - Father	1899	1958		
FLINCHPAUGH, Jeanette - Mother	1902	19--		
FLINCHPAUGH, Herbert C. Ohio Pfc 319 Repair Unit MTC WW I	6-25-1896	4-24-1952		
FLINCHPAUGH, Lawrence (L.) Son	6-13-1933	3-15-1985		
WHEELER, William [LO 1869]	----	----	69	3
WHEELER+, Erminie/Minnie bur pos W1 (b. & res Miami, OH; of disease of brain; d/o W. F. & Phidilla)	5-18-1867*	4- 5-1868*		
WHEELER*+, Phildela bur pos W2 (b.Harrison, OH; of consumption; res Miamitown, OH; d/o Lester LEWIS)	10- 1-1848*	2- 1-1870*		
WHEELER*+, Grace bur pos E8 (b. & res Miamitown, OH; of acute cerebral spinal meningitis; d/o William F. & Mary E.)	2-10-1878*	8- 1-1880*		
MOORE, Abram [LO 1873]	----	----	70	3
SMITH, Asa [LO 9-20-1873]	----	----		
CROWELL, Mary E.	1832	1905		
GILKS, Julia CROWELL	1867	1898		
KIEHBORTH, George - Father	10- 3-1876	10-31-1936		
KIEHBORTH, Mamie - Mother [LO]	4-14-1881	4-13-1954		
KIEHBORTH, Joan D.	1912	----		
" ssa , Melvin R.	1912	2-17-1982x		
KIEHBORTH, Ralph W.	9-10-1907	8-12-1973		
BAER, Philip H.	1863	1928		
BAER, Alice CROWELL	1865	1925		
WEBSTER, Wild F.	1884	1926	71	3
FLOWERS, Edward [LO] (b. MD; of inflammation of lungs; res Mimitown, OH; s/o Samuel & Cazier)	8-20-1802x	4- 4-1866x		
" ssa , Malinda	1814	1888		
" ssa , Amasa [LO 1867]	1837	1897		
SCHREIBER, Bessie Mae - Daughter	1921	1936	71.5	3
SCHREIBER, Bessie Mae - Mother	1886	1940		
SCHREIBER, George, Jr.- Husband & Father [LO & no date of transfer from Mary HEY]	1881	1973		
SCHREIBER, Ann - Wife	1891	1961		
BUNNELL, Warren - F. & A.M. emb	1867	1936		
BUNNELL, Mary (HEY) [LO 1934]	1870	1947		
JOHNSON, Catherine	12- 7-1879	11-14-1967	72W	3
JOHNSON, Charles L. [LO 1914]	5-27-1876	4-14-1959		
JOHNSON, Esther	1906	1913		
STRIMPLE, Aaron [LO 1934]	1859	1940	72E	3
STRIMPLE, Eliza B. [LO 1934]	1857	1940		
THOMPSON, Lambert	1875	19--		
Lot 73 is now lot 73.5 & 74A.				
DRAKE, Charles [LO]	----	----	73.5	3
DRAKE, G. Edith - Our Mom	1897	1962		
NOERR, George William	10- 9-1867	10-10-1948	74A	3
"ssa , Zitella ISGRIG	10- 8-1872	5-28-1971		
ROEVER, ----- [LO]	----	----	74.5	3
ROEVER, Edith May	1899	1969		
ROEVER, Adolph H.	1871	1948		
" ssa , Rachel N.	1875	1945		
ROEVER, Beryl Vera	1908	----		
ROEVER, John Henry	1907	1965		
SCHILD, Dorothy C. WILCOX ROEVER	1911	----		
ROEVER, Lawrence Raymond	1904	1960		
ROEVER, Clifford William	1897	1971		
ROEVER, Lydia Elizabeth	1898	1972		
HAHN, Howard J.	1915	----		
HAHN, Ruth ROEVER	1917	----		
McDONALD, Ethel ROEVER	1910	----		
McDONALD, Frank G.	1913	----		
McDONALD, Louise ROEVER	1910	1943		
POTTENGER, Thomas L. F. & A.M. emb [LO 1934]	1865	1946	74SW	3

NAME	BD or AGE	DD	Lot	Sec.
POTTENGER, Hope CAMPBELL w/o Thomas L.	1867	1954		
POTTENGER, Elizabeth MILLER	74y 4m 2d	1-10-1908	74E	3
" ssa , James R. [LO, NW & E, 1867]	81y 3m	6-23-1914	&NW	
" ssa , Meade M.	24y	8-25-1891		
" ssa , Royal J.	22y 7m	11- 8-1891		
" ssa , Gussie M. INGERSOLL w/o Meade C.	1896	1963		
" ssa , Meade C. - F. & A.M. emb	1897	1972		
POTTENGER, Maggie M.	26y 4m	9-20-1882		
POTTENGER, Mary (Isabell) (b. & res Crosby Twp.; of typhoid fever; d/o James R. & Elizabeth M.)	9y 3m 4d	3-13-1867		
MILLER, Thelma	1902	1963	75A	3
MILLER, Richard C.- Ohio Pfc Co.M 145 Inf WW I Vet.	3-12-1899	1-21-1966		
MILLER, Archie E. - Jr Ord emb	1890	1931		
MILLER, Elizabeth	1865	1944		
MILLER, Edwin B. - Jr Ord emb [LO 1931]	1863	1942		
SHEPPARD, Lida MILLER	1897	1947		
GLAUSER, ----- [LO]	----	----	75.5	3
GLAUSER, John E. - Tec 4 U.S.Army WW II Amer Legion mkr	1922	1- 1-1980x	N	
" ssa , Margie L.	----	----		
GLAUSER, Sandra Gaye	12- 9-1946	6- 7-1961		
OTTO, ----- [LO]	----	----	75.5	3
OTTO, Gussie	1894	1956	S	
" ssa. Ethel J.	1903	11-28-1977x		
GEIST, Edward H. - Husband [LO 1940]	1894	1946	76	3
GEIST, Clara - Wife	1897	19--		
HEY, Walter E. [LO]	1-25-1883	2- 2-1957	76.5	3
"ssa, Adele W.	10-11-1893	1-12-1985	W	
SWINGLE, ----- [LO]	----	----	76.5	3
SWINGLE, Jesse H. - Brother	1903	1963	SE	
SWINGLE, Alice R. ARMSTRONG	1907	6- 4-1985x		
SWINGLE, Donald "Jack"	1901	10-18-1978x		
COFFEY, ----- [LO]	----	----	76.5	3
COFFEY, Myrtle b.	3-13-1893	2-23-1971	NE	
WALKER, Reeves [LO]	----	----	77	3
REEVES, Anna B.	1855	1924		
WALKER, Carrie - Mother	1876	1919		
LAEHR, Harry S. - F. & A.M.	1896	6-21-1982x	77.5	3
"ssa , Edith M. [LO]	1897	5-11-1987x	NW	
REIK, Helen LAEHR - OES emb [LO]	1915	----	77.5	3
REIK, Elmer A., Sr. - F. & A.M. emb [LO]	1905	1957	SW	
MONROE, ----- [LO]	----	----	77.5	3
MONROE, Gerald C.	10-18-1932	4- 3-1957	E	
Lots 78 & 29 are not on cemetery map.				
In aisle between lots 77.5 & 78.5;			A77.5	3
BERNING, Raymond M. - Son	1963	1968	&78.5	
W part of lot is designated "Babies"			78.5	3
LITTLETON, April Jean	one date	3-29-1965	W	
LITTLETON, Marion Franklin	one date	2-13-1966		
GOETZ, Stephen Daniel	3-23-1975	3-24-1975		
WEISBRODT, Pauline Marie - Baby	one date	1968		
YOUNG, Betty Carol	1964	1966		
LOCKWOOD, Clifford [LO]	1907	1957	78.5	3
" ssa , Mildred [LO]	1908	8-25-1985x	E	
LOCKWOOD, Robert Carl - Pfc U.S.Army Korea	12-18-1927	11- 5-1984		
STEPHENSON, ----- [LO]	----	----	79.5W	3
WORKMAN, George C. [LO]	1895	3-10-1978x		
" ssa , Elizabeth A. [LO]	1895	----		
BALDWIN, Martha nee FICHTNER - Mother	1906	1943	80	3
BALDWIN, Eva May	1880	1951		
" ssa , John W. - Spanish American War Vet. [LO 1943]	1879	1951		
_____, ----- My Beanie S.H.	1903	1972		
ILIFF, FLora May	1910	1965		
GILBERT, George - Husband	1898	1975		
" ssa , Estelle (Ida Estelle) Wife	1908	7-21-1985x		
JOHNSON, William A. - Husband [LO]	1-21-1909	4-25-1978	80.5	3
" ssa , Margaret - Wife [LO]	5-23-1916	7-12-1987	NW	
GRIFFIN, Charles [LO]	1901	6- 7-1982x	80.5	3
" ssa , Frances (D.) [LO]	1902	4-15-1983x	5SW	
METZGER, George [LO]	1899	1958	80.5	3
METZGER, Ruth BUTLER [LO]	1901	1957	E	
SCHARDINE, Donald [LO 1934]	----	----	81	3
YAGODICH, ----- [LO]	----	----	81SW	3
YAGODICH, Emery D., Jr. - Son	1930	19--		
YAGODICH, Sally A. - Wife	1908	1964		
YAGODICH, Emery - Husband	1897	1969		
MINGES, Jimmy [LO, E half, transferred from Donald SCHARDINE 1964]	----	----	81E	3
MARTIN, Elwyn Lamont- Ohio Pvt U.S.Marine Corps WW I	6- 2-1894	7- 6-1973	81SE	3
MARTIN, Edna nee HUGHES [LO 1964]	12-22-1900	7-11-1981		

NAME	BD or AGE	DD	Lot	Sec.
WEISBRODT, ----- [LO]	----	----	81N	3
WEISBRODT, Andrew G.-Ohio Tec 5 Medical	8-17-1916	5-17-1964		
Corps WW II-"Married Aug.7,1943"				
" ssa , Dorothy E. - Mom	1924	1985		
DEAN*, Dorothy	----	5- 9-1985*	81NE	3
NEIDHARD, E. J. [LO]	----	----	81.5W	3
BAILEY, Joseph	1885	1963		
" ssa , Mary	1882	1968		
KLENK, ----- [LO]	----	----	81.5E	3
KLENK, Charles	1886	1969		
"ssa , Anna	1890	1957		
HEY, Peter [LO 1888] Civil War Vet. Co.K	10-31-1843	1-17-1912	82W	3
106 Ohio Inf.				
"ssa, Anna M.	9-17-1840	9-25-1930		
HEY, William s/o Peter & A.M.	12-19-1868	11-15-1894		
HEY, Susie d/o Peter & A. M.	5-10-1875	12- 5-1894		
KLEINFELDER, Jacob - Father [LO 1888]	1-28-1817	12- 2-1890		
" ssa , Elizabeth - His Wife - Mother	8-27-1821	4- 6-1898		
SCHUNK, ----- [LO]	----	----	82.5NW	3
KORTE, ----- [LO]	----	----	82.5SW	
WALKER, Andrew [LO]	1890	1967	82.5E	3
"ssa , Gladys	1898	3-26-1986x		
LITTELL, George E. "Sonny"	1929	1957		
HINE, Henry [LO]	----	----	83	3
KNOSE, Wm. [LO 1888]	----	----	84N	3
KNOSE, Nancy A. - Mother D of A mkr	1843	1912	84S	3
KNOSE, Sallie	----	----		
" ssa, Omer	----	3-23-1978x		
TUCKER, Baby	----	----	85	3
TUCKER, Frank B. [LO 1934]	1913	1974		
" ssa , Ruth K. "Married Apr.12, 1935"	1914	1-14-1988x		
MEYER, ---- [LO]	----	----	86NW	3
MEYER, Frederick J. "Rick"	1936	1973		
"ssa , Marilyn L. "Pete"	1940	----		
HEYOB, ----- [LO]	----	----	86SW	3
HEYOB, Robert F. - Tec 5 U.S.Army WW II	1916	3-16-1976x		
MUIRHEAD, Marguerite M. - Mother	1892	1963	86E	3
BECKETT, Chas. [LO]	----	2-18-1989x		
Lots 87-91 are not on cemetery map.				
NEELEY, ----- [LO]	----	----	92NW	3
NEELEY, Norman - Our Son	4- 3-1944	5- 8-1979		
GALLAMORE, George W. - Father [LO]	3- 9-1849x	1905	92E	3
(b. IN; of heart failure; res Hamilton Co. OH; sawyer)				
GALLAMORE, Maria BURNS - Mother	1854	1908		
CADY, Joseph [LO 1879]	----	----	93	3
GIERINGER, Daisy [LO 6-13-19--]	----	----		
GIERINGER, Victor [LO 5-27-1961]	----	----		
KERN, Warren M. - F. & A. M. emb	1909	1961	94	3
KERN, George H. [LO 1933]	1864	1946		
KERN, Florence	1868	1933		
MATLACK, Phoebe J.	1849	1938		
HINE, Alma W. - Wife	1890	1968	95N	3
HINE, Frederick L. - Husband [LO]	1879	1958		
KASHBAUM, ----- [LO]	----	----	95S	3
KASHBAUM, Frank W. - F. & A. M. emb	1869	1953		
KASHBAUM, James A. Ohio Reg Sgt Maj Postal Exp Svc WWI	1890 -	1952		
KASHBAUM, Helen L.	1872	1956		
KASHBAUM, Lillian L.	1907	1954		
ANDREWS, Granville Chidlaw s/o Joseph C.	12- 2-1887	10-10-1889	96	3
& Jennie K.				
ANDREWS, Theresa (Florence) d/o Joseph H.	8-30-1875	2-22-1878		
& Rachel V. (b. U.S.; of brain fever; res Whitewater Twp.)				
HENRIE, Sarah C. A.	----	----		
FRANK, Rachel V.	1869	1928		
FRANK, Joseph M.	1857	1924		
ANDREWS, Samuel H.	1871	1942		
STILES, Inf s/o Phil & Edna	----	7--- 1922		
ANDREWS, Rev. Hugh	10-22-1774	9- 1-1822		
" ssa , Sarah d/o Gen. Johnithan CILLEY	1- 6-1789	10- 7-1862		
a Rev. War Vet.				
" ssa , Joseph H. [LO 1868]	1- 6-1821	10-28-1889		
" ssa , Rachel V. w/o Joseph H.	5-13-1840	11- 5-1892		
" ssa , Harriet d/o H. & S.C.	1-13-1813	2-13-1814		
" ssa , Jonathan s/o H. & S. C.	9-17-1816	8-31-1835		
ssa BARTLETT, Eliza A. w/o Dr. W. H.	9- 3-1813	7-28-1841		
" ssa ANDREWS, Amanda d/o H. & S. C.	11- 4-1818	7-13-1839		
ANDREWS, Joseph C.	1864	1938		
" ssa , Jennie K.	1865	1948		
STEVENS, Mary (E.) ARTHURS	1837(DI-7-24-1881)			
ANDREWS, Arthur Hugh - Husband	6- 2-1886	3- 2-1965		
" ssa , Virginia HORNE - Wife	8- 9-1886	4-25-1972		
PUGH, Cary R.	1859	1933		
PUGH, Sarah C.	1867	1926		
ANDREWS, Joseph, Sr. [LO 1868]	----	----	97	3

NAME	BD or AGE	DD	Lot	Sec.
ANDREWS, Marie	1900	1-30-1977x	97	3
ANDREWS, Joseph, Jr. - Jr Ord emb	1889	1954		
NEIDHARD, Mary E. - OES emb	1873	1947		
_____, ----- Baby	----	----		
NEIDHARD, George J. - F. & A. M. emb	1868	1961		
BACHMAN, Eugene L.	12-10-1928	11-26-1984	97S	3
" ssa , Mabel L.	3- 5-1929	----		
HAMMITT, George W. s/o Wm. S.	7- 4-1864	10-24-1866	98	3
HAMMITT, William [LO 1867]	5- 5-1828	7-27-1888		
" ssa , Hannah (b. America; res Colerain	5- 1-1834	9-15-1905x		
Twp.; d/o Benj. & Nancy LAW)				
" ssa , James	6-10-1869	6-10-1869		
" ssa , Ella M.	3-29-1874	4-16-1877		
ssa HAUSER, Esther E.	1-24-1893	7-25-1893		
ssa HAUSER, David S.	1894	1909		
HAUSER, Jacob	1860	1944		
HAUSER, Margaret H.	1861	1928		
In aisle between lots 98 & 114:	----	----	A98&	3
REAVES, Danny Lee	10-11-1961	8-18-1984	114	
WADSWORTH, John [LO 1925]			98.5	3
_____, ----- Father	1861	1928	NW ¼	
_____, ----- Mother	1867	1924		
WADSWORTH, -----	----	----	SW ¼	
USLEMAN, Edith	----	----	98.5	3
" ssa , Charles	----	----	NE	
SATER, Nellie (b. OH; of diptheria & croup;	4- 2-1871x	11- 5-1872x	99	3
res Crosby Twp.; d/o M.V.B. & Mary E.)				
SATER, Infant (b. Crosby Twp.; of	1-25-1869x	2-21-1869x		
congestive chill; res Hamilton Co. OH; infant of M.V.B. & M.E.)				
SATER, Mattie	1866	1867		
SATER, Dr. P. M.	1869	1921		
SATER, Milton (s/o Martin & Mary E.; b. & res	1875	11-11-1876x		
Crosby Twp. Hamilton Co. OH)				
SATER, Martin V. B. [LO 1867]	1842	1940		
SATER, Mary Ellen	1843	1920		
SATER, Martin [LO 1925]	----	----	99.5	3
BROWN, Daisy S.	1873	1956		
BROWN, Robert S. - Lt. Colonel	1900	1944		
_____, Lowry F.	1867	1935		
_____, Katharine M.	1869	1950		
OYLER, Etta E.	1877	1966		
_____, Dr. Clinton H.	1878	1949		
HILL, Jessie M.	1876	1892	100	3
HILL, Hannah M.	1865	1866		
HILL, Jennie E. w/o J. T.	12-10-1849	6-21-1885		
HILL, Margaret F. w/o J.T.	8-17-1844	11-25-1866		
HILL, Jethro T. [LO 1869]	----	----		
HILL, Harry J.	1891	1892		
HILL, Jessie M.	1893	1893		
HILL, Grace	1871	1908		
HILL, Harry	1871	1955		
In aisle between lots 100 & 112:			A100	3
TOLLE, Lee J. - SP 5 U.S.Army Korea	10- 3-1936	1-26-1984	&112	
ALLEN*, Lula	----	7-16-1984*		
LITTLETON*, Tilford	----	9-13-1984*		
HEDGER*, Charles	----	10-18-1983*		
BEST, Ruth HEUBACH	1900	9-11-1978x	100	3
HEUBACH, Ella - Mother	1869	1939	.5W	
HEUBACH, Val - Dad F. & A. M. emb [LO 1928]	1870	1950		
HEUBACH, Paul W. - 1st Sgt U.S.Army WW II	1914	5-16-1981x		
NOES, Wm. & Ruth - [LOs]			SE 100.5	3
RACE, Henry Francis [LO] Sgt US Army WW II	1922	5- 8-1986x	NE	
" ssa, Lillian B. [LO]	1925	----		
FLOWERS, Lulu	1893	1912	101	3
FLOWERS, Addie	1862	1895		
HAMMITT, Margaret nee SCHREINER D of A emb	1877	1930		
& IOOF - F.L.C. embs				
" ssa , Samuel, Sr. Jr Ord & D of A embs	1870	1950		
HAMMITT, R. C. - D of A mkr [LO 1873]	----	----		
" ssa , Margrette w/o Richard C. 33y8m11d	8-27-1839	5- 8-1873		
GRIES, Sandra Ann	1943	5- 2-1979x		
In aisle between lots 101 & 111:	----	----	A101&	3
LEWIS, Hermetta	----	9- 7-1983x	111	
CAMPBELL, David J. - SP 4 U.S.Army Vietnam	7-28-1950	10-17-1983		
HAUSER, Cassie - No LO listed	1854	1932	101.5	3
HAUSER, John - Civil War Vet.	1846[10-17]	1930		
SCHAFER, Edward	1872	1904	102	3
RAISCH, Estelle CORSON - Sister	1893	1941		
SCHAFER, John - Father [LO]	1839	1926		
" ssa , Eliza - Mother	1844	1926		
" ssa , Edward	1872	1904		
WHITEHEAD, Edith CORSON	1890	1913		
MANTHEY, Elnora M. - Mother	1876	1966	103	3
MILLER, Florence E. [LO 1892]	1868	1951		
MILLER, William E.	1867	1940		

NAME	BD or AGE	DD	Lot	Sec.
MILLER, Matilda J. - Mother	46y 6m22d	11-27-1892	103	3
" ssa , John W. - Father-Civil War Vet.	1844	1899		
ORR, Luvadia M.	1874	1908		
MELIN, Marie	1906	1951		
MELIN, John - D of A mkr	1880	1946		
SAMMONS, Arthur L. - Father	1869	1939		
" ssa , Sophia J. - Mother	1870	1957		
SAMMONS, Calvin L.	1897	1918		
SAMMONS, Ray C.	----	7-26-1896		
SAMMONS, Ralph A.	----	7-11-1896		
SAMMONS, Edith P.	----	5-18-1914		
GIERINGER, Martha	1870	1959	104	3
CASE, Elmira C.	1908	1937		
CASE, Clifford R.	1861	1926		
HAHN, Dorothy M.	1904	1963		
RUNK, Clarence R.-Father F. & A.M. emb	10-28-1897	3-16-1970		
Ohio Sgt U.S.Army WW I - American Legion mkr				
"ssa, Ruth A. - Mother	6-11-1900	6-11-1985		
RUNK, Stacy B. [LO 1909]	1866	1936		
"ssa, Pearl I.	1874	1909		
SHEPPARD, Chester R. - U.S. Inf WW I Vet.	1893 [6-2]	1925	105	3
SCUDDER, Mary E. McALISTER w/o Wm. F.	7-18-1853	3-17-1893		
" ssa , Wm. F.	3-16-1837	10- 2-1912		
ssa , McALISTER, James [LO 1892]	1-17-1823	4-12-1902		
ssa , McALISTER, Elizabeth	1-19-1825	8-28-1897		
SHEPPARD, Charles E. - Father	1861	1943		
" ssa , Margaret A. - Mother	1860	1946		
HAMMITT, Katherine - Mother	1858	1939	106	3
" ssa , John W. - Father - Jr Ord emb [LO 1893]	1857	1913		
HAMMITT*, Infant bur pos W1	----	----		
"In Memory of Isaac WRIGHT & Family"			107	3
WRIGHT, Isaac - 57 Reg Co. B Civil War Vet. [LO 1891]		----		
YANSEY+, Elizabeth bur pos W1	----	----		
CRAIG+, Ida bur pos E7	----	----		
WRIGHT+, ---- bur pos E8 (Isaac?)	----	----		
HAMFT, Dorothea	1818	1889	108	3
HAMFT, John - Father [LO 1889]	1847	1930		
HAMFT, Harriet - Mother	1857	1939		
HART, W. (Washington) D. [LO 1897]	----	----	109	3
HART, Anna - Mother	1830	1908		
HART, Mathies - Father	1829	1897		
CAMPBELL, Jeanetta E.	4-14-1847	3-22-1897	110	3
" ssa , George P. [LO 1897]	6- 1-1837	2- 2-1915		
CAMPBELL, Margaret - Mother	1869	1921		
CAMPBELL, James - Father	1867	1940		
STOREY, Louise	1870	1942		
McHENRY, Van [LO 1871]	----	----	111SW	3
McHENRY+, Abbie bur pos W3	----	----		
McHENRY+, Van's child - bur pos W3	----	----		
McHENRY+, Van's child bur pos W4	----	----		
LAWYER, Raymond S. s/o Wm. & Nancy	1886	1929	111E	3
LAWYER, Edmund J. s/o Wm. & Sarah - F. & A.M. emb	1902	1954	&NW	
LAWYER, Bernadine L. nee TOWNSEND	1905	12- ?-1987x		
LAWYER, William S. - F. & A.M. emb [LO 10-3-1887]	1855	1925		
LAWYER, Nancy E. w/o William S.	10-29-1855	9-29-1887		
LAWYER, Sarah C.	1865	1941		
LAWYER, Sidney	1893	1915		
in aisle between lots 111 & 118:			A111	3
STAMPER, Elizabeth (VOELKER)	3- 4-1916	12-11-1982	&118	
ROWE, Linda Jean	1-10-1950	11- 7-1982		
INGERSOLL, John [LO 1871]	----	----	112	3
INGERSOLL+, Betsey bur pos W1	----	----	NE	
INGERSOLL+, Elsie bur pos W2	----	----		
CAMPTON, Paul W. [LO]	1913	4-30-1984x		
"ssa , Agnes L. [LO]	1911	----		
In aisle between lots 112 & 117:			A112	3
RADER, Alma	1- 2-1910	5- 1-1986	&117	
RADER, Clayton	12-21-1910	2-28-1983		
REEVES, Reene (cowboy scene on stone)	1932	1-25-1988x	113	3
GAULT, James [LO] (b. 1-6-1839 America;	35y 8m 23d	9-29-1874		
of inflammation; res Miamitown, OH; s/o Samuel & Elizabeth)				
RISDON, Thomas C. - Father- F. & A.M. emb	1931	----		
" ssa Ruth K. - Mother	1921	10- 6-1987x		
RUDISELL, Herbert R. (Rae)	2-17-1929	1-12-1988		
" ssa , Dorothy V. MECHTENSIMER	2-21-1924	----		
In aisle between lots 113 & 116:			A113	3
OSBORNE, LOvie R. - Mother	1900	4- 6-1983	&116	
WININGS, Sarah A. [LO 1867]			114	3
DAVIS, Henry C. - Co. K 6 Ohio Inf-Civil War Vet.	----	[12- 2-1913]		
FETHERLIN, Mary	5-15-1833	2- 2-1913		
ssa , DAVIS, Matilda [LO 11-10-1913]	2-28-1851	5- 9-1932		
ssa , WININGS, Matilda - Mother	In 64th yr.	7-22-1867		
(b. 1803 VA; of cholera; res Miami Twp.; d/o John & Mary PRICETT				

NAME	BD or AGE	DD	Lot	Sec.
In aisle between lots 114 & 115:			A114	3
BRUESHABER, Ernest L. Pfc U.S.Army WW II	1-13-1918	5-20-1983	&115	
HEDGER, Marion F., Jr. Pfc U.S.Army WW II	8- 8-1922	5- 5-1983		
ROHR, Johannes [LO 1868]	4-27-1810	6-26-1871	115	3
ROHR*, Catherina (b. & res Hamilton Co. OH;	7-19-1854*	7- 8-1868*		
of flux; d/o John & C. Veronika)				
In aisle between lots 115 & 127:			A115	3
SCHULTE, Robert C. - Husband - Cpl U.S.Army	12-16-1929	5- 6-1982	&127	
BROXTERMAN, Richard E. - U.S.Army	12-17-1927	1-13-1982		
COLUMBIA, Chas. [LO 1870]			116	3
COLUMBIA*+, Child bur pos W1 (Ann Laurie,	12-10-1868*	1-30-18??*		
b. & res Whitewater Twp.; of inflammation of brain, d/o Chas. & Emma COLUMBIA)[year of d. not recorded, could be from 1869-1871]				
LAW, FLora L.	1874	1913		
In aisle between lots 116 & 127:			A116	3
MARTIN, Viola	one date	5-16-1980x	&127	
LAMBING, Glenn J. - Son & Brother &	1955	1-15-1980x		
emb:"a wheel with wings"				
____, ----- (illegible) Brother	----	----	117	3
ADAMS, William - Our Father [LO 1870]	64y 11d	3-21-1875		
(b. Germany 3-10-1811; of dropsy; res Taylors Creek, Green Twp.; s/o S.R. & Josephine(				
WHITLOCK*+, Nancy bur pos W4 (b. Fredericks-	2-14-1798*	9-24-1879*		
burg, VA; of dropsy; res near Cleves, OH)				
ADAMS, Mary B. d/o W. & E.	10- 8-1872	4- 3-1891		
ADAMS, Jacob s/o W. & E.	7- 4-1870	4-27-1893		
In aisle between lots 117 & 126:			A117	3
LAMBING, John J.- Father-Cremains	1- 3-1919	12-17-1986	&126	
SMITH, Rev. Logan	1911	5-14-1980x		
SILVER, James T. [LO 1873]	12- 7-1807	12-21-1873	118	3
DUNN, Cleves Silver s/o J.W. & L.A.	4m 4d	4- 4-1877		
(b.11-30-1876 Hamilton Co. OH; of brain fever; res Dent, OH; s/o Lizzie & J.W.)				
STRUBLE, R. [LO]	----	----	119	3
PITTMAN, William G. - Father; F. & A.M. emb	1894	1951		
STRONG, John L., Jr.	1896	1953		
BAILEY, Nellie - Mother	1847	1926		
" ssa , Byron - Father - [LO] Co. A 83 Ohio Inf-Civil War Vet.	1846	1908		
BAILEY, James B.	1883	1958		
BAILEY, George	1877	1967		
PRAGER, Laura C. - Mother	1880	1968		
PRAGER, William - Father	1879	1917		
SCHARDINE, Catherine M.	1877	1906	121	3
SCHARDINE, Louise	1856	1944		
SCHARDINE, Fred [LO 1906]	1843	1925		
SCHARDINE, William	8-11-1872	9-22-1937		
" ssa , Elizabeth	6- 3-1886	2- 7-1972		
SCHARDINE, John V.	1880	1952		
" ssa , Tensia	1887	1971		
HORSLEY, Leo [LO 1906]	----	----	122	3
HORSLEY, Mattie May	----	----		
HORSLEY, Jefferson L.	1862	1916		
HORSLEY, Susie E.	1869	1918		
DEAN, Andrew J. - WW I Vet.	1886	1966	123A	3
DEAN, William H.	1922	1930		
DEAN, Edward - Father [LO]	1848	1920		
DEAN, Jennettie - Mother	1850	1929		
STATEN, Bessie B.	1883	19--		
ADAMS, William - Civil War Vet. [LO 1905]	1840[3- 6]	1922	123	3
" ssa, Esther Jane - His Wife	1845	1928		
ADAMS, John H. - Spanish American War Vet.	2-28-1868	2- 2-1920		
TOPH, FLora C. d/o J. & E. 8y6m8d	3-19-1874	9-27-1882	124	3
TOPH, Eliza S.	1846	1926		
"ssa, John W. [LO 1882]	1837	1928		
TOPH, Ettie M.	1870	1937		
NEEL, John J.	1910	1962		
"ssa, Rev. William G.	1889	1958		
"ssa, Nora TOPH	1884	1961		
KLEINFELDER, John [LO 1877]			125	3
SMITH, Clyde L. - Father - 32nd F. & A.M. emb	1892	1953		
KLEINFELDER, Martha w/o John (d. of	3-11-1855	2-18-1877		
typhoid fever; res Venice, OH)				
FAGALY, Jessie - Mother - D of A emb[LO 9-24-1923]	1873	1948		
FAGALY, John - Father - Jr Ord emb	1870	1961		
JONES, Charlotte [LO 1905]			126W	3
JONES, Lester	1826	1873		
"ssa", Martha (b. Colerain Twp.; of	11-30-1855x	8- 8-1877x		
phthisis; res College Hill, OH; d/o S? or J? L. & Charlotte)				
HETTEL, George	1894	1920	126E	3
" ssa , Lydia [LO 1921]	1888	1978		
HETTEL, Florence	----	7-24-1978x		
____, Louisa M.	----	----	127	3

NAME	BD or AGE	DD	Lot	Sec.
____, Benj. A.	----	----	127	3
NEIDHARD, Edward J. - F. & A.M. emb	1875	1960		
NEIDHARD, Catherine E.	1877	1960		
____, Elizabeth	----	----		
____, Elmer Markland	one date	1892		
NEIDHARD, Cheryl Lynn	9-30-1945	10- 1-1945		
NEIDHARD, William	1852	1942		
NEIDHARD, Charles	1859	1949		
NEIDHARD, Christina	1859	1940		
NEIDHARD, Andrew [LO 1875]	1832	1918		
NEIDHARD, Mary	1831	1909		
NEIDHARD, Raymond G.	1902	1954		
NEIDHARD, Naomi	1907	1932		
ALTHAUS, Frederick - Father [LO 1879]	1831	1887	128	3
" ssa , Verena - Mother	1828	1901		
ALTHAUS, Albert	1860	1914		
ALTHAUS, Catherine	1859	1945		
DUGAN+, Mrs. ----- bur pos W1	----	----		
ALTHAUS*+, Frederic A. bur pos E5	1-23-1877*	4-13-1879*		
(b. Hamilton Co. OH; of scarletina; res Taylors Creek, Hamilton Co. OH; s/o Frederic, Jr. & Christena)				
ALTHAUS*, John (b. & res Taylor's Creek, Hamilton Co. OH; of Brain fever; s/o Albert & Catherine)	11-20-1880*	4-15-1881*		
LOCKWOOD, Fredrick [LO 1934]	1881	1960	129	3
" ssa , Emma	1886	1966		
LOCKWOOD, Virginia Claire	one date	11-19-1939		
MINGES, ----- "Babies" [LO]			130A	3
MARTIN, H., Jr.	----	----	NW	
BREEDEN, ----- [LO]	----	----	130A	3
MYERS, John - Baby	one date	1965	SW	
ELLIS, Jeffrey Scott	6-13-1964	9-13-1964		
HAYNES, ----- [LO]	----	----	130A	3
HAYNES, Henry A.	2-11-1906	11-27-1960	E	
KAPPES, Bessie B. [no LO listed]	7- 7-1889	8-30-1976	130W	3
EICKBUSCH, Albert G. - Father- Cremains	1894	1982		
" ssa , Nellie E. - Mother	1894	1960		
SMITH, ----- [LO]	----	----	130SE	3
SMITH, Mildred - Wife	1901	1960		
BICKERS, ----- [LO]	----	----	130NE	3
BICKERS, Richard L. - Ohio Pvt Btry A 5 FA Regt WW I Vet.	10-22-1898	9-16-1969		
SCHUESLER, ----- [LO]			131W	3
SCHUESLER, Nick	1881	1964		
" ssa , Barbara	1880	1962		
BRUG, Henry	1879	1966		
"ssa, Irene W.	1891	1966		
GEORGE, ----- [LO]			131SE	3
GEORGE, Harry P.	1889	1966		
" ssa , Anna L.	1894	10-10-1986x		
GLAUSER,----- [LO]			131	3
GLAUSER, Viola B. (Barbara) nee FEITH;w/o John	5- 5-1904	12-14-1986		
GLAUSER, John, Sr. - American Legion mkr Ohio Pvt 10 Co. 3 Training Bn WW I Vet.	5- 5-1895	2-12-1966		
Lots 132-144 are not on cemetery map.				
APPLEGATE,----- [LO]			145W	3
SCHROTH, Horace P. "Jack"	1899	1965		
HOERST, Gilbert A. - Son	1950	1968	145E	3
BUCK, Lewis, Jr.	1881	1968		
GEERS, Harry A.	1890	1962		
Lot 146 & 147 are not on cemetery map.				
MERRILL, ----- [LO]			148W	3
BALASH, Charlotte M.	1920	1975		
ssa , SCHLEMMER, Irene M.	1917	6- 7-1981x		
MERRILL, Leslie C. - Father	1894	1961		
" ssa , Bertha - Mother	1897	1- 4-1984x		
KOPP, ----- [LO]			148SE	3
KOPP, Jonas - Father	7-25-1898	1-27-1961		
RUTZ, ----- [LO]			148NE	3
RUTZ, Agnes H. - Mother	1893	9-21-1984x		
BARNES, Freeman E. [LO]	1911	7- 5-1983x	149	3
" ssa , Edith M. [LO]	1910	----		
SHANKS, Roy G. [LO]	1903	1974	150	3
" ssa , R. Rae	1902	----		
McNEELY, Rae - Our Baby - Fred & Margaret	3- 2-1957	9-24-1960		
SCHARDINE,----- [LO]			151W	3
SCHARDINE, Ben	9- 5-1894	6-16-1967		
WHITNEY & MYERS [LO]			151E	3
WHITNEY, Moses - Father	1886	1960		
" ssa , Blanche - Mother- Cremains	1887	5-15-1981x		
MYERS, Bruce David - Husband	1877	1960		
"ssa , Katherine - Wife	1889	1962		
MINGES, Billy - Boy Scouts - Troop 118	1923	1937	152	3
MINGES, Mae - Mother	1888	1958		
MINGES, Theodore, M.D. - OES emb	1889	1972		

NAME	BD or AGE	DD	Lot	Sec.
MINGES, Virginia M.	1904	10- 6-1977x	152	3
MINGES, Ellanora - Mother OES emb	1887	1972		
[Between Ellanora's & Michael's stones is a mkr: "Knights of Pythias Mill Ohio 634"]				
MINGES, Michael - Daddy F. & A.M. emb	1886	1923		
MINGES, Joseph - F. & A.M. emb	1879	1971		
MINGES, John - Father F. & A.M. emb [LO 1899]	1838	1923		
MINGES, Rosa - Mother	1845	1899		
MINGES, John [LO 1882]			153	3
WEBER, Mary	one date	1889		
WEBER, Mary	one date	1894		
WEBER, Raymond	1897	1898		
MINGES+, B----(illegible) bur pos E8	----	----		
BUNNELL, Daniel [LO 1875]	----	----	154N	3
" ssa . Elizabeth	----	----		
BUNNELL, Isaac N.	1858	1936		
CONRAD, Edw. [LO]	----	----	154S	3
RICE, Elizabeth M. nee GILLEY [LO 1878]	1826	1912	155W	3
RICE, Uriah (b. Granville, VT; of disease of heart; res Whitewater Twp.)	4-18-1808x	4-16-1878x	&SE	
RICE, Ben G. [LO 2-14-18--]	1852	1930		
RICE, Sue V. nee SIMMONDS	1858	1902		
RICE, Ben H. - d. in Service WW I Vet.	1892[4-22]	1919		
RICE, Edna S.	1882	1882		
RICE, Goodeno	1857	1860		
GERWE, Charles W. [LO] Pfc U.S.Army WW II	1-11-1915	1-29-1980	155NE	3
"ssa , Thelma J.	1919	----		
SIMPSON, Samuel R.	1915	11-12-1984x		
" ssa , Mae	1917	11- 5-1985x		
BACON, Denn [LO 1885]	78y---14d	2-11-1888	156	3
BACON, Denn - Father	1852	1929		
BACON, Kate - Mother	1854	1945		
BACON, May	1876	1885		
BACON, Oscar E. - Husband	1887	1973		
"ssa , Alpha M. - Wife	1885	1973		
ADAMS, Archibald [LO 1884]			157	3
KNOSE, Benton [LO 4-24-1909]				
CREGAR, Harry [LO 4-2-1911]				
KNOSE, Jacob E.	1872	1947		
"ssa , Florence STRIMPLE - His Wife	1875	1937		
STRIMPLE, T. (Tobias) [LO, NE ¼, 9-11-1923]	1847	1926		
BACHMAN, Louis F.	1897	1960	NE¼	
" ssa , Leona M.	1901	----		
CREGAR, Emma	1891	1960	157S	3
CREGAR, Louise	1875	1959		
CREGAR, Harry [LO, S½, 4-2-1911]	1869	1926		
GAINS, Wm. & Mary [LOs 1886]			158	3
FLOWERS, Caroline	1906	1909	158A	3
FLOWERS, Victor - Father [LO 1909]	1882	1968	N	
" ssa , Elizabeth - Mother	1884	1969		
NEIDHARD, E. J. [LO 1-1-1934]			158A	3
JUNKERT, Philip - Ohio Cpl Co.B 1 Repl Regt Engrs WW I Vet.	6- 4-1890	12- 7-1963	S	
" ssa , Jessie - VFW Ladies Aux emb	1884	1935		
LISTERMAN, Henry C. - Father	1876	1950		
" ssa , Emma M. - Mother	1884	1935		
SMITH, Ruth	1918	1935		
CADY, Naham	1855	1934		
"ssa, Catherine	1860	1937		
WRIGHT, A. [LO]			158B	3
WAKEFIELD, Anne	1898	1947	159A	3
ROESSLER, Paul [LO 1907]	1874	1970		
" ssa , Alice	1875	1960		
MENNINGER, Albert J. - Ohio Cpl 330 Inf WW I	9-11-1895	9-15-1967		
HAYES, H. Jarvis	1886	1976		
" ssa, Edna R.	1897	4-11-1979x		
LEUGERS, Annie E.	1869	1950		
SMITH, Anthony - Co. D 83 Ohio Inf-Civil War Vet.	1843	1913		
WISSEL, Frederick J. - Husband	1883	1926	159B	3
WISSEL, Emma L. LOCKWOOD [LO 1908]	1879	1952		
LOCKWOOD, James M. - Father	1873	1908		
LOCKWOOD, Lee O.	1895	1933		
" ssa , Lulu I.	1894	19--		
LOCKWOOD, James M. - Father [LO 1908]	1851	1928		
" ssa , Margaret - His Wife - Mother	1854	1916		
LOCKWOOD, Lulu	one date	1917		
Lots 160-165 are not on cemetery map:				
BEST, ----- [LO]			166	3
BEST, Charles F.	35y	11-30-1887		
MAXFIELD, Ralph W. - Husband [LO 1939]	1881	1949	167	3
" ssa , Henrietta - Wife	1876	19--		
BURRIS, Wm. [LO 1911]			168	3
SCHUBERT, Alma [LO 1927]			168.5	3

NAME	BD or AGE	DD	Lot	Sec.
OTTO, Joseph D. - Husband - WW I Vet.	1897	[9-2] 1933	168.5	3
KING, Edna OTTO [LO 9-10-1933]	1898	1967		
SCHUBERT, Elsie - Mother	1903	1926		
AUBLE?, James H. [LO 1911]			169	3
NEIDHARD, E. J. [LO 1931]				
GREINER, John - Co.F 138 Ohio Inf Civil War Vet. [LO 1904]	1832 [3-11]	1908	170	3
" ssa , Rosa	1835	1915		
WALKER, Henry	2-27-1837	10- 3-1902	171	3
" ssa , Barbara [LO 1902]	3-17-1844	5- 3-1930		
SCHUBERT, Ella - Mother	1874	1910	172W	3
SCHUBERT, N. (Nicholas) J. - Father [LO1902]	1873	1921	&NE	
SCHUBERT, Elmer A. - Husband - F. & A.M. emb	1900	----		
SCHUBERT, Katherine L. - Wife - OES emb	1902	5- 8-1983x		
No LO listed			172SE	3
NEIERT, John - Father [LO]	1824	1898	173	3
" ssa , Margaret - Mother	1827	1908		
NEIERT, Louisa	12-29-1861	11-10-1956		
NEIERT, John	1885	1975		
CONRAD, Edward [LO 1900]			174	3
BECKETT, Lillian N.	1911	1969	175	3
NOES, Lillie May	1880	1947		
"ssa, Andrew J. [LO 1934]	1862	1936		
BACHMAN, John [LO 1900]			176	3
BACHMAN, Peter - Father - Anchor emb	4-14-1828	6-21-1900		
REISINGER, Lulu	1886	1902	177	3
REISINGER, Anna E. - Mother	1849	1916		
REISINGER, Jacob - Father [LO 1902]	1846	1930		
REISINGER, Linc.	1879	1959		
REISINGER, Emma	1887	1973		
APPLEGATE, Jennie - Mother	1868	1949	178	3
" ssa , Sherman - Father [LO]	1866	1950		
APPLEGATE, Orman M. - Jr ord UAM 129 emb	1894	1943		
APPLEGATE, Alma BUTKE	1898	1920		
CORSON, William H.	1874	1952	179	3
DAVIS, Dollie M. [LO]	1872	1953		
LOESCH, Carrie E. nee CORSON - Wife	1-26-1881	8-28-1964		
LOESCH, John, Jr. - Ohio Pvt 2 Bn FA Regt WW I Vet.	8- 1-1889	12-27-1958		
FLOWERS, Mamie Klots [LO 10-22-1935]			180	3
FLOWERS, Louisa KLOTS - Mother [LO 1901]	1862	1936		
HUGHES, Clarence J. - Ohio Pfc Btry K 19 Coast Arty WW II Vet.	7-15-1907	9- 6-1953		
WOLFRAM, Edward L.	1898	1953		
WOLFRAM, Anna L.	1889	3-18-1976x		
McCREADIE, Edward	1881	1940	181	3
McCREADIE, Rachel R. [LO 1903]	1851	1929		
McCREADIE, Andrew - Co.F 138 Inf Ohio-Civil War Vet.	1840	1903		
McCREADIE, Howard - Dad	1883	1944		
HONEGGER, Carl	1882	1948		
" ssa , Daisy	1876	1970		
KLEINFELDER, Albert J. - Father	1853	1903		
" ssa , Anna M. - Mother [LO 1903]	1858	1935		
NEUFARTH, Henry	1878	1956		
NEUFARTH, Ella	1891	11- 6-1980x		
CROUSE, Annie [LO 1903]	----	----	183	3
CROUSE, Mabel	1887	1903		
CROUSE, Jacob	1855	1907		
GROLL, Edith	10-21-1897	12-13-1975	184	3
____, Earl	4-18-1902	3-24-1904		
____, Raymond	6-25-1900	1- 8-1902		
HETISIMER, William [LO 1902]	7- 6-1871	1-18-1956		
" ssa , Mary	12- 9-1876	2- 7-1956		
Lots 185-198 are not on cemetery map.				
HAYS, Dr. Harmon H., Sr.	1856	1945	19or199	3
WRIGHT, Alma [LO 1909]	----	----	199	3
FLINCHPAUGH, ----- [LO]	----	----	199N	3
FLINCHPAUGH*, Evelyn	----	11-25-1983*		
BATES, ----- [LO]	----	----	199S	3
AYERS, Charles Edward	1874	1945		
REECE, Joe K. (KERR)	1893	5-29-1977x		
PHELPS, ----- [LO]	----	----	200NW	3
PHELPS, Robert	1890	1971		
"ssa , Nellie	1904	4-11-1977x		
RISSE, ----- [LO]	----	----	200SW	3
RISSE, Manuel W.	1909	1971		
" ssa, Helen L.	1917	11-17-1982x		
LITTELL, ----- [LO]	----	----	200E	3
LITTELL, John F.	1914	11-23-1982x		
" ssa , M. Elizabeth	1916	1971		
LINNEMAN, James E.	12-11-1956	11- 4-1972		
LINNEMAN, Ronald M.	10-20-1961	9-10-1983		
WEITZ, ----- [LO]	----	----	201	3

NAME	BD or AGE	DD	Lot	Sec.
PURVIS, Claude Allen - Ohio Cpl 186 QM CoWW2	10-12-1917	6-21-1971	202	3
PURVIS, ----- [LO]	----	----	202	3
PURVIS, Garry A. - Son	2-22-1950	9- 9-1971		
[No lot owner listed]			203	3
GABBARD, Claude	1901	8- 2-1978x		
GABBARD, Hilda	1910	----		
There are two lots numbered 204 on cemetery map; one located in NW area of Sec. 3 between lots 166 & 210 and the other is located in SW area of Sec. 3 between lots 85 & 86.				
[No lot owner listed, north lot between 166 & 210]			N204	3
KRAMER, Casper	1903	12-17-1983x		
" ssa , Viola K.	1902	----		
FRANK, ----- [LO, NW ¼, south lot 204]	----	----	S204	3
FRANK, Beatrice	1901	1973	NW	
FRANK, Bernard	1894	1974		
ILIFF, ----- [LO, SW ¼, south lot 204]			S204	3
SHELDON, Benjamin	1901	1973	SW	
" ssa . Eva A.	1901	4-23-1984x		
ROSS, ----- [LO, SE ¼, south lot 204	----	----	S204	3
ROSS, Cleat C. (Chatus)	1909	5- 9-1977x	SE	
MYERS, ----- [LO, NE ¼, south lot 204	----	----	S204	3
MYERS, Harry	1908	1973	NE	
"ssa , Hazel	1906	1-31-1979x		
"ssa , Inez	1928	----		
ROESSLER, ----- [LO]	----	----	205NW	3
ROESSLER, Arthur E.	1908	5-22-1987x		
" ssa , Alice C.	1911	1973		
ROESSLER, Tina Renee [bur at foot of grd mother]one date		7-24-1978		
HENSLEY, ----- [LO]	----	----	205NW	3
HENSLEY, Lester (John Lester)	11-18-1896	10-26-1978		
HENSLEY, Verona	3-28-1908	10-18-1983		
TAYLOR, ----- [LO]	----	----	205SE	3
TAYLOR, Sylvester	1910	1973		
" ssa , Loretta	1916	6-28-1988x		
INSPRUCKER, ----- [LO]	----	----	205NE	3
INSPRUCKER, Clarence - Father	1902	11-30-1981x		
" ssa . Anna Marie - Mother	1910	1973		
MENNINGER, ----- [LO]	----	----	206NW	3
MENNINGER, Geraldine B. - Mother	1931	1972		
JACOBS, ----- [LO]	----	----	206SW	3
LEWIS, ----- [LO]	----	----	206SE	3
LEWIS, Roscoe N.	1896	1974		
" ssa, Elizabeth V.	1902	1972		
SCHAUMLOEPPEL, ----- [LO]	----	----	206NE	3
FLICK, ----- [LO]	----	----	207W	3
FEMRITE, ----- [LO, SE, single burial]	----	----	207SE	3
FEMRITE, Margaret V. nee MILTON - Mother	1918	1973		
MURPHY, ----- [LO,NE part]	----	----	207NE	3
MURPHY, Dennis M.	9-14-1955	8-27-1972		
EVANS, ----- [LO]	----	----	208NW	3
EVANS, William H. - Father -"Married June 22,1957"	1931	1972		
"ssa , Rosemary E. - Mother	1932	1972		
SEILER, ----- [LO]	----	----	208SW	3
TUCKER, ----- [LO]	----	----	208E	3
SNEED, ----- [LO]	----	----	209W	3
SNEED, William C. - Father	1927	1972		
SHARP, ----- [LO]	----	----	209SE	3
SHARP, James F. - Father	1944	1972		
BIEHLE, ----- [LO]	----	----	209NE	3
BIEHLE, Edward J. - Father	1908	1971		
COFFIN, ----- [LO]	----	----	210NW	3
COFFIN, Clinton O. (Otto) - Husband	1903	7-13-1978x		
" ssa , Sarah A. - Wife	1901	3-26-1985x		
FUGATE, ----- [LO]	----	----	210SW	3
TUCKER*, Rosie (SW corner of lot)	----	3-13-1979		
MEYER, ----- [LO]	----	----	210SW	3
SANDMAN, ----- [LO]	----	----	210NE	3
SANDMAN, Chester	1904	1971		
" ssa , Hazel	1905	----		
KLENK, ----- [LO]	----	----	211NW	3
KLENK, Charles - Husband	1925	3- 8-1977x		
" ssa, Eva - Wife	1915	1974		
SPIVEY, ----- [LO]	----	----	211SW	3
SPIVEY, Lorell M.	1916	11-19-1980x		
SPIVEY, Louis B. - Pvt U.S.Army WW II Vet.	5- 6-1912	3-26-1974		
BERNING, ----- [LO]	----	----	211SE	3
BERNING, Henry W.	1907	1973		
" ssa , Jeanne E.	1912	----		
WEAVER, ----- [LO]	----	----	211NE	3
WEAVER, Harold H. - Husband	1909	----		
" ssa , Hilda L. - Wife	1912	----		
JAWORSKI, ----- [LO]	----	----	212W	3
JAWORSKI, Donald J. - MSG U.S.Army	10-31-1920	9- 9-1974		

NAME	BD or AE	DD	Lot	Sec.
JAWORSKI, Ethel M. (On same stone as Donald)	1914	11-8 -1976x	212W	3
" ssa , Kenneth A.	1954	----		
BENTEL, W. [LO]	----	----	212E	3
BENTEL, Howard J.	1910	1974		
" ssa , Iva	1917	----		
POWERS, ----- [LO]	----	----	213NW	3
POWERS, James C. - U.S. Air force	8-17-1935	8-16-1974		
THREM, ----- [LO]	----	----	213SW	3
TAYLOR, Anna M. MINNICH THREM _ Mother	1907	7-10-1981x		
SAMMONS, ----- [LO]	----	----	213SE	3
SAMMONS, Lyle	1905	1974		
" ssa , Marie	1902	19--		
STEWART, ----- [LO]	----	----	213NE	3
STEWART, Charles C. - Pvt. U.S.Army	12- 5-1889	7- 4-1974		
STEWART*, Dorothy	----	5- 8-1979*		
SAMMONS, ----- [LO]	----	----	214NW	3
SAMMONS, Henry C.	1902	1975		
" ssa , Vera A.	1908	1974		
BRENNER, ----- [LO]	----	----	214SW	3
MORGAN, ----- [LO]	----	----	214E	3
FRONDORF, ----- [LO]	----	----	215W	3
MURRAY, ----- [LO]	----	----	215E	3
MURRAY, Barbara Jean - Wife & Mother	9-23-1950	10-11-1974		
SCHULER, ----- [LO]	----	----	216NW	3
SCHULER, Tucker E.	3-12-1904	9-15-1983x		
" ssa , Viola M.	3-31-1910	6-29-1976		
FELIX, ----- [LO]	----	----	216SW	3
FELIX, Everett L. - Pop	1922	----		
"ssa , Rosella A. - Mom	1920	1975		
BALDWIN, ----- [LO, single burial]	----	----	216SE	3
BALDWIN, John W. - Pvt. U.S.Army	3-14-1929	6- 2-1974		
SULLIVAN, ----- [LO]	----	----	216E	3
SULLIVAN, Thomas I. "Married May 16, 1942"	1920	----		
" ssa , Margaret H.	1921	1974		
MURPHY, ----- [LO]	----	----	216NE	3
FRANK, ----- [LO]	----	----	217NW	3
FRANK*, Carl A.	----	9-18-1876*		
SCHULER, ----- [LO]	----	----	217SW	3
DOYLE, ----- [LO]	----	----	217E	3
DOYLE, Augustine C. - Husband	1907	4-18-1986x		
" ssa, Rose K. nee GUETHLEIN - Wife	1911	1975		
ADAMS, Earl [LO?]	1906	1-15-1977x	218A	3
BROMWELL, ----- [LO]	----	----	218W	3
BROMWELL, Orville J.	1895	10-16-1976x		
" ssa , Ura R.	1901	3-21-1988x		
SPIVEY, ----- [LO]	----	----	218SE	3
WEBER, ----- [LO]	----	----	218NE	3
WEBER, Earl E.	1913	8-30-1977x		
WEBER, Catheryn K.	1911	1959		
Lot 219 is not on cemetery map.				
TIERNEY, ----- [LO]	----	----	220NW	3
TIERNEY, Edward	1908	10- 8-1987x		
BROXTERMAN, William M.	1897	2- 1-1976x		
" ssa , Elizabeth H.	1907	----		
FAGALY, -----, Jr. [LO]	----	----	220SE	3
FAGALY*, Darlene	----	1-19-1976*		
FAGALY, ----- [LO]	----	----	220NE	3
FAGALY*, Mildred	----	1-18-1976*		
FAGALY*, Harold, Sr.	----	12-11-1980*		
TYGRETT, ----- [LO]			221NW	3
TYGRETT, James Harold - F. & A.M. emb - Husband,	1918	1975		
Father, Businessman, Sportsman, Human Being-Presented As An Unfeigned Tribute By The Family, Mar. 11, 1967				
" ssa , Marjorie E.	1919	----		
ZEEK, ----- [LO]	----	----	221SW	3
ZEEK, Robert M. - Husband	1914	1975		
DRUMMOND, ----- [?LO, SE ¼]	----	----	221SE	3
ANDREWS, G. & J. [?LO, NE ¼]	----	----	221NE	3
BURGESS, ----- [LO]			222	3
BURGESS, Floyd R. _ A 1/Cl U.S.Air Force	11-13-1921	9- 7-1976		
WW II - Korea				
HAYNES, Delton A. [LO N. third]	4-15-1908	9-17-1985	223N	3
" ssa , Margaret nee MURPHY	10-10-1906	----		
WELSH, Betty [LO center third]	----	----	223C	3
WELSH, James S. - F. & A.M. emb	1934	11- 4-1981x		
WOOD, Ralph [LO S. third]	1911	----	223S	3
"ssa, Nola	1927	7- 8-1982x		
SUNDERMAN, August J.	1906	7-29-1981x	224N	3
" ssa , Edith H. [LO N. part]	1914	----		
SCHALK, William - Dad	1905	11- 7-1980x	224S	3
" ssa , Hazel - Mom	1907	7-11-1981x		

NAME	BD or AGE	DD	Lot	Sec.
The following lot is reserved for veterans & has no number on map:				
KEETHLER, Charles - Ohio Sl USNR WW II	1910	1959	Vets	3
ROWE, Roscoe - Ohio Pfc Co C 264 Inf	12-12-1925	1-24-1960		
66 Inf Div WW II BSM-PH				
LEWIS, Arthur B. - Ohio Cpl Sup Co.	1-12-1889	12-25-1960		
41 Infantry WW I				
OSBORNE, James E. - Ohio Pvt U.S.Army	7- 1-1930	3- 9-1963		
HENRY, Roy A. - Ohio Pvt U.S.Army WW II	4- 7-1908	1-21-1964		
Am Vets WW II mkr				
TUCKER, Raymond L. - Ohio Pvt HQ Co 7	12- 4-1901	6- 7-1964		
Infantry WW I				
RUTZ, Herschel L. - Ohio Pfc Co C 44 TK	5-14-1933	4-29-1966		
Bn Disabled American Vet. mkr				

SOUTH SECTION

NAME	BD or AGE	DD	Lot	Sec.
PIERSON, David A., Sr. (77y 7m25d)	3-18-1835	11-13-1912	1	S
PIERSON, David A., Jr. (28y 4m20d)	8-30-1885	1-19-1914		
POWELL, Laura E. nee PIERSON (27y5m15d)[LO]	1-29-1890	7-14-1917		
DAVIS, C. M. [LO]	----	----	1NE	S
BAUER, Lottie [LO 1917]	----	----	2	S
BAUER, W. J.	1871	1917		
BLACK, Leonard C. - Ohio Cpl Co A 148 Inf WWI-PH	4-18-1895	1-9-1957		
MARKLAND, Flowers D.	1892	1966	3W	S
MARKLAND, Faye OYLER	1894	1962		
MARKLAND, Mintie FLOWERS	1858	1933		
MARKLAND, T. J. - IOOF emb [LO 1928]	1851	1931		
MINGES, J. [LO]	----	----	3E	S
LAW, Baby	one date	1928	4W	S
LAW, Carlisle C. - American Legion 40/8 emb	1894	1951		
[LO 12-3-1928]				
MINESINGER, Lee (Edw. Lee)	1898	2-13-1980x		
WW I U.S. 1917-1918 mkr				
KNOSE, Benton - Dad [LO 1928]	1868	1944	4E	S
KNOSE, Lillie - Mom	1871	1960		
KNOSE, Minnie M.	1877	1929		
ARNOLD, Michael - Father	1848	1928	5W	3
" ssa , Margaret - Mother [LO 1928]	1853	1929		
ESTRIDGE, ----- [LO]	----	----	5SE	S
FAGALY, Clifford [LO 4-19-1971]	----	----	5NE	S
HUSS, Bertha	1905	1963	6	S
HUSS, Frank	1864	1927		
"ssa, Elizabeth - His Wife [LO 1927]	1859	1937		
HUSS, Frank	1894	1967		
HUSS, Joseph	1897	1974		
HUSS*, Theresa	----	1-10-1989*		
In aisle between lots 6 & 7:			A6	S
LANSAW, Edward	1906	----	&7	
LANSAW, Virgil	1903	----		
In aisle between lots 6 & 7:			A6	S
BROWN, Billie Jo - Daughter	7-28-1971	12-12-1987	&7	
KUPFER, Harry J. [LO 3-1935]	1891	1973	7W	S
" ssa , Phyllis M. [LO 1934]	1892	1964		
GLAZIER, William C.	1909	1975	7E	S
KUPFER, Edward H. [LO 1925]	1880	1961		
KUPFER, Mayme ROBERTS	1870	1925		
INGERSOLL, John - Ohio Cpl Co L 330 Inf	12-21-1894	6- 2-1966	8	S
WW I Vet.-American Legion mkr				
INGERSOLL, Helen Marie	5-25-1918	6-18-1984		
_____, Charles I. - on stone with Daniel-next name	1899	1965		
INGERSOLL, Daniel H. - Father [LO 1924]	1853	1936		
INGERSOLL, Emma C. - Mother - D of A mkr	1865	1939		
INGERSOLL, Edwin - Our Son	1888	[12-30-1923]		
WW I Vet. - American Legion mkr				
FLICK, Leslie L.	1909	1939	9	S
FLICK, Louis J. [LO 1928]	1876	1964		
FLICK, Bessie J.	1881	1966		
FLINCHPAUGH, Vivian	1898	1907	10W	S
FLINCHPAUGH, Charles [LO 1928]	1871	1961		
" ssa , Julia	1874	1973		
WILLSEY, Owen - F. & A.M. emb	1898	3-11-1984x		
" ssa , Ethel	1901	12- 3-1982x		
FLINCHPAUGH, Forest	1904	1958	10NE	S
FLINCHPAUGH, Verna	1905	----		
FLINCHPAUGH, Shirley Irene	1929	1933		
BRAMLETT, L. & R. [LOs]	----	----	10SE	S
DEAN, Ed [LO 1929]	----	----	11W	S
DEAN, Eva E.	1874	1928		
"ssa, Anca E.	1873	1964		
GROTHAUS, Ada W.	1892	1971	11E	S
GROTHAUS, Olive S.	1884	1970		
HOWARD, Susan B. - Mother [LO 1933]	1859	1938		
LEWIS, Jessie M.	1888	1942		

NAME	BD or AGE	DD	Lot	Sec.
SHIRE, John M. [LO-NW eighth]	1902	----	12NW	S
TREE, ----- [LO SE eighth]	----	----	12SE	S
SMITH, Sarah - Mother	1859	1941	12	S
SMITH, Frank - Father	1852	1938		
THAMANN, Joseph - Father	1908	1944		
THAMANN, Pearl	1913	----		
SMITH, Clarence L. [LO 1930]	1890	1974		
" ssa, Dora A.	1894	1974		
LACEY, Dora nee OTTO - Mother	10-29-1874	2-15-1931	13	S
LACEY, John R. - Father [LO 1931]	12-19-1869	5- 1-1941		
STRIMPLE, Pierce J.	1892	4- 1-1977x		
" ssa , Doris L.	1897	4- 9-1982x		
ROBERTS, Seth E.	7-22-1921	----		
"ssa , Helen M.	8- 2-1928	----		
LACEY, John C.	1900	1-13-1988x		
"ssa , Hilda M.	1906	----		
LITTLE, W. S. [LO 1931]	----	----	14	S
KOPP, Richard I. - Ohio S1 U.S.Navy WW II American Legion mkr	6-29-1919	4-18-1970	15W	S
KOPP, Charles A., Jr. - Ohio LCDR USNR WW II Jr. Ord? emb	12-20-1912	4-22-1966		
KOPP, Hazel B. - Mother - OES emb	7-17-1890	8-21-1980		
KOPP, Charles A., Sr. - Father - F. & A.M.emb [LO 1931]	1887	1958		
KOPP, Charles A. [LO 1931]	1852	1931	15E	S
KOPP, Elizabeth [LO]	1858	1937		
KOPP, John	1857	1932		
"ssa, Wilhelmine	1862	1936		
McDONALD, C. & T. [LO]	----	----	16NW	S
WHITNEY, William - F. & A.M. emb	1902	1-11-1977x	16SW	S
" ssa , Florence [LO]	1903	----		
SWISHER, ----- [LO]	----	----	16E	S
PETERS, Minnie B. - Mother	1887	1970		
HAYES, Luella SWISHER	1885	1969		
VAN BLARICUM, Minnie May	1879	1945	17W	S
MURPHY, Alice	1874	1940		
MURPHY, Robert A. [LO 1940]	1859	1947		
VAN BLARICUM, Ollie	1873	1941		
" ssa , Mabel [LO]	1873	1948		
VAN BLARICUM, Will	1891	1949		
" ssa , Eva	1893	9-22-1979x		
McCORMICK, Edna [LO]	1894	1957	18W	S
KUPFER, Lucy	1864	1951		
KUPFER, John	1877	1944		
MORGAN, Chester & Ruth [LOs 1940]	----	----	18E	S
MORGAN, Lydia F. - Mother	1887	1941		
In aisle between lots 18 & 19:	----	----	A18	S
SIMONSON, Ann	1895	1944	&19	
STEPHENSON, Marie B. (BARKER)	1893	5-23-1977x	19	S
STEPHENSON, Charles - Indiana Pvt 8 Co 159 Depot Brigade WW I Vet.	4-19-1892	12- 8-1954		
BARKER, Joseph H.	1866	1949		
"ssa , Mary A.	1861	1947		
HAMOND, Winfield S. (Bud) [LO 1942]	1895	12-18-1981x		
"ssa , Myrtle E.	1893	6-15-1983x		
VONDERHEIDE, Arnold E.	1903	----		
" ssa , Barbara	1871	1958		
CADY, Richard E. - Pfc Co C 62nd A.I.B. emb: Lightning bolt crossed with a bar, on a triangle, with "14" at the top, "O" on the left at crossed bolt & bar & "D" on the right of crossed bolt & bar.	11-20-1920	11-22-1944	20W	S
CADY, Benjamin E. - Father [LO]	1885	1956		
CADY, Matilda M. - Mother	1894	1974		
CADY, C. & J. [LOs]	----	----	20E	S
GUTZWILLER, Amelia C. nee CADY [LO]	1888	4- 5-1977x	21	S
GUTZWILLER, Henry W. [LO]	1892	1958		
BELL, Mary L. [LO]	1905	1960	22	s
BELL, William E.	1900	1945		
HILL, Glenna BELL	1895	1962		
SCHALK, Wanda E.	1900	1959		
HAUER, ----- [LO]	---	----	23	S
HAUER, Addie M. OES emb	1881	1967		
HAUER, CHarles E. F. & A.M. emb	1880	1954		
VOLTZ, Ivan R. [LO]"Married Jan. 16,1926"	1903	2-18-1980x	23A	S
" ssa, Luella	1906	3- 1-1985x		
VOLTZ, Sherri L.	1960	1962		
VOLTZ, Terry Wm.	1951	1952		
PRUITT, Herbert [LO] "Married Sept. 2,1948"	1918	5-16-1986x	23B	S
"ssa , Helen J.	1924	12-24-1982x		
VANCLEVE, Elysah [LO 1909]	----	----	24	S
STEPHENSON, Walter H. "Married Jan.16, 1928"	11-25-1902	3-23-1982	24W	S
" ssa , Pauline B. [LO]	8-19-1910	----		
McCRACKEN, ----- [LO]	----	----	24SE	S

NAME	BD or AGE	DD	Lot	Sec.
McCRACKEN, Ralph K. - Father	1919	6-11-1979x	24SE	S
" ssa , Margaret L. - Mother	1927	9-14-1979x		
HELTON, ----- [LO]	----	----	24NE	S
KNOSE, Joy E.	1905	1912	25	S
SCHAICH, Frances L.	1906	19--		
KNOSE, Mintie M. - His wife	1879	1914		
"ssa , Willis J. - Jr Ord & K of P embs-[LO1912]	1878	1963		
SCHAICH, Gilbert H. - F. & A.M. & Kof P embs	1899	19--		
BORTLEIN, Frank E.	1890	7-14-1977x		
" ssa , Violet G.	1900	1943		
_____, Edward	1921	1942		
WOERTHWINE, Jacob	1864	1914	26W	S
" ssa , Belle - Pythian Sisters mkr [LO1914]	1856	1940		
McDONALD, James A.	1852	1915		
McDONALD, Mrs. Rebecca [LO 2-15-1915]	----	----	26E	S
McDONALD, Cecil	1917	1918		
" ssa , John	1877	1942		
" ssa , Minnie	1883	1974		
" ssa , Eugene	one date	1921		
_____, Lollie - no surname, on stone with Elsie	1870	1891		
_____, Baby Elsie	one date	1891		
ANDERSON, ----- [LO]	----	----	27	S
ANDERSON, Raymond	1924	----		
ANDERSON, Florence W. - American Legion Aux mkr	1895	1962		
ANDERSON, Charles T. - Ohio Cook U.S.Army WW I World War U.S. 1917-18 mkr	1890	1958		
ANDERSON, Dorothy	one date	1920		
" ssa , Jean	1922	1923		
ANDERSON, John	1866	1951		
" ssa , Lucy	1871	1919		
SCHARP, Julius [LO 1917]	----	----	28W	S
STATEN, John T. - F. & A.M. emb [LO]	1888	1956	28SE	S
" ssa , Anna M.	1887	1951		
FICHTNER, Carl [LO 1917]	----	----	29W	S
FICHTNER, Anna M. - Mother - D of A mkr	1884	1939		
FICHTNER, Paul A. - Father	1876	1924		
WALTHER, H. Kenneth - Husband	1903	1963	29E	S
SMITH, Marcella M. - Wife	1913	12- 5-1984x		
COVERT, Howard A. - F. & A.M. emb	1911	1?-12-1986x		
" ssa , Marie E. [LO]	1910	8-10-1988x		
SNYDER, W. T. [LO 1920]	----	----	30	S
GUETHLEIN, Lue Rosa - Mother	1888	1952		
" ssa , Harry H. - Father	1884	1963		
SNYDER, Louisa - Mother	1845	1920		
SNYDER, Valentine - Father	1838	1921		
McHENRY, Ella [LO 1923]	----	----	31	S
ORR, William [LO, no date,transferred W. ½ to Mr. G.P. BEVIS]				
MORFORD, W. [LO]	----	----	31NW	S
STUTZMAN, Bernice L.	1-23-1909	----		
STUTZMAN, Milton M.	1-28-1908	6-20-1986		
BEVIS, Mrs. George P. [LO 4-12-1928]	----	----	31SW	S
BEVIS, Bessie M. - Mother	1868	1933		
BEVIS, Floyd E. "Hap"	6-22-1900	2-12-1971		
In aisle between lots 31W & 32W:			A31W	s
PEABODY, ----- [LO]	----	----	A31W	S
BEVIS, Cora P. (PEABODY)	12-16-1900	12-24-1978		
DOERR, Esther M. (McHENRY) Daughter, w/o H.E.	1897	1960		
ssa " McHENRY, Junius C. - Son	1895	1953		
ssa " McHENRY, Elmer C. - Father	1864	1923		
ssa " McHENRY, Ella C. - Mother [LO 1923]	1864	1944		
In aisle between lots 31E & 32E:			A31E	S
OTTO, Clifford L. [LO 1923]	1909	----	&32E	
"ssa, Cartha D. [LO]	1919	----		
"ssa, Josephine	1868	1923		
"ssa, August	1850	1929		
CORSON, Mary E.	1865	1944	32	S
CORSON, Joseph W.	1858	1939		
CORSON, Walter H. - F. & A.M. emb [LO 1923]	11-11-1888	6- 7-1967		
CORSON, Frances B.	3-27-1890	5-31-1979		
In aisle between lots 32E & 33 E:			A32E	S
WILLIG, William L. (Lawrence) Tec 5 U.S. Army WW II - "Married April 24, 1954"	9-15-1924	12-22-1979		
" ssa , Thelma L. [LO]	3-24-1924	----		
SCHWING, Romana - Mother	1907	1963	33N	S
BEILMAN, Leona - Mom	1888	19--		
BEILMAN, William - Dad [LO 1928]	1878	1959		
BEILMAN, Henry [LO 1928]	1854	1929	33S	S
" ssa , Annie WILLSEY - His Wife	1851	1935		
BEILMAN, Pearl C.	1886	1953		
MARKLAND, Mrs. T. [LO 1928]	----	----	34S	
GIERINGER, Ezra Z.	1894	1949		
" ssa , Mayme M.	1897	5- 2-1988x		
MARKLAND, Cleaves - Father - Jr Ord emb	1870	1928		

NAME	BD or AGE	DD	Lot	Sec.
MARKLAND, Matilda - Mother	1872	1960	34	S
WEBSTER, Art [LO 1930]	----	----	35	S
WEBSTER, Glen	1909	8-18-1984x		
WEBSTER, Arvilla I.	1922	----		
PANCERO*, Viola	----	7-17-1984*		
WEBSTER, Flowers W.-Ohio Pfc 5 Qtrmaster Co. WW II	8-17-1919	7-31-1953		
WEBSTER, Forest	1903	1930		
BEILMAN, Nelson - Son	1886	1971	36	S
BEILMAN, Albert - Son	1880	1962		
KELLER, Amy - Wife	1896	2- 9-1977x		
KEELER, Paul - Husband	1904	1964		
BEILMAN, Everett - Son	1883	1934		
BEILMAN, John - Father [LO 1934]	1850	1939		
BEILMAN, Anna - Mother	1852	1935		
BEILMAN, Clara - Daughter	1876	1960		
KRAUSE, Joe [LO 1931]	----	----	37W	S
RABENSTEIN, Chester	1888	1947		
" ssa , Chrystn	1884	1946		
SCHUSTER, Fred [LO 1931]	1866	19--	37E	S
" ssa , Emma - D of A emb	1859	1931		
KRAMER, Anna C. - Wife	1902	11-20-1981x	38S	S
" ssa , Arthur P. - Husband - Jr Order em.[LO1934]	1898	9-20-1986x		
" ssa , Amelia - Mother - D of A emb	1867	1940		
" ssa , George - Father - Jr Ord UAM 26 emb	1863	1936		
ECKEL, Clarence	1886	1938	39	S
ECKEL, Elizabeth [LO 1938]	1885	1971		
SPRINGMYER, Louise M. [LO]	----	2-16-1969	40W	S
SPRINGMYER, Walter G. [LO]	11- 4-1902	10-27-1978		
WYMER*, Evelyn	----	11-26-1984*		
SPRINGMYER, Charles W. [LO 1939]	1872	1948	40E	S
SPRINGMYER, Louise J. [LO 1939]	1875	1969		
LEMON, Dorothy M. [LO 1943]	1882	1972	41W	S
LEMON, Jesse N.	1879	1943		
LINNENKOHL, Mrs. Wm. [LO 1942]	----	----	41E	S
LINNENKOHL, William G.	1885	1942		
COVERT, Opal ARNOLD	1925	----	42W	S
ARNOLD, Edith M.	1900	1973		
ARNOLD, Bryan [LO 1942]	1896	10- 8-1980x		
ARNOLD, Elmer N.	1898	1971	42E	S
ARNOLD, Anna F.	1898	----		
ARNOLD, Edward T. - Father [LO 1942]	1866	1944		
ARNOLD, Jessie B. - Mother - D of A mkr	1876	1942		
PURVIS, Donald W. - Son	1- 9-1947	3-10-1966	43	S
ELLIS, Charles M. - Husband	4-18-1924	3-28-1964		
WILLOUGHBY, Clifford - Our Son	1940	1959		
WILLOUGHBY, Vernon - Our Son	1926	1943		
WILLOUGHBY, Danny Ray	1963	1964		
PURVIS, Marvin L. - Son	2- 8-1949	3- 6-1949		
SEARS, Corrine - Sister	6-25-1936	7-21-1966		
BRADLEY, Floyd e. - Son	1- 7-1947	3-24-1969		
WILLOUGHBY, Claude V. - Husband [LO]	3-15-1895	5- 9-1977		
WILLOUGHBY, Sarah E. - Wife	6- 8-1900	6-21-1980		
In aisle between lots 43 & 44:			A43	S
WILLOUGHBY, J. [LO]	----	----	&44	
WILLOUGHBY, Claude V., Jr. "Babe"	3-26-1943	10-14-1980		
KRESS, Harold [LO]	----	----	44	S
KRESS, Ethel K. - Wife	1907	1943		
SEFTON, Samuel - Father	12- 3-1861	2- 8-1944	45W	S
" ssa , Lucy - His Wife - Mother	12- 8-1870	9-27-1955		
CORMICAN, Chester A. [LO]	1892	7-22-1984x		
" ssa , Florence	1894	1971		
STREIT, ----- [LO]	----	----	45E	S
STREIT, Marie E. - D of A emb	1910	1955		
STREIT, Joseph F. - Father	1885	1956		
" ssa , Selma K. - Mother	1884	1944		
DEAN, E. [LO]	----	----	46W	S
WABNITZ, V. [LO]	----	----	46E	S
PHILLIPS, ----- [LO]	----	----	47W	S
PHILLIPS, M. Pearl	1887	1962		
PHILLIPS, Chester A. - WW I Vet.	1891	1952		
CARTER, E.M& G. [LOs]	----	----	47E	S
CARTER, Edward Scott	1907	1958		
"ssa , Edna Blanche	1907	4- 6-1987x		
Lot 48 is not on cemetery map.				
_____, Theodore	1915	1915	49	S
_____, Martha	1910	1910		
_____, Clifford	1910	1911		
WHITNEY, Carl Edwin - Emb "A", tow "E"s within overlapping circles, & I on a geometric figure.	1907	4-16-1982x		
WHITNEY, Marguerite ROESSLER - emb "Z-T-A" on a shield	1911	----		
ROESSLER, Caleb - Father [LO 1910]	1868	1958		
ROESSLER, Margaret - Mother	1877	1955		

NAME	BD or AGE	DD	Lot	Sec.
ALTHAUS, Francis - [LO 1913]	One date	1957	50W	S
ALTHAUS, Henry	One date	1913		
ALTHAUS, Lorene	One date	1920		
GREULICH, John - Father - F. & A.M. emb & K of P mkr [LO 10-8-1915]	1882	1947	50E	S
" ssa , Rose - Mother - OES? emb	1891	1933		
GREULICH, Stanley W.	1912	1915		
GREULICH, Gordon - musical notes emb	1915	12-15-1984x		
" ssa , Ann	1917	----		
American Legion mkr beside "MINGES" monument			51	S
MINGES, Kate	1847	1916		
MINGES, Carl - Father	1906	1967		
"ssa , Cecilia - Mother	1915	----		
MINGES, Charles - Father [LO 1916]	1853	1925		
" ssa , Amelia - Mother [LO 1916]	1867	1934		
MINGES, Henry C. - Father	1903	1960		
RUDISELL, Melissa	1869	1954	52	S
RUDISELL, Everett [LO 1916]	1864	1916		
RUDISELL, Ida E.	4-23-1890	6-13-1973		
RUDISELL, Howard A.	1-19-1892	11-10-1982		
RUDISELL, Everett C. - Father	1890	1959		
RUDISELL, Goldie - Mother	1890	3-22-1976x		
In aisle between lots 52 & 53:	----	----	A52	S
YORK, Joseph H., Sr. - Ohio Pfc U.S.Army WW I - American Legion mkr	7-23-1890	6-12-1969	&53	
YORK, Myrtle - [LO]	2- 2-1897	7-26-1987		
WENTZEL, Benjamin [LO 1916]	1856	1932	53W	S
" ssa , Lillian - His Wife	1867	1920	&SE	
WENTZEL, Maud	1891	1916		
SCHARDINE, Earl - F. & A.M. emb [LO]	1917	6-28-1981x	53NE	S
" ssa , Mary V. - OES emb [LO]	1908	9-12-1982x		
In aisle between lots 53 & 54:			A53	S
BERNING*, William B.	----	2-25-1988*		
ARNOLD, Edna - Mother	1894	12-13-1979x	54	S
ARNOLD, Clifford C. - Father	1892	1937		
HINE, William L. - Father [LO 1917]	1847	1934		
"ssa, Charity - Mother	1852	1939		
PHARES, Edith	2- 1-1891	8-18-1983	55	S
GRESCHEL, Louis	1902	----		
" ssa Emma M.	1902	9- 7-1987x		
ZIMMERMAN, Peter N. - Father [LO 1919]	9-12-1864	7-20-1953		
ZIMMERMAN, Kate HEY - Mother	8- 3-1867	12-24-1953		
HEY, John - F. & A.M. emb [LO 1919]	1871	1961		
"ssa, Helen - OES emb	1875	1950		
WOOD, Edwin E. - F. & A.M. emb [LO 1924]	1871	1927	56	S
"ssa, Emma M. - OES emb	1882	1948		
LACEY, Charles & Isabelle [LOs 1926]	----	----	57	S
LACEY, Katie POE - Mother	1868	1935		
LACEY, Jacob C. - Father	1862	1941		
In aisle between lots 57 & 58:			A57	S
PETERS, Edna nee HOLLOWAY	1899	1963	&58	
RUNCK, Dora	1882	1961	58	S
RUNCK, Henry - [LO 1929]	1877	1964		
HOLLOWAY, Vera	1909	1973		
HOLLOWAY, Ohmer	1895	1965		
SCHAEFER, Charles J.	4-22-1891	6-18-1943		
CROWEL, Jennie - Mother	1862	1929		
ssa HOLLOWAY, Johnnie - Son	1901	1929		
ssa HOLLOWAY, Charles E. - Son	1899	1954		
LYNCH, Cecil W. - Husband	1907	1974	59W	S
"ssa , Virginia B. - Wife	1913	2-15-1989x		
SPARKS, Leonard - Father	1878	1932		
" ssa , Ethel - Mother [LO 1932]	1890	1968		
KING, SHirley - [LO]	One date	8-16-1935	59SE	S
RECTOR, Frank [LO]	3-16-1894	5-12-1978		
OWENS, Marshall	1865	1930	59NE	S
OWENS, Lucinda [LO 1930]	8-30-1869	6-16-1954		
FLINCHPAUCH, Ruth	1913	1931	60W	S
FLINCHPAUGH, Simon	1908	1937		
FLINCHPAUGH, Chris [LO 1931]	1874	1957		
" ssa , Helen	1877	1965		
SCHUBERT, Pearl [LO 1931]	----	----	60E	S
SCHUBERT, George - F. & A. M. emb	1879	1931		
ALSTON, Pearl	1886	1968		
ALSTON, Minor G.	1884	1951		
WALSH, Charles	1868	1933		
HAUSS, Frances	1914	----	61	S
HAUSS, Wilbur	1910	6- 6-1978x		
HAUSS, Augusta	1889	1965		
HAUSS, Carl [LO 1934]	1885	1966		
HAUSS, Fred [LO 1934]	1859	1938		
HAUSS, Barbara RAUH	1866	1935		
KRATZEL, Wm. [LO 1937]	----	----	62W	S
_____, ----- Mother	----	----		

NAME	BD or AGE	DD	Lot	Sec.
LONG, Lester [LO 1939	1911	2- 6-1987x	62W	S
"ssa, Alice	1915	6-12?-1986x		
SCHUSTER, Floyd "Abe"	1905	1973	62E	S
" ssa , Mildred P. [LO 1937]	1909	----		
WILLIS, Mildred	1888	1937		
MORGAN, Harry [LO 5-31-1938]	1887	1949	63W	S
" ssa , Lulu - D of A mkr	1896	1938		
WILLSEY, George	1863	1938	63E	S
" ssa , Sallie C. [LO 1938]	1871	1939		
ALLEE, Charles [LO 1942]	---- -	----	64	S
DAVIS, Charlene [LO 7-11-1973]	----	----		
WALLACE, Margaret E. (ALLEE)	7-21-1909	12-17-1986		
ALLEE, Edwin Oscar	6- 5-1941	3-16-1942		
STEHR, Harry F. - Ohio Pvt U.S.Army WW I	3- 2-1888	10-30-1961	65W	S
STEHR, Henry	1862	1942		
"ssa , Barbara [LO 1942]	1866	1948		
RADEL, Fred & Minnie [LOs 1942]	----	----	65E	S
HELCHER, E. & E. [LOs]	----	----		
WASH, Martha S. - Mother [LO 1942]	1875	1957	66	S
WASH, John	1865	1937		
WASH, George W.	1899	1961		
DICKINSON, William H.	1903	1972		
SNEED, Nellie [LO 1942]	----	----	67	S
LEISRING, Lawrence A. "Tony"	10-30-1929	6-29-1963		
SNEED, Marvin Taylor	9-16-1903	10- 9-1942		
EDWARDS, John W. - Father	1863	1943		
EDWARDS, Lula A. - Mother	1882	1952		
EDWARDS, Raymond L.	7-31-1903	5-23-1970		
EDWARDS, Mae - Mother	6-16-1910	8-29-1975		
HUSSEL, Gesena S.	1881	1972	68	S
HUSSEL, William A. [LO]	1883	1959		
TOOLEY, Samuel B. [LO]	1887	1948	69	S
" ssa , Mary L.	----	----		
" ssa , David W.	1848	1935		
" ssa , Mary E.	1852	1940		
KUHN, Albert - Pvt U.S.Army WW I	6-22-1893x	6-15-1978x	70A	S
KUHN, Frederick	1899	10-23-1978x		
KUHN, Philip [LO]	1897	5-13-1981x		
ROESSLER, Hattie	1884	1950	70B	S
ROESSLER, Fred [LO]	1878	1964		
[LO not listed]			70C	S
CLARK, Robert E.	1918	1973	70D	S
" ssa, Norma E. [LO]	1922	----		
DOERR, J. M. [LO]	----	----	70E	S
DOERR, William	1906	11-10-1983x		
"ssa , Minnie	1912	11-19-1982x		
TUCKER, W. [LO]	----	----	71W	S
TUCKER, Liddie G.	11-30-1886	9-10-1945		
MINNICH, Peter J.	1871	1963	71E	S
" ssa , Magdalena	1874	1972		
SEIM, William H. - Husband	1863	1946		
SEIM, Margaret - Wife [LO]	1875	1961		
KRAMER, John A.	1894	1913	72	S
KRAMER, John - Father [LO 1913]	1860	1927		
KRAMER, Margaret - Mother	1868	1947		
FLINCHPAUGH & VARLEY [LOs 1910]			73	S
FLINCHPAUGH, Lulu	----	----		
FLINCHPAUGH, Sarah SWAIN	----	----		
FLINCHPAUGH, Simon	1835	1910		
VARLEY, Anderson E.	----	----		
VARLEY, Minnie M.	----	----		
VARLEY, Violet	----	----		
NOSE, Barbara - Mother	1875	1911	74N	S
NOSE, William H. - Father [LO 1911]	1855	1946		
METZGER*, Charles (NE Corner of lot)	----	9- 1-1979*		
STEINMAN, Walt [LO 1911]	----	----	74S	S
STEINMAN, Frank [LO 9-23-1947]	----	----		
NEIDHART, George [LO 1915]	----	----	75	S
HEARN, Clara	1879	1938		
HEARN, Holley L. "Babe" [LO]	3-18-1877	8-11-1961		
BOHNING, Anna - Mother	1889	1955		
BOHNING, Charles J. - Father	1882	1975		
KNOSE, Leslie - WW I Vet.	9-30-1891	2-24-1955	76	S
KNOSE, Mary - Mother	1865	1930		
" ssa, Philip - Father	1857	1943		
WENTZEL, Edward D. - Husband [LO 1917]	8- 3-1884	9-21-1951		
WENTZEL, Minnie A. - Wife	3-11-1885	1-16-1973		
WENTZEL, Edward G.	1912	1920		
In aisle between lots 76 & 77:			A76	S
OSBORNE, Amon E. Pfc U.S.Army WW II	11-21-1923	4-10-1988	&77	
In aisle between lots 76 & 77:			A76	S
MURRAY*, Winfred	----	7-30-1988*		
HEY, Helen E. (d. 9-27-1981)	One date	10- ?-1981	77	S

NAME	BD or AGE	DD	Lot	Sec.
HEY, James George - F. & A.M.? emb	6-27-1903	11-26-1973	77	S
HEY, William M.	7- 6-1907	10-10-1947		
HEY, Jacob F. - Father [LO 1919]	2-15-1877	3-17-1955		
HEY, Elizabeth - Mother	5-15-1878	1- 1-1968		
STOREY, Mattie [LO 1921]	1868	1936	78	S
" ssa , Harry S.	1864	1921		
_____ , ----- (empty foundation)	----	----		
WEBER, Edwin W.	1889	1965		
"ssa , Hazel G.	1892	6-15-1981x		
STOREY, W. Howard	1902	1951		
LOHREY, Mildred E. [LO]	1913	----	79NW	S
SIEGERT, George [LO 1924]	1884	1951	79SW	S
" ssa , Carrie M. - D of A emb	1886	1924		
SIEGERT, Mamie	1895	12-23-1979x		
LOHREY, Henry [LO 1924]	1889	1964	79E	S
" ssa , Hilda	1889	4-30-1980x		
ALBRECHT, Walter T. - Ohio Tec 3 U.S.Army WW II Vet.	8-27-1922	7- 5-1973		
JOYCE, Margaret - Mother	1862	1941	80	S
" ssa. Elias [LO 1926]	1857	1932		
JOYCE, Clifford - Ohio Pvt Sup Co 151 Inf WW I Vet.	8-24-1886	11-14-1953		
HEARN, James H. - Father [LO 1930]	1875	1953	81	S
" ssa, Welthy A. - Mother	1879	1951		
HEARN, Lucile	1909	----		
HEARN, Edward	1909	1971		
HOGRAEVER, Malinda R.	----	19--	82	S
" ssa , Frank V. [LO 1930]	----	19--		
ssa EVANS, Robert L.	----	1954		
ssa " , Minnie M.	----	1931		
SCHREIBER, George - Husband [LO]	7-23-1914	----	83A	S
" ssa , Addline - Wife	10- 6-1916	6-26-1979		
" ssa , Albert - Son	5- 6-1941	----		
DAVIS, John A. - Dad "Married May 9,1934"	1911	6-25-1978x	83B	S
" ssa, Bessie M. - Mom [LO]	1917	----		
BEAVER, Hannah [LO 1931]	1869	1943	83C	S
" ssa , William	1856	1930		
KITTLE, H. & D. [LOs]	----	----	83D	S
[LO not listed]			83E	S
BERRY, S. [LO]	----	----	83F	S
BERRY, Ida M.	----	5- 5-1984x		
"ssa , Dennis C. - F. & A.M. emb	1899	1978		
ROESSLER, William	1871	1934	84N	S
ROESSLER, Mary SCOGGINS [DO 1934]	1871	1937		
BITTNER, John, Jr.	4-11-1894	2- 8-1977	84S	S
BITTNER, Ruth G.	11-29-1903	10-26-1979		
ROESSLER, Martha - Mother	1884	1966		
ROESSLER, Charles - Father [LO 1934]	1872	1945		
MILLER, Mary L.	1871	1935	85A	S
" ssa , Emery A. [LO 1934]	1864	1937		
BROXTERMAN, Joseph M. [LO]	1911	11- 7-1983x	85B	S
" ssa , Ruth F. [LO]	1917	----		
McDONALD, J. & M. [LOs 1934]	----	----	85C	S
DORSCH, Amelia J. - Mother	1877	1961	85D	S
DORSCH, John - Father [LO 1934]	1875	1940		
JOYCE, Benjamin - Father	1882	1937	86W	S
" ssa, Frieda - Mother [LO 1937]	1884	1961	&SE	
GERWING, Edna	1895	1972	86NE	S
" ssa , John [LO]	1893	1974		
KRESS, Robert	1925	1938	87	S
KRESS, Edward [LO 1938]	1898	1970		
"ssa , Emma	1900	----		
KRESS, Henry	1872	1952		
"ssa , Dorothea	1877	1956		
JUTZI, Louis [LO 1941]	1911	19--	88W	S
"ssa , Minnie	1913	1941		
JUTZI, Louis - Pop	1874	1951	88SE	S
JUTZI, Anna T. - Mom [LO 1941]	1886	1964		
STACY, Emery [LO]	1915	3-27-1979x	88NE	S
" ssa, Polly	1911	11-10-1979x		
HANAWAY, Rosa P.	1908	1941	89A	S
HANAWAY, Madge E. - OES emb [LO 1941]	1887	8-11-1980x		
HANAWAY, George E. - F. & A.M. emb [LO 1941]	1883	1965		
WOODS, Robert H. [LO]"Married Feb.16, 1935"	1916	----	89B	S
"ssa , Mary E. - [LO]	1916	----		
HANAWAY, C. & D. [LOs]	----	----	89C	S
PEASLACK, Marian [LO 1942]	----	----	90	S
DUDLEY, Stanley Durbin - Cpl U.S.Army WW II	8-18-1916	4-17-1981	90	S
BERKMYER, George R. - Sgt U.S.Army WW I [LO 1942]	1-14-1895	1-13-1976	91	S
BERKMYER, Albert J.	1867	1942		
BERKMYER, Ellen J.	1868	1947		
BERKMYER, Marie H.	1893	1972		

NAME	BD or AGE	DD	Lot	Sec.
In aisle between lots 91 & 92:			A91	S
CRONE, Frank [LO]	1896	1972	&92	
CRONE, Irma (D.) KNOSE	1903	10-21-1981x		
BRISBIN, Walter F. & A.M. emb [LO]	12-21-1915	1975	92	S
BRISBIN, Lulu C. Mother	1876	1944		
BREESE, Lewis	7-10-1874	4-22-1959		
KNOSE, Meade, Sr.-Daddy [& Nimetta LO's]	10- 2-1901	8-26-1953	93	S
KNOSE, Anna - Mom	12-14-1904	1-20-1988x		
LACEY, Edna	7- 7-1909	6-24-1966		
HELMS, Emery L. - Pvt U.S.Army WW II	11-30-1907	9- 6-1982		
LACEY, Jim (James C.) 25 yr. vet. IOOF & D of A embs	1903	6-19-1976x		
OTTO, Ruth	9-11-1915	8-17-1981	94	S
OTTO, Dora - Mother [LO]	1873	1966		
OTTO, Frank - Father	1870	1946		
OTTO, Vernor - Tec 4 U.S.Army WW II	12-28-1904	3-17-1988		
OTTO, Hazel	11- 9-1906	4- 2-1957		
WILLIAMS, Albert A.	1859	1914	95	S
" ssa , Belle C. - His Wife [LO 1914]	1860	1940		
NOSE, Martin [LO 1910]	1864	1936	96	S
"ssa, Margaret	1869	1939		
Children:				
"ssa, Leah	1892	1910		
"ssa, David	1897	1919		
"ssa, Charles	1891	1918		
LEMMON, David - Ohio Sgt 11th Inf Co B U.S.Army WW I Vet.	1872	1- 7-1930		
" ssa , Elmira	1884	1931		
METZGER, Edward - Father [LO 1911]	1859	1914	97	S
" ssa , Magdalena - Mother	1861	1911		
METZGER*, Magdalena	----	8-16-1980*		
SMITH, Hattie C.	1892	1970	98	S
SMITH, Joseph F.	1888	1966		
_____, Patsy - Baby	One date	1932		
"WULLENWEBER" on monument:				
____, Hattie	1864	1933		
____, Christian [LO 1912]	1862	1917		
SMITH, John Paul	1921	1929		
_____, Ivy	One date	1923		
_____, Carl	One date	1915		
_____, Earl	One date	1912		
GIERINGER, Mrs. C. P. [LO 3-18-1936]			99	S
MINGES, Peter - F. & A.M. emb - Civil War Vet. [LO 1917]	1840	12-21-1923		
MINGES, Amanda - OES emb	1848	1917		
ADAMS, M. & J. [LOs]	----	----	100NW	S
KUPFER, Charles - Father [LO 1918]	4- 4-1888	3-14-1968	100E	S
KUPFER, Katherine - Mother - D of A emb	7-26-1881	4-27-1947	&SW	
_____, Alma Louise	1916	1917		
STYONS, Cecil Bray,III	6-18-1967	11-28-19--		
In aisle between lots 100W & 101W:			A100W	S
KUPFER, Ralph M. [LO]	1912	11-30-1982x	&101W	
" ssa , Della F.	1912	----		
KUPFER, E. [LO in aisle between lots 100E & 101E]			A100E &101E	S
HILEMAN, James - Father	1866	1949	101	S
" ssa , Eva - Mother	1870	1953		
OWENS, Jesse H. (Bub) Tec 3 U.S.Army WW II	4-27-1915	12-20-1977		
OWENS, Naomi M.	1898	6-19-1982x		
"ssa , Jesse M. [LO 1919]	1891	10-25-1978x		
OWENS, Mabel - Mother	1884	1919		
OWENS, Charles J. - Ohio Sgt Coast Arty Corps WW II - Jr Ord UAM #26 mkr	9- 5-1917	6-25-1944		
KNAU, M. & J. [LOs]	----	----	102A	S
WILLIAMSON, Anna Maria [LO 1921]	1853	1934	102B	S
WILLIAMSON, James	1853	1921		
MOZENA, Floyd L. [LO]	1912	4- 5-1984x	102C	S
"ssa , Helen R. [LO]	1913	----		
KNAU, Michael C.-"Married Sept. 19, 1931"	1910	11- 2-1976x	102D	S
"ssa, Mildred M. [LO 1976?]	1911	10-10-1978x		
WILLIAMSON, Joseph [LO 1921]	1859	1945	102E	S
WILLIAMSON, Caroline D.	1860	1927		
GILB, William Henry [LO 1976?]	11- 2-1914	10-30-1985	102F	S
"ssa, Odie Jewel [LO]	1-27-1925	----		
HETTERSIMER, Hazel - Daughter	1910	1965	103	S
HETTERSIMER, Emma - Mother [LO 1922]	1882	1956		
[D of A stone mkr behind headstone may belong here or on lot 126]				
HETTERSIMER, Harry - Father	1882	1922		
HETTERSIMER, Roy - Ohio Tec 5 883 Ord Ham Co WW II	4-25-1915	2-20-1973		
WERTZ, E. & R. [LOs]	----	----	104A	S
SEAL, Howard L., Sr. - S1 U.S.Navy WW II	7-14-1913	11-26-1982		
STURGILL, R. [LO]	----	----	104B	S
STURGILL, Winfrey R.	8-19-1908	1-20-1982		

NAME	BD or AGE	DD	Lot	Sec.
MILTON, C. [LO]	----	----	104C	S
LINZY, Gary Lee - Sgt U.S.Marine Corp Vietnam	11-30-1950	11-9-1981		
MONTGOMERY, William T. - Dad	5-30-1914	12-22-1981		
" ssa , May R.-Mom-Married Nov.28,1933	6- 6-1915	----		
MINGES, Daisy - Mother	1878	1955	104E	S
MINGES, Fred - Father [LO 1922]	1875	1968		
HETERSIMER, Herman	1860	1940	105	S
HETERSIMER, Joseph	1864	1950		
ENNIS, Edward - Husband [LO 1922]	1868	1944		
ENNIS, Ida - Wife	1873	1961		
MINGES, William [LO 1922]	1877	1922		
MINGES, Elizabeth	1869	1936		
HETERSIMER, William - Father-Civil War Vet. emb	1841	[7-29]1929		
HETERSIMER, Mary - Mother	1843	1924		
SNYDER, Henry J.	1912	1957	106	S
SNYDER, Mary - Mother	1875	1947		
SNYDER, Gertrude	1898	1969		
SNYDER, John [LO 1923]	1890	19--		
SNYDER, Cornelia	1847	1923		
WEBER, E. [LO aisle between lots 106 & 107]	----	----	A106 &107	S
BRATER, Walter	1908	1936	107	S
SNYDER, Charles [LO 1925]	1877	1963		
" ssa , Elsie	1881	1963		
SNYDER, Dorothy M.(d.10-14-1986 & stone has yr 1987)	1912	1987		
SNYDER, Harry	1904	1925		
SHINKLE, John	1882	1959	108	S
" ssa , Pearl	1887	1959		
WEBER, Michael - Father	1856	1926		
WEBER, Anna - Mother [LO 1926]	1862	1956		
WEBER, Leona - Daughter	1885	1975		
KRAUS, Robert G.	1900	1974	109	S
"ssa , Nellie M.	1900	1973		
POE, Edythe L.	1897	1941		
POE, William E.- Spanish American War Vet.	1869	10-23-1927		
"ssa, Martha A. - His Wife [LO 1927]	1870	1955		
KRAUS, George A.	1861	1930	110	S
"ssa , Anna M. [LO 1930]	1862	1959		
KRAUS, Edna F.	1892	1954		
_____, John Richard "Dick"	11-22-1942	4-24-1943	111	S
HYLAND, Howard H.	5-12-1917	12- 8-1979		
HYLAND, Wilhelmina "Minnie"	10-23-1886	10- 1-1966		
HYLAND, Howard T.	4-23-1888	8-24-1967		
HYLAND, John H. [LO 1931]	3- 2-1862	9-19-1943		
HYLAND, Mary A.	8-27-1862	5- 2-1943		
HYLAND, Nellie B.	11- 3-1884	2- 6-1959		
VOGT, C. & BORTHLEIN, E. [LOs 1938]	----	----	112	S
VOGT, Lottie - Mother	1886	19--		
VOGT, Charles F. - Father	1881	1938		
VOGT, Charles A. - Father	1907	11-14-1976x		
VOGT, Elnora K. - Mother	----	----		
TEATS, Marguerite	1903	----	113	S
"ssa , Thomas D.	1901	1967		
KRUEGER, Otto J. - F. & A.M. emb	1913	1974		
SPAETH, Fred [LO 1940]	1879	1963		
" ssa , Martha	1881	1941		
SCHLENK, Matilda NINISH	1857	1942		
STOCKHOFF, ----- [LO-aisle between 113 & 114]	----	----	A113	S
STOCKHOFF, Emma F.	1908	3-27-1977x	&114	
STOCKHOFF, Clifford - Pvt U.S.Army WW I	1896	8- 4-1977x		
JACKSON, Bernard Dale - Sgt U.S.Army WW II[LO]	8-2-1924	1- 5-1981	114A	S
PICKENS, Amos E. - 1939	----	----	114B	S
GIERINGER, Earl A.	One date	4-18-1908		
ssa PICKENS, Amos [LO 1938]	6- 4-1862	8-14-1941		
ssa GIERINGER, Albert F.	One date	12-26-1884		
ssa PICKENS, Elizabeth	5- 6-1866	4-22-1940		
ssa GIERINGER, Cora M.	One date	2-28-1885		
SCHOEMER, R. & W. [LOs]	----	----	114C	S
SCHOEMER, Edward M. - Sgt U.S.Army WW I	2- 6-1891	12-22-1979		
YOUNG, Ralph [LO]	----	----	115A	S
YOUNG, Helen K. w/o Ralph [LO]	5-23-1913	1- 2-1979		
SAMMONS, A. [LO]	----	----	115B	S
SAMMONS, William A. - Cpl U.S.Army WW II	2-10-1917	5- 6-1979		
ASHCRAFT, Marcus	1915	5-10-1979x	115C	S
" ssa , Jessie [LO]	1917	----		
COLWELL, Lannie - Dad [LO]	1949	6- 8-1979x	115D	S
In aisle between lots 115 & 116:	----	----	A115	S
HEINTZ, Carl R. - Jr Ord emb	1912	1943	&116	
HEINTZ, Mike	1924	1979	116	S
" ssa , Helen	1924	----		
HEINTZ, Walter E.	1908	1965		
" ssa , Elva B.	1912	----		
HEINTZ, William [LO]	1882	1963		
" ssa , Freda	1888	1952		

NAME	BD or AGE	DD	Lot	Sec.
HEINTZ*, Earl L.	----	6-18-1979*	116	S
In aisle between lots 116 & 117:	----	----	A116	S
? , Vaunda	1921	1944	&117	
CLARK, John M. - Father	1912	1943	117	S
"ssa , Mary A. (WILLIAMS) [LO]	1910	5- 8-1986x		
[No lot owner listed]			118	S
RACK, Dorothy R. - Mother	1930	1974		
REHFUES, Carl [LO 1911]	----	----	119	S
GLAUSER, Mary	1869	1912		
KROCKER, Emma - Aunt	1865	1944		
SCOGGINS, George	----	----	120W	S
" ssa , Isabel	----	----		
" ssa , Doris [LO 1911]	----	----		
CADY, Isaac [LO 1911]	10-28-1848	7-17-1922	120E	S
"ssa, Laura - His Wife	3- 7-1852	3-21-1935		
LOCKWOOD, ----- [LO 1915]	----	----	121	s
LOCKWOOD, Joseph A. - Our Son	1915	1915		
LOCKWOOD, Ottilia	1878	1956		
LOCKWOOD, Oliver - Father	1876	1954		
" ssa , Ivy M. - Mother	1876	1929		
LOCKWOOD, Dorothy M. - Our daughter	1915	1930		
FRANK, Hugo B. - Husband	1896	1968	122	S
MILLER, Mabel E. - Wife	1885	1955		
MILLER, Ward B. - Husband - F. & A.M. emb	1879	1962		
MILLER, Victoria B. - Our Daughter	1869	1963		
MILLER, Charles W.-Father [LO-1917] **Civil War Vet.**	**1835**	12-31-1923		
MILLER, Angeline P. - Mother	1843	1927		
SHEAR, Ed [LO 1918]	----	----	123	S
WUEST, Stephen C.	1877	1946		
WUEST, Cora	1886	1972		
ARNOLD, Leslie L. - F. & A.M. emb	1894	1960	124	S
ARNOLD, Emma B.	1895	3-27-1984x		
BETSCHER, Emil L. - K of P [LO 1918]	1862	1918		
BETSCHER, Etta S. - Pythian Sisters emb	1867	1947		
GIERINGER, Carolyn B.	1887	1972		
BETSCHER, Edwin O. - Rotarian	1897	5-28-1976x		
BETSCHER, Christine M.	1901	1972		
RUDISELL, E. & M. [LOs]	----	----	125A	S
GIERINGER, Edward - F. & A.M. emb [LO 1920]	1880	1969	125B	S
GIERINGER, Bertha L. - OES emb	1878	1920		
BOHNERT, William - Father	1847	1920	126	S
BOHNERT, Margaret E. - Mother [LO 1920]	1850	1934		
[D of A stone mkr at foot of grave may belong here or on lot 103]				
BOHNERT, Dora - Sister	1888	1975		
MYERS, Jeannette M.	1904	1954	127	S
"ssa , John J.	1873	1962		
"ssa , May E.	1877	1954		
WOOD, Marshall S. - Father	1890	1972		
WOOD, Lida - Mother	1844	1922		
"ssa, Fayette M. - Father [LO 1922]**Civil War Vet.**	**1843**	6-29-1924		
WOOD, Ida M. - Mother	1892	1972		
ROLFES, Richard Edwin	1911	9-23-1981x	128	S
WOOD, Harry A. - Father [LO 1922]	1868	1944		
WOOD, Ada B. - Mother	1874	1943		
ROLFES, Mary Emily	8-30-1913	10-16-1956		
BRAMER, Henry [LO 1925]	----	----	129A	S
SHAFFER, D. & M. [LOs]	----	----	129B	S
SHAFFER, Earl R.	1909	5-14-1981x	129C	S
"ssa , Ruth W. [LO]	1910	----		
In aisle between lot 129 & 130:	----	----	A129	S
MIENTENKOETTER, Ivy Glenn - OES emb	1902	1954	&130	
WOOD, Mary A. - OES emb	1877	1972	130W	S
WOOD, William J. - F. & A.M. emb [LO 1934]	1872	1958		
WOOD, George P. - F. & A.M. emb [LO 1934]	10-10-1874	8-18-1961	130E	S
WOOD, Mina M. - OES emb	6-14-1888	10- 5-1984		
BALSER, George W. [LO 1927]	1868	1953	131	S
" ssa , Julia M.	1878	1927		
MARSHALL, David H.	1890	1929		
BALSER, Richard D. "Dickie" Son	1942	1953		
WERNER, ----- [LO]	----	----	132A	S
RUEBER, Martha	1861	1930	132B	S
RUEBER, Andrew	1859	1929		
KLENK, Susie C.	1891	1960		
" ssa, Harry R. [LO B & C 1929]	1892	1969		
KLENK, Harry F. - SSM 3 U.S.Navy WW II	3-17-1921	7-12-1987	132C	S
KLENK, William - Ohio S2 U.S.Navy WW I	9-12-1896	3- 9-1962		
American Legion mkr				
In aisle between lots 132 & 133:	----	----	A132	S
GETZ, Martin C.	12- 9-1896	4- 1-1973	&133	
KIDWELL, Margaret Lula - Mother & Grandmother	1883	8-15-1984x	133	S
GETZ, Clara E. - Mother	11-19-1894	11-21-1977		
GETZ, Joseph H.	7-25-1891	4-26-1936		
GETZ, John - Father [LO 1931]	1862	1931		
"ssa, Emma - Mother	1863	19--		

NAME	BD or AGE	DD	Lot	Sec.
SEILER, Irvin C.	1909	12-27-1977x	134A	S
"ssa , Myrtle M. [LO]	1912	3-30-1988x		
McJILTON, S. (Stuart) Hylan	1902	12- 4-1979x	134B	S
" ssa , Anna Lee [LO 1934?]	----	----		
MARSH, Alice - Aunt [LO 134C] "Sisters"	1908	12-28-1980x	134C	S
ssa REED, Minnie - Mother [LO 135A]	1905	7- 4-1977x	&135A	
THOMAS, Leola [LO 1934]	1891	1974	134D	S
THOMAS, Eunice L. - Mom	1867	1948		
THOMAS, Enoch H. - Pop	1867	1935		
ECKLAR, J. & V. [LOs]	----	----	134E	S
ADDISON, A. & H. [LOs]	----	----	135B	S
ADDISON, Eugene	1926	12-31-1981x		
" ssa , Dorothy	1922	----		
CADY, Rose M.	1891	1940	135C	S
CADY, William A., Jr. [LO 1940]	12- 1-1890	10-24-1973		
Ohio Wagoner U.S.Army WW I				
CAMPBELL, Edna V. - D of A emb	1894	1941	136W	S
CAMPBELL, Luther M. - Ohio Pvt 20 Co 158	5-16-1897	11-24-1970		
Depot Brig WW I				
BENNETT, Florence A. - Cremains	1887	11-21-1978x		
BENNETT, Thomas T. [LO 1941]	1880	1955		
MAHOOD, Fred G. - Jr. Ord emb [LO 1941]	1889	1966	136E	S
MAHOOD, Annie - Mother	1864	1947		
HOLDERER, George	1899	12-20-1982x	137	S
HOLDERER, Mildred	1909	----		
ALTHAUS, Anna	1886	3-30-1979x		
ALTHAUS, Fred [LO 1942]	1884	1971		
ALTHAUS, Charles - Father	1880	1942		
ALTHAUS, Sophia Sue - Mother	1883	1959		
STOCKHOFF, Ronald C.	1939	1967	138	S
LOHR, Jacob	1900	1964		
CARTMELL, James E. - Son	9- 9-1963	7-11-1967		
JOHNSON, Grover C. - Ohio Pvt 6 Casual	2-24-1893	3- 1-1968		
Det WW I Vet.				
_____, ----- foundation but no gravestone	----	----		
WEISEL, Valentine G. [LO]	1884	7- 3-1977x	139A	S
" ssa , Louise A.	1890	1974		
FLICK, Jacob	1872	1956		
"ssa , Louise [LO]	1875	1964		
[LO not listed]	----	----	139C	S
LUECK, Herman - Father - F. & A.M. emb	6-26-1882	2-28-1958		
PRICE, Lillian - Wife [LO]	1895	2-27-1979x	139D	S
PRICE, Ralph E. - Husband	1894	1958		
SHECKLER, Arthur R. [LO] "Married Oct.31,1926"	1899	1970	140W	S
" ssa , Lulu M. (Myrtle)	1908	3- 8-1985x		
SHECKLER, Amy -[Infant twins buried at foot of	1976	8- 3-1976x		
" ssa , Adam grandmothers grave]	1976	8- 5-1976x		
DOWNEY, E. [LO]	----	----	140E	S
DOWNEY, Herbert	1906	1944		
DOWNEY, Pensy - Mother	1-21-1878	1-28-1975	141	S
RUHLMAN, Harry L. [LO]	1899	11-17-1978x		
" ssa , Irma "RADENHEIMER" on E side of stone	1903	1971		
NEWMAN, (James?) Roger [LO]	1912	6-11?-1986x	142N	S
" ssa , Hilda [LO]	1919	----		
ADAMS, Pearl - Daughter [LO 1912]	1879	1944	142S	S
" ssa. Mary - Mother	1854	1912		
MAXFIELD, C. (Charles) H. [LO 1914]	1836	3- 4-1917	143	S
Civil War Vet. mkr				
MAXFIELD, Helen	1840	1926		
ARNOLD, Albert & Louise [LOs 1916]	----	----	144	S
LEWIS, Romaine C. - Ohio Cp. HQ Co 30	3-30-1889	10- 3-1969	145	S
Inf 9 WW I - "LEWIS" with F. & A.M. emb on monument				
LEWIS, William Paul	1894	1918		
LEWIS, William	1864	1918		
LEWIS, Mary Elizabeth nee CARR [LO 1918]	1863	1931		
LEWIS, Elsie W.	1892	1945		
RAIBLE, C. & L. [LOs]	----	----	146A	S
RAIBLE*, Charles	----	2-28-1988*		
ALTHAUS, Edith M.	1899	1918	146B	S
ALTHAUS, George [LO 1919]	1868	1934		
ALTHAUS, Anna	1873	1928		
MEISBERGER, William N.	1901	8-14-1980x	146C	S
" ssa , Marie V. [LO]	1902	----		
METZGER, ELsie- OES emb	1899	1972	147	S
METZGER, John - F. & A.M. emb	1894	1-18-1989x		
METZGER, William B.	1853	1939		
JONES, Joseph [LO 1920]	1869	1935		
JONES, Laura B.	1903	1920		
FAGALY, Matilda	1850	1945	148	S
FAGALY, John N. [LO 1920]	1846	1924		
FAGALY, Arthur C.	1888	1945		
FAGALY, Stanley E. [LO]	1890	6- 6-1984x		
" ssa , Beverly Ann - Our Baby	One date	1938		
" ssa , Lucy C.	1910	----		

NAME	BD or AGE	DD	Lot	Sec.
STRONG, John L.	1870	1937	148	S
STRONG, Lida K.	1873	1937		
THOMPSON, May M.	1879	1920		
SPRINGMYER, Louise A. - Mother	5-29-1879	10- 3-1945	149	S
SPRINGMYER, Edward J. - Father	9-12-1872	7-29-1958		
JUTZI, Nora M. - Mother	12- 6-1875	11-15-1951		
JUTZI, John H. - Father	5- 2-1873	1-16-1953		
JUTZI, Martha L.	1-11-1901	5-22-1959		
SPRINGMYER, John [LO 1920]	1845	1935		
SPRINGMYER, Katherine	1851	1920		
MILLER, Clara J. - OES emb & Pythian Sisters mkr	1863	1932	150	S
MILLER, Harry B. - F. & A.M. emb [LO 1922]	1864	1932		
STICKSEL, William [LO 1923]	1849	1923	151W	S
STICKSEL, Wilhelmina	1849	1924		
STICKSEL, William, Jr.	1875	1954		
STICKSEL, Grace	1993	1963		
ADDISON, ----- [LO]	----	----	151E	S
HYDEN, Sandi Joyce d/o Oakley & Beulah ADDISON	7-12-1947	7- 4-1965		
WEICKEL, Jacob	1883	1957	152	S
WEICKEL, Mina	1890	1967		
WEICKEL, Fred	1888	1951		
PFAU*, Ethel - Cremains (DI between 1-25 & 2-13	----	1984?)		
PFAU, Emma	1875	1936		
WEICKEL, Anna B.	1878	1956		
WEICKEL, ELise - Mother	1847	1924		
" ssa , Jacob - Father - [LO 1924]	1848	1926		
WEICKEL, Katherine	1880	1930		
FAGALY, Patricia L.	One date	10-30-1948	153	S
FAGALY, Carl L. - Baby	3 mos.	1925		
FAGALY, Edna HARRIS	1904	1925		
FAGALY, Dorothy Anne - Daughter	11-26-1962	1-26-1963		
FAGALY, Albert E.	1905	12-31-1980x		
" ssa , Helen H.	1913	7- 5-1985x		
FAGALY, Roy G.	1901	12- 7-1977x		
" ssa . Dorothy M.	1912	12- 4-1979x		
FAGALY, Royal G. [LO 1925]	1875	1968		
" ssa , Anna B.	1874	1966		
JUNKERT, Lora R.	1875	1947	154	S
JUNKERT, Margaret	1850	1928		
JUNKERT, John D.	1916	1925		
JUNKERT, John P. [LO 1925]	1880	1966		
" ssa , Ella M.	1886	1975		
KRAMER*, Elmer	----	12- 3-1987*	155	S
KRAMER, Eugene - Father - F. & A.M. emb	1- 4-1903	4-18-1978		
KRAMER, Louis E. - Ohio Pvt Stu Army Tng Corp WW I	2-16-1897	11-14-1955		
KRAMER, Jacob - Father [LO 1937]	1867	1939		
KRAMER, Katie - Mother	1867	1951		
KRAMER, Leroy	6- 6-1893	5-29-1965		
HENRIE, Gordon G.-K of P mkr between these	1917	1947	156W	S
HENRIE, George W. - two stones	1890	1938		
" ssa , Elsie E. [LO 7-1938]	1894	19--		
HUFFMAN, Charles	1857	1938	156E	S
LEEDS, Frank	1880	1968		
BEALL, Claud [LO 1938]	1877	1949		
BEALL, Mary	1878	1956		
FEIGE, Wm. [LO 8-15-1940]	----	----	157W	S
FEIGE, Caroline - Mother	1858	1940		
STOCKHOFF, Frank [LO 1939]	1900	1964	157E	S
" ssa , Rose	1906	10-19-1982x		
STOCKHOFF, Alma Rose	1925	1939		
ALLGEIER, Henry C. - F. & A.M. emb [LO 2-1941] American Legion mkr	1895	1941	158W	S
WOOD, Mildred B. - Wife & Mother	1914	1955		
GUTZWILLER, Jessie E. - "Cass"	1891	1942	158E	S
" ssa , Fannie M. RININGER	1885	1947		
GUTZWILLER, William C.	1863	1949		
" ssa , Louise [LO]	1866	1940		
HATHAWAY, Arthur - Brother - Jr Ord emb	1887	1960	159W	S
HATHAWAY, Fannie - Sister - OES emb	1884	11- 1-1976x		
HATHAWAY, Ray - F. & A.M. emb [LO]	1877	1955		
" ssa , Clara B. - OES emb & D of A mkr	1875	1954		
HAYHOE, Thomas J.	1863	1943	159	S
HAYHOE, Jennie R. [LO]	1874	1969		SE
WITTENBERG, William A. [LO]	1924	2-11-1981x	159	S
" ssa , Erma L. [LO]	1923	----		NE
MAHANEY, R. & F. [LOs]	----	----	160W	S
_____, ----- Mother - (Minnie?)	1886	1978	160E	S
HUFFMAN*, Minnie [Minnie & Eliza LO's]	----	3- 8-1978*		
_____, ----- Dad	1886	1948		
ALDRICH, Blanche & Harry [LOs]	----	----	161	S

NAME	BD or AGE	DD	Lot	Sec.
ALDRICH, Harry Ralzamon - Dad -Born Union, Conn Died Birmingham, MI - Husband & Father - F. & A.M. emb	11-29-1892	5- 7-1960	161	S
HALLAM, Edwin M.	1912	11-12-1988x	162W	S
" ssa , Mary A. [LO]	1911	11-16-1980x		
SAYERS, D. [LO]	----	----	162SE	S
BUTTS, Roy O. [LO]	1890	1-29-1977x	162	S
"ssa , Alice C.	1884	1969		NE
ROLFES, William F.	1881	1958	163W	S
" ssa , Emma L.	1885	9-18-1987x		
BIGGS, Gustave W. - Jr Ord emb [LO]	1879	1954	163	S
" ssa, Irene B.	1881	1958		
BIGGS, Gustave W. - F. & A.M. emb	1910	----		
" ssa, Dorothy E.	1913	11-21-1986x		
There are two lots numbered 164. This one is between lots 141 & roadway:				
ASHCRAFT, Troy	4-27-1908	9-23-1974	164	S
" ssa , Lucy (Lucy Ashcraft REESE) [LO]	6-20-1908	6- 6-1982		
Second lot numbered 164 is S of lot 163:				
HOWARD, H. & R. [LOs]	----	----	164W	S
HOWARD, Nelly BARKER	7-14-1906	5-20-1975		
STAAT, August [LO]	1880	1974	164E	S
"ssa , Mary E.	1885	1972		
LOOS, N. & R. [LOs]	----	----	164A	S
LOOS, Clifford	1901	4-21-1986x	164A	S
"ssa, Lillian	1905	----		
MARTIN, Earl [LO]	1912	9-16-1984x	165A	S
" ssa , Catherine	1912	5-31-1980x		
DURRETT, M. [LO]	----	----	165B	S
DURRETT, Ronald Keith - Ssgt U.S.Marines WW II	1912	4- 8-1981		
No lot owner listed	----	----	165C	S
WILLSEY, Viola M.	1907	1918	165D	S
WILLSEY, Samuel E. [LO 1918]	1864	1934		
" ssa , Dora A.	1871	1958		
_____, Raymond	1914	1925	166W	S
LOCKWOOD, Jacob [LO 2-10-1927]	1878	1935		
" ssa , Ida (Louise)	1883	9-14-1983x		
FLICK, John [LO 1920]	1879	1952	166E	S
" ssa, Margaret	1885	1966		
REHFUES, Edward [LO 5-15-1924]	1871	1943	167W	S
" ssa , Martha - His Wife	1860	1924		
" ssa , Lilah M. - His Wife	1884	1934		
WOOD, Janet M. - Baby	11- 6-1940	1- 4-1941		
ALTHAUS, Edward [LO 1920]	1855	1921	167E	S
" ssa , Mattie	1852	1920		
ALTHAUS, Mary	1878	1944		
PFALGRAF*, Marion	----	5-20-1988*	168	S
KRAUS, Frederick [LO 1922]	1859	1933		
" ssa, Katherine	1869	1954		
KRAUS, Alfrieda	1903	1922		
FLOWERS, Elsie	1886	1962	169	S
FLOWERS, John E.	1856	1939		
DEAN, Clarence, Sr. - Father [LO 1922]	1879	1929		
DEAN, Mattie - Mother	1884	1973		
DEAN, Mildred - Daughter	1909	1925		
DEAN, Clarence W., Jr. - Son	1912	1922		
MOODY, Inez M.	11-17-1901	11-10-1985	170W	S
MOODY, Carl O. - Tenn Pfc U.S.Army WW I	6-13-1899	6-26-1969		
GRABEL, William [LO 1922] [Wm's individual stone gives b. yr 1872]	1873	1958	170E	S
" ssa , Anna E. SNYDER - His Wife	1875	1921		
GWALTNEY, Edith G.	1905	1929		
HORNING, Mary [LO 1923]	1873	1951	171	S
HORNING, Valentine	1864	1923		
HORNING, Anna K.	1894	1963		
HORNING, Albert J.	1894	1968		
HORNING, Fred	1911	1975		
" ssa , Hilda	1900	7-21-1981x		
HORNING, E. Stanley	1918	1974		
ZIND, Mary H. - Mother [LO 1923]	1861	1926	172	S
LEVY, Katherine Z.	1890	1971		
LEVY, Leon	1887	1944		
LEVY, Jeanette	1916	----		
ZIND, Edward	1886	1947		
ZIND, Emma B.	1887	12- 3-1982x		
DARBY, Clara G. - Mother	1863	1923	173	S
DARBY, Allen M. - Father [LO 1923]	1861	1935		
DARBY, Allen G. - Father	1904	----		
DARBY, Elizabeth T. - Mother	1909	6-17-1985x		
LAKE, Lawrence [LO 1931]	----	----	174	S
REESE, Roy - Father	1885	1936		
REESE, Olga - Mother	1885	1975		
GOSLING, Cora B. [LO 1932]	1863	1936	175N	S
GOSLING, John E.	1858	1932		
ALTHAUS, Raymond	1889	1958	175S	S
ALTHAUS, William V.	1866	1934		

NAME	BD or AGE	DD	Lot	Sec.
ALTHAUS, Hannah E. [LO 1934]	1865	1957	175S	S
DETERS, Clara E. (Edith)	1891	4- 8-1982x	176	S
TRAUD, Edith A.	1901	5- 2-1986x		
TRAUD, Valentine G.	1887	1939		
WEIGEL, Gertrude M.	1909	----		
DETERS, Edward C. - Father [LO 1934]	1869	1937		
DETERS, Rose N. - Mother	1876	1935		
DETERS, Elizabeth R. (Rose)	1904	1- 8-1980x		
MATHIAS*, Noah **E.-WWI** & WWII Vet.[LO 1938]	9-10-1897	1-22-1989*	177	S
ULLOM, Randall Paul - Our Son	1956	9-18-1981x		
MATHIAS, Georgiena V.	1900	1975		
MATHIAS, Edward - BSA Troop 201 Eagle emb	1921	1938		
RABENSTEIN, Otto P.	1875	1944	178	S
" ssa , Emma L. [LO]	1882	1953		
HASTINGS, John F. (Franklin) T/Sgt U.S. Army WW II	4-19-1912	8-18-1976	179	S
FAGALY, Abbie A.	1891	10-31-1980x		
" ssa , William E. [LO]	1882	1955		
BENTER, Ella H. w/o Fred E.	1901	1969	180W	S
BENTER, Frederick E. - Cpl U.S.Army WW I	12- 1-1896	9-17-1984		
HODGES, Sallie D.	1882	1959		
HODGES, William R. [LO]	1871	1949		
SCHWARTZ, ----- [LO]	----	----	180E	S
SCHWARTZ, Robert L. f/o Robert, Jr., Sally & Larry - North Bend Fire Dept. mkr	1919	1948		
KIRK, Michael Wm.	One date	1950		
SCHWARTZ, Larry L.	1948	1972		
GETTLES, Harlan E.	1883	1949		
" ssa , Imo Faye [LO]	1893	1969		
JACKSON, Art [LO]	----	----	181E	S
JACKSON, Baby	One date	11-23-1948		
GILLESPIE, Shirley [LO]	----	----	182W	S
GILLESPIE, Ralph E. - Husband & Daddy	1923	1950		
GETZ, Chas. - [LO]	----	----	182E	S
GETZ, Linda F.	8-27-1950	9-13-1950		
MYERS, James T. (Todd) [LO]	4-24-1910	11-20-1986	183W	S
"ssa , James, Jr.	One date	1951		
"ssa , Frances P.	7- 8-1926	----		
SHARP, Arthur G. [LO]	1897	4-21-1976	183E	S
" ssa, Marie A. [LO]	1901	----		
KREBS, Ralph - Son [LO]	1898	1969	184W	S
KREBS, Nora - Mother	1877	1959		
KREBS, Fred - Father	1871	1953		
KREBS, Helen	1904	1963	185W	S
KREBS, Charles (A.) [LO]	1902	1968		
HERBERT, Elizabeth C.	1887	10-16-1976x		
MILLER, Collins J. - Father [LO]	1865	1950	185E	S
MILLER, Hattie B. - Mother	1876	1953		
TUCKER, Charlotte (NW Corner of lot)	1909	6- 1-1980x	186A	S
CLARK, Robert M. - Indiana Pvt 102 Inf WW I	8-25-1893	12-25-1963	186A	S
CLARK, Emmett	1899	8-31-1984		
CLARK, Robert Milton [LO]	1863	1951		
"ssa , Louella	1864	1951		
WHEELDON, Joseph E.	1912	----		
" ssa , Carrie J.	1915	1974		
DOWNEY, George	1899	3-20-1976x	186B	S
" ssa , Myrtle [LO]	1902	12-12-1983x		
WILLIAMS, B. [LO]	----	----	186C	S
WILLIAMS, Herbert L. - Pfc U.S.Army	6- 5-1902	1- 2-1975		
KATZEL, John - Father- Civil War Vet. Co M 5th O.V. Cav.	1845	[12-19]1924	187	S
" ssa , Amelia [LO 1925]	1865	1956		
KLEEMAN, Walter Philip [LO]	11- 9-1905	3- 4-1981	187	S
" ssa , Amelia Elizabeth	5- 9-1910	----	SE	
MERCER, Robert V.	1934	1956	188	S
BACHMANN, Amanda - Mother	1872	1947		
BACHMANN, Theodore - Father [LO 1934]	1863	1951		
BACHMAN, Theodore	4-18-1901	7-26-1984		
BACHMAN, Dorothy V.	1929	1934		
BACHMAN, Matilda C.	8-23-1908	2-15-1989		
HOLDEN, Ronald R. "Prince of Shadows"	1926	12- 5-1980x	189	S
HOLDEN, Raymond E. [LO 1925]	1890	1948		
" ssa , Alice P.	1892	1969		
_____, Beatrice - These 3 names on one stone:	1912	1925		
_____, Raymond	1914	1925		
_____, Sylvia	1922	1925		
BAUSCHER, Charles W. - Father	1885	1950		
BAUSCHER, Effie J. - Mother	1875	1950		
WELSH, ----- [LO]	----	----	190W	S
WELSH, Flora	7-23-1892	10-17-1980		
WELSH, Robert M. - D.A.V. WW I	10- 7-1892	7-25-1972		
BELLMAN, Fred - Father [LO 1925]	1880	1962	190E	S
BELLMAN, Lillie (Lillian) Mother	1882	11- 7-1983x		

NAME	BD or AGE	DD	Lot	Sec.
BELLMAN, Irma - Daughter	1912	1931	190E	S
BELLMAN, Edith - Daughter	1908	1924		
BACHMAN, Naomi (Age 4y 2m)	11-19-1920	1-21-1925	191A	S
BACHMAN, Violet F.	1897	1961		
BACHMAN, George H. [LO 1925]	1895	1973		
TAYLOR, Ernest V. "Married June 26, 1935"	1912	1974	191B	S
" ssa , Dorothy P. [LO]	1918	----		
COVERT, Bertha K. - Wife & Mother [LO]	1905	4-13-1988x	191C	S
COVERT, Edward W. - Husband & Father	1903	1974		
SULLIVAN, Mildred [LO] "Married Jan. 13,1932"	1915	8-15-1984x	191D	S
" ssa , George T. [LO]	1903	2-12-1989x		
LINNENKOHL, Catherine - Mother	1861	1927	192	S
LINNENKOHL, George - Father CL,122 [LO 1927]	1857	1942		
WILSON, Otto	1895	1970		
" ssa , Lillian	1896	7-24-1983x		
HALLMAN, Louisa A.	1864	1949	193W	S
HALLMAN, Alfred T.	1862	1955		
HALLMAN, Myrtle M. [LO]	1898	1962		
HORNING, Loretta	1896	6-30-1981x	193E	S
HORNING, Louis [LO 1931]	1857	1955		
HORNING, Mary L.	1862	1931		
HAMILTON, Mrs. John [LO 1931]	----	----	194	S
DETERS, Charles J. [LO 1934?]	1892	1968		
"ssa , Stella M.	1891	8-17-1988x		
DETERS, Charles W.	1917	1959		
NIMMO, William L. [LO]	1875	1954	195	S
" ssa, Pearl M.	1880	1958		
NIMMO, Donald Stewart - American Legion mkr	1929	1947		
WOODS, Eugene Shirley [LO] Ohio Ssgt U.S. Marines WW II	3- 5-1920	9- 7-1972	196W	S
KING, Samuel - Father [LO]	1891	1961	196E	S
"ssa, Margaret - Mother	1892	1947		
SAMMONS, Stanley A. - F. & A.M. emb	2-26-1910	7-19-1973	197	S
" ssa , Luella A. [LO]	3-19-1910	12-22-1977	NW	
ABBOTT, Leroy R. - Virginia S2 U.S. Navy WW II	7-29-1909	11- 1-1973	197	S
" ssa , Martha A. [LO]	1914	----		
HENDRICKSON, R. & G. [LOs]	----	----	197E	S
TAYLOR, Lee Light - Son	6-29-1954	8-30-1973		
BRAUNE, Bruno Emil [LO] "Saxony, Germany"	4-16-1870	10-29-1949	198	S
" ssa , Olga C. nee FRÖBE	1-23-1876	10- 2-1955		
BRAUNE, Alice D. - Mother	2-14-1910	2-23-1965		
MARTIN, Elizabeth O. nee BRAUNE - Sister	7-17-1901	3-23-1988		
BRAUNE, Judy Ann	One date	7-20-1974		
BRAUNE, Siegfried H. [LO]"Married Feb.6,1971"	1917	----		
" ssa , Cecilia nee SCHALLICK	1928	----		
REINKING, Carrie & Sons [LOs]	----	----	199	S
REINKING, Arthur W.	1922	12-29-1978x		
REINKING, Carrie A. - Mother	1879	1961		
REINKING, William C. - Father	1874	1949		
REINKING, Erwin W. - Son - A.S. of C.A.P.	1918	1960		
SCHISLER, Corinne - Niece	1914	1961		
MEACHAM, John I. - Uncle	1882	1967		
REINKING, Wilbert G. - Husband	1910	1967		
HEARNE, Elizabeth - Daughter	1903	10-12-1980x	200	S
HEARNE, Mattie - Mother	1873	1949		
HEARNE, George R. - Father [LO]	1872	1952		
HEARNE, Helen - Daughter	1901	----		
HEARNE, Russell E. [LO]	1907	10- 5-1976x	201W	S
" ssa , Marie C.	1909	----		
SHAVER, Hortis Augustus "Married Aug.25,1945"	**10-4-**1906	3- 6-1983	201E	S
"ssa , Evelyne Marie nee MATHIAS [LO] b. Hamilton County, OH & Hortis A. b. Gallia County, OH	9- 2-1920	----		
REATHERFORD, Wm. "Chess"	1900	8- 4-1976x	202W	S
WILLIAMS, Reba - Mother	1906	----		
REATHERFORD, Julius [LO]	1870	1954		
" ssa , Alice [LO]	1868	1956		
HAYES, Nixon [LO]	----	----	202E	S
WILLIS, John Henry	1888	1952	203W	S
"ssa , Sara Mabel [LO]	1889	1970		
FOYSTER, ----- [LO]	----	----	203E	S
SWAFFORD, Geneva	1905	1952		
JACKSON, Mary [LO]	----	----	204W	S
JACKSON, Erna - Mother	1888	1957		
JACKSON, Charles J. - Father	1885	1962		
COOKENDORFER, ----- [LO]	----	----	204E	S
COOKENDORFER, William A.	12-31-1873	9- 7-1952		
TROUTMAN, Mary J.	1904	5-10-1979x		
COOKENDORFER, William E.	12-25-1907	9-29-1955		
BINGLE, R. [LO]	----	----	205	S
BINGLE, Carl E. - Ohio Sgt Co F 422 Regt WW II	10-18-1919	12-22-1963	NW	
COX, Frank - Dad	1909	1962	205	S
COX*, Lillian [LO]	----	3- 9-1988x	SW	

NAME	BD or AGE	DD	Lot	Sec.
BAIN, Forest [LO]	----	----	205E	S
BAIN, William H.- BSA mkr "In Memoriam,	6-16-1939	7-24-1953		
William H. BAIN, Miamitown, OH 2nd Class Troop 53"				
JANICKE, Leo [LO]	----	----	206W	S
JANICKE, Berniece C.	3-10-1901	6-26-1966		
CLINKSCALES, Edgar H.	8- 6-1881	2-28-1954		
HAMPSON, Robin Ray	One date	1953	206E	S
JACKSON, Andrew L. - Father	1888	1953		
JACKSON, Marie E. - Mother [LO]	1891	1961		
STRIMPLE, P. & D. [LOs]	----	----	207	S
HOWARD, Samuel E. [LO]	11-19-1880	11-29-1964	208W	S
" ssa , Maud E.	5-20-1883	6- 2-1955		
HOWARD, Pearl BARR	8- 1-1885	7-26-1968		
HOWARD, Elmer E.	2-21-1908	3-27-1973		
DUCKWORTH, B. [LO]	----	----	208	S
DUCKWORTH, Arthur Lee - Ohio Cox USNR WW II	11-10-1925	10-18-1954		SE
DUCKWORTH, Charlotte M. [LO]	1902	----	208	S
" ssa , Arthur J. [LO]	1901	8- 5-1979x		
ROLFES, Fred [LO]	----	----	209	S
ROLFES, Albert W.-Ohio SSgt Army Air	10-11-1915	9-22-1964		
Force WW II				
ROLFES, Albert - Ohio Cook Co D 138 Inf WW I	1-10-1890	4-16-1968		
WEST, Judy Mae - Daughter	1-31-1950	11- 6-1955		
GAEBEL, Harold F., Sr.	1922	1974	210	S
" ssa , Elsie M.	----	----		
BUNNELL, Reda M.	1932	9-29-1984x		
BUNNELL, James D.	1928	----		
BUNNELL, Dr. W.A. - Father	3- 7-1885	1-11-1957		
BUNNELL, Elsie (HORSLEY) Mother [LO]	8-21-1892	12- 8-1982x		

SOUTHWEST SECTION

NAME	BD or AGE	DD	Lot	Sec.
In aisle N of lot 1:				
BALLARD, Albert W.-Ohio GM2 USNR WW II	6- 1-1923	1- 9-1968	A1	SW
BENTEL, William, Jr [LO]	1874	1952	1	SW
" ssa , Matilda	1882	19--		
SEARS, Clarence A.	1-16-1886	12- 3-1950		
SEARS, Carrie RUEHL [LO]	12- 9-1885	9-10-1970		
SEARS, Lucille	11- 5-1912	11-21-1965		
SEARS, Lee E. - VFW mkr	2-22-1894	4- 9-1961		
HINE, Olive	1898	1969	2	SW
HINE, Louis R.	1873	1950		
HINE, Susie [LO]	1893	1955		
LAMB, Ernest	1915	1960		
HINE, Leslie A.	1897	1974	3N	SW
"ssa, Naomi V. [LO]	1898	12- 3-1988x		
GETZ, Minnie [LO]	----	----	3S	SW
NUGENT, Hilda E. - VFW Ladies Aux mkr	5- 7-1905	6- 4-1971		
NUGENT, Joseph H.	6-14-1898	8-19-1969		
(Joseph Harris NUGENT d. 12-3-1977)				
SCHARDINE, Ethel A.	1910	1956		
HOPPING, Mary [LO]	----	----	4	SW
HOPPING, Edwin - F.& A.M. emb - Cleves Vol Fire	1893	1944		
Dept. mkr				
CAMPBELL, Infant	----	----		
HOPPING*, George	----	3-15-1976*		
GOODMAN, Henry - Husband	1873	1945	5	SW
GOODMAN, Fannie - Wife [LO]	1883	1969		
PARKER, Harry [LO]	----	----	6	SW
GABEL, Edna M. nee LINNENKOHL - Mother	1899	1952		
BERTRAND, Lauretta	9-15-1888	9-23-1956		
BERTRAND, Louis J.	1- 1-1882	11- 2-1945		
MYERS, Laura B.	1862	1951	7	SW
"ssa , William F. [LO]	1863	1946		
PEACOCK, Samuel M.	1888	1961		
" ssa , Edna M.	1890	1974		
LAKE, Laura R.	1894	1975	8	SW
"ssa, Laurence P. - F. & A.M. emb [LO]	1888	1973		
"ssa, Ruth C.	1892	1931		
"ssa, William H. - Ohio SSgt 301 Bomb GP	10-13-1924	6-19-1968		
AAF WW II AM & 2 OLC				
WENDLING, Dorothy M. - Mother	1917	1975	9	SW
MYERS, Electra B. - Mother [LO]	1893	1957		
MYERS, Elijah C. - Father	1890	1947		
ANDERSON, Estella V. - Mother	1895	1971	10	SW
ANDERSON, William N. (Norbert) Father	1894	5-29-1981x		
MECHTENSIMER, Margaret BACHMANN [LO]	1897	1- 5-1985x		
MECHTENSIMER, Henry	1880	1948		
ANDERSON, Marjorie G.	2- 5-1918	8- 2-1978		
BURDSALL*, Carolyn (KRAMER)	----	3- 7-1988*	11	SW
KRAMER, Walter C. [LO] Ohio CY U.S.Navy	10- 7-1894	5- 1-1948		
WW I - American Legion mkr				
COMBS, R. [LO]	----	----	12W	SW
COMBS, Alma PRUITT - Mother	1915	1955		
HALLETT, Pauline [LO]	----	----	12E	SW

NAME	BD or AGE	DD	Lot	Sec.
HALLETT, Anthony - Father	1903	1955	12E	SW
HALL, D. [LO]	----	----	13NW	SW
HAEFNER, Alma - Mother [LO]	1892	1971	13SW	SW
HAEFNER, Louis - Father	1893	1955		
COWELL, John W. - F. & A.M. emb	1881	1955	13E	SW
COWELL, Catherine [LO]	1891	7- 1-1984x		
RHOADES, William M. - Father [LO]	1878	1961	14	SW
" ssa , Minnie Goldie - Mother	1884	1956		
SMITH, Adrian [LO]	----	----	15W	SW
SMITH, Elverna F. - Mother - OES emb	6- 5-1915	7-26-1956		
HERBSTREIT, Elsie I. (ROESSLER) [LO]	1913	3-31-1986x	15E	SW
ROESSLER, Ezra C.	1913	1956		
No lot owner listed:			16A	SW
JOHNSON, Melvin C. - Ohio Wagoner U.S.Army	5-31-1901	11- 8-1965	16B	SW
WW I - VFW mkr (? Yr of d. on government stone is 1900)				
" ssa , Ruth W.	1901	12-26-1985x		
MOLONEY, Marie M.	1908	1967	16C	SW
MOLONEY, John J. [LO]	1904	3- 9-1987x		
CORMICAN, Robert P. [LO]	1890	1971	16D	SW
" ssa , Muriel I. [LO]	1891	1967		
SPARKS, Jonas T., Jr. [LO]	1916	12- 4-1985x	17W	SW
SPARKS, Elinore	1-11-1920	11-20-1956		
STUMPF, Ruth G. - Mother [LO]	1894	11- 8-1977x	17E	SW
STUMPF, Edward J. - Father	1887	1956		
SCHUETZ, Henry [LO]	----	----	18W	SW
SCHUETZ, Joseph C. - Fabber	1882	1966		
" ssa , Lydia - Mother	1880	1957		
HIGGINS, Lee	5-22-1873	6-22-1957	18E	SW
" ssa , Nannie [LO]	12- 6-1878	6-21-1970		
WESTERMAN, Lea	3- 5-1898	7-20-1987		
ROE, Bee [LO]	6- 8-1893	----	19W	SW
"ssa, Delia	12-17-1905	10-17-1958		
ALLEN, Elizabeth	1875	1968		
MERKLE, Ray J. [LO]	1905	12-26-1983x	19E	SW
" ssa , Millie	1914	----		
MERKLE, Eleanora O. - Mother	1911	1971		
MERKLE, David L. - Son	1939	1958		
KOLB, ----- [LO]	----	----	20NW	SW
JONES, J. [LO]	----	----	20SW	SW
GETZ, Betty J. [LO]	----	----	20E	SW
GETZ, Edward Lee - Ohio Pfc HQ & HQ Co	6- 7-1923	3- 4-1958		
67 Armd Regt WW II BSM-PH				
BRADLEY, Cecil [LO]	----	----	21W	SW
BRADLEY, Martin W.	One date	6-11-1959		
LITTELL, Marvin [LO]	----	----	21E	SW
_____, ----- [small log memorial stone]	----	----		
HENSLEY, Della [LO]	----	----	22W	SW
STAPLETON, Catherine - Mother	1868	1965		
HENSLEY, Paul A.	6-15-1914	6- 5-1961		
GOLDSMITH-BROGLE [LOs]	----	----	22E	SW
GOLDSMITH, Joseph H. - Father	1897	1959		
" ssa , Marie L. - Mother	1899	1966		
BROGLE, SYlvester H.	1905	1965		
"ssa , Irene C.	1906	1959		
No lot owner listed:	----	----	23W	SW
WINTER, Edward P. - Ohio S2 USNRF WW I	12- 9-1895	5-30-1963	23E	SW
WINTER, Irene B. [LO]	2- 5-1904	1- 7-1985		
[No lot owner listed]	----	----	23W	SW
JACKSON, E. & L. [LOs]	----	----	24W	SW
DAVIS, Ruth L.	1915	1964		
JACKSON, Richard C. - Son	1938	12-24-1979x		
JACKSON*, Edward	----	9- 2-1987*		
Lots 25 & 26 are not on cemetery map.				
In aisle N of lot 27:				
BAILEY, James B. - Ohio Pvt U.S.Army	9-14-1935	2- 7-1969	A27	SW
GRADY, S. & M. [LOs]	----	----	27W	SW
WOODYARD, Newton S.	1877	1954		
" ssa , Jane D.	1878	1963		
SEAL, Catherine - Mom	1886	1952	27E	SW
SEAL, Russell E. "Russ" Tec 5 U.S.Army [LO]	1-26-1912	9-16-1974		
Disabled American Vet mkr				
SEAL, Raymond W.	2-15-1922	11-23-1984		
HEID, Jacob E.	1900	1972	28W	SW
HEID, Ida nee GUTZWILLER [LO]	6-14-1874	12-28-1955		
HEID, Jacob J.	10-28-1879	6-17-1950		
MINGES, Ralph, M.D. [LO]	1920	9- 3-1987x	28E	SW
MINGES, Annette - Mother	1922	1950		
BOHANNON, Eva	12-23-1870	10-22-1962	29	SW
BOHANNON, Bennett	8- 1-1873	12-14-1953		
WEBER, Stanley [LO]	1901	5-12-1984x		
"ssa , Geneva (Mary Geneva)	1905	1- 3-1982x		
HOPPING, George E. [LO]	11-11-1890	3-15-1976	30	SW
MATSON, Edith (?d.2-2-1976)	11- 8-1889	3- 3-1976		
MATSON, J. Emery	1891	1954		

NAME	BD or AGE	DD	Lot Sec.
HOPPING, William B.	1859	1909	30 SW
" ssa , D. Wilbur	1897	1901	
HOPPING, Carrie L.	1862	1951	
STRATEGER, Pearl nee SLAUGHTER - Mother	1892	1925	31 SW
STRATEGER, Joseph Arnold - Father [LO]	1885	1966	
STRATEGER, Harry	1877	1946	
STRATEGER, Mayme	1887	1975	
In aisle between lots 31 & 32:	----	----	A31 SW
POWERS, Infant	One date	6-17-1947	&32
POWERS, Ethel M.	1921	11-30-1987x	
KELLER, John P.	1889	9-23-1977x	32W SW
" ssa , Elizabeth K.	1893	1969	
HEY, John Korbett - Ohio Tec 4 Engrs	12-20-1917	3-27-1962	
WW II [LO]			
JUMP,C. [LO]	----	----	32SE SW
STRATEGER, Helen K.	1879	1969	32NE SW
STRATEGER, Louis G. [LO]	1881	1950	
SCHOCKEY, ----- [LO]	----	----	33W SW
BATES, Fred J. - Ohio Pvt U.S.Marines WW I	11-12-1899	11-14-1962	
EDWARDS, Charles [LO]	3-16-1885	1-22-1960	33E SW
EDWARDS, Dorothy T.	5- 4-1900	1- 3-1985	
KRAUSE, George L.	1928	1965	
"FOREMAN-VAN PELT" on monument	----	----	34 SW
VAN PELT, M. (Milton) Basil - Father [LO]	1891	2-26-1976x	
VAN PELT, Minnie - Mother	1894	1954	
PASELEY, Mary H. - Mother	1879	1958	35 SW
PASELEY, John F. - Father [LO]	1879	1966	
PASELEY, Lee H.	1908	1954	
PATTON, S. [LO]	----	----	36NW SW
PATTON, Claude - Cpl U.S.Army WW II	3-22-1926	10- 6-1979	
HOFFMAN, Edward J. - Father	1891	1956	36SW SW
" ssa , Rose L. - Mother [LO]	1897	5-20-1984x	
SCHMITT, George M.	1902	1956	36E SW
SCHMITT, Iva [LO]	1907	1964	
BORTLEIN, Joseph	1884	1958	37W SW
BORTLEIN, Anna [LO]	1881	1959	
TAYLOR, Leslie A. - U.S.Army WW I	1894	1957	37E SW
TAYLOR, M. Isabelle - Mother [LO]	2- 1-1904	----	
TAYLOR, L. James - Son	2-17-1944	----	
STOCKHOFF, Johnny - Son	1942	1958	38NW SW
STOCKHOFF, John (B.) [LO]	One date	11-14-1977x	
No LO listed;			38SW SW
NADICKSBERND, Harry J. - Husband	1912	1974	38E SW
NADICKSBERND, Virginia F. - Wife [LO]	1912	----	
HOLMAN, Pete	1889	1958	
BIGGS, C. [LO[	----	----	39NW SW
BIGGS, Edna M.	1920	1959	
BIGGS, A. & A. [LOs]	----	----	39SW SW
COLLIER, Ernest E.	1893	1958	39E SW
" ssa , Stacy V. [LO]	1896	1974	
TROYER, Maude	1893	1967	
WYMER, Evelyn A.- Wife "Married July 14,1942"	1917	11-26-1984x	
"ssa , Lewis B. - Husband [LO]	1914	1975	
TRICKEL, Rachella H. "Friend of God's Creatures"	1924	10- 6-1982x	
WYMER, Margaret	1885	1959	
WHEELER, Earl [LO]	----	----	40E SW
WHEELER, Vera D. - Mother	1824	1958	
BARTLEY, Anna M. - Wife [LO]	3-24-1897	10-14-1980	41W SW
BARTLEY, Stanton T.-Ohio Sgt Co D 329	2- 5-1896	1- 7-1960	
Inf WW I			
MORRIS, Alvin S. [LO]	----	----	41E SW
BRONOLD, John B.	3- 5-1880	11- 1-1959	
" ssa , Hollie	10-28-1891	10-24-1959	
KRAUS, Martin C.	1897	1961	42W SW
"ssa , Inez F. [LO]	1908	----	
BENESCH*, Alice E. [LO]	----	2-24-1985*	42E SW
WARD, Robert	3-28-1897	11-21-1964	43NW SW
"ssa, Gertrude [LO]	8- 9-1909	7-20-1984	
KRAMER, Alma E. [LO]	9-28-1900	10-14-1980	43SW SW
KRAMER, Avery W.-Ohio Sgt Co E 6	10-10-1892	4-23-1965	
Ammunition Tn WW I - American Legion mkr			
LAIL, Clarence L. - Father - Ohio Pvt	4- 5-1898	5-15-1961	43E SW
Co C 105 Engrs WW I - U.S. War Vet. mkr			
"ssa, Bertha E. - Mother [LO]	1898	1975	
HUGHETT, James R. - Ohio GY Sgt U.S.Marines	1-25-1925	2-10-1968	
WW II Korea			
HUGHETT, Jessie A. nee LAIL w/o James	11- 5-1927	----	
CLARK, Stephen B. - Pop [LO]	1898	1967	44NW SW
"ssa , Nellie M. - Mom	1904	1965	
CAUDILL, Elmer - F. & A.M. emb	1906	1970	44SW SW
" ssa , Hazel [LO] OES emb	1910	----	
WAVRA, Leroy C. - Husband [LO]	1915	----	44SE SW
"ssa , Carol E. - Wife	1913	1981	

NAME	BD or AGE	DD	Lot Sec.
SAMMONS, Charles C. - Dad [LO]	1875	1971	44NE SW
" ssa , Carol J. - Mom	1886	1966	
STIER, Irene F. [LO]	1901	1970	45NW SW
STIER, John Peter - Ohio Pvt U.S.Army WW I	12-22-1893	2- 1-1966	
American Legion mkr			
No Lot owner listed;			45SW SW
HAEN*, Hallie - Cremains	----	9-11-1979*	
BLACK, C. & E. [LOs]	----	----	45SE SW
BLACK, George O.-Ohio Pvt Camp Hospital	1-16-1895	1-13-1968	
43 WW I - American Legion mkr			
BERGNER, Paul F.	1897	1966	45NE SW
BERGNER, Viola D. - Mother [LO]	5-30-1904	8- 9-1979	
HEARN, W. P. [LO]	----	----	46 SW
HEARN, Pauline-1st Lt. Army Nurse Corps WW II	2- 1-1920	10-24-1976	
WILLSEY, Merida [LO]	1901	1974	47 SW
" ssa , Lillian	1897	1973	
HARBAUGH, Lael - Sister	1896	1966	
Lot 48 thru 52 are not on cemetery map.			
SCHARDINE, Chris - "Married May 23,1923"	1904	----	53W SW
" ssa , Bertha B.	1908	4-28-1983x	
SCHARDINE, Clara A. [LO]	3-27-1900	6- 4-1965	
SCHARDINE, Kenneth	9-18-1896	11- 4-1961	
JAMES, Harold S. [LO]	1893	1- 9-1986x	53E SW
"ssa , Leila V.	1897	1-31-1983x	
JAMES, Melvin Peary - U.S.Army WW II -VFW mkr	1-11-1917	2-24-1985	
HAUCHE, Cora [LO]	----	----	54W SW
ENNEKING, Margaret - Wife	1902	1963	
ENNEKING, William (C.) Husband	1898	9-12-1978x	
LANE, Mary [LO]	----	----	54E SW
PICKENS, Edith [LO]	----	----	55W SW
PICKENS, Virgil E.	2-15-1892	11-12-1966	
DOWNEY, Leonard	1897	1962	55E SW
" ssa , Demy [LO]	1903	19--	
GETZ, Catherine E. - Mother	1891	1962	56W SW
GETZ, John - Father [LO]	1844	6-26-1984x	
In aisle between lots 56 & 57:			A56 SW
TURPIN, Elmer H. - Ohio Pfc 15 Bn U.S.Guards WW I	1894	1962	&57
HOLMES. George F. - Dad - F. & A.M. emb	1899	1962	56E SW
HOLMES. Evelyn M. - Mom OES emb [LO]	1902	1968	
ALLEN, Bessie M. - Mother	1889	1962	57W SW
ALLEN, Warren D. - Father [LO]	1890	1973	
HUNGLER, Charles G., Sr.-U.S.Army WW II	4-13-1925	12-14-1985	57SW SW
GEILER, William [LO]	1895	1974	57E SW
" ssa , Shirley	1896	1966	
MARVIN,------ [LO]	----	----	58NW SW
BAILEY,------ [LO]	----	----	58SW SW
BAILEY, Mark Alan	12-11-1960	12-10-1987	
BAILEY, Michael "Toddy" Our Baby	9-28-1962	2-22-1963	
MOHRHAUS, Bernard - Father [LO]	1899	3- 8-1985x	58SE SW
" ssa , Cecilia - Mother	1902	1974	
BERNARD, ----- [LO]	----	----	58NE SW
SCHMITT, Valentine - Father	1871	1962	
" ssa , Cecilia - Mother	1876	1963	
CRAMER, G. Charles - F. & A.M. emb [LO]	1895	8-17-1988x	59W SW
" ssa , Emilie - OES emb	1896	1971	
HARPER*, Grace (Opal) [LO]	----	10-24-1980	59E SW
SOARD*, Eileen (M.) Baby	----	4-28-1983*	
WRIGHT, Barney W. [LO]	1919	1964	60NW SW
" ssa , Betty (Jo)	1927	6-10-1981x	
CARTMELL, M. Earl	2-21-1910	7- 1-1964	60SW SW
" ssa , Wilma L. [LO]	8-21-1908	----	
MILTON, ----- [LO]	----	----	60NE SW
MILTON, Tammy Jean	7-10-1963	7-18-1963	
INGLIS, S. [LO]	----	----	60SE SW
INGLIS, Robert F. - Son & Brother	1960	10-23-1979x	
ROSS, I. & A. [LOs]	----	----	61W SW
ROSS, Irvin B., Sr. - Ohio Tec 5 U.S.Army	4- 2-1919	5-13-1973	
WW II			
ROSS, Oscar	1889	1963	
"ssa, Katherine	1888	1940	
ALTHAUS, Loretta [LO]	----	----	61E SW
ALTHAUS, Ralph H.	1898	1963	
ADDISON, Gracie	1902	1970	62W SW
" ssa , Finley	1900	4-10-1986x	
CHASE, Wilford [LO] "Married Nov.18, 1942"	8- 6-1918	4- 4-1969	
Sgt 1560 SVC COMD Unit WW II - VFW mkr			
" ssa, Myrtle	1923	----	
STAUTBERG, George - Husband - [LO]	1900	1-13-1092x	62E SW
" ssa , Edna M. - Wife	1900	1963	
WILSON, E. [LO]	----	----	63NW SW
WILSON, Herbert Allen - Father - Ohio RD	4-17-1931	8-29-1967	
3 U.S.Navy Korea;			
HUNT, Rosemary	1917	1967	63SW SW
HUNT, Thomas J. [LO]	1912	1969	

NAME	BD or AGE	DD	Lot	Sec.
MILLER, William H.	1886	1967	63E	SW
" ssa , Clara N. [LO]	1890	1981		
ZWICK, L. [LO]	----	----	64NW	SW
ANDERSON, Hattie - Aunt	1881	1973		
EVANS, Miles N., Jr. [LO] Ohio Sfc U.S.	11-12-1927	1- 1-1967	64SW	SW
Army Korea				
WILLIAMS, C. & D. [LOs]	----	----	64E	SW
WILLIAMS*, Dorothy	----	11- 3-1987*		
EARLY, E. & R. [LOs]	----	----	65NW	SW
EARLY*, Elmer	----	11-23-1985*		
BETTS, A. & G. [LOs]	----	----	65SW	SW
LINDE, ----- [LO]	----	----	65E	SW
LINDE, Richard V. - Ohio Pfc 1 Bn 1 MAR	12-20-1940	12-21-1966		
1 MAR Div Vietnam PH VFW mkr				
LINDE, Elmer	1-22-1921	----		
"ssa , Geraldine F.	5-19-1923	----		
R.S.R. [LO]	----	----	66NW	SW
CR----, C. [LO]?	----	----	66SW	SW
HETISIMER, William D. - Father [LO]	1886	1967	66SE	SW
" ssa , Mamie - Mother	1903	1970		
RILEY, L. [LO]	----	----	66NE	SW
RILEY, Thomas M. - Ohio Pfc 1462 SVC	7-28-1925	11-14-1966		
COMD Unit WW II PH - VFW mkr				
RILEY, L. [LO]	----	----	67NW	SW
No LO listed	----	----	67SW	SW
FIEGE, William H. - Father	1882	1966	67SE	SW
"ssa , Marie M. - Mother -[LO]	1885	1974		
"ssa , Marie H. - Daughter	1911	3-15-1989x		
ASHCRAFT, J. [LO]	----	----	67NE	SW
ASHCRAFT, John D.	1883	1967		
SMITH, Mary M. [LO]	1905	1968	68	SW
"ssa , Arthur [Lo]	1898	7-31-1976x		
SCHROEDER*, Margaret	----	6- 3-1978*		
[No LO listed]	----	----	69	SW
VEIT, Walter "Steve"	1917	7-22-1981x		
"ssa, Violet "Belle" nee HOCKMAN	1922	12-17-1984x		
[No LO listed]	----	----	70	SW
[No LO listed]	----	----	71	SW
CHANEY, Frank E. - Father - F. & A.M. emb [LO]	1906	2- 5-1979x	72	SW
"ssa , Clara P. [LO]	1910	----		
Our children Kenneth, Robert, Shirley, Gary, Sharon				
[No LO listed]	----	----	73W	SW
TOLER, Thelma E. - Mother [LO]	1914	11-14-1981x	73	SW
GROVE, Louise D. - Mother	1896	1963		SE
OTTO, Evelyn J(ean) GROVE - OES emb [LO]	7-18-1917	5- 9-1985	73NE	SW
WOLFE, D. & R. [LOs]	----	----	74NW	SW
THOMAS, C. [LO]	----	----	74SW	SW
COLEGATE, William (C.) [LO]	1881	1965	74E	SW
" ssa , Barbara	1889	5-15-1978x		
BAIN, Beverly C. - Father	8- 6-1908	6- 4-1964		
LACEY, William S. - Husband [LO]	1890	6-20-1981x	75NW	SW
"ssa , May C. nee SMITH	1887	1964		
WILLIAMSON, ----- [LO]	----	----	75SW	SW
WILLIAMSON, Joseph	1888	1975		
" ssa , Anna S.	1891	1965		
GIERINGER, ----- [LO]	----	----	75SE	SW
GIERINGER, Robert - Ohio Pvt 31 Artillery	9-17-1896	10- 7-1964		
CAC WW I				
GIERINGER, Ethel - Wife	2-28-1896	5-23-1968		
MYERS, Walter F. - Ohio Wagoner U.S.	1-31-1895	9-29-1964	75NE	SW
Army WW I				
MYERS, Anna C. - Mother [LO]	1898	3-23-1980x		
HAMMOND, W. & B. [LO]	----	----	76	SW
HENSLEY, James M. - Dad	4-14-1863	9- 4-1967		
LIPPS, Maude B.	8-10-1900	----		
"ssa , Philip D.	8-25-1895	6- 8-1978		
FRONDORF, H. [LO]	----	----	77W	SW
FRONDORF, Alvera M.	1912	1975		
In aisle S of 77W"			A77W	SW
FRONDORF, James H. - Ohio Sp/4 569	4-18-1944	1- 8-1968	&78	
Engr Co - VFW & American Legion mkrs				
LUCKETT, Robert T.	1899	1967	77SE	SW
" ssa , Lucille V. [LO]	1915	----		
COOKENDORFER, John R. - Ohio Tec 5 HQ	10-20-1917	11- 2-1967	77NE	SW
Co 34 infantry WW II - U.S.War Vet mkr				
COOKENDORFER*, E. Jean [LO]	----	8-23-1988*		
HEIL, F. [LO]	----	----	78W	SW
HEIL, David R. - Our Son	6-23-1949	9-15-1968		
ARMACOST, James	1906	1968	78SE	SW
" ssa , Clara (Marie) [LO]	1898	8-17-1979x		
SCHARDINE, ----- [LO]	----	----	78NE	SW
[No LO listed]	----	----	79NW	SW
ROTH, Richard L. R.,Sr.-Father [LO]	1915	1970	79SW	SW
HAYS, Rose Mary - Mother [LO]	1929	1974	79E	SW

NAME	BD or AGE	DD	Lot	Sec.
HAYS, Nelson William [LO] Ohio RCT Co H	1-24-1928	9- 5-1972	79E	SW
Infantry Korea				
HAYS, Nelson W., Jr. - Son "Sonny"	1951	1968		
GARRETT, R. & L. [LO]	----	----	80W	SW
GARRETT, Michael Allen - Son	6- 4-1961	8- 7-1968		
WRIGHT, ----- [LO]	----	----	80E	SW
PITSLER, B. [LO]	----	----	81W	SW
SIEBEIN, Louis H. [LO]	1914	----	81E	SW
" ssa , Evadeane M.	1908	12- 9-1977x		
ssa SMITH, Edna Mae - Daughter	1931	1968		
HEIL, F. [LO]	----	----	82W	SW
MURRAY, Henry [LO]	1892	6-12-1978x	82	SW
MURRAY, Nora	1896	1968		SE
ADKINS, O. [LO]	----	----	82NE	SW
ADKINS, Charles	1886	1970		
ADKINS, Clara	1906	1968		
[No LO listed]	----	----	83W	SW
SHOCKLEY, George P. - 32nd F. & A.M. emb	1909	1966	83SE	SW
SHOCKLEY, Marjorie K. ISON - Wife [LO]	----	11-18-1977		
SIMMONDS, R. E. [LO]	----	----	83NE	SW
WALKER, H. Clifford - mkr: Spanish War Vet	1877	1967		
1898-1902 United Army/Navy-Cuba-Phillipine Islands-Puerto Rico-U.S.A.				
WALKER, Minnie F. nee HUNT	1886	1969		
[No LO listed]	----	----	84	SW
[No LO listed]	----	----	85	SW
Lot 86 not on cemetery map.				
JERGENS, H. [LO]	----	----	87	SW
CALLOWAY, E. [LO]	----	----	88N	SW
CALLOWAY, Okla M. "DO"	1903	1968		
UPCHURCH, N. & D. [LOs]	----	----	88S	SW
UPCHURCH, Gregory A. "Drummer Boy"	1960	9-29-1976x		
LUTZ, Elmer L. [LO]	1897	3-17-1982x	89NW	SW
"ssa, Bertha E. [LO]	1896	1970		
POLI, William V. [LO]	1887	1974		
"ssa, Dora	1886	1970		
KING, Thomas W. [LO]	1891	1972	89SE	SW
KING, Ruby C.	1895	1970		
H-----, P. [LO]	----	----	89NE	SW
[No LO listed]	----	----	90NW	SW
IVEY, Alex William - Tenn S2 U.S.Navy WW I[LO]	3- 8-1900	11-16-1971	90SW	SW
RUSKAMP, H. [LO]	----	----	90E	SW
MEDENDORP, Helen	1920	1970	91NW	SW
MEDENDORP, Fay B. [LO]	1915	6- 1-1976x		
ENDRESS, E. [LO]	----	----	91SW	SW
ENDRESS, Frank P. - Ohio TM2 U.S.Navy WW II	8-28-1911	10-25-1970		
GROW, May V. [LO]	1908	6-12-1985x	91	SW
GROW, Everett - Husband	1898	1970		SE
MADJE, Frank	1883	1970	91NE	SW
" ssa, Margaret [LO]	1884	1971		
EGBERT, Christian	1887	1969	92SE	SW
" ssa , Minnie [LO]	1888	9-14-1977x		
WILLIAMSON, Chester C. [LO]	1904	7- 5-1976x	92W	SW
" ssa , Violet M.	1904	1969	&92NE	
MARKINS, Andrew J. [LO]	10-30-1884	8- 2-1969	93NW	SW
[No LO listed]	----	----	93SW	SW
KRUSE, M. [LO]	----	----	93SE	SW
[No LO listed]	----	----	93NE	SW
MILLER, Lillian K. - Wife	1907	1969		
[No LO listed]	----	----	94W	SW
HOPPING, Clarence - F. & A.M. emb	1886	1969	94SE	SW
" ssa , Ethel M. - OES emb [LO]	1893	19--		
PURVIS, C. [LO]	----	----	94NE	SW
PURVIS*, William	----	8-25-1979*		
HEBBE, J. [LO]	----	----	95N	SW
HEBBE, Arthur L. "Bud" American Legion mkr	5- 1-1925	4- 5-1969	95N	SW
[No LO listed for 95S, 96, 97, 98, 99 ....& 104, 105.]				SW
CARR, H. & B. [LOs]	----	----	100W	SW
HARTMAN, Harry A. [LO]	1894	----	100E	SW
" ssa , Ida V. [LO]	1898	12- 1-1981x		
BUTSCH, ----- [LO]	----	----	101W	SW
BUTSCH, Thomas J. - Son	1954	1970		
BUTSCH, David - Son	1962	1973		
POPE, S. & M. [LOs]	----	----	101E	SW
POPE, Steven D. - Son	1954	3-23-1976x		
POPE, Gregory - Son	1956	1970		
[No LO listed]	----	----	102W	SW
REATHERFORD, Oscar E. [LO]	1904	----	102	SW
" ssa , Alice J.	1919	----		SE
COLLIER, John D. [LO]	1916	----	102	SW
" ssa , Mary E. [LO]	1918	----		NE
STOECKEL, Julius J. [LO]	1899	11-10-1977x	103N	SW
" ssa , Hattie [LO]	1907	2-13-1979x		
[No LO listed]	----	----	103S	SW
STRAUB, Leola F. - Mother	1903	1971		

MEMORIAL SECTION

NAME	BD or AGE	DD	Lot	Sec.
ENNIS, Mary R. (d. between 3-1 & 4-6-1877 of childbirth, res. Miamitown, OH)	1840	1877	1W	M
ENNIS, John J. [LO #137, 1877][Originally lot #137 in Sec. 3]	1829	1899		

The following burials were first listed on page 59 in "Plat of Lots" as four unnamed graves on the west side of lot #223 (No Sec. listed) & LO was A.E. WEST. On page 159 in "Plat of Lots", A.E. WEST is listed as LO of lot 139, Sec. 3 & no burials indicated on lot. Lot 139 is no longer on cemetery map. Three WEST burials (unnamed) are listed in "Deaths & Interments" as children of A.E. & ---- H. WEST; with these remarks, "Taken up & deposited in lot 223, Sec. 4, 12-5-1864. Removed from Wesleyan Cemetery, Cumminsville and temporarily deposited until the new grounds are laid out.

NAME	BD or AGE	DD	Lot	Sec.
WEST, Augustus E. [LO 1865]			139	-
WEST, Eddy (d. of dysentery, res Harrison, OH, s/o Augustus E. & Amy)	?6-30-1866	8-27-1868	1E	M
"ssa, John A.	7-15-1850	8- 8-1850		
"ssa, Francis T.	5- 7-1854	8-23-1854?		
"ssa, Frances L.	9- 3-1858	2- 5-1860?		
"ssa, Manning S. (Seymore) (b.Hamilton Co. OH, of pseudo or membranous croup, res Harrison, OH, s/o A.E. & Amy H.)	12-21-1862	12- 1-1866		
RESS, Philip [LO]	1926	9-23-1982x	2W	M
"ssa, Maria [LO]	1928	----		
"Baby Plot"			2E	M
FOHL, Joseph Brian	5-17-1982	5-20-1982		
STURGILL, Tiffany Nicole	One date	11- 4-1983		
MOORE*, Gary Berry	1day	2-13-1984*		
[No LO listed] [This lot may possibly be #141 sold to Michael DEAN, 1866. Three DEANS are listed in the "unknown" Sec.; some may be buried on this lot.]			3	M
AGEE, ----- [LO]			4N	M
AGEE, Mildred L.	1918	5- ?-1982		
"ssa, Robert	1920	----		
[No LO listed]	----	----	4S	M
METZLER, R. & I. [LO]	----	----	5N	M
SIEGLE, Earl R. [LO]	4-14-1914	1- 1-1983	5S	M
"ssa , Anna E. [LO]	11-25-1914	2-17-1986		
W., E. & R. [LOs]	----	----	6N	M
CRAMER, Charles G. [LO]	1921	12-23-1983x	6S	M
" ssa , Dorothy M. [LO]	1922	----		
EDWARDS*, Ethel	----	12- 1-1982*	7N	M
H.F. [LO]	----	----	7S	M
FARWICK, James J. - Emb: rifle, deer & fish	1959	10- 7-1983x		
L. & G.H. [LOs] (recent burial)	----	19--	8	M
HUNT, Weller D. (David)	1915	2-27-1985x	9N	M
"ssa, Kathryn M. [LO]	1912	----		
MORROW, Arthur I.	1913	2?-10-1986x	9S	M
"ssa , Fern C. [LO]	1920	----		
E. M. [LO]	----	----	10N	M
MARTIN, Howard - Pfc U.S.Army WW II	8-30-1914	10- 5-1984		
ADAMS, E. Ray - Pvt U.S.Army	11- 9-1945	12-25-1984	10S	M
R.B.L. [LO] (11 & 12S)	----	----	11	M
GEOPP, Ralph F. "Married Dec. 20,1952"	1914	1- 5-1983x	12N	M
"ssa *, Lillian [LO]	----	12-10-1985*		
P.K. [LO]	----	----	13N	M
C. & V.H. [LO]	----	----	13S	M
K. & I.P. [LOs]	----	----	14N	M
PHILLIPS, Maryanne - Daughter	11-13-1972	9- 8-1986		
CAMPBELL, Damon - Husband & Father [LO] WW II Vet. - "Married July 9, 1948"	3-13-1927	----	14S	M
" ssa , Ruthene - Wife & Mother & Teacher	3-30-1928	7-11-1987		
PETERS, Clifford L. - Father [LO] "Married Apr. 20, 1933"	2-12-1910	2-20-1988	15S	M
" ssa , Alma L. - Mother [LO]	1- 3-1910	----		
EVANS, Miles R. - Pvt U.S.Army WW I	3- 9-1896	12-28-1986	16N	M
BOWLES, John M. - Son (Cremains DI 2-5-1987)	1956	1987	16S	M
" ssa , Betty Ann - Mother [LO]	1921	----		
P. & J.F. [LOs]	----	----	17N	M
D. R. [LO]	----	----	17S	M
RUSKAUP, Edward A. - SSgt U.S.Army WW II	8-23-1923	2-26-1987		
MULLENIX, Charles Lee - U.S. Air Force [LO]	10- 3-1937	5-27-1988	18N	M
L. H. [LO]	----	----	18S	M
HASTE*, Thelma A.	----	8-30-1988*		
HETISIMER*, Cecil	----	10-23-1988*		
GREGG, Edgar W. [LO] "Married May 28, 1965"	5- 8-1941	----	19N	M
"ssa , Suzanne M.	3- 5-1947	1- 5-1988		
BLAIR, Arlin D. [LO] "Married Jan.13, 1945"	1922	----	19S	M
"ssa , Pansy	1923	2- 5-1988x		
H. & E.W. [LO]	----	----	20N	M
WILLIS, Hubert (C.)	----	2-14-1989x		
K. & C.T. [LO]	----	----	20S	M

NAME	BD or AGE	DD	Lot	Sec.
HORN, Robert, Jr. - Son [LO]	1945	3-28-1987x	21N	M
[No LO listed]	----	----	21S	M
HENSON, Paul [LO] Emb: two deer	1935	3-22-1987x		
" ssa , Linda [LO] Emb: a horse	1948	----		
OUELLETTE, Helen (K.)	11-29-1918	7-18-1987	22S	M
LaFOLLETTE, Gladys - Mother & Sister [LO]	1-21-1928	----	23N	M
L. M. [LO]	----	----	23S	M
MARTIN, Robert, J. - Pvt U.S.Army WW II	6-11-1922	4- 1-1988		
STANTON, Beverly L. - Mother	7- 9-1967	----	24	M
" ssa , Jimmy Lee - Son	6-17-1986	8-30-1988		
" ssa , Novin C. - Father [LO]	10- 5-1964	----		
FITE* , Robert Noel	----	10-27-1988*	25N	M

MAUSOLEUM

NAME	BD or AGE	DD	Lot	Sec.
BITTNER, John C.	1931	----		
" ssa , Esther M.	1933	----		
RUNK, Clifford C.	1936	----		
"ssa, Myra J.	1935	----		
GIERINGER, James S, Sr.	1921	----		
" ssa , Margaret H.	1921	----		
COLEGATE, Milton A.	1915	----		
" ssa , Mildred C.	1919	----		
BAUER, Paul W.	1926	----		
BAUER, Edith M.	1927	----		
WALTAMATH, Gordon H.	1909	----		
WALTAMATH, Marian J.	1916	----		
WEBER, Pearl R.	1901	----		
STURGILL, Charles W.	1962	7- 7-1988x		
MEYN, William E. -(Cremains DI 2-5-1986)	1914	1986		
"ssa, Dorothy G.	1913	----		
GIERINGER, James S., III - Cremains	One Date	9- 7-1988		
FAGALY, Clifford G.	1903	----		
" ssa , Marie M.	1907	----		
McARTHUR, Melvin	1926	5-14-1986x		
" ssa , V. Ruth	1929	----		
DAVIS, David W.	1915	----		
" ssa, Ruby F.	1919	----		
McKENZIE, Kenneth	1915	----		
" ssa , Pauline	1926	----		

BURIALS ON UNKNOWN LOTS

The following burials are from the Sec. "Plat of Lots" in Book #1 which diagrammed lots and burial sites. The lot diagram for these burials did not give the lot and/or Sec. number. It is uncertain where they are presently buried.

BAXTER, Charles, buried on Wm. THACKERA lot (Bur. possibly W2-3)

DEAN, Unnamed, buried on Michael DEAN lot (Bur. possibly W4)

JOHNSTON, Samuel, (shown as a lot owner only), (north-south burial indicated without any name) with notation "empty grave, old plot def--- so the ----- is gone" [lot 74 Sec. 2?]

METZER, John Wm., (also listed as Wm. METZER), "separate interment" (no lot owner was shown)

THACKERA, W.'s Child, buried on Wm. THACKERA lot (Bur possibly W4)

The following list of names is from "Deaths & Interments" in Book #1. They do not have a lot & Sec. number listed, their names do not appear on the "Plat of Lots" diagrams and no matching tombstone was found in the cemetery. The lot/Sec. numbers within parentheses ( ) are questionable and must not be assumed as correct.

ALTHAUS, Unnamed - d. between 11-19-1879 & 4-2-1880 (May be a duplicate entry for Frederick A. ALTHAUS on lot 128, Sec. 3?)

ALTHAUS, Infant - b.11-4-1905 d.11- 4-1905, stillborn, b. & res. Green Twp. Hamilton Co. OH; ch of Fred & Anna ALTHAUS (Lot 137, Sec. 5?)

ARNOLD, Arthur - b. Miamitown, OH d. 10-1-1876; res Brookville, IN; s/o G. & Hattie ARNOLD (Lot 48S, Sec. 2?)

BARTHOLOMEW, Unnamed (Mary E.B.?) d. between 8-1 & 11-26-1880 (Lot 9,Sec.1?)

BAXTER, Chas. - b.Miamitown,OH d. between 9-30 & 10-19-1879; res Whitewater Twp.; Bur. on Wm. THACKERA Lot; Lot No. is unknown)

BENSON, Zach - b. 3-10-1810 MD; d. 4-3-1875 of paralysis; res Miamitown, OH (Lot 14,Sec. 1?)

BUNCE, Emily A. - b. 4-14-1814 NY; d. 2-3-1873 of consumption; res Miamitown, OH; d/o ----- & Elizabeth BROWN (Lot 47, Sec. 3?)

BUNNELL, Daniel, Sr. - b. Aug., Miami, OH; d. 8-4-1905 of old age; res Hamilton Co. OH; farmer; s/o Daniel & Mary BUNNELL.

BUNNELL, Unnamed - d. between 3-24 & 4-15-1867

CHAMBERS, J. H. - b. 1-5-1867 Miami; d. 5-21-1875 of heart; res Taylor's Creek; OH; ch of Ben & Adline CHAMBERS (Lot 25, Sec.2?)

COLEGATE, Albert E. - d. 12-5-1988

CONE, Mrs. Mary - Bur. 3-24-1881 (same as Mary CONE on Lot 13, Sec.2?)

CROLLEY, Charles - d. 11-26-1880 of brain fever; b. & res Miamitown, OH

CROWELL, Arch (no date of birth) d. 9-4-1875; b. & res Green Twp.

CUTTER, Burrus - b. 4-19-1880 America; d. 4-21-1881 of measles; res So 282 Western Ave., Cincinnati, OH; ch of Abijah & Amanda CUTTER (Lot 42,Sec.2?)

NAME NAME

BURIALS ON UNKNOWN LOTS CONTINUED

CUTTER, Francis M. - b. 9-29-1872 Hamilton Co., OH; d. 9-5-1873 of cholera infantum; res Bevis, OH; s/o A.W. & Amanda CUTTER (Lot 42, Sec.2?)
DAVIS, F.F. - b. 10-1-1855 Taylor's Creek, OH; d. 7-23-1880 of consumption; res Cheviot, OH; clerk; ch/o John A. & Rachel DAVIS (Lot 49, Sec.2?)
DEAN, Ed. - Bur. 9-20-1877 d. of consumption
DEAN, Mary Ann - b. 11-27-1863; d. 12-7-1864 of diptheria; b. & res Hamilton Co., OH; d/o Michael & Margaret DEAN, (Lot --, Sec. 4 (Lot 3,M Sec?)
DEAN, Michael - d. between 10-25-1867 & 2-10-1868 (Lot 3, Memorial Sec,?)
FAGALY, Anna M. - b.10-24-1833 Hamilton Co., OH; d.12-29-1873 of consumption; res Miami Twp.; d/o J (?) & Elanor YANNEY
FRANKHOUSE, Unnamed - d. between 10-25-1867 & 2-10-1868 (Lot 62E, Sec.2?)
GALLIGER, Toty - b. 6-1-1867 Cincinnati, OH; d. 9-7-1873 of teething; res 196 E. 6th St. (Cincinnati ?); ch of James & Louisa GALLIGER.
GANT, Amanda - b. 1818 IN; d. 12-11-1905 of paralysis; res Miamitown, OH.
GANT, William - b. America - d.10-1-1905 of old age; res Miamitown, OH farmer
GERARD, Daniel - b. 2-23-1874 Cincinnati, OH; d. 2-23-1874; res 159 Race St., (Cincinnati ?); s/o Danniel & Mrs. GERARD
GERHARDT, Dan - b. & res Cincinnati, OH; d. 8-21-1875
HAENA, John - b. 6-22-1867; d. 3-4-1868/1871 of inflammation of lungs; (yr. of d. uncertain due to mixing of entries); b. & res Whitewater Twp.; s/o Chas. D. & Barbara HAENA
HAMMITT, William S. - b. 2-23-1800 North Bend, OH; d. 1-3-1875 of general debility; res Colerain Twp.; s/o Wm. & Hannah HAMMITT
HART, Unnamed - d. between 12-1880 & Apr. 1881; (Lot 39, Sec. 1?)
HENERY, (HENRY?), Wm. - d. 12-25-1876; b. & res Green Twp.
HILDRETH, Eva - b. 12- 9-1877 Cumminsville, OH; d. 5-23-1879 of congestion of brain; res Harrison, Hamilton Co., OH.
HINE, Martha - b. 6-25-1864; d. 7-13-1864 of bowel complaint; b. & res Colerain Twp.; d/o Henry & Rachel HINES.
HINES, Unnamed - d. between 12-1880 & 4-21-1881 (Lot 14E, Sec. 1?)
HOWARD, Andrew P. - b. American d. 1-2-1905 of old age; res Cincinnati,OH; carpenter
HOWARD, Elaine E. - b. 7-22-1879 Hamilton Co., OH; d. 7-24-1879; res Colerain Twp.; d/o Chas. & Susan B. HOWARD (Lot 66, Sec. 2?)
HUMES, Mrs. - Bur. 3-15-1881
INGERSOLL, Elizabeth - b. 5-4-1806 Virginia; d. 8-24-1850 of cholera; res Miami, OH; d/o Thomas & Nancy TATTERSHALL, reinterred 2-16-1870. (Lot 112, Sec. 3?)
INGERSOLL, Elsa P. - b. 6-2-1805 Mass.; d. 2-15-1868/1871 of consumption; (Yr. of death is uncertain due to mixing of entries); res Miami, Hamilton Co., OH; d/o Henry & Naomi ATHERTON (Lot 112, Sec. 3?)
ISGRIGG, Elizabeth - b. 1-1-1800 PA; d. 3-23-1879 of senile decay; res. Dearborn Co., IN; d/o J. & ---- SCHOTT
ISGRIGG, Tom - d. 8-14-1876 Cincinnati, OH; s/o Dan & Mrs. ISGRIGG (Lot 39, Sec. 3?)
JAMISON, Unnamed - d. between 3-24 & 4-15-1867 (Matie?) (Lot 59, Sec.2?)
JONES, James - d. between 5-1 & 7-22-1867 (Lot 17, Sec. 1?)
JONES, Eliza - b. 9-2-1866 College Hill, OH; d. 12-21-1872 of hemmorhage of lungs; res Whitewater Twp.; d/o Sam'l L. & Charlotte JONES
KNOSE?, Maud - b. 5-1868; d. 10-8-1904 of kidney trouble; b. & res Miami, OH; d/o Isaac WRIGHT (Lot 78, Sec. 2?)
LUKENS, John G(?) - b. 7-24-1869 Cincinnati, OH; d. 3-24-1874 of Scarlet Fever; res No.2 Dorsey St., Cincinnati, OH; s/o Thomas LUKENS; (Lot 1, Sec. 2?)
MARTIN?, Unnamed - b. 4-22-1875; d. 4-24-1875 of gastritis; b. & res Whitewater Twp.; ch/of Jacob & Mary MARTIN (Lot 117, Sec. 2?)
McMINN, Dellie B. - b. 5-22-1875; d. 7-20-1877 of whooping cough; b. & res Cincinnati, OH; d/o Fred & Sarah (McMINN?) (Lot 31, Sec.3 or Lot 45,Sec.2)
McMINN, Willie - b.12-24-1873; d. 6-13-1881 of drowning; b. & res Cincinnati, OH; s/o Frederick & Sarah McMINN (Lot 45, Sec. 2? or Lot 31, Sec. 3?)
METZER, (METZGER?), William - b. 5-13-1847 Germany; d. 4-10-1878 of concussion of brain; res Whitewater Twp.; s/o Wm. & Rosina METZER
METZGER, Infant - d. between 6-13 & 7-18-1881 - stillborn
MILLER, Fannie b. American; d. 8-15/17-1904 of insanity (phthisis culumulis); res Longview Hospital, Cincinnati, OH.
NOSE, Frank - Bur. 11-10-1881
NUGENT, Child of Andy's; d. 6-7-1876; b. & res Whitewater Twp.
NUGENT, Wm. - b. & res Crosby Twp.; d. 9-13-1875
ORR, Ida E. - b. 10-28-1856; d. 1-20-1867 of typhoid fever; b. & res Cincinnati, OH; d/o Joshua W. & Frances ORR (Lot 32, Sec. 2?)
ORR, Mary frances - b. 2-8-1866 Green Twp.; d. 10-25-1867 of whooping cough; res Cincinnati, OH; d/o J.W. & Fanny ORR (Lot 32, Sec. 2?)
PERRY, Bessie - b. 1-18-1875; d. 3-11-1875 of congestion of brain; b. & res Miamitown, OH; d/o B.C. & Mrs. PERRY
POOL, Child of R.'s - d. 5-25-1876; b. & res Colerain Twp. (Lot 13,Sec. 3?)
POOL, John - b. 3-3-1877; d. 6-22-1880 of whooping cough; b. & res Green Twp.; s/o Richard & Mary POOL (Lot 13, Sec. 3?)
POOL, Nellie - b. 1-26-1879; d. 6-23-1880 of whooping cough; b. & res.Green Twp.; d/o Richard & Mary POOL (Lot 13, Sec. 3?)
POPE, Infant - d. between 7-24 & 9-24-1879; b. & res Whitewater Twp.
POUDER, FLora E. - b. 3-24-1880; d. 6-22-1880 of cholera infantum; b. & res Springfield Rd., (Hamilton Co., OH?); d/o Henry & Dora POUDER
RITTENHOUSE, Unnamed - d. between 5-1 & 7-22-1867 (Lot 37, Sec. 3?)
SCOGGIN, Unnamed - d. between 9-21 & 11-10-1881; b. & res Whitewater Twp.
SHARDINE, Child - d. between 6-2 & 7-22-1875 (Lot 89, Sec. 2?)
SHEAR, John - b. American; d. 1-18-1905 of old age; res Cincinnati, OH teamster (Lot 4, Sec. 2?)
SHEPPARD, Emma G. - b. 12-15-1872; d. 3-9-1873; b. & res Dent, OH; d/o Charles & Mary SHEAPPARD (Lot 56, Sec. 2?)
SNICKEY, John - b. 4-1-1874; d. 6-1-1875 of brain fever; b. & res Lexington, KY; s/o Lewis & Elizabeth SNICKEY/SNICKY
STRUBLE, Ethelbert - d. between 8-1 & 11-26-1880
TAYLOR, Chas. E. - b. 11-25-1873 Delhi, OH; d. 4-20-1880 of Scarlet Fever; res Pleasant Ridge, OH; s/o Robert & Jane TAYLOR (Lot 52, Sec.2?)
WALKER, Edward B. - b. 11-1-1799 Maryland; d. 2-25-1875 of broken hip; res Colerain Twp.; s/o Christopher & P. WALKER (Lot 29, Sec. 1?)
WILSON, David C. - b. 5-1-1849 (IL crossed out); d. 5-1-1867; res Hamilton Co., OH; adopted son of Solomon WALKER (Lot 65A, Sec. 3?)
WILSON, John G. - b. 12-29-1810 Maresfield, England; d. 9-2-1869 of typhoid dysentery; res Green Twp.; farmer
WILSON, Mary - b. 7-5-1809 Chapel Frith, England; d. 12-30-1873 of heart disease; res Dent, OH; d/o George & Sarah MELLER (MILLER?)
WOOD, Olive/Oliver R. - b. 8-1905; d. 9-19-1905; b. & res Westwood, OH; ch/o Edward & Emma WOOD (Penciled in over Edward: "Edwin" & over WOOD "HEYWOOD")

No lot owners listed for 104 & 105 in the Southwest Section.

The following few entries were missed in typing the respective page and noticed in proof reading:

THOMPSON*+, Ann M. - Bur. possibly W3-4 4-16-1790* 9- 6-1866* (Mrs. Ann Magdalen Thompson, b. PA; of rheumatism; res Miamitown,OH; d/o Conrad & Catharine VANTREESE; confined to her house & entirely helpless for 8 or 10 years.) Lot 23 Sec.1
FARMER*, Willerd (b. Miamitown, OH; of consumption; res Springfield Twp.; s/o Henry & Emily FARMER Lot 23 Sec.1 8-13-1847* 2-10-1875*
COX, John - Father [Lot 43 Sec. 1] 39y 5m 5-28-1851
WOOD, Earl - Father [Lot 106 Sec. 2] 1891 1911

The following two names were submitted by Mrs. Mary J. Sefton as they do not have gravestones and were not found in the records.

HENRIE, Dollie WILKINSON - b. 26 Nov. 1860 d. 6 Feb. 1930 w/o Benjamin F. Henrie - Buried in lot 127, section 2.
WILLSEY, Leslie A. - b. 16 Aug. 1884 d. 6 Sept. 1956 s/o Thomas Willsey & Anna HENRIE - Buried in lot 126, section 2.

Public Cemetery, number 2 is located in Section 6 of Whitewater Township, Hamilton County, in Miamitown, Ohio. It is on the south side of Mill Street, between State Route 128 and the Methodist Church. The Miami (Miamitown) Cemetery is next to this cemetery on the south side and there is no fence between the two. This cemetery is maintained by the township trustees. Mrs. Hazel L. Berry copied the gravestone inscriptions in August 1982. The rows of gravestones were copied from west to east and each row from north to south. The exact date for establishment of this cemetery is not known but it does consist of one acre of land with burials prior to 1850. This is the first time for these records to be published.

(Following stones are approximate in relationship to "rows".)

GREIFF, August - 11th ---- ---- Row 1
Ohio Batt'y - Civil War Vet. mkr
STOUT, Margareth 6-12-1833 5-22-1879 Row 1
J.H.W. (Initials on a footstone leaning against west fence.)
JOHNSON, Thomas Jay 7-23-1958 7-25-1958 Row 1
BANNISTER, Wm. - Co. D ---- ---- Row 1
Benton Cadets MO. Vols. - Vet.of Civil War mkr
KOPP, Elizabeth 1889 1895 Row 2
KOPP, Julius One date: 1897 Row 2
BROWN, Elvera 1880 19-- Row 2
" ssa, James 1874 1954
OSWALD, John - Ohio Pfc One date: 1- 4-1956 Row 2
Co. H 28 Infantry WW I SS-PH
PENNINGTON, Thelma 1-26-1930 9-26-1931 Row 2
GRISLEY, Mary 1846 1922 Row 3
GRISLEY, Geo. - Co. F 46th Ohio Inf.[Civil War] ---- Row 3
FRAZEE, Noah - Co. A 5th Ohio Cav.[Civil War] ---- Row 4
BUNNELL, Semantha 4y 1m 11d 10-22-1857 Row 5
d/o Josiah & Rachel BUNNELL (stone is broken off base)
HOMER, Jonas 3- 8-1783 4-26-1845 Row 5
MILTON, Robert L. 1862 1932 Row 5
" ssa , Margaret J. 1890 1957
FAUVER, Joseph - Co. D ---- ---- Row 6
39th Ohio Inf. - Civil War Vet. mkr
PURVIS, Russell 1936 1937 Row 6
PETERS, Walter - Father 1882 1932 Row 7
PETERS, Roy 7- 9-1930 10- 2-1931 Row 7
PETERS, Dora 11- 8-1927 8- 1-1933 Row 7
BUNNELL, Benj. In 86th yr. 10-3-1847 Row 8
BOGART, Helmus 2-23-1785 8-20-1847 Row 8
BOGART, James W. 1-13-1821 9- 6-1886 Row 8
BOGART, Wm. Henry - Co.C 5th Ohio Inf. 3-23-1862 Row 8
PIERSON, Emely Jane 6y 10m 2d 4-19-1849 Row 9
PIERSON, Jacob C. 16y 6m 14d 4-22-1849 Row 9
FRAZY, Ann Marie d/o 5-25-1845 5-22-1848 Row 9
John & Mary FRAZY
COLLINS, Ephraim In 76th yr. 10-30-1845 Row 9
" ssa , Catharine w/o In 86th yr. 4- 4-1857
E. COLLINS
" ssa , Robert In 93rd yr. 3- 1-1829
SMITH, Helena - Mother 1885 1938 Row 9
COVERT, Johnny One date: 4- -1936 Row 9
JOHNSON, William s/o A. & H. 4y 1m 22d 2-15-1839 Row 10
HILL, Patsy Ann One date: 1939 Row 10
Following 2 stones are loose and leaning against Wm. JOHNSON'S stone in Row 10. They probably belong on a double foundation in Row 11, west of Leah STEVENS' stone in Row 12.
STEVENS, Frances E. d/o 5y 10m 11d 7-20-1849 Row 11
John W. & Mary
STEVENS, James W. s/o 2y 11m 6d 11-19-1848 Row 11
John W. & Mary
STAIGER, John - A native In 30th yr. 7-14-1857 Row 15
of Germany who was drowned in the Great Miami River at Miamitown, OH

TURNER, John V. s/o M.P. & 8-25-1822 8-25-184(3?) Row 12
F. TURNER
ssa , BAIRD, Mary P. 2-22-1801 10-30-1850
TURNER b. at Newbrg, NY - Mother - Erected by her dau Emma (?)
ssa , BAIRD, Martha U. d/o 10-11-1833 2-14-1856
M.P. & J.H. BAIRD
STEVENS, Leah w/o James B. In 52nd yr. 8-15-1840 Row 12
NUGENT, Margaret w/o Thomas 43y 2-15-1825 Row 12
SMITH, Catharine consort In 28th yr. 7-30-1821 Row 12
of Patrick
SMITH, Patrick - Father 39y 22d 8-31-1831 Row 12
RAMSAY, Agnes w/o Robert 61y 9-19-1846 Row 12
" ssa , Robert - F. & A.M. emb. 58y 10-16-1846
Natives of Farforshire, Scotland
____, ____ (Top of stone ?2y 6m 4d ------1853 Row 13
broken off through the age & dates.
VANTREES, Pamela d/o 32y 3m 5d 6-28-1843 Row 13
E. & Hannah
SHAW, Bathsheba w/o W.M.SHAW 36y 4d 3- 8-1848 Row 13
BARNS, Wm. John s/o Alvy T. 10- 1-1848 7-17-1849 Row 13
& Eliz----- (broken off) Age 8m 17d
WHEELER, Alvin - Co.B 57th Ohio Inf. ---- Row 13
Civil War Vet.
INGERSOLL, Henry In 40th yr. 8-24-1838 Row 13
____, ____ fieldstone, no inscription Row 13
____, ____ fieldstone set in concrete ---- Row 13
____, ____ fieldstone set in concrete ---- Row 13
____, ____ fieldstone set in concrete ---- Row 13
WILSON, Sedney S.-bottom 2- 4-1818 4-13-184(5?) Row 13
of stone is set in concrete & yr. of death uncertain
DUNLAP, Jos.- Co.I 5th U.S.C.T. ---- ---- Row 13
Civil War Vet.
CHAMBERS, Lydia 66y 2-20-1846 Row 14
WHEELER, James C. s/o illegible 11-20?-1839 Row 14
Alvin & Catharine
" ssa , Elizabeth d/o illegible 10-25-1841
Alvin & Catharine (These 2 are probably on the same lot as Alvin WHEELER in Row 13.)
____, ____ fieldstone - no inscription ---- Row 14
(May be on same lot with Henry INGERSOLL in Row 13.)
WILSON, Paine s/o S. & 7-12-18?1 1-12-18?3 Row 14
Catharine (Yr. of birth may be 1811 or 1841 & yr. of d. may be 1813 or 1843; stone probably on same lot as Sedney WILSON, Row 13.)
WILE, James A. s/o Andrew 6-31-1848 7-16-1849 Row 15
J. & Mary A. (Birthday of "31" is engraved on stone)
WILE, Mary A. - Consort of 1- 2-1831 7- 5-1849 Row 15
Andrew J. WILE; d/o Charles & Ann WILLIAMS
COLUMBIA, Sarah w/o William 46y 4m 22d 11-10-1853 Row 15
COLUMBIA, Wm. - Father 12-27-1804 1-22-1899 Row 15
COLUMBIA, Ephraim 28y 3m 9d 4-27-1861 Row 15
HILL, John In 72nd yr. 9-15-1851 Row 15
"ssa, Hannah w/o John HILL In 47th yr. 6- 5-1845 Row 15
KIHL, Peter - Father ---- ---- Row 15

INDEX

Other Heritage Books by Hamilton County Chapter of the Ohio Genealogical Society:

CD: Hamilton County, Ohio Burial Records, Volumes 1-9:

Hamilton County, Ohio Burial Records:
** Volume 1: Wesleyan Cemetery, 1842-1971 (1984)*
** Volume. 2: Anderson Township Cemeteries, 1800-1989 (1990)*
** Volume 3: Vine Street Hill Cemetery, 1852-1977 (1991)*
** Volume 4: Miami Township (Primarily Maple Grove) (1993)*
** Volume 5: Crosby and Whitewater Township Cemeteries (1993)*
** Volume 6: Colerain Township Cemeteries (1994)*
** Volume 7: Springfield Township Cemeteries (1994)*
** Volume 8: Sycamore Township Cemeteries (1994)*
** Volume 9: Union Baptist African American Cemetery (1997)*

Hamilton County, Ohio Burial Records:
Volume 4: Miami Township Cemeteries
Volume 5: Crosby and Whitewater Township Cemeteries
Volume 7: Springfield Township Cemeteries
Volume 8: Sycamore Township Cemeteries
Volume 9: Union Baptist African American Cemetery
Volume 10: Green Township
Volume 11: Columbia Township
Volume 12: Calvary Cemetery
Volume 13: First German Protestant Cemetery of Avondale and Martini United Church of Christ Records
Volume 14: Harrison Township

Hamilton County, Ohio Church Death Records, 1811-1849

Index of Death Lists Appearing in the Cincinnatier Zeitung, *1887-1901*

Index of Death Notices Appearing in the Cincinnati Daily Times, *1840-1879*

Index of Death Notices Appearing in the Cincinnati Volksblatt, *1846-1918, [Hamilton County]*

Restored Hamilton County, Ohio Marriages, 1808-1849

Restored Hamilton County, Ohio Marriages, 1850-1859

Restored Hamilton County, Ohio Marriages, 1860-1869

Restored Hamilton County, Ohio Marriages, 1870-1884

Other Heritage Books by Jeffrey G. Herbert:

Index of Death Notices and Marriages Notices Appearing in the Cincinnati Daily Gazette, *1827-1881*

Index of Death and Other Notices Appearing in the Cincinnati Freie Presse, *1874-1920*

Index of Death Notices Appearing in the Cincinnati Commercial, *1858-1899*

Restored Hamilton County, Ohio Marriages, 1808-1849

Restored Hamilton County, Ohio Marriages, 1860-1869

Restored Hamilton County, Ohio Marriages, 1870-1884

CD: Restored Hamilton County, Ohio Marriages, 1860-1869

www.ingramcontent.com/pod-product-compliance
Lightning Source LLC
Chambersburg PA
CBHW080522090426
42734CB00015B/3131

9781556139178